Upstate Cauldron

SUNY series in Western Esoteric Traditions

David Appelbaum, editor

Upstate Cauldron

Eccentric Spiritual Movements in Early New York State

JOSCELYN GODWIN

excelsior editions
AN IMPRINT OF STATE UNIVERSITY OF NEW YORK PRESS

Published by
STATE UNIVERSITY OF NEW YORK PRESS
Albany

Printed in the United States of America

Excelsior Editions is an imprint of State University of New York Press

For information, contact
State University of New York Press
www.sunypress.edu

Production, Laurie D. Searl
Marketing, Anne M. Valentine

Library of Congress Cataloging-in-Publication Data

Godwin, Joscelyn.
Upstate cauldron : eccentric spiritual movements in early New York State / Joscelyn Godwin. — Excelsior editions.
pages cm. — (SUNY series in Western Esoteric traditions)
Includes bibliographical references and index.
ISBN 978-1-4384-5595-2 (hardcover : alk. paper)
ISBN 978-1-4384-5594-5 (pbk. : alk. paper)
ISBN 978-1-4384-5596-9 (ebook)
1. New York (State)—Religion. 2. Occultism—New York (State) I. Title.

BL2527.N64G63 2015
200.9747—dc23 2014020301

10 9 8 7 6 5 4 3 2 1

Contents

Acknowledgments

This book is the outcome of a gradual discovery of the spiritual archaeology of Upstate New York. It began in the late 1960s when my mother, Stephanie Allfree Godwin, introduced me to Woodstock's Old Catholic Archbishop (Father Francis) and to devotees of Meher Baba, and when I discovered Anthony Damiani in his Ithaca bookstore (see chapter 25). In 1989 I met John Patrick Deveney, an authority on spiritualist history, to whom I am most grateful for reading this book in manuscript, and for his and Dr. Penny Asbell's hospitality in New York City. At the same time, I met Leslie Price, founder of the journals *Theosophical History* and *Psypioneer* and encourager of my work from that day to this. Much later, Marc Demarest added his rich fund of data in the website "Chasing Down Emma," and his ever-ready willingness to mine it for his friends' benefit. Madis Senner helped to define my project with his website *Mother Earth Prayers: Places of Prayer in Greater Upstate New York*, and his short-lived Spirit House Society inspired my first phase of research. Tom Tryniski's online collection of local newspapers at *fultonhistory.com* was an enormous help in this.

Others have helped through conversations or correspondence: Joseph Caezza and Mark Stavish with their deep knowledge of esoteric traditions; Eugenia Victoria Ellis with her dissertation on Claude Bragdon; John Gallucci and Tom Klenck, companions on long drives around the state; Layne Little, with materials on Mormonism; Mildred E. Logan and Wade Jacobson at the Temple of Truth in Freeville. For their many comments, hints, and ideas, some that they themselves may not recall, I thank Milton Chapin, Deborah Belle Forman, Cathy Gutierrez, Brenda and Rosemary

Hayes, Alvin Holm, John Leidenfrost, Jack Loop, Thom Metzger, Zac Moore, Bruce Moser, John Nelson, John Patane, Einar Petander, Marjorie Roth, James A. Santucci, Avery Solomon, Carl Stearns, Pringle Symonds, Andy Tetlow, Hugh Urban, John Anthony West, Judith Wellman, Thomas Willard, Peter Lamborn Wilson, Mason Winfield, Anthony Wonderley, and Melanie Zimmer. Among the friends no longer with us, Phyllis Benjamin, John Michell, and Nicholas Goodrick-Clarke all took an interest in this, as in my previous projects.

At Colgate University, the Upstate Institute has generously supported this project, especially through publishing my study of the Spirit House in Georgetown, for which I thank Ellen Kraly, Meika Loe, and Julie Dudrick. I also thank Colgate University's Research Council for grants in support of my travel around the state, and the Division of the Humanities for enabling me to give papers on this topic at the conferences of the European Society for the Study of Western Esotericism in Strasburg and the Association for the Study of Esotericism in Davis, California.

Among the libraries and historical societies of New York State, I especially thank Christian Goodwillie, Curator of Rare Books and Special Collections at Hamilton College, for opening the resources of the Communal Societies Collection to me and for providing many of the illustrations in the present book. Andrea G. Reithmayr, Curator of Rare Books at the University of Rochester Library, shared her intimate knowledge of Claude Bragdon and gave me access to his papers. I also thank Norman Carlson of the Fenton History Center, Jamestown; David Corson of the Kroch Library, Cornell University; Jerry Dale and Phyllis Evans of the Georgetown Historical Society; Holly Hewitt of the Marion Skidmore Library, Lily Dale; Sarah Keen of Colgate University Library's Special Collections; Barbara Kittle of the Daniel A. Reed Library of SUNY Fredonia; Denise A. Roe of the Madison County Archives, Wampsville; Joyce Hackett Smith of the Cayuga-Owasco Lakes Historical Society, Moravia; John Paul Wolfe of the McClurg Museum, Westfield; and the guides at the visitors centers of the Mormon sites at Palmyra and the Whitmer Farm. My son, Ariel Godwin, designed and drew the four maps. My wife, Janet, read the book in manuscript and suggested many improvements of style and expression. Neither she nor anyone else named above is responsible for any infelicities, solecisms, or errors that remain.

Hamilton, New York, February 2014

Upstate Cauldron

ILLUSTRATION 1.1. Sir William Johnson. Statue in Johnstown by Pioggi, with assistance of Edward Lamson Henry, erected by the Aldine Society, 1904.[1] *Author's photograph.*

CHAPTER I

The Historical Background[2]

During the first century of American independence, at least thirty spiritual movements, cults, utopian communities, or new religions started in Upstate New York. The Shakers, the Mormons, the Oneida Community, and spiritualism are merely the best known. The others range from the obscure to the ephemeral; all were "eccentric," in the sense of being outside the political and social norms of the era, and in rejecting the Protestant churches that supposedly formed its spiritual bedrock. The whole phenomenon, with its concentration in time and space, is without parallel in social or religious history.

In trying to account for it, historians have turned to the Christian revivals of the "Burned-over District," as the central and western region came to be known; the mass emigration of New Englanders cut loose from their home churches; the mushrooming towns along the Erie Canal and the opening to the West, with its sense of a new world dawning; and the growing disgust with institutionalized racial and gender injustice. Others see a "psychic highway" across the state, nourished by native spirits, earth energies, and other intangibles.[3] In an epilogue I will reconsider these ideas, but for now this book is more about facts than theory. It emphasizes the lesser-known personalities and, when possible, goes to the primary sources. Each succeeding chapter begins with an original statement, a credo, or an account of some extraordinary happening. It is for the reader to wonder at these outer reaches of human experience, which some call folly, others the broaching of boundaries between worlds.

I find this study by turns fascinating, comical, and moving. Besides its value as a human document, it is a laboratory for the study of religious origins. Here are recent cases of men and women who had visions or encounters with divine beings, assumed missions of cosmic importance, received doctrines or sacred books, attracted disciples, and started movements. Some blazed for a moment, then fizzled out like the ancient religious radicals Apollonius of Tyana, Marcion the Gnostic, al-Hallaj, or Sabbatai Zevi.[4] Others, like Moses, Jesus, or Mohammed, succeeded in planting an inextinguishable root. What determines the difference? I do not know, any more than I know why one particular acorn becomes an oak tree. My principle is always to respect, and usually to credit, the experience that lit the fuse, but not its interpretation or the doctrinal baggage train that follows it. That is a study in itself, reflecting the character, limitations, prior beliefs, and motivations of the person reporting the experience.

Readers familiar with Western esoteric traditions will notice many echoes among our provincial visionaries, such as astral journeys like those recounted in Plato's *Republic* and the Hermetic *Poimandres*, the search for hidden meanings in the books of Genesis and Revelation, and the mythic origins of Freemasonry and the Rosicrucians. Early Mormonism owes a distant debt to alchemy, as does spiritualism to Swedenborg, while the Theosophical Society and the occultist movement that appeared in the later nineteenth century were explicitly rooted in Egyptian tradition.

On a more mundane level, every character portrayed in this book had to deal with historical and geographical realities. They all had ancestors, parents, a childhood, and some sort of education. Like everyone else they needed money, companionship, and a home. Many of them started as dirt-poor subsistence farmers. Yet unencumbered by today's legal and governmental controls, they could move around freely, reinvent themselves, and live quite well on next to nothing. To consider their material conditions brings them to life, and often earns our sympathy. So this chapter continues by sketching the main events and currents of their world.

We begin with geography. Tourists are often surprised to find that New York's two major attractions, Manhattan and Niagara Falls, are at either end of a state the size of England. Everything in between is considered "up" with respect to New York City and Long Island, but exactly where the Upstate region begins will depend on whom you ask. In Manhattan they may answer, "Yonkers." Others will exclude the commuter belt, the Catskills, even the Hudson Valley up to Albany. As a longtime resident I have my own definition, which suits the subject matter of this book: Upstate begins where the magnetism of New York City no longer affects the mental compass.

In the period of this study, which is roughly from the Revolution of 1776 until the First World War, the region was transformed from a wilderness into an economic powerhouse. At least, that was the point of view of the colonists and their descendants. The whole territory originally belonged to the Six Nations of the Iroquois Confederacy: from east to west the Mohawk, Oneida, Tuscarora, Onondaga, Cayuga, and Seneca.[5] Both natives and colonists had long traded in animal furs: otter, mink, wildcat, bear, and especially beaver, which supplied the felt hat industry on both sides of the Atlantic. The Indians trapped the animals and provided the pelts in exchange for tools, cottons, firearms, and liquor. This arrangement faltered when the colonists coveted the Indians' lands as well. During the eighteenth century their settlements crept up the Mohawk River to its navigable end at Fort Stanwix (in present-day Rome), and up its southern tributaries to Schoharie and Cherry Valley. Many of the pioneers were German refugees from the Palatinate, dispossessed by European wars. Others emigrated out of opportunism, like the Irish-born magnate Sir William Johnson, who became the British Superintendent of Indian Affairs and accumulated about 170,000 acres. The Van Rensselaers, Dutch patroons, owned even more, including the present capital district. Among their innumerable tenants were Ann Lee and her Shaker community (see chapter 3). The oldest churches and mansions of the Mohawk Valley are rare survivals of this semi-feudal frontier period.[6]

In the eighteenth century, the native tribes were dragged into the rivalries of French and English colonists, themselves the reflection of wars in Europe. It was largely Sir William Johnson's diplomacy and empathy for the Indians that enabled the settlers along the Mohawk to live in peace. This was not to last. At the Revolution the Oneidas and the small Tuscarora nation sided with the rebels, advised by their missionary, the Rev. Samuel Kirkland.[7] The other four Iroquois nations took the British side and helped to harass the rebels, spreading a reign of terror among the settlers. Following the massacre of Cherry Valley, where Mohawks, unrestrained by their Tory leaders, scalped and mutilated men, women, and children, George Washington ordered a punitive expedition. In the summer of 1779, Generals John Sullivan and James Clinton set out, Sullivan marching from Pennsylvania and Clinton from Schenectady. Both made use of the Susquehanna River, Clinton with a celebrated damming of its source in Otsego Lake to generate enough flow to carry his transport boats.[8] The two generals converged at Tioga with a force of about four thousand and proceeded to destroy the Iroquois settlements of central New York, driving the surviving inhabitants into British-held territory and burning houses and crops to prevent their return. Much the same happened to the Mohawks, as their valley became the scene of raids and atrocities, and by the end of the war was virtually a wasteland. Broken and demoralized, the Iroquois Confederacy dissolved, though ironically it served as a model for Franklin, Jefferson, and their colleagues as they designed their own union of states.

The Sullivan Expedition returned with news of the potential richness of the Finger Lakes region. Once the war was over, it served to reward veterans with their promised grants of land. In true military fashion, the area from Manlius to Geneva and from Watkins Glen to Lake Ontario was divided on a regular grid into townships, and these into plots of about five hundred acres. A clerk in the surveying office baptized the towns with classical names, to match the new nation's self-identification with republican Rome and democratic Athens, and threw in some English cultural heroes for good measure: hence the place names of Ithaca, Hector, Scipio, Camillus, Cincinnatus, Locke, Dryden, and the rest.

The Military Tract, as it was called, ended at the Preemption Line that ran north-south from Sodus Point, just clearing Seneca Lake. Present-day roads still follow it and bear its name. Whether by chance or by geodetic intention, it is the exact meridian of Washington, D.C. (77°02'E). During the 1780s the region to the west of the line, officially Seneca country, hatched a new breed of speculators and land agents, and new complications of ownership. Jemima Wilkinson's utopian community (see chapter 3) was both a beneficiary and a victim of these. Some of the deals beggar the imagination. For instance, in 1788 Oliver Phelps and Nathaniel Gorham bought preemptive rights to the entire tract of about six million acres from the Commonwealth of Massachusetts, whose title went back to pre-Revolutionary times. This gave them the right to sell it, once they had persuaded the Indians to sell *their* title. The company's land office in Canandaigua made their village into an economic hub for the region. After Phelps and Gorham had failed to complete their deals, the Holland Land Company, owned by investors from the Netherlands, took over and did the same for the village of Batavia, named for their native land. Nor was the process limited to the west. To the north, the state disposed of millions of acres of wilderness and Black River country to Alexander Macomb and other investors. This is where Charles Grandison Finney (see chapter 2) turned from lawyer to revivalist firebrand. We will be hearing later (see chapter 13) of a central New York land agent, Gerrit Smith, who stood at the nexus of the radical and spiritualist movements. He sold former Oneida acreage from his red-brick office in the village of Peterboro. A very few land agents chose to settle Upstate and build mansions in Georgian style, such as William Constable, Jr.'s Constable Hall in Constableville (!), or Lorenzo, the house of John Lincklaen in Cazenovia.

While fortunes were made and lost during this redistribution, the greatest losers were the Indians themselves. Those who had not already fled the state at the Sullivan campaign were either induced to leave for reservations in Wisconsin or Kansas, or confined to a few widely separated reservations in New York: Buffalo Creek and Tonawanda near Buffalo, Cattaraugus on Lake Erie, Allegany on the Allegheny River, tiny Oil Spring on Cuba Lake, Onondaga south of Syracuse, and Oneida south of that city. The latter four remain in tribal possession to this day. This set the stage for the appearance of Handsome Lake (see chapter 4), the Seneca prophet whose personal life paralleled his tribe's descent into wretchedness. The new religion he brought them was a first step toward reasserting their racial and spiritual identity.

This is where our history really begins. A flood of emigrants left the New England states, where the farmland was poor and scarce and there were few opportunities for younger sons to set up on their own. A number of our characters belonged to such families. The Mormon leaders Joseph Smith and Brigham Young (see chapter 6) were both born in Vermont in the early years of the century, left as children, and were raised respectively in Wayne and Chenango counties. The spiritualist and world traveler James Peebles (see chapter 21) was also born in Vermont and raised on the Chenango River. Rachel Baker (see chapter 5), the sleeping preacher, was born in Massachusetts and raised in Onondaga County. Others came from Pennsylvania, Canada, or directly from Europe, like the German Inspirationists (see chapter 9), who emigrated as a group and bought land near Buffalo. Ann Lee (see chapter 3) came from England as a religious refugee with her first Shaker companions. The parents of Thomas Lake Harris (see chapter 16), leaving England for reasons unknown, set up shop in Utica. Mary Andrews (see chapter 13) came from famine-struck Ireland to work as a servant, until her mediumistic talents made her a celebrity in Moravia and beyond.

The motives of those who arrived Upstate as adults were more varied. John Humphrey Noyes (see chapter 10) and John Murray Spear (see chapter 15) left New England on their own initiative, finding New York a less hostile environment for their social experiments and theological heresies. Spear's community at Kiantone was short-lived and he returned to Massachusetts; Noyes's at Oneida made social history. Paschal Beverly Randolph, medium and sexologist (see chapter 14), came from Boston to Peterboro because Gerrit Smith was giving farmland to free blacks. Timothy Brown, the builder of the Spirit House in Georgetown (see chapter 17), sold his sawmill and land holdings in Vermont and joined relatives already in Madison County.

Some of our characters were born in the state and felt its influences from an early age. Parley Pratt (see chapter 7) came from Burlington, a hamlet in Otsego County, and encountered first the Shakers, then the Mormons. Cyrus Teed, proponent of the concave earth theory (see chapter 19), came from an equally obscure corner of Delaware County, where his father built waterwheels. He discovered the speculative blend of magnetism, electricity, and alchemy that was still taken seriously outside the dominant institutions. Among the spiritualists and mediums, Andrew Jackson Davis (see chapter

11) was born a cobbler's son and grew up on the Hudson among Swedenborgians and mesmerizers; the Fox sisters came of age in the radical hotbed of Rochester. Theirs must have been a different experience from life on the inland routes, like Amanda Theodosia Jones's in East Bloomfield (see chapter 17), Amelia Bloomer's in Homer, or Cora Richmond's in distant Cuba. Of those mentioned so far, only Noyes had a privileged upbringing and a Yale education. Somehow that did not matter as it might have in stuffier parts of the country, or in Europe. Snobbery came late to a region without an aristocracy or venerated institutions.

The first challenge facing Upstate pioneers was to turn forest into farmland, unless they were fortunate to own areas that the Indians had already cleared and cultivated. The very trees that stood in their way yielded a first cash crop: they were felled, burned, and the ashes soaked in water and dried to make potash. An acre of virgin forest produced two tons of this chemical compound,[9] essential for making soap and glass and in high demand by European countries that had already destroyed their forests. Potash and beaver pelts were the foundation of Upstate's prosperity, but the farmers dreamed of fields of waving wheat and contented cattle. It was one thing to be a homesteader, supplying one family's needs, and another to be an investor. Many of the settlers had sunk considerable cash into their land purchases, and expected to become rich through them.

Two of the main requirements for development were a sawmill and a gristmill: the first, to cut trees into manageable and saleable lumber, and the second, to grind grain into flour. In a region of lakes, rivers, and streams there was no lack of free power from falling water. The building of mills on every available watercourse seeded many of the villages, towns, and indeed cities. The radical and spiritualist capital of Rochester would never have arisen without the falls of the Genesee River. Once a surplus was produced, a market for it had to be found, and here nature was less obliging. The Appalachian mountain chain, which stretches from Alabama to the Adirondacks and beyond, forms a barrier between the inland states and the East Coast, with its cities and ports. The first and only river to cut through the range is the Mohawk. If the newly settled regions were to flourish, they had to find a way to use this river for access to the Hudson, and thence to New York City and the world.

Transportation might seem to have little to do with spiritual matters, but the protagonists of this book owed their mobility and consequent renown to its improvements. The Mohawk itself was not a perfect river for commerce. The first obstacle was the ninety-foot drop of Cohoes Falls near its mouth. Goods coming downriver had to be unloaded at Schenectady for an eighteen-mile wagon ride to the port of Albany. Further upriver there were stretches of shallow rapids and waterfalls, especially where the Mohawk passes its narrowest defile at Little Falls. The boats and their cargoes were landed and lugged along a well-worn portage route. At Rome, where the Mohawk effectively ends, the Indians had long operated a "Carrying Place" to the head of Wood Creek, one or two miles away depending on the season. From there they could paddle down a sluggish and convoluted stream to Oneida Lake. Such portage routes suited the Indians' canoes, but they severely limited the size of boats, as did the creeks whose waters might be only inches deep. The wonderfully readable journal of Simon Desjardins and Nicolas Pharoux, who were sent in 1797 to survey lands in the Macomb Purchase bought by a French consortium, describes the hazards of such a journey.

During the 1790s the Western Inland Lock Navigation Company took the situation in hand.[10] By digging short stretches of canal around the various obstacles, it made navigation possible—though still far from easy—from Schenectady to Oneida Lake, and then down the Oneida and Oswego rivers to Lake Erie. Meanwhile there was competition, as the land routes were greatly extended and improved. The turnpike system allowed entrepreneurs to improve a stretch of track, paving it with cinders, planks, or a bumpy "corduroy road" of logs, and to charge a toll for its use. Today's Routes 5, 20, and 80 trace the principal turnpikes between Albany and the Finger Lakes. Along with the turnpikes came stagecoaches on regular schedules. In winter, wheels and mud gave way to snow and sleds. Many of the older houses along these routes were once taverns, serving everyone from land speculators to cattle drovers.

The Erie Canal, completed in 1825, lowered the cost of freight by an order of magnitude compared to the land routes. Forced through the legislature by the energetic DeWitt Clinton, planned and engineered by complete amateurs, and dug at first by local labor, it was the most ingenious and effective example of water management since Roman times. European travelers especially admired the aqueducts that carried the canal over natural streams and rivers.

The canal enabled the produce of the interior—iron ore, lumber, salt, potash, furs and hides, grains and flour, pork and cattle, hops, liquor, cheese, ginseng[11]—to be sold in the coastal cities or exported. In the other direction it brought manufactured goods, machinery, bricks, window glass, clothing, luxury items. In time the Upstate cities became manufacturing centers in their turn, and the exchange more complex. Additional canals brought Pennsylvania coal to fuel their factories, which shipped their products down the Delaware to Philadelphia and the Susquehanna to Baltimore. The consequences went far beyond the commercialization of the Upstate region. The Erie Canal helped to open up Ohio to settlement and to make Cleveland and then Chicago into industrial cities, to say nothing of Buffalo as its prime loading station. At the other end it made New York City the financial center of the nation and its busiest port. As if a cork were pulled from a barrel, the natural wealth of the American interior now spilled out upon the whole world.

Second in importance were the railroads, which passengers preferred to the tedium of endless locks and the company of the notoriously rough "canawlers." The first trains in the state rattled from Albany to Schenectady in little more than an hour, while the canal boats spent all day circumventing Cohoes Falls. In 1851, when the state, jealous of its canal profits, at last allowed freight trains, the Erie Railway completed the southern route from the Hudson to Lake Erie, restoring opportunity to a region that the canal had somewhat drained. The golden years of the Upstate region saw both canals and railroads running at full capacity, providing a network of public transport with no equivalent today. It accounts for the surprising mobility of some of our characters, such as Paschal Beverly Randolph (see chapter 14), who in one February day rode from Syracuse to Utica (fifty miles, presumably by train), then twenty-four miles by sleigh to Edmeston, arriving in time for tea and a séance.

Alongside the economic and demographic boom came the social revolution. Although New York was fifty years late in abolishing slavery—Vermont had led the way in 1777—during the 1830s and 1840s many of its citizens defied the Fugitive Slave Law of 1793, which obliged northern states to return runaway slaves to their southern masters. After the passing of a sterner act in 1850, the Underground Railroad developed as an informal system of hosting escaped slaves and helping them to reach Canada. Until the Civil War, the abolitionists worked hand in hand with those campaigning for women's rights. Both movements could accuse the nation's lawmakers of infidelity to the Constitution, which proclaimed the equality of all before the Creator. Gerrit Smith, William Lloyd Garrison, Elizabeth Cady Stanton, and Matilda Joslyn Gage are some of the radical leaders who will play an important part in our narrative (see chapters 13 and 20). Their first victory was New York's Married Women's Property Act, passed on April 7, 1848. It allowed married women to retain property they had owned before marriage and earned during it, but still left much to be won, such as the right to divorce abusive husbands, obtain custody of children, administer estates as widows, and of course, to vote.

These were heady times. The Californian gold rush had started in January 1848. On February 21 Karl Marx published the *Communist Manifesto*. Revolutions broke out in the Italian states in January, in France in February, and in the Austrian empire and German states in March, plunging continental Europe into turmoil for the rest of the year. On April 27 France abolished slavery in her colonies. Closer to home, on March 1 the first Perfectionists arrived to form the Oneida Community. On March 31, the Fox sisters launched the spiritualist movement in Hydesville, and Andrew Jackson Davis heard a voice saying, "Brother, the good work has begun."[12] On July 9 the first women's rights convention was planned (see chapter 13). It was announced on the eleventh and held on the nineteenth and twentieth of the same month, bringing some three hundred participants to Seneca Falls.

One hesitates to play down such a momentous episode as the Civil War, but it did not interrupt the processes described up to now. New York State was far from the battle lines. Its industries and farms prospered by supplying the Union Army with weapons, uniforms, and food, while its bankers loaned money to the government at high interest. The economic historian Peter Bernstein writes that the New York canal network and the consequent industrial revolution "helps to explain northern superiority" when the war came.[13] The state emerged from the war richer and more powerful than ever. This was little comfort to the more than forty-six thousand volunteers and draftees from New York who had lost their lives, though spiritualism flourished as the bereaved turned to it for solace.

The postwar settlement granted freedom to former slaves and voting rights to the males among them, but not to women of any color. This irked the women's movement, which felt that it had helped both abolition and the war effort and received nothing in return. It turned its energies inward or to other causes such as temperance, as the freed blacks continued their equally unfinished struggle for true civil rights. While all the movements that we shall study here favored women's equality, they tended to avoid public activism. Instead, the Oneida Perfectionists, the Fourierists, and the "free lovers" of Harmonia practiced equality within their own communities (see chapters 9, 10, and 15) in ways more radical than anything imagined at Seneca Falls. In theory they also favored racial equality, but black membership in these groups was close to nil, and the only Indians present were spirit guides. As for state and national politics, and all the emotions and ambitions they created in the wider world, our groups virtually ignored them. They had more important matters to get excited about, such as commerce with higher planes of existence and the pursuit of immortality. This chapter has concentrated on the material and geographic environment with which, however unworldly, they had to contend.

This suggests one explanation for why so many eccentric spiritual movements did arise in Upstate New York. Those with the gumption to set out for virgin territory and carve a livelihood out of its natural riches were unbound by authority or tradition. They knew the resilience and resistance

ILLUSTRATION 1.2. Ruins of the Richmond (or Montezuma) Aqueduct, 1849, the second-largest construction on the Erie Canal, on which the canal crossed the Seneca River. *Author's photograph.*

of the physical world more keenly than town dwellers. They were building a civilization from the ground up, and along with that endeavor came a freedom in the construction of their mental worlds. Into this wilderness came the Erie Canal. Defying the skeptics and city politicians, overcoming all the obstacles nature had put in its path, its completion was an achievement of mythic dimensions. To ride the canal from Albany to Buffalo, to see its booming towns and cities and then perhaps to visit Niagara Falls, must have given a sense of the grandeur of nature and of human ingenuity and power that we can hardly imagine. In such a state of mind, anything seemed possible, in heaven as well as on earth.

Easier to explain is the decline of such movements in the twentieth century. By 1900 the Upstate cities had all the appurtenances of cities elsewhere: tall buildings, crowded streets, hospitals and lawyers, local politicking, the very rich and the very poor. Outside the Adirondacks the state was almost deforested in favor of farming.[14] The examples I have drawn from this period, Elbert Hubbard, Gustav Stickley, and Claude Bragdon (see chapters 22, 23, and 24) had quite different motivations from the visionaries and mediums of the pioneer generations. Familiar with the industrial system, even compromised by it, they longed for the real or imagined values of the past, such as craftsmanship, self-reliance, and an honest aesthetic.

Today, Upstate is in transition once again. Its cities have lost their industrial base and have yet to find a comparable source of wealth. The Barge Canal that replaced the Erie is almost unused. Family farms are vanishing. The small towns and villages offer little in the way of employment or encouragement for ambitious youngsters. Yet if there is a special product or a tourist attraction, the state's very decline has been to its advantage. Outside the large cities, with their irreparable scars of urban renewal, there are places scarcely altered since the nineteenth century, with all the grace and variety of its domestic and public architecture. One finds them along the canals and the turnpikes; in the wine country and the Finger Lakes; in the college and university towns; in Cooperstown with its museums. Tourists may well feel nostalgic for the quality of life that they imagine to exist there. And in between there are miles upon miles of field, forest, and lake, much of it without a human habitation in sight. There one may sense the inexplicable spirit of place that transcends the ups and downs of human history.

ILLUSTRATION 2.1. Charles Grandison Finney, preacher of the Second Great Awakening. From Finney's *Memoirs*, New York: A. S. Barnes & Co., 1876. *Courtesy of Special Collections, Hamilton College Library.*

CHAPTER 2

The Religious Background

There was no fire, and no light, in the room; nevertheless it appeared to me as if it were perfectly light. As I went in and shut the door after me, it seemed as if I met the Lord Jesus Christ face to face. It did not occur to me then, nor did it for some time afterward, that it was wholly a mental state. On the contrary it seemed to me that I saw him as I would see any other man. He said nothing but looked at me in such a manner as to break me right down at his feet. . . . Without any expectation of it, without ever having the thought in my mind that there was any such thing for me, without any recollection that I had ever heard the thing mentioned by any person in the world, the Holy Spirit descended upon me in a manner that seemed to go through me, body and soul. I could feel the impression, like a wave of electricity, going through and through me. Indeed it seemed to come in waves and waves of liquid love; for I could not express it in any other way. It seemed like the very breath of God. I can recollect

> distinctly that it seemed to fan me, like immense wings. No words can express the wonderful love that was shed abroad in my heart. I wept aloud with joy and love: and I do not know but I should say, I literally bellowed out the unutterable gushings of my heart. These waves came over me, and over me, and over me, one after the other, until I recollect I cried out, "I shall die if these waves continue to pass over me." I said, "Lord, I cannot bear any more;" yet I had no fear of death.[1]
>
> *Experience of Charles Grandison Finney, 1821*

During the eighteenth century, while New England and Pennsylvania were seething with religious revivals, Upstate New York was a heathen land. In the previous century, the Jesuits had tried to convert some of the Iroquois nations and made martyrs of themselves, as we will read in chapter 4. In 1710 a deputation of Mohawk chiefs visited England and were received by Queen Anne, afterwards sitting for their portraits in full regalia. The queen ordered chapels to be built at her own expense for the Mohawks and Onondagas,[2] providing them with magnificent communion silver that still survives.[3] Sir William Johnson's Indian Castle Chapel at Fort Plain (1769) is the last witness to the hopeful fantasy of transforming Indians into Anglicans. But no one seems to have tried very hard. After meeting the settlers and fur traders who had made Albany into a commercial center, Dr. Alexander Hamilton wrote in his 1744 travel diary that, "As to religion they have little of it and enthusiasm not a grain."[4]

The Anglicans and the Dutch Reformed Church were the two officially sanctioned sects of colonial New York, and the only ones allowed to manage property and borrow money. The rest were tolerated. By 1775 they included (in order of prevalence) Presbyterian, Lutheran, Quaker, Congregational, Baptist, German Reformed, and French Protestant churches.[5] The Lutherans, obviously, followed the teachings of Martin Luther (1483–1556). The Dutch and German Reformed churches, the French Protestants, and the mainly Scottish Presbyterians descended from the French reformer John Calvin (1509–1564). The Congregationalists were also Calvinist in doctrine but maintained the autonomy of each congregation, unlike the Presbyterians who were regulated by presbyters or elders. The Baptists' distinguishing features were adult, rather than infant, baptism and a rejection of any state authority in religious matters. The Quakers, or the Religious Society of

Friends, were a quietist, humanitarian sect with roots in English Protestant mysticism.

Apart from the Quakers, who were nondoctrinaire, all these sects shared three things: repudiation of papal authority and the Church of Rome, reverence for the Bible as the literal Word of God, and the belief that after death, human beings are either saved or eternally damned. The leaders of the Protestant Reformation accepted St. Augustine's doctrine that all humans deserve eternal damnation on account of sin, originally committed by Adam and Eve and passed down as an inborn depravity in all their descendants. Calvinism held that Christ's atonement earned salvation for some but not for others, and that every person is predestined for either heaven or hell, no matter what they do. The Lutherans, on the other hand, believed that one can voluntarily participate in Christ's saving sacrifice through faith. Most Methodists and Baptists were of the same opinion. This belief is sometimes called Arminian, after the Calvinist dissident Jacobus Arminius (1560–1609), who taught that salvation is not predestined but a personal choice open to every all.

While all the sects under consideration, and virtually all of their eccentric offshoots, were Protestant by ancestry, the reader may sense an "elephant in the room" in the shape of the Roman Catholic Church. Our characters tended to deplore, demonize, or more often ignore it, and the Vatican returned the compliment. Unlike the Protestants, the Catholics could put their trust in good works, the intercession of the Virgin Mary and other saints, and the sacraments, especially confession and absolution. In Luther's time they could also buy indulgences to shorten their time in purgatory, the probable destination of all but the very saintly and the irredeemably wicked. Unpleasant as the purgative process might be, it guaranteed eventual entry into paradise. The Protestants had no such middle ground; rejection of the doctrine of purgatory was another of the reformers' sticking points.

Today, when most churches outside the Bible Belt tend to downplay the threat of eternal punishment, we heirs to the Enlightenment can only imagine its psychological effects. Apart from the terror of spending eternity in physical and mental agony, whether through deficiency of faith or through God's all-powerful whim, there was always the worry about one's nearest and dearest. Were they already roasting in hell? How could one love with all one's heart a God of such inhumanity who, besides, blamed his victims? That some dared to think such thoughts was the mainspring for most of the developments within American Protestantism.

Three of these developments form the background to our studies: (1) the (first) Great Awakening, from the late 1730s through the 1740s; (2) the New Light Stir of the Revolutionary years, 1776–1782; (3) the

Second Great Awakening, from 1826 through the 1830s. Although the first Great Awakening did not directly affect the Upstate region, it set the style for evangelical revivals ever after. Its movers were itinerant preachers in the mold of John Wesley (1703–1792), the founder of Methodism. The leading figure in America was Wesley's associate George Whitefield (1714–1770). He preached up and down the East Coast, touching New York in 1739 with revivals in Manhattan, Staten Island, Flatbush, and Westchester County.[6] Whitefield was famous for his ability to draw crowds of thousands and harangue them with his stentorian voice. He forced sinners to face their condition and the terrible danger they were in. Salvation had to be felt as a transformative experience and to bring about a permanent change from one's former way of life. Weeping, trembling, and groaning were all part of the process. Along with this basic evangelical principle went a confidence that in revivals God's grace would descend with extraordinary force and bring about mass conversions.[7]

Not everyone fell under the revivalist spell. Anglican and other clergy who saw organized religion as an adjunct to a well-ordered society feared for their congregations, if not their jobs. "Enthusiasm" became a term of contempt in Enlightened minds.[8]

The next wave of revivals began in 1776 in Maritime Canada, then spread to New England. The name "New Light Stir" comes from the division between revivalists and the "Old Lights" who remained within the conventional churches. The New England groups went under names such as "Annihilationists," "Nothingarians," "Merry Dancers," and "Come-Outers." The first two held that the non-elect suffer no eternal punishment but are simply snuffed out at death; the latter two, that the elect must sin before grace can be obtained. Like some Gnostic sects of antiquity or the Anabaptists of sixteenth-century Münster, the Merry Dancers of Sanford, Maine, indulged in drunkenness and promiscuous sex, meanwhile "hooting the Devil" and scaring their neighbors by screaming, "Woe! Woe! Woe!" into the stillness of the night.[9]

Two symptoms of the New Light Stir in the Upstate region were Jemima Wilkinson's migration from Rhode Island to the Finger Lakes, and the prophecies of Joseph Meacham (1742–1796), a lay Baptist preacher in New Lebanon (see chapter 3). As always in times of political turmoil, some were sure that the Last Judgment was at hand. Meacham proclaimed that Christ would return to earth before 1779 was out. His congregation prepared for the event with an orgy of visions, prophecies, and speaking in tongues. The disappointment at the year's close plunged him and his group into a state of depression and self-questioning, until the Dark Day of May 19, 1780.

This well-documented event, which affected most of New England, is thought to have been due to forest fires in New Hampshire. At the time it seemed to have a far different cause. It began at mid-morning, and by noon it was too dark to read. Birds went to bed; frogs started to chirp. The air smelled of a malt house or a coal kiln. The Connecticut legislature in Hartford continued working by candlelight, determined that if this were the Day of Judgment, it ought to find them in the line of duty.[10] The New Lebanon enthusiasts knew that this was what they had been waiting for. They joined forces with Ann Lee's Shakers, henceforth to live out the millennium in their own way.[11]

Both the Shakers and Wilkinson's group were Perfectionists, believing it possible to live a sinless life here and now. Simply by entering the community and living by its revealed teachings, they had demonstrated that they were of the elect, and the fate of the "world's people" did not trouble them overmuch. God had his own plans, and they would come to fruition very soon.

The antipode of these divisive doctrines is Universalism, the belief that all humans will eventually attain salvation. It has a long history, perhaps going back to the sayings of Jesus himself, as its proponents would amply demonstrate. It came to America with the English ex-Calvinist John Murray (1741–1815), an itinerant preacher and chaplain in the Revolutionary army. Murray formed the first Universalist church in Gloucester, Massachusetts, in 1779, then in 1793 one in Boston. The sect's principles were, first, the authority of the Bible as revelation of God's nature and of human duty and destiny; second, the nature of God as love, who will finally restore all people to holiness and happiness; third, the obligation to live a good life in this world.[12] The Bostonian minister Charles Chauncey (1705–1787), a fierce opponent of the revivals, came to believe that all humans are saved, but he warned that "many of them will be miserable in the next state of existence, and to a great degree, and for a long time, in proportion to the moral depravity they have contracted in this."[13] No Protestant seems to have remarked that this was exactly the Catholic doctrine of purgatory.

A more radical view was proclaimed by Hosea Ballou (1771–1852), who occupied John Murray's former pulpit in Boston. Ballou's study of scripture convinced him that upon the death of the body, God reveals himself to the soul, which "immediately ceases to confer with flesh and blood, beholds with inexpressible admiration the heavenly beauties of the new nature, is moulded into its likeness, and experimentally [i.e. experientially] becomes a child of God; the flaming sword is removed from the place of light; the way to the tree of life is opened, and the soul enters by the anchor of hope within the veil . . ."[14] So the only wages of sin are paid in this life. The Universalists would suffer more than one schism over this question.

The Unitarians had a different ancestry[15] deriving from denial of the trinitarian doctrine that God is three equal persons, Father, Son, and Holy

Spirit. In England, thinkers of the stature of John Milton, Sir Isaac Newton, and John Locke found no warrant in the Bible for the dogma of the Trinity or the divinity of Jesus. Nor did Joseph Priestley (1733–1804), equally renowned as a scientist (he discovered oxygen), a theologian, and an admirer of the French Revolution. The latter opinion brought him under suspicion of treason, and in 1794, after a mob had destroyed his house, he left England and settled in Northumberland, Pennsylvania. Two years later he founded the first American Unitarian church in Philadelphia.

Unitarianism appealed to educated liberals who had already discarded Calvinist predestination.[16] The revivalists' harping on God's wrath and man's total depravity repelled them, as did the emotionality of mass conversions. Some had heard of the "higher criticism," the historical-literary approach to scripture coming from Germany, and agreed that the Bible, though undoubtedly inspired, could be studied in a rational and scholarly way. Above all, they wanted a theology of a loving God, not an angry one. It followed that Jesus' mission was not atonement through his death, but his exemplary life and the promise of his resurrection, in which all believers would share.

The great proponent of American Unitarianism was William Ellery Channing (1780–1842), a minister in Boston from 1803. His sermon on Unitarian Christianity, delivered in Baltimore in 1819, urged a rational approach to scripture, the acceptance of Jesus' humanity, and the infinite benevolence of God.[17] It enraged the conservatives, unleashed a pamphlet war, and made Channing America's most famous preacher. It also precipitated a flight from Congregationalism into the new sect. By 1825, almost all the Congregationalist churches in Boston had become Unitarian.[18] Ralph Waldo Emerson (1803–1887) and Theodore Parker (1810–1860) began as ministers in this environment before moving on to still more radical departures from New England's Calvinist roots.

The leading figure of the Second Great Awakening, Charles Grandison Finney (1792–1875), was a typical product of the New England emigration. When he was two years old his family moved from Warren, Connecticut, to take advantage of the cheap land in Oneida County. They went first to Brothertown, then to Hanover, where they stayed until 1808.[19] For the last two of those years, Finney may have attended the Hamilton-Oneida Academy in Clinton (refounded as Hamilton College in 1812).[20] The family then moved north to Henderson, near Lake Ontario. Finney went back to the Warren Academy to prepare for Yale or Princeton, but did not continue there. Instead, he taught school in New Jersey for two years, then returned to Jefferson County to clerk for an attorney in Adams. Soon he was a lawyer in his own right.

Jefferson County, according to Charles Hambrick-Stowe, was mainly settled by western Vermonters who had brought with them a "penchant for emotional extremism in their religion" that went back to the revivals of forty or fifty years before.[21] Whether or not this infected Finney, or whether the catalyst was his pious girlfriend, Lydia Andrews, the upwardly mobile, handsome attorney started to worry about his soul. He worried to the point of agony, until the memorable events of October 10, 1821. Shy of being seen praying, he sought solitude in the woods north of Adams, and there experienced eight or nine hours of "missing time."[22] Later that evening he had the mystical experience narrated at the head of this chapter.

Finney now abandoned the law and turned to the ministry under the informal guidance of the local Calvinist pastor, George Gale. In 1824 he was ordained in the Presbyterian Church, married Lydia, and for a few unsettled years preached revivals around Jefferson County. His breakthrough came in spring 1827, when Gale, now retired to Westernville in Oneida County, invited him to preach there. Keith Hardman points out that he did not do so in a void: the Erie Canal was creating an economic boom, and revivals were already in progress along its route. Finney just happened to have the right touch. "Rough-cut and self-educated" as he was, "his preaching was paralyzing in its intensity and its ability to rivet an audience and bring it under quick conviction."[23] He also had the right physique: like Washington, Jefferson, and Lincoln, he was well over six feet tall.

In 1826 Finney moved his campaign to the canal junction of Rome. He might preach for hours on end, or, like the Ancient Mariner, buttonhole a single victim. The goal was to bring about a conversion experience, maybe not as titanic as his own but powerful enough to save its subject from eternal damnation. Adjuncts to the process were giving up alcohol, tea, coffee, tobacco, evening parties, dancing, and attractive female dress. A gruesome innovation was the "anxious bench" for people who were not sure whether they could honestly declare themselves saved. There they would sit, the eyes of the congregation upon them, as Finney tore at their souls. He also held "anxious meetings," usually at night and in darkened rooms, stalking around and whispering to each one, "Do you love Jesus Christ? Don't you feel awful?" and similarly loaded questions.[24]

Finney's genius now found its full scope, as he preached revivals all around central New York. In New York Mills, where Lydia's brother was superintendent of a textile factory, he preached to the mill owners and the workers, most of them young women, and converted almost all. Auburn was another success story, twenty years before it would take fire again with spiritualism. Troy, Wilmington, and Philadelphia came next, then some years in New York City with a church of his own. In 1830 he accepted an invitation to preach in Rochester. There, nearer to his home ground, his revivals reached their climax. One result was the addition of about five thousand people to the church rosters of central New York,[25] but it went much further than that. Finney's example inspired other revivalist preachers, and the movement became a national one, touching all the Protestant denominations. It lives on today, as witnessed in the success of Billy Graham and later televangelists.

Finney's triumphant progress was opposed both by the Calvinists, for Finney was now an out-and-out Arminian, and by Unitarians and Universalists who thought his methods crude, bullying, and with no lasting result. His campaign in their stronghold of Boston (1831–32) was a flop. He worked a few more years in New York City, becoming increasingly involved with the abolitionist movement. This brought an invitation to the new antislavery college in Oberlin, Ohio, where Finney spent the rest of his working life, first as a professor and then as president.

After the Second Great Awakening, someone christened the region from Utica to Buffalo the "Burned-over District," as though a spiritual forest fire had swept it clean. The analysis of this process, its causes and conse-

ILLUSTRATION 2.2. Indian Castle Church, near Herkimer. An Episcopalian chapel built for the Mohawk Indians by Sir William Johnson, 1769. *Author's photograph.*

quences, is something we must leave to historians of the "centric" movements, i.e., the Christian sects. A suitable emblem would be the town of Palmyra, where four churches stand at the four corners of the main intersection: Methodist, Baptist, Episcopal, and Presbyterian, each eager, no doubt, to swell its congregation. Yet outside the town center, each summer a cast of hundreds, watched by a crowd of thousands, stages a sacred drama upon a hill topped by a golden statue of an angel.[26] The rest of this book will be about the sacred dramas enacted in the Upstate region, some as consequential as Mormonism (see chapter 6), others as modest (but no less consequential) as the revelation of how to preserve fruits and vegetables (see chapter 17).

ILLUSTRATION 3.1A.
Mother Ann Lee, founder of the Society of Believers in Christ's Second Appearing (Shakers). A "psychometric portrait" drawn by Mr. Milleson of New York and identified by a test medium as being of Ann Lee. From *The Phrenological Miscellany*, New York: Fowler & Wells, 1883. *Courtesy of Special Collections, Hamilton College Library.*

ILLUSTRATION 3.1B.
Jemima Wilkinson, the Publick Universal Friend. From *Memoirs of Jemima Wilkinson, a Preacheress of the Eighteenth Century*, Bath, N.Y.: R. L. Underhill & Co., 1844. *Courtesy of Special Collections, Hamilton College Library.*

CHAPTER 3

The Female Face of God

In watchings, fastings, tears and incessant cries to God, she labored, day & night, for deliverance from the very nature of sin. And under the most severe tribulation of mind, and the most violent temptations and buffetings of the enemy, she was often in such extreme agony of soul as caused the blood to perspire through the pores of her skin. Well might her sufferings and trials be compared with those of the Lord Jesus, when he was in the wilderness, tempted of the Devil.

As she was ordained of God, to be the first Mother of all souls, in the work of regeneration she had not only to labor and travel for her own redemption, through scenes of tribulation, and to set the example of righteousness, and mark out the line of selfdenial and the cross for her followers; but also to see and feel the full depth of man's loss, and the pain and judgment which every description of lost souls were under.

Hence she was destined to pass through inexpressible sufferings for their redemption. Sometimes, for whole nights together, her cries, screeches and groans were such as to fill every soul around her with fear and trembling, and could be compared to nothing but the horrors and agonies of the damned in hell, whose awful states were laid upon her, and whose various agonies she was, by turns, made to feel.

By such deep mortification and sufferings her flesh wasted away till she became like a mere skeleton. Elder John Hocknell, who had been a member of the Society under James and Jane Wardley, and was well acquainted with Mother Ann, through all her sufferings, testified, that he had known her to be under such power and operations of God, attended with such severe sufferings, for six weeks together that her earthly tabernacle was so reduced that she was as weak as an infant; and was fed and supported by others, being utterly incapable of helping herself; though naturally of a sound and strong constitution, and invincible fortitude of mind.

Though Ann was wrought upon in this manner, more or less, for the space of nine years; yet she had intervals of releasment, and was, at times, filled with visions and revelations of God. By this means, the way of God, and the nature of his work, gradually opened upon her mind, with increasing light and understanding. At length, about the year 1770, after a scene of deep tribulation, and the most excessive sufferings and cries to God, she received a full revelation of the root and foundation of human depravity; and of the very transgression of the first man and woman, in the garden of Eden. Then she clearly saw whence, and wherein all mankind were lost and separated from God, and the only possible way of recovery.

By the immediate revelation of God, she henceforth bore an open testimony against the lustful gratifications of the flesh, as the source and foundation of human cor-

> ruption. Her testimony was delivered with such power of God, and accompanied with the word of prophecy in such a marvellous and searching manner, that it entered into the very secrets of the heart; by which means the most hidden abominations were brought to light. She testified in the most plain and pointed manner, that no soul could follow Christ in the generation, while living in the works of natural generation, and wallowing in their lusts.
>
> The light and power of God revealed in Ann and through her, administered to those who received her testimony, had such sensible effect, in giving them power over all sin, and filling them with visions, revelations and gifts of God, that she was received and acknowledged as the first spiritual Mother in Christ, and the second heir of the covenant of life in the new creation. Hence she received the title of Mother; and hence those of the Society who received and obeyed her testimony, found a great increase in the power and gifts of God; while those who rejected it, lost all their former light and power, and fell back into a state of darkness, and into the common course of the world.[1]
>
> *From the experiences of Mother Ann Lee,*
> *founder of the Shakers*

Modern psychology casts a sympathetic eye on the heartbreaking experiences of Ann Lee (1736–1784), founder of the Shakers. Born in working-class Manchester, England, at the dawn of the Industrial Revolution, she feared and loathed the idea of marriage, but her family forced her into it. Eight pregnancies followed: four stillbirths and four live-born children who died in infancy. No wonder she blamed sex as the cause of her misery and the "root and foundation of human depravity."

Living as she did in a very restrictive but religious society, Ann's protest took the form of anorexia and spiritual exhibitionism, as described above.

In punishing herself, she punished everyone around her. They must have been relieved when she left Manchester to join a small sect of breakaway Quakers in Bolton. These dissidents had been influenced by the Camisards, an extremist sect of the Huguenot diaspora.[2] Called the "French Prophets," their rites included trances, speaking in tongues, and violent physical motions.[3] Ann's transgressions continued: she was several times arrested and imprisoned for breaking the Sabbath and for blasphemy (a crime in England until 2008). But a few friends and relatives were drawn to her. They imitated her ecstatic singing and the trembling that would turn into a dance, earning them the nickname of the "Shaking Quakers."

Persecuted in England, Ann and her followers decided to emigrate. Legend tells that on August 6, 1774, just off the boat in New York City, she knocked on the door of a Mrs. Cunningham on Pearl Street and announced: "I am commissioned by the Almighty God to preach the everlasting gospel to America, and an angel commanded me to this house and to make a home for me and my people."[4] (Mrs. Cunningham's reply is not recorded.) The proto-Shakers worked in menial jobs until they managed to lease some swampy land from Stephen Van Rensselaer[5] in Niskayuna, south of the Mohawk River.[6] They moved up there in 1776 and spent the next four years working their plot and keeping their heads down.

Mother Ann Lee taught that her community was witnessing the Second Coming of Christ; hence their official name, the United Society of Believers in Christ's Second Appearing. She also taught a form of Perfectionism, which held that once Believers had made a full confession and embraced the celibate life, they would be free from sin. Thus she banished the besetting fear that whatever one did, one might be predestined to damnation. Most importantly, Ann Lee's God had a dual nature as both male and female, which was the basis of the Shakers' gender equality. Mother Ann was not quite the first woman to lead a spiritual movement in America—Anne Hutchinson (1591–1643) has that distinction—but she was the first to establish a lasting sect.

After the Dark Day of May 19, 1780, Ann Lee went public, proclaiming the gospel of Christ's second appearing, and the call was answered far and wide. Among those who converted were Joseph Meacham (see chapter 2), who had previously visited and admired the Believers. Now he brought his congregation with him. However, the world around them happened to be at war, and the Shakers' pacifism and British origin went down badly with the Patriots. Several Believers were arrested; Ann herself spent months in Albany Jail. After the fighting ended in 1781 she was free to proselytize again, and spent two tumultuous years in New England.

Something about the Shakers drove otherwise normal citizens to frenzy, and time and again mobs stormed their houses, dragged them out, and beat both men and women.[7] One of the worst assaults happened in New Lebanon, later to become a Shaker stronghold. Mother Ann had only one quiet year back at Niskayuna when on July 21, 1784, her brother William died. Thereupon she went into a decline, and died on September 8.

James Whittaker, then only thirty-four years old, took charge and immediately tightened up the rules. Celibacy was enforced, married couples could no longer cohabit, property must be common, and public evangelism cease.[8] The legacy of a large farm in New Lebanon enabled Whittaker to make a fresh start there, and this now became the heart of Shakerdom. Meacham was the next head of the Believers and the first American-born. In conformity with the principle of sexual equality, he divided Shaker leadership by gender, directing the men himself and putting Mother Lucy Wright (died 1821) in charge of the women. Meacham also instituted a threefold hierarchy modeled on his vision of the Second Temple, as described in Ezekiel 40–42. Believers in the "Outer Court" dealt with the outside world; those in the "Middle Court" worked in production; the "Inner Court" were the leaders, who never left the property and dictated its practical and spiritual activities.[9] Most importantly, he regularized the turning, spinning, rolling, and other violent movements:

> It was to Father Joseph in vision that the revelation came of the peculiar movements and exercises called among Believers "laboring." He saw the hosts of Heaven worshiping in these ways and was taught the movements, which he gave to the people. They have ever since been cherished and honored as their beautiful meanings have been fathomed; the spiritual assistance and stimulus found in their use have been realized by all who in faith and simplicity have practised them in union with the gift and leading of the Spirit.[10]

The designs of Shaker furniture, much prized by the "world's people," were also revealed in visions. Plato spoke lightly about beds and tables having their archetype in the world of Ideas;[11] the Believers (though they probably never read Plato) brought them down to earth.

The Shaker machine was now ready to go, and it ran efficiently through the end of the century, supplying the world's people with seeds, farm produce, furniture, vehicles, and clever, labor-saving devices. To avoid the suspicion attendant on secrecy, the Believers allowed visitors to watch their devotions.[12] The New Lebanon settlement was especially popular because it was a short drive from Lebanon Springs, a fashionable watering place. Tourists came in the hundreds to see the Sunday worship with its choreographed dancing and spontaneous outbursts. Many came to gawp and scoff, but the

Believers were above mockery, confident that they alone were saved. An elder told visitors at Enfield, Connecticut, in 1821:

> Knowing the depravity of the human heart, we do not suppose that you have come here for any good purpose; but God, with whom all things are possible, may turn it to good. We do not wish to give offense, but we feel it a duty to speak plainly to you. We are sensible that we are a despised people, yet God has been pleased to manifest himself to us, and to raise us up in this latter day as a light unto many. There is no salvation without a belief in the testimony of the *second appearance* of Christ, and we are the only people who believe that testimony. We are the only righteous and the only happy people.[13]

While Ann Lee, in her own lifetime, had been regarded as a prophet and visionary, the mythology surrounding her grew after her death. By 1787 she was identified as the "Woman Clothed with the Sun" of Revelation 12:1 and the "Elect Lady" of II John; she was "everywhere present, as God himself is."[14] In 1808, during a revival in New Lebanon, there came the revelation that Ann Lee was the female manifestation of Jesus and that his Second Coming had been in Mother Ann herself.[15] This made her a real presence, who, like Jesus, was intimately concerned with the lives of believers. For instance, in 1832 Joshua Stone, a Shaker imprisoned in Albany for refusing military service, saw his cell illuminated as bright as noonday, and beheld the heavenly host, with Mother Ann Lee among them.[16]

The year 1837 was a crucial one for energizing the Shakers, as visions came thick and fast. On August 12, 1837, at Watervliet, Gideon Kibben saw the heavenly host with Ann Lee at the head, marching through the village three to four feet off the ground.[17] On November 7, Ann Mariah Goff traveled with a spirit companion to a large square building, and there met Mother Ann Lee and Lucy Wright in shining white robes with crowns on their heads. The next day, during a five-hour trance, Goff was warned by Mother Ann of the great Day of Judgment that was coming, in which the wicked would be tormented until they repented, and included advice and reproofs to specific individuals.[18]

Goff's revelations set a dangerous precedent of using visions for delivering personal messages, supposedly from a higher source. One can imagine how this could be abused. In 1837 some Shaker girls at Watervliet launched a free-for-all, dignified as "Mother Ann's Work," with "powerful shakings, quakings, testimonies, promisings, threatenings, warnings, predictions, prophecies, trances, revelations, visions, songs, and dances."[19] Some gave out accusations of individuals that led to expulsions and poisoned the atmosphere of the Watervliet community. Others lay entranced for days on end, and returned with tales of meeting Lafayette, Washington, Napoleon, and Indian chiefs.[20] Another phenomenon of this revival period was possession by "Indians" who would jabber in pidgin English and act in a "savage and boisterous" way:[21] a degrading parody of how Indians were seen by whites, but also an anticipation of the native spirit guides who would become a fixture of spiritualism.

In 1841 the Shakers decided it would be prudent to exclude visitors from rites that had taken such a bizarre turn. On May 4, 1842, Philemon Stewart of the New Lebanon community was summoned to the Holy Fountain of the Shaker village, where for fourteen days he wrote at the dictation of an angel. The resulting scripture, called *A Sacred and Divine Roll*, claimed authority equal to the Bible, and confirmed Ann Lee's status as the second Christ.[22] It was sent to all the Shaker groups and regarded as a new revelation of principles and directives. All in all, the 1830s and 1840s were the Shakers' most creative period, from which date their enigmatic and beautiful spirit drawings and many of their songs. It also prepared them to accept the message of spiritualism when it arrived in 1848, for contact between worlds was what they had maintained all along.

Jemima Wilkinson, the Universal Friend (1752–1819)

> On the fourth Day of the 10th Month, on the Seventh Day of the weak, at night, a certain young-woman, known by the name of Jemima Wilkison was seiz'd with this mortal disease. And on the 2d. Day of her illness, was render'd almost incapable of helping herself.—And the fever continuing to increase untill fifth Day of the Weak about midnight, She appear'd to meet the Shock of Death; which [illegible] the Soul.
>
> *From Memorandum of the "Columbus" or Typhus fever, found in Jemima Wilkinson's Bible and preserved with her papers*[23]

Her Case was Like no other he knew of that the fever being Translated to the head. She Rose with different Ideas that what She had when the fever was General, and she Conceived the Idea that she had been Dead and was raised Up for Extraordinary Purposes, and got well fast,—but, that She had been Dead none of her friends or Attendants had any apprehension or thought of her having been Dead, but She was for some time After Considered by her friends not to be in her right Mind.

Account of Dr. Man, of Attleboro,
who treated Jemima Wilkinson[24]

The heavens were open'd And She saw too Archangels descending from the east, with golden crowns upon there heads, clothed in long white Robes, down to the feet; Bringing a sealed Pardon from the living God; and putting their trumpets to their mouth, proclaimed saying, Room, Room, Room, in the many Mansions of eternal glory for Thee and for everyone, that there is one more call for, that the eleventh hour is not yet past with them, and the day of grace is not yet over with them. For every one that will come, may come, and partake of the waters of life freely, which is offered to Sinners without money, and without price.

And the Angels said, The time is at hand, when God will lift up his hand, a second time, to recover the remnant of his People, whos [*sic*] day is not yet over; and the Angels said, The Spirit of Life from God, had descended to earth, to warn a lost and guilty, perishing dying World, to flee from the wrath which is to come; and to give an Invitation to the lost Sheep of the house of Israel to come home; and was waiting to assume the Body which God had prepared, for the Spirit to dwell in. . . . And then taking her leave of the family between the hour of nine & ten in the morning dropt the dying flesh & yielded up the Ghost.

> And according to the declaration of the Angels,—the Spirit took full possession of the Body it now animates.[25]
>
> *Jemima Wilkinson's account of her vision in 1776*

Jemima Wilkinson, like Ann Lee, began as a Quaker and came to be revered as God in female form. In every other respect, Jemima had an easier life, with her prosperous Rhode Island family, the unmarried state that was obviously her preference, her tough and active physique, her doctrines, and the latitude she allowed to her followers. Her father, Jeremiah Wilkinson, farmed a large estate in Cumberland, Rhode Island, and in the normal course of things, Jemima would have married and led a good Quaker life. Whether or not it was George Whitefield himself, on one of his many preaching tours,[26] who set her on a different path, in her late teens she fell under the influence of the New Light Stir. By 1776 she had joined a separatist group and the Quakers had disowned her.

Jemima's solution, whether conscious or not, was to disown herself. Her spectacular vision (see above) features the New Light themes of direct inspiration, the potential salvation of all, and the imminent millennium, but it went much further—outrageously so. The New Lights had touched the fringes of Perfectionism, but none had dared claim that their humanity had been completely scoured away, leaving them a pure vessel for the Divine Spirit.

Jemima's new condition required a new name, the "Publick Universal Friend," and a new costume of black or purple robes, a white cravat, and flowing hair beneath a broad-brimmed Quaker hat: masculine, in effect, down to the waist. Although not learned, she had the entire Bible stored in her memory and instant access to the appropriate quote. She must have struck an impressive figure. A memoir of her mentions "arched black eyebrows and fierce looking black eyes, darting here and there with penetrating glances throughout the assembly, as though she read the thoughts of people . . . [occasionally] uttering words of wondrous import, with a masculine-feminine tone of voice, or kind of croak, unearthly and sepulchral."[27]

During the Revolutionary years, the Universal Friend moved around New England as though on a higher plane than worldly events. Royalists and Patriots alike tolerated her. They let her preach in prisons and comfort condemned men. She gained some well-placed disciples, notably Judge William Potter, who added a fourteen-room wing to his mansion in Kingston, Rhode Island, to house her and her attendants. This annoyed the clergy and others who thought a preaching woman either blasphemous or clownish.

But her unflappable disposition and earnest, magnetic personality brought her more allies than enemies.

As soon as the war was over, the Friend was on the road again, making several preaching trips to the capital, Philadelphia. Her well-mounted, oddly dressed entourage always attracted attention, and she sometimes showed clairvoyant insight into the hearts of her individual hearers. Any attempt to involve her in theological controversy foundered against her evasive, measured, moralizing answers.

The Dark Day of May 19, 1780, was a memorable one in the Friend's calendar, for on that day Judge Potter's beloved daughter Susannah "left time," dying in her arms. After that the Friend seems to have lost her sense of an imminent millennium. As the decade wore on, she tired of the city and the preaching circuit, and began looking for a place to plant her community. A first posse of her scouts left in 1785 to prospect the newly opened Genesee and Finger Lakes region. In due course some of the wealthier members put up the money for land on the western shore of Seneca Lake, and a colony began the arduous work of clearing, planting, building, and working a gristmill and a sawmill in preparation for the Friend's advent.

Herbert Wisbey, her biographer, suggests that the Friend's community was modeled on the Ephrata Cloister.[28] This was a German Seventh-Day Baptist community northwest of Philadelphia, founded in 1732 by Conrad Johann Beissel. It included a core of celibates who followed a strict, ascetic lifestyle and an outer circle of married members, all working at crafts or farming. There were no articles of belief, vows, or confessions of faith, but a sense of an elect, utopian society that went back to the Rosicrucian ideals of early-seventeenth-century Germany. Absolute belief in the Bible, friendliness and hospitality to outsiders, a partial community of property, and Saturday worship were common to both Ephrata and the Universal Friend's sect. Another influence may have been the Shakers, but Niskayuna and New Lebanon lay well outside Jemima's field of activity, and there were radical differences in their theology and sexology.

The Friend set out from Worcester, Pennsylvania, in 1790, traveling in her carriage emblazoned with the signs of the Sun, the Cross, and the initials "U. F." It was shipped up the Susquehanna River, then drawn overland to where Keuka Lake empties into Seneca Lake: present-day Dresden, in Yates County. The disciples had built her a log house where she lived for four years, surrounded by their own cabins or houses, according to their means, and by the fields in which she was by all accounts a willing laborer.

The Friends' Settlement, as it was called, comprised about three hundred people in sixty families and was the largest settlement of its time in western New York. What exactly they did in the spiritual line is vague. They listened to the Friend's Sabbath-day homilies, consulted her on every aspect of life, health, and conduct, but did not baptize or celebrate the Lord's Supper, like the established sects. Nor did they sing in harmony like the Ephratans or whirl like the Shakers. Most of them were married, but celibacy was held out as a superior state. They abstained from alcohol and, as far as they could, from sex, but the Friend forgave lapses and was fond of children. She followed Quaker principles of opposition to slavery, causing Judge Potter to free his own slaves, and rigorous honesty in dealing with the Indians who remained in the area. Early biographers, mostly disaffected members or outsiders with theological objections,[29] told stories of Jemima trying to raise the dead, walk on water, having secret lovers, and obtaining forced gifts with the words, "The Lord hath need of it." In that insanitary age, even her habit of daily bathing and liking for clean linen was held against her. At this distance of time, her main fault seems to have been trusting people who did not deserve that trust.

The Seneca Lake community suffered endless troubles with faulty land deeds, poor surveying, and shady agents. In 1794 they cut their losses and left for a new home a dozen miles away, north of the West Branch of Keuka Lake. Here they bought fourteen hundred acres in the township aptly named Jerusalem. The Friend lived in another large log house, together with the needier members of the society who could not build for themselves. Her immediate entourage was of about fifteen women, celibate like herself. This is where the Duc de la Rochefoucauld-Liancourt and his party stopped on their way back from Niagara Falls. The Frenchmen were bored by the Friend's preaching but declared the dinner the best since they had left Philadelphia.[30]

The Jerusalem community flourished for twenty years, and its example drew many other settlers to the region between Seneca Lake and the Genesee River. In 1809 the disciples started building a new residence and meetinghouse: a frame house in Federal style, five-bayed on each side, which they finished in 1815. This marked the apogee of the movement, after which the Friend's health began to decline. On April 19, 1819, her sister Patience died. The Friend was carried to the funeral service, where she preached her last sermon. She herself left time on July 1, following her sister just as Ann Lee had followed her brother. The devotees placed her body in a vault in the cellar, perhaps hoping for its resurrection. Later they buried it according to Quaker custom, in an unmarked grave, so the house on Friend Hill Road remains her only visible memorial.

The Friend's last will directed that the poorer disciples be supported from the general funds, and this was done until the last one died in 1874.[31]

ILLUSTRATION 3.2. The Wilkinson House at Jerusalem, Keuka Lake. The home of Jemima Wilkinson, the "Publick Universal Friend," and her close associates from about 1809 until her death in 1815. *Author's photograph.*

Unfortunately, due to her conviction that Jemima Wilkinson had died in 1776, she had always refused legal ownership of anything. The communal property of more than four thousand acres was held in trust by her faithful disciple, Sarah Richards, who died in 1793. Sarah's will was contested by her son-in-law, and, in Wisbey's words, "Before the legal battle was over, all the principals in the case . . . were dead; thousands of dollars were expended in litigation; and the assaults of those who coveted her lands had warped the public image of the Universal Friend and her followers almost beyond recognition."[32] Unlike the Shakers, who continued to produce powerful and charismatic figures, there was no one to replace the Universal Friend, and the community soon withered and dispersed.

That the divine has both male and female aspects is obvious to polytheists, whether ancient Greeks or modern Hindus, who can worship a god, a goddess, or both. It is more difficult for monotheists whose sacred books depict a decidedly masculine God. In the Middle Ages, the Catholic Church compensated by de-emphasizing the Old Testament and exalting the Virgin Mary, whom many found more approachable and responsive than any person of the Trinity. For Protestants, this was not an option, so that those with a dual-gendered notion of God had to find other havens. We will meet several of them in the chapters that follow. Eventually a "Mother-Father God" became the norm for Christian Scientists, Unitarians, and Universalists, while esoteric doctrines taught, as they always have, that the Absolute is beyond any human conception of gender.

ILLUSTRATION 4.1. Tomb of Handsome Lake, Seneca chief and revealer of the Gaiwi'io religion. Onondaga Nation, Nedrow. *Author's photograph.*

CHAPTER 4

The Indian Tragedy

So they proceeded on their journey and it happened that a vision appeared unto them. They seemed to be advancing toward an approaching man. Soon they met him and passed. Now when they were a distance apart they turned and he was facing them. So they greeted each other. Then said the man, "Sedwa:go'wanê, I must ask you a question. Did you never hear your grandfathers say that once there was a certain man upon the earth across the great waters who was slain by his own people?" That was what he said when he spoke.

Then answered Sedwa:go'wanê, "It is true. I have heard my grandparents say this."

Then answered the man, "I am he." And he turned his palms upward and they were scarred and his feet were likewise and his breast was pierced by a spear wound. It appeared that his hands and his feet were torn by iron nails. All this was true. It could be seen and blood was fresh upon him.

> Then said the man, "They slew me because of their independence and unbelief. So I have gone home to shut the doors of heaven that they may not see me again until the earth passes away. Then will all the people cry to me for succor, and when I come it will be in this wise: my face will be sober and I shall turn it to my people. Now let me ask how your people receive your teachings."
>
> He answered, "It is my opinion that half my people are inclined to believe in me."
>
> Then answered he, "You are more successful than I for some believe in you but none in me. I am inclined to believe that in the end it will also be so with you. Now it is rumored that you are but a talker with spirits (djîs'gä^{n}dâtâha`). Now it is true that I am a spirit and the one of him who was murdered. Now tell your people that they will become lost when they follow the ways of the white man."
>
> So that is what he said. Eniaiehuk.[1]
>
> *From the Visions of Sedwa:go'wanê*
> *(Handsome Lake), 1799*

In Nichols Pond County Park, south of Canastota, a New York State historical marker commemorates the earliest European incursion into central New York. It reads:

SITE OF
CHAMPLAIN BATTLE
HERE CHAMPLAIN AIDED BY
HURON INDIANS ATTACKED THE
STOCKADED ONEIDA VILLAGE
OCT. 10–16, 1615.

Samuel Champlain (c. 1567–1635) was the explorer after whom Lake Champlain is named, and the founder of the city of Quebec. The more he discovered of "New France," as Canada and the Northeast were then called (at least by the French), the more entangled he became in Indian affairs. The colonists needed the cooperation of the natives, who quickly learned the superiority of European weaponry—steel swords and the arquebus (a primitive but effective musket). While the Indians found themselves unwillingly involved in the rivalries between French, Dutch, and English colonizers, the reverse was also true. Schiavo and Salvucci, in their introduction to *The Iroquois Wars*, write that "[Champlain] and the French were drafted almost immediately into a complex intertribal system of alliance, trade, blood feud, and warfare that long predated any serious establishment of European colonies."[2]

As this historical marker indicates, the Hurons had persuaded the French to support them in their ongoing war with the Iroquois. Champlain wrote a long description of his journey from Quebec to attack a stronghold of the Oneidas or Onondagas,[3] though archaeologists no longer identify it with the Nichols Pond site.[4] During the skirmishes en route, the Hurons captured some Iroquois women and immediately cut off a finger from one of them. They were surprised when their French ally objected to this "beginning of their usual punishment." The Iroquois would do the same to them, they said.[5] When the war party finally reached the enemy stronghold and attacked, the stockade resisted all their attempts to batter or burn it down. Champlain had an up-to-date European solution: a siege tower that would enable the arquebusiers to fire on the enemy from above. The Hurons built it under his direction, and two hundred men carried it into place. Once there, however, they lacked the discipline needed to support his strategy, and the siege failed. Champlain had a painful retreat, wounded in the leg by arrows, trussed like a turkey, and carried on an Indian's back.[6]

In the wake of the colonizers came God's warriors, the Jesuit missionaries. Their written reports in the *Jesuit Relations* are a priceless source for the early period of contact, but do not always make pleasant reading. Both Hurons and Iroquois enjoyed the prolonged torture of their captives, and the Jesuits who had installed themselves with the tribes watched these procedures and sent detailed accounts to their headquarters. While they found them shocking, the missionaries' job was to convert the natives to Christianity. Better behavior would then follow, or so they believed. In any case, the Jesuits themselves had volunteered for this dangerous work fully prepared for martyrdom. If they succeeded in converting a victim, his reward (and theirs) would be great in heaven. In 1668, one Father Millet attended the slow burning of a baptized captive at Onondaga, and after describing it, adds:

> This occupation of helping the Captives that are burned alive and eaten, in the Missionaries' presence, is an exercise demand-

> ing great courage; and as one naturally has a horror of seeing people burned and eaten, it is, for a new Missionary, a strange spectacle, and one in which he has great need of being fortified by grace. Among these races, the victorious find their diversion in the custom; but this cruelty can but cause much pain to persons brought up in the Christian religion.[7]

The editors of *The Iroquois Wars*, who neither condemn nor whitewash the Indians' practices, write:

> Thus we are compelled to take seriously the traditionalist notion of cruelty as a motivating factor—not, as with Parkman,[8] with any sense of racial determinism that the Iroquois were bound to act cruel because they were Iroquois, but rather that they were prey to human vices, and their society had instituted an outlet for one particular vice to such an extraordinary degree.[9]

The Jesuits' conduct and motives puzzled the Indians. How could men who called themselves "fathers" refuse sexual relations? What did they really want? Their spells and rites looked suspiciously like sorcery.[10] Occasionally the missionaries fell foul of their hosts, with fatal consequences. The Mohawks killed Father René Goupil (1608–1642) in September 1642. His colleague Father Isaac Jogues (1607–1646) suffered six months' captivity in 1642–43, with tortures and mutilations horribly described in the *Jesuit Relations*. The Dutch helped him to escape, but in 1646 he returned to his missionary field and was killed.

Iroquois culture and Catholic belief may not qualify as eccentric movements, but their clash left a mark—some would say a lasting spiritual presence—on the Upstate region. Its visible memorials are the Catholic shrines on opposite banks of the Mohawk. In Auriesville, the Shrine of Our Lady of Martyrs commemorates St. Isaac Jogues, St. René Goupil, and the other six North American martyrs. All were canonized in 1925. On the other side of the Mohawk, near Fonda, is the National Kateri Tekakwitha Shrine, dedicated to an Indian woman who lived most of her life in a village on this site. St. Kateri (1656–1680) converted to Christianity and insisted on living as a virtual nun within Mohawk society. Although not martyred, she was cruelly used by her people, to which she added self-inflicted pains. In 2011, Pope Benedict XVI accepted the two miracles required for canonization: the disappearance of her smallpox scars after her death, and the healing of an American boy whose parents had prayed for Kateri's intercession. It drew worldwide attention to the Mohawk Valley shrines as places of pilgrimage and the renewal of religious life. Others may be less reassured. Despite the natural beauty and serenity of the sites, the martyrs' shrines remind them of the lengths to which fanatics are driven by the certainty that theirs is the only true faith, and of the recurrent torture and burning of "heretics" by their fellow Christians.

A happier atmosphere surrounds the three mansions and the chapel built by Sir William Johnson (see chapter 1), the colonial government's agent to the Indians. His charge and achievement was to keep them on the British side during the various mid-century wars against the French. Johnson had charm and great persuasive power. The Indians, by all accounts, were always in and out of his houses, camping on the grounds, and accepting him as lover of their daughters: he had eight children by Molly Brant, sister of the educated Mohawk leader Joseph Brant. The baronet's attitude to religion was pragmatic. Born an Irish Catholic, he had joined the Anglican Church, without which political advancement in the colony would have been impossible. Likewise, he encouraged Indian converts to embrace Anglicanism, rather than the Catholicism of the French enemy. Indian Castle Church, which he built on land donated by the Brants, speaks of reconciliation rather than martyrdom. With its lack of imagery and unmarked Indian graveyard, it more resembles a Quaker meetinghouse.

The Quakers had a different approach. Because they respected the "inner light" as latent within people of all races and faiths, it was not so important for them that the Indians should accept Christian dogma. Their missionary strategy was not to thrust the Gospel down heathen throats, accompanied with threats of hellfire, but gradually to make Quakers of them. Those young Friends who, like the Jesuits of old, chose to live among the Indians taught by example: they built neat houses, planted tidy fields, erected mills, and led a quiet, sober, hard-working life. If only the Indians would see the sense of this, live in nuclear families, have their menfolk take up farming and their women industrious crafts, and eventually graduate to private ownership of house and land . . . these were the Quakers' ideals. But however kindly meant, it was a program of cultural genocide, and it failed.

Like all Native Americans, the Iroquois already had a theology, a cosmology, and effective ways of communicating with the spirit world. Everyday messages came through dreams, which were taken seriously, interpreted, and their instructions acted upon. Special ones occurred during the male initiation rites, in which a youth would spend two weeks or more in the forest, fasting and alone. The ordeal was expected to culminate in a vision of his guardian spirit, who would replace his parents as his protector and counselor.[11] Some youths were marked out for a closer connection with their guardian spirit, and would become clairvoyants, shamans, even witches. The terms vary, but all represent mediators between worlds or states of being. The shaman uses his access to the spirit world for the interpretation of dreams and for healing; the witch, at least in the Iroquois understanding of the term, for doing ill.

At a higher level were the prophets or messianic figures, whose message was for the whole tribe. Two appeared in 1762, the unnamed Onondaga Prophet and the Delaware Prophet called Neolin, meaning "the enlightened one," who lived on the Cuyahoga River near Lake Erie (now in Ohio). The "Master of Life" instructed him in a vision and revealed a written code of laws, then sent him from village to village, preaching. Since Neolin's listeners were illiterate, he gave the code a graphic form and displayed it on a large sheet of parchment: part prayer sheet, like the ones white men used, part mnemonic symbols such as the Indians wove into their wampum belts. Like every prophet, Neolin urged repentance. He told his people what they must do to recover the Creator's favor: drive out the white man and reclaim their own land. Anthony Wallace, the chronicler of Seneca history, comments that for all Neolin's claim to restore tradition, "he was advising the abandonment of many old cultural elements, such as 'medicine songs,' war rituals, polygyny; and he was introducing various quasi-European concepts, such as a high-god common to both whites and Indians, written prayers, and a written 'Great Book.'"[12]

Every tribe underwent a degree of religious crisis after the encounter with the whites and their missionaries. Sometimes this led to conversion, as with the Stockbridge Indians under Samuel Kirkland. More often the result was a syncretism such as Wallace describes. There was also a pagan resistance. The Oneidas, for example, split along Christian and pagan lines. Blacksmith, leader of the pagan party in the mid-1790s, told a white traveler that "the objects of his devotion were the rocks and mountains which he believed were animated by some invisible Power, which had a superintendency over human affairs. . . . This had been his religion from his youth, and he had never failed of receiving answers to his prayers . . . and he regarded the Oneida stone as an image of the deity which he worshipped."[13]

Most Oneidas of the Christian party immigrated to Green Bay, Wisconsin, following an eccentric, part-Mohawk missionary called Eleazar Williams (1787–1858). Vast territories were promised them, and the largest of the three Oneida communities still exists on their diminished remnant.[14] The Oneida Stone, being a pagan relic, was left behind. In 1849, the newly founded Forest Hill Cemetery in Utica offered it a home.[15] Utica was nearing the height of its prosperity, and the local Oneidas, reduced to a hundred or so destitute souls,[16] consented. For a century and a quarter the stone rested on a plinth near the cemetery entrance, with a bronze plaque reading as follows:

SACRED STONE OF THE ONEIDA INDIANS
THIS STONE WAS THE NATIONAL ALTAR OF THE
ONEIDA INDIANS AROUND WHICH THEY GATHERED
FROM YEAR TO YEAR TO CELEBRATE SOLEMN
RELIGIOUS RITES AND TO WORSHIP THE GREAT
SPIRIT
THEY WERE KNOWN AS THE TRIBE OF THE
UPRIGHT STONE. THIS VALUABLE HISTORICAL
RELIC WAS BROUGHT HERE FROM STOCKBRIDGE
MADISON CO., N.Y. IN 1849.

In 1974 the Indians of Madison County decided that it was time to repatriate their sacred stone.[17] They brought it to their reservation, now the Oneida Indian Nation, where it sits opposite the circular Council House. Meanwhile Oneida fortunes have skyrocketed, thanks to the success of their Turning Stone Casino in Verona. Few of the gamblers and golfers who flock to that resort know that its name derives from the travels of this midsize glacial boulder.

Whether converted or not, the Iroquois found that Christianity had left an ineradicable mark on their ethics, cosmology, and eschatology. These found a new codifier in a chief of the Seneca tribe originally named Hadawa'ko ("Shaking Snow," c. 1735–1815). He had already played a large part in the pre- and post-Revolutionary eras, both as warrior and negotiator. By the time the dust had settled and the new nation was forging ahead, the Indians' hopes for a restoration of their homeland had come to nothing, and Hadawa'ko himself had fallen into depression and alcoholism. One day in 1799, already bedridden, he became unconscious, his body temperature dropped, and he was thought to be dead. He returned to consciousness with the tale of a tremendous vision, which was followed by two more and by a lifelong series of minor revelations. Like many who have been spiritually reborn, he adopted a new name: Sganyodaiyo, which translates roughly as "Handsome Lake."

Handsome Lake describes a Swedenborgian (or, to anticipate, a spiritualist) heaven, in which the dead retain their personalities and have affairs of their own to pursue. For instance, George Washington, strolling with his dog, declares that the Iroquois should "go back to the places that are theirs for they are an independent people." Then comes a cosmological vision of the "veil over all," a white object whose revolutions affect the earth and are in turn regulated by the four messengers. These suggest the four archangels of Judeo-Christian tradition,[18] to whom esoteric sources attribute a cosmic regulatory function. Next, Handsome Lake meets Jesus, who speaks with him man to man, as in the extract at the head of this chapter.

Handsome Lake was more than a seer: he founded a religion. It was called Gaiwi'io, the "Good Word" addressed to the Indians, just as the Gospel, in his view, was destined for the white men. Thus, like the female messiahs discussed in chapter 3, Handsome Lake claimed a role complementary to that of Jesus. The process much resembles the legendary beginnings of Islam. Doctrinal messages came to the Seneca Prophet over a span of years from the four angels who appeared to him in vision. He recited the messages to his adherents, who memorized and passed them down in different lineages. Some time after Handsome Lake's death a canonical, written version was compiled, which has been ritually recited ever since. Arthur Parker, writing in 1913, relates,

> The present form of the Gai'wiio` was determined by a council of its preachers some fifty years ago. They met at Cold Spring, the old home of Handsome Lake, and compared their versions. Several differences were found and each preacher thought his version the correct one. At length Chief John Jacket, a Cattaraugus Seneca, and a man well versed in the lore of his people, was chosen to settle forever the words and the form of the Gai'wiio`. This he did by writing it out in the Seneca language by the method taught by Rev. Asher Wright, the Presbyterian missionary. The preachers assembled again, this time, according to Cornplanter, at Cattaraugus where they memorized the parts in which they were faulty. The original text was written on letter paper and now is entirely destroyed.[19]

The Gaiwi'io is a blend of visions with moral instructions. It defines four cardinal sins: drinking alcohol, practicing witchcraft, the use of love charms, and abortion. Matthew Dennis has pointed out that the three latter prohibitions were aimed at women, who were traditionally powerful members of the tribe and the holders of matriarchal lineages. For instance, upon marriage a man would join his mother-in-law's household, and the woman was free to throw him out if he misbehaved. It was women who concocted love charms, regulated birth, and enjoyed relative sexual freedom. Handsome Lake's visions, on the contrary, depicted terrible punishments for women's sexual lapses, while those of men were excused and erased by confession. Dennis comments: "They look like cultural imports from the patriarchal and misogynous society that surrounded the Senecas, at odds with Iroquois tradition."[20]

The confession of sins was imported from Christianity, as was the whole notion of sin, formerly absent from Indian as from most pagan ethical systems. This required a reinterpretation of the Twins, whom Iroquois mythology placed at the origin of the material world. The Good Twin was its creator;

the Evil Twin, the spoiler who envied the creation and claimed it as his own work.[21] Iroquois tradition paid the Evil Twin his due, mainly through the periodic rituals of the False Face Society, whose members would don masks and run amok. As in old European solstice customs like the Saturnalia with its Lord of Misrule, along with their potential for healing, these controlled eruptions served as a safety valve for repressed desires. Handsome Lake's eschatology recast the Evil Twin in the role of the Christian Satan, and threatened sinners with something that Indian tradition had never contemplated: posthumous torture in an eternal hell. On the pagan side, in 1799 he revived the White Dog Sacrifice, celebrated at the midwinter full moon that marked the Iroquois New Year. A pure white dog was strangled, decorated, hung on a pole, burned, and eaten in a spirit of thanksgiving. In one of his visions, Handsome Lake meets his former pet who had been sacrificed in this way and who greets him joyfully. Christian disapproval suppressed this rite, which was unsettlingly similar to its own traditions of Mass and Communion, but it was still being celebrated in the twentieth century.[22]

Handsome Lake's triumph over his own alcoholism and his efforts to woo his people away from hard liquor won universal respect. As in Islam and Mormonism, it was abstinence that most distinguished his followers from the surrounding community of hard-drinking Christians. A less healthy obsession was with witchcraft, a fear that the whites had suppressed since Salem but was still rampant among the Indians. According to Mary Jemison (1743–1833), witches had been executed nearly every year since she had lived with the Seneca, i.e., since her capture in 1758 and decision to integrate with the tribe.[23] Dennis describes the mental climate that resulted from such beliefs: "An unsuspecting husband could learn that his wife was, in fact, *Ka-tar-hwat,* a fabulous reptile; friends or foes might turn out to be secret witches; trees might talk, and during sleep people's disembodied spirits might roam the landscape."[24]

By 1800, Handsome Lake had been persuaded by his angelic messengers that his mission was not just to preach but "to judge the earth and cure diseases."[25] When his niece fell ill and failed to respond to ritual treatments, he blamed his Delaware neighbors for bewitching her, took a hostage, and prepared to execute him in revenge. The girl's recovery only served to prove the truth of the accusation: it had scared the Delaware witches into desisting. Wallace writes that after this, "He believed that, as the angels told him, witches were the agents of the Evil Spirit, responsible for almost all sickness and disease and working to destroy the world itself. If they were not checked by good men who believed in Handsome Lake's message, the world would come to an end."[26]

A council at Buffalo Creek in 1801, impressed by Handsome Lake's transformation and charisma, made him the supreme leader of the Six

Nations. When the eminent orator Red Jacket (c. 1750–1830) objected to Handsome Lake's growing despotism, the prophet disclosed a vision of Red Jacket eternally tormented in hell.[27] In 1802 he accused his rival of witchcraft and actually brought him to trial, as memorably depicted in a later painting by James Mix Stanley (1869).[28] Red Jacket in turn planted rumors that Handsome Lake was a fraud perpetrated by Cornplanter (c. 1730s–1836), the prophet's half brother, who conveniently "remembered" revelations when the prophet's memory of them failed.[29]

During an epidemic in 1807 that struck down many of his tribe, another obsession gripped Handsome Lake. The cause, he declared, was a great underground beast, and he set groups digging after it. When no such animal was found, he put the blame, as usual, on witchcraft.[30]

We do not know how many women were executed as witches under Handsome Lake's leadership, but certainly some were, for around 1808–09 Cornplanter declared that such killing must stop, and the Quakers expressed relief at the decision of the Indians "to take no more lives on that account."[31] Yet this was not the end. One last killing occurred in 1821, when Tommy Jemmy, a Seneca, cut the throat of an accused woman. This led to a cause célèbre hinging on the question of whether the Indians were free to apply their own laws within their reservations, or whether federal law applied

ILLUSTRATION 4.2. Council Stone of 1615, Nichols Pond. Near the reputed site of the tribal battle in which Samuel Champlain fought and was wounded. *Author's photograph.*

there. After some legal wrangling the killer went free, but it was clear that a repetition would not be tolerated.

Handsome Lake's mission had begun in Cornplanter's tract along the Allegheny River, but the rivalries and resentments that he caused forced him to relocate, first upriver to Cold Spring on the Allegany Reservation, and then to Tonawanda, a reservation now swallowed by Buffalo. At the time of his death he was visiting the Onondaga Reservation, and was buried there. As memories of his excesses faded, the positive result of his prophetic career developed. The Gaiwi'io was treasured as the unconverted Indians' guide to maintaining their identity and, in modified form, their spirituality. But none of this could prevent the next act of the tragedy.

As the nineteenth century progressed, the Indians lost more and more of their land. The Senecas' largest reservation, at Buffalo Creek, stood inconveniently astride the Erie Canal's route. In 1838 they were displaced in what Laurence Hauptmann calls "one of the major frauds in American Indian history."[32] Some Oneidas had already gone to Wisconsin. The plan for the Senecas was to resettle them—perhaps "dump" is a truer word—in Kansas.

The followers of the Gaiwi'io opposed this vigorously, with the encouragement of a second generation of prophets at Buffalo Creek and Tonawanda. These seers confirmed Handsome Lake's revelations through visions of their own, claiming that they received annual visits from the same four angels as he. The Buffalo Creek Prophet was taken on a tour of hell, where he saw the punishments meted out to the chiefs supporting the Kansas resettlement. The Tonawanda Prophet warned of a pestilence that would only be averted through a ritual feast and dance, and a special sort of medicine he had prepared. Thanks to this new wave of religious enthusiasm, the 1840s saw the constant recitation of Handsome Lake's teachings and the accumulation of a large body of legends and texts.[33] Thus the Gaiwi'io survived through a similar process to the one that revivified Shakerism at about the same time, namely the acceptance of a fresh prophetic dispensation.

None of this touched the white man's world. The Indians had vanished, for all practical purposes, into the romanticized past of James Fenimore Cooper's *Leatherstocking Tales*. Readers could indulge a moment of sympathy for the "Last of the Mohicans," and in Cooperstown itself they may still notice the curious mound on the corner of Route 33. A single tree grows on it, and the stone plaque set into its side is just legible:

> White Man Greeting!
> We near whose bones you stand
> Were Iroquois. The wide land
> Which now is yours was ours.
> Friendly hands have given back
> To us enough for a tomb.

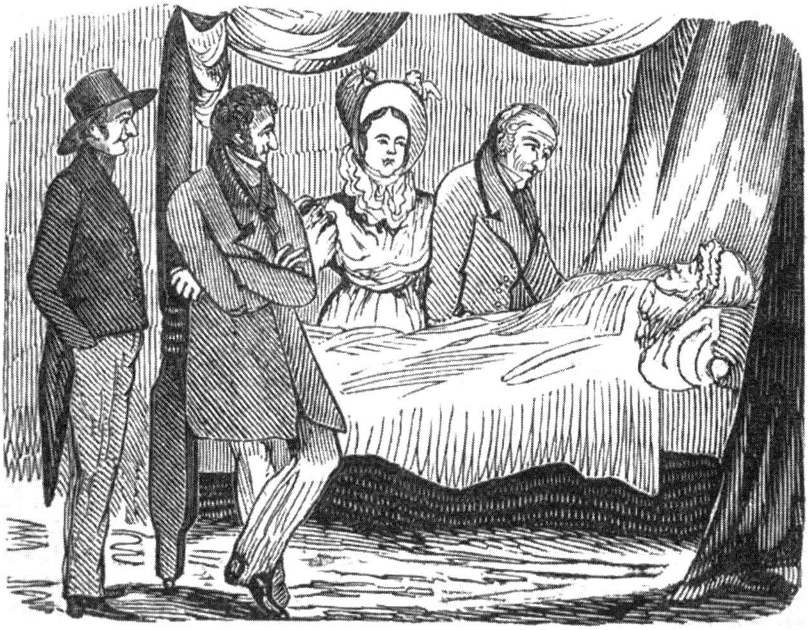

ILLUSTRATION 5.1. Rachel Baker, the sleeping preacher. From J. E. Smith, *Legends and Miracles, and Other Curious and Marvellous Stories of Human Nature*, London: B. D. Cousins, 1837.

CHAPTER 5

Sleeping Preachers

The intermittent disorder which Miss Baker suffers, seizes her in bed or in her chair if she sits up. After a few moments of torpor or somnolency, at the usual hour she loses her consciousness and begins to speak in an audible and frequently a forcible tone. She is usually found lying in a supine posture and so free from all voluntary action save that of her organs of speech, and a little inclination of her neck, that she stirs neither hand nor foot from the beginning to the termination of the attack. Except the lips, throat, and neighbouring parts there is not more action discoverable in her than if she was totally disabled by palsy. She may be literally said to lie still. Thus this modest damsel falls into a devotional exercise as soon as she loses her consciousness. It would be improper to consider her asleep tho' her body and limbs are so quiet and her eyes steadily closed.

The exercise consists of three parts: the first an incipient or opening prayer to God, similar to those of our reformed preachers; the second an addres [*sic*] or exhortation as to a human audience present, and listening to her; and the third a closing supplication to the Supreme being resembling

> in its principal points the final offering of confession and thanksgiving from the pulpit. She neither sings nor selects a text, but occasionally recites verses from the hymns of Watts.
>
> It has been remarked that the topics of these exercises are strictly conformable to the Calvinistic faith. In them she manifests an extensive acquaintance with the doctrinal parts of the scriptures, and readily cites the several books. . . .
>
> On one occasion I observed, during her sermon, that she ought to be silent and not talk so long and so loud in her sleep. She heard me and denied that she was asleep. Her eye lids were, as usual, accurately closed, and there was no sign of winking. She declared herself awake, and in confirmation of her opinion, described in vivid and glowing strains the spectacle then bright in her view; consisting of the angels, saints, and souls of just men made perfect, ministering before the throne of the Almighty, clothed in robes white as snow, and without spot or blemish, and looking like fine linen wrought by skilful hands, and with curious and cunning workmanship.[1]
>
> *From an account of Rachel Baker,*
> *the sleeping preacher, 1814*

The peculiar syndrome of Rachel Baker (1794–1857) lasted only five years. She made no extraordinary claims and no sect formed around her, but it earned her abiding, if unwelcome, fame. Her case was examined by experts[2] and widely reported in the popular and scientific press, becoming a fixture in the annals of abnormal psychology, sleep studies, and spiritualism.

Rachel was born in Pelham, Massachusetts, in 1794, the daughter of Ezekiel Baker (1764–1842) and his wife, Hannah Rachel Sears (1766–1841).[3] She came to New York State in 1803 when her father, a Presbyterian farmer, settled in Marcellus, Onondaga County. Contemporary biographers say that as a girl she was neither well schooled nor particularly bright. However, in June 1811, she attended an adult baptism somewhere in Scipio township, and returned home in a deeply depressed state. After some months, her mother induced her to say what was upsetting her: it was the certainty that she was the greatest sinner on earth and was going to hell. This was the theme of the sleep talking that began shortly after, becoming more and more nightmarish until the crisis of January 27, 1812: "Awful terrors seemed to have taken possession of her; her affrighted imagination seemed haunted with dreadful spectres; she said that one of the infernal fiends was grasping her, and would drag her down to the bottomless pit!"[4] The household, as one can imagine, was very much alarmed by the spectacle. But as Rachel told them afterward, she had given herself up to God and, in a classic salvation experience, heard the words, "Daughter, be of good cheer, thy sins are forgiven thee."

From then on, Rachel was a changed woman. She continued to talk in her sleep, but now it was with confidence in God's goodness to repentant sinners. In January 1813 she moved to Scipio to live with an aunt and learn dressmaking. There she joined the local Baptist church. Her sermons continued nightly and word of them spread. They were the standard mixture of platitudes, emotional outbursts, and exhortations to repent and be saved.[5] Although one report says that her preaching was "strictly conformable to the Calvinistic faith,"[6] its talk of salvation through being born again[7] puts it more on the Arminian side.

In October 1813 Rachel visited New York City for medical advice on how to rid herself of a faculty that may have been edifying to witnesses but gave her no pleasure. A stenographer who had taken down some of her sermons in shorthand published them the next year, along with Rachel's answers to questioners, some of them trivial ("What dress do you like best?"), others searching. Curiously, when asked what she had to say to the people of New York City, where she was at the time, she answered that she was in Scipio among her brothers and sisters.[8]

The learned men of the city found Rachel Baker's case fascinating, and by 1815 they had compiled a treatise of nearly three hundred pages,[9] a monument in itself to scientific ideas on sleep, dreams, and trance states. Like experts the world over, when faced with an enigma they coined an impressive-sounding term for it. This, said Dr. Samuel L. Mitchill,[10] was a rare case of *somnium cum religione*, or "devotional somnium," one of a variety of states between sleep and waking.

After the investigation, Rachel returned to Scipio unchanged and continued her preaching, which now attracted crowds of a hundred or more. Despite her waking belief that "it is not apostolical for a woman to be a public teacher of holy things,"[11] she simply could not help herself. When awake, she insisted that she could remember nothing of what she had said, and certainly showed none of the authority, eloquence, and command of scripture that marked her sermons. In 1815 Rachel was sent back to New York City at the expense of some kindly women, so that she could attend a respectable boarding school. But her health suffered and she soon returned

Upstate, still seeking a cure. Success came in September 1816, thanks to a friend and relation, Dr. Rowland Sears of Norway, Herkimer County. His therapy involved dashing cold water on her and dosing her with camphor, castor, asafoetida, and especially opium,[12] and that was the end of Rachel Baker's preaching career.[13]

What happened to her after that, no one seems to know, but a clue may lie in the obituary of one James Sears Baker (1822–1875). He graduated from Geneva Medical College in 1843 and practiced as a physician in Tully and Collamer, then as a dentist in Marcellus from 1851–65. He was then ordained as a Congregationalist minister, and preached to congregations in Madison (which dismissed him), Otisco, and the Onondaga Valley.[14] The official necrology of Congregational ministers records him as having been born in Marcellus, "son of ——— [*sic*] and Rachel Baker." In all other cases, as one would expect, the father is named and the son has his surname, not his mother's. Noting James's middle name, one can't help suspecting that Dr. Sears had a more than professional relationship with his patient.

Rachel's case was far from unique, and may have given rise to some less sincere copycats. For example, a short notice in the *Northern Post* of Salem, New York, slyly states on November 2, 1815, "The success of Miss Rachel Baker in N. York has produced a beautiful sleeping preacher in England." Nor was she even the only Rachel Baker: Dr. Mitchill mentions *a young lady of the same name*, presently in Maryland, whose specialty was *somnium cum musica*, singing in the trance state.[15]

Keeping now to the Upstate region, three cases reported in the local newspapers during the years following Rachel Baker's cure are probably only the tip of the iceberg. An exhaustive search would surely turn up more, and there must also have been unreported cases, either because they were slight, ephemeral, or irregular, or because the families did not want publicity.

The three cases follow much the same pattern. The first was in Sodus, Wayne County. Joseph Howard, aged seventeen, had been laboring under a similar disorder for a year when the *Palmyra Register* reported on him on December 2, 1818:

> His fits of devotional somnium come on regularly every day, between the hours of 2 and 3 o'clock P.M. and last about one hour and a half. We were last Sabbath gratified by witnessing his somnium exercises. His fits commence with slight twitches of the extremities and the muscles of his face, and in a few moments his whole system becomes agitated with the most violent contortions. From this state, in which he remains about ten minutes, he appears to fall into a deep sleep, when he commences his devotional services.[16]

Joseph Howard's devotions began with a psalm and continued in very orderly fashion with a homily, a concluding blessing, and an invitation to questioners. In all of this he spoke with a fluency and an authority beyond his age. Asked about the salvation of infants, he was definite: they are innocent of sin and justified by Christ, so they go to heaven. After more convulsions and contortions, he would awaken with no memory of what he had said.

The next year, 1819, a correspondent to the *Cooperstown Watch Tower* reported on "Another Sleeping Preacher" in Exeter, Otsego County. This was Joseph Ball, who was apparently able to turn his ability on and off at will, as later types of mediums and channelers would do.

> There is now living with Mr. Amos Thomas, in the town of Exeter, a young man about 20 years of age, named *Joseph Ball*, who, like the celebrated Rachel Baker, preaches, prays, exhorts, &c. in his sleep, or in a particular state of the system, and answers questions to all who call to see him. As he is a young man not versed in public speaking, and of moderate abilities, this is the more surprising. He is different from Rachel Baker in one respect, viz. he does not preach or exhort every night, but gives regular appointments, and is punctual to them—sometimes two nights in succession, and at others, one in three or four nights.
>
> As I consider this case similar to Rachel Baker's, which I think the faculty called a *somnium*, my inducement to publish this is principally to awaken the curiosity of some of the profession to visit him. Perhaps he may be cured. I have understood that doctor Willoughby [*sic*] effected the cure of Miss Baker after doctor Mitchill and others had failed.[17]

A third example from 1826 lived in Otisco, Onondaga County, practically on Rachel's home turf, and was somewhat older than the others:

> *Simeon Watson* a hard laboring industrious man, aged about 30, of athletic habits, and sanguine temperament, about a month since commenced preaching in his sleep. The *fit* (as it is unquestionably a disease) commences immediately after lying down in the evening, and continues until the usual religious exercises of a meeting are concluded. Mr. Watson is a pious, respectable member of the Baptist society, and during the past winter has been much engaged in an awakening which has existed in that vicinity. Soon after retiring to rest he apparently falls asleep. In a few moments he is seized with strong spasmodic contractions of the muscles of the chest and limbs—always groans, and sometimes as if in great

ILLUSTRATION 5.2. *Invitation to the Spirit World* by Josiah Wolcott. From John W. Edmonds and George T. Dexter, *Spiritualism*, New York: Partridge & Brittan, 1856. *Courtesy of Special Collections, Hamilton College Library.*

distress: and when this paroxysm subsides, commences preaching, or rather praying. Our informant terms it preaching, because in his "somnium" he always terms it so himself, whereas Miss Baker when in that state always declined having her exhortations termed preaching, assigning the scriptural reason, that women ought not to teach. Mr. Watson commences with a prayer of ordinary length—then names some passage of scripture as a text, from which he discourses fluently, and quite connectedly, and closes with another prayer. He is totally insensible as to what is passing around, nor can he be awakened until the paroxysm leaves him. Some at first were skeptical; but trials were made sufficient to convince the most incredulous. During the existence of the paroxysm his hands are so firmly clenched together as deeply to indent them with his fingers, and cause the blood to stagnate under his nails. Miss Baker's hands used to be motionless by her side, yet she, like Mr. Watson, used to move her head on the pillow as if addressing an audience. In the midst of an exhortation, Rachel would pause to answer a question, and then correctly proceed; but Mr. Watson cannot be diverted from his subject. In short, this state of the human body, and mind, must be deemed one of great singularity and interest; and one which, as it has never been fully investigated and explained, opens a wide field for the religious and philosophical enquirer.[18]

It does indeed. The history of sleeping preachers reaches back into the eighteenth century[19] and continues up to the end of the nineteenth, by which time it merges with trance-speaking, mediumship, experiments in hypnotism, and early examples of channeling. One such hybrid case, related by John Buescher, is that of Benjamin Scovil Hobbs, who began preaching in Walton in 1844. Three years later he joined the Chenango Universalist Association and worked as a pastor in South Bainbridge and Webster. Hobbs had a problem of falling into trances while preaching, whereupon the spirits would take possession of his voice and hands. Whatever happened next, he had to be removed to the Utica Lunatic Asylum, from which he emerged as an itinerant spiritualist lecturer.[20]

Dr. Mitchill writes candidly about the spectrum of opinions concerning such phenomena, and his categories hold good to this day:

> The observers of the symptoms and occurrences were divided into three classes; first, those who supposed the young woman an impostor, and all her performances a deception; secondly, those who considered her divinely inspired to preach the word miraculously, and warn sinners to repentance; and thirdly, those who thought her prayers and sermons but the symptoms of a disease, of which she might be cured as radically as of an intermitting fever, an epilepsy, or of any periodical malady. To the latter of these classes, I belonged.[21]

Nowadays few would disagree with another member of the third class, quoted in the 1815 report: "That all that Rachel expresses in her state of somniloquism, is the result of preconceived ideas and opinions, but delivered with a readiness and fluency which is very far above her waking state."[22] Moreover, all these characters would most likely be diagnosed with MPD (multiple personality disorder). That may well be part of the explanation, but it does not remove the essential mystery of how and why these things happen.

With the benefit of hindsight and a glance forward to chapter 12, we can see the whole phenomenon as a kind of proto-spiritualism. Like mediums of the post-1848 generation, sleeping preachers spoke in a trance state, as though possessed by another consciousness with superior knowledge and an agenda of its own. Their gift, or affliction, was soon turned into a public performance. None of them had earned the official license to preach (and as a woman, Rachel Baker never could), but they circumvented this by operating in private homes. There was debate over whether Rachel was a fraud, then, just like the Fox sisters, she was taken to New York City to be examined and evaluated. However, the time was not ripe, the climate of belief not ready, for her ability to be seen as anything other than a disease with a fancy name.

Illustration 6.1. *Joseph Smith Receives the Golden Plates from the Angel Moroni.* Sculpture by Torleif Soviren Knaphus on the Hill Cumorah Monument, Palmyra, 1935. *Author's photograph.*

CHAPTER 6

Mormon Roots

What do we hear? Glad tiding from Cumorah! Moroni, an angel from heaven, declaring the fulfillment of the prophets—the book to be revealed! A voice of the Lord in the wilderness of Fayette, Seneca county, declaring the three witnesses to bear record of the Book. The voice of Michael on the banks of the Susquehanna, detecting the devil when he appeared as an angel of light. The voice of Peter, James, and John in the wilderness, between Harmony, Susquehanna county, and Colesville, Broome county, on the Susquehanna river, declaring themselves as possessing the keys of the kingdom, and of the dispensation of the fullness of times. And again, the voice of God in the chamber of old father Whitmer in Fayette, Seneca county, and at sundry times, and in divers places through all the travels and tribulations of this Church of Jesus Christ of Latter Day Saints.[1]

From Joseph Smith's address to his church, 1842

While the sleeping preachers of the preceding chapter downplayed their own personalities and taught more or less orthodox Christology, the visions of Ann Lee, Jemima Wilkinson, and Handsome Lake raised them to virtual equality with Jesus Christ. With varying degrees of humility they taught that while Jesus had done his part (manifesting the masculine side of God; giving a law to the white man), the divine mission had now passed to them. The same is claimed for the Mormon prophet, Joseph Smith, Jr. (1805–1844), and more: according to Mormon theology God the Father was a man in flesh and bone, and every believer may eventually become a god like him or a goddess like his wife or wives.[2] Such doctrines put Mormonism beyond the pale of Christian ecumenism. As surely as Christianity parted from Judaism while claiming to fulfill it, and Islam, with similar claims, from both Judaism and Christianity, the Church of Jesus Christ of Latter-day Saints is a new religion, the fourth of the Abrahamic family.

Joseph Smith had a keen sense of place, as the above quotation shows, and his religion acquired its own sacred geography, mirroring the westward colonization of the new republic. By birth, he was a Vermonter. After the disastrous harvest of 1816, the "year without a summer," his parents joined the emigration to western New York. The Smith family stayed there until the exodus of the Mormons to Kirtland, Ohio, in January 1831.

The three theaters of early Mormon activity were (1) around the Smith homestead near Palmyra, (2) the farm of Peter Whitmer between Cayuga and Seneca lakes, and (3) along the Susquehanna River into northern Pennsylvania. The Catskill Turnpike made travel between them relatively easy. Following today's routes 7 and 79, this early state route started at Bainbridge and passed the southern ends of Cayuga and Seneca lakes. From Ithaca one could sail up the lake and join the Erie Canal, which had reached Palmyra by 1822. Both northern and southern regions are rich in historic sites, and are here listed in the order in which they figure in Mormon history:[3]

1. The Sacred Grove south of Palmyra, where in the spring of 1820 Joseph Smith had his first vision. While praying alone in the forest for guidance as to which of the competing Christian sects he should join, a pillar of light descended on him. Two beings appeared whom he later identified as God the Father and Jesus Christ. God told him that his sins were forgiven, and that he should join none of the churches, for they were all "an abomination in his sight."[4]
2. The Smith log house, where on September 21, 1823, Joseph, tormented by spiritual doubts, had a nighttime vision. Three times the angel Moroni appeared, floating in

brilliant light. He told Joseph of a book written on golden plates buried nearby, together with a pair of stones to aid in translating it, called the Urim and Thummim.[5]

3. Hill Cumorah, north of Manchester, where on the next day, September 22, 1823, Joseph found a stone box containing the golden plates, the reading device, and a breastplate.[6] He returned each year, finally being permitted to remove them on September 22, 1827.[7]

4. Site of Isaac Hale's home and tavern in Harmony (now Oakland), Pennsylvania, where Joseph arrived in November 1825, commissioned to search for a Spanish silver mine.[8] Nearby were the cabin and smallholding that Joseph and his first wife, Emma, bought from her family, the Hales, and occupied on and off from December 1827 until the end of August 1830.[9] This was the chief place of translation of the Book of Mormon. In the woods on May 15, 1829, Joseph and Oliver Cowdery witnessed the descent of a personage in a cloud of light who said he was John the Baptist, sent by Peter, James, and John (see the quotation above), and who ordained them in the priesthood of Aaron.[10]

5. Josiah Stowell's house, near Afton. Stowell (also spelled Stowel or Stoal) was Hale's contact with the Smiths, for he went to Palmyra every year to buy grain from them and had heard of Joseph's talents. He helped to finance Hale's treasure hunting.[11]

6. Joseph Knight's house, near Nineveh, Colesville Township. Knight accompanied Stowell to Palmyra on his grain-buying trips. Both men were staying with the Smiths when Joseph retrieved the golden plates,[12] and gave Joseph casual employment during his stays in the south. At Knight's house, in April 1830, Joseph organized the first branch of his church and performed his first miracle, casting out an evil spirit from Knight's son Newel.[13]

7. Site of the "Mormon House" of Zechariah Tarbill (or Tarble) in Afton, where Joseph and Emma Hale were married on January 18, 1827.[14]

8. Site of Martin Harris's farm, near Palmyra. Harris helped the young Smith couple and financed the printing of the Book of Mormon, published in 1830.[15]

9. Peter Whitmer's home, south of Waterloo, where Joseph and Emma Smith stayed for some months in 1829 and finished translating the Book of Mormon.[16] In early July, Joseph led three witnesses (David Whitmer, Oliver Cowdery, and Martin Harris) to the nearby woods. There, on a table, an angel displayed the golden plates, the Urim and Thummim, the Sword of Laban, and the Liahona, a miraculous ball with a compass that had enabled the prophet Lehi to find his way through the wilderness.[17] A few days later at an outdoor location in Palmyra, Joseph showed the golden plates to eight members of the Whitmer and Smith families. They all signed a statement saying that they had "seen and hefted" the plates.[18]
10. The Grandin Press in downtown Palmyra, where the Book of Mormon was typeset and printed in 1830.

Each of these events presents problems to the impartial historian. As background, it helps to know something of the milieu into which Joseph was born. The prophet's father, Joseph Smith, Sr. (1771–1841), was, by all objective standards, both a credulous and a shady character. Before leaving Vermont he had been involved in two or perhaps three cases of counterfeiting, "certainly as a victim, and possibly as an accomplice."[19] In rural New England and early New York, counterfeiting money and divining for buried treasure often went hand in hand; John Brooke calls them "opposite sides of the same debased alchemical coin."[20] Both activities were risky, one being criminal, the other involving unfriendly spirits. Joseph Sr. shared the popular belief that pirates, Spaniards, or Indians had buried chests of treasure that could be discovered through dowsing or "scrying." Dowsing or divining with rods or forked sticks is a well-testified method of finding underground water or, in central New York, the profitable salt springs. As for scrying, Joseph Sr. used a method that his son later made famous: staring at a special stone placed in his hat. This goes back to an equally venerable practice of staring into a stone, mirror, crystal ball, pool of ink, etc., as a means of inducing visions and spirit communications.

As Joseph Sr. told his neighbor Peter Ingersoll, summer was the best time to dig for the chests: "You notice, said he, the large stones on the top of the ground—we call them rocks, and they truly appear so, but they are, in fact, most of them chests of money raised by the heat of the sun."[21] But the owners of such chests had bewitched them, so that if disturbed, they would sink back into the ground, out of reach of the digger.[22] They had evil spirits bound to them, which could only be outwitted by nocturnal rites involving magic circles, incantations, even animal sacrifice.[23] The slightest fault or ritual slip-up would cause, and excuse, failure of the operation. For instance, at Joseph's first attempt to remove the golden plates, "he saw in the box something like a toad, which soon assumed the appearance of a man, and struck him on the side of his head."[24]

That some people could make a living at treasure hunting is a measure of the eternal hope for sudden wealth, exploited in a less superstitious age by the state lottery. Responsible Mormon historians such as Richard Bushman no longer try to conceal Joseph Jr's. involvement in it. In 1825 both Josephs, father and son, worked on Josiah Stowell's quest for the Spanish silver mine, and were contracted to receive a share of any eventual profits. Joseph Jr. seems to have been more of a scryer than a dowser. He used "peepstones" (stones naturally or artificially holed) to find lost objects and to describe scenes at a distance, and it was this ability that got him into trouble in March 1826.[25] New York's lawgivers, hoping to enlighten a recalcitrant population, had decreed it illegal to pretend to such powers. On complaint from a neighbor, Joseph was arraigned in Bainbridge on the charge of being a "disorderly person and an impostor," judged guilty, and fined two dollars and sixty-eight cents.[26]

Beside money digging and its associated folk magic, three other influences had saturated the regions of Vermont in which Joseph Sr. grew up. Freemasonry was a powerfully mythopoeic idea, even to those who were not initiates. Millennialism, which expected the scenario described in the Book of Revelation to begin in one's lifetime, was another. The third was the New Israelite movement, which identified the Native Americans as descendants of the ten lost tribes of Israel. All three would leave distinctive stamps on Mormon scripture and doctrine.[27] Moreover, Joseph's forebears were no strangers to vivid spiritual experiences. His maternal grandfather, Solomon Mack, was converted in his old age by "fiery lights in the night and mysterious voices calling him by name, terrifying him until he understood that the Lord had taken this direct means to call him to redemption."[28] In 1803 Joseph's mother, Lucy Mack Smith (1775–1856), while near death from consumption, heard the voice of Jesus, and from that moment she recovered.[29] Joseph Sr. had a series of archetypal dreams recorded by Lucy, which resurfaced in the Book of Mormon as visions of the patriarch Lehi.[30] All of this demonstrates that Mormonism, for all its originality, did not come out of a void.

In any new religion's foundation myths, the most important would be the first calling of the prophet. But immediately the difficulties multiply. I have given the standard account (see no. 1, above), but it is neither the only one nor the earliest. There survives a handwritten account of 1831 or 1832 in which Joseph Smith recounts that in his fourteenth year he met "the Lord," obviously Jesus because he mentioned having been crucified, who forgave Joseph's sins and promised to come quickly.[31] Second, in his diary of 1835–36, Smith describes a "personage" who appeared in the pillar of flame, then a second personage who "said unto me thy sins are forgiven thee, he testifyed unto me that Jesus Christ is the Son of God; and I saw many angels in this vision." This time, neither personage is identified as Jesus. Third, in his manuscript *History of the Church*, Smith writes: "I received the first visitation of angels, which was when I was about fourteen years old."[32]

No one in the church heard of this first vision until 1838, and it was not published until 1842.[33] By then, the "personages" appearing in the pillar of light had been identified as God the Father and Jesus Christ, the former announcing: "This is my beloved Son, hear Him." Until then, the Mormon community had based their faith on Joseph's vision of the angel Moroni (see no. 2, above). Dale Morgan, an agnostic researcher, points out the oddity of the situation: that Joseph should have long concealed his first vision, with its far loftier summons by the Father and the Son, together with their incendiary message that all the churches were corrupt. Equally odd is that he should have still been unsure of the existence of God three years later, when the second vision occurred.[34] Morgan's conclusion is that by 1838, with the church well under way, Joseph felt confident in rewriting his history through "a conception investing him with an ineffable dignity, for in all recorded history, to what other men have the Father and the Son appeared?"[35] Here Morgan was mistaken, for as later scholars have shown, Joseph's vision was far from unique in the revivalist milieu. Bushman and Michael Quinn cite a dozen or more cases in which visionaries have claimed the sight of God the Father and/or Jesus Christ.[36]

A middle ground between accepting Joseph's visions as veridical, as Mormon historians must do, and dismissing them as fictions, belongs to researchers into paranormal and anomalous phenomena. Walter Evans-Wentz, an authority on Celtic mythology and Tibetan Buddhism, recognized Joseph's visions as encounters with the same "shining beings" as appear in Celtic fairy lore and in the vision quests of Native Americans. He also compared the finding of the Book of Mormon with the Tibetan tradition of *tertons*, hidden scriptures awaiting discovery by the right person.[37] Jacques Vallee, most intelligent of ufologists, compares the two visions to similar ones reported by UFO contactees. He notes that in the first vision Joseph describes a "pillar of light exactly over my head [. . .] which descended gradually until it fell upon me," and in the second (a typical "bedroom visitation"), the shocks felt in his body and the light that formed "a conduit right up into heaven" into which Moroni disappeared.[38] I would add, on the basis of the Tanners' research, that the pillar of light is the one constant in all three accounts. Vallee writes that the experiences of UFO contactees and abductees are nothing new, but a perennial phenomenon that each age accommodates to its own belief system. How one interprets it is another matter. Vallee concludes:

> It is futile to engage in a debate concerning the truth or falsity of the statements made by Joseph Smith. We are looking here for indications of a higher order, and we can define as a miracle any event, real or imagined or even faked, which creates certain paranormal but verifiable effects. The transformation of an ordinary farmboy from rural New York State into an unchallenged leader of multitudes is an unusual fact that deserves attention even if we doubt the story. When we trace the turning point of this man's life to the sighting of a strange light and to contact with an entity inside the light, I believe the account needs to be preserved along with those we have already found in other faiths and other lands.[39]

After the visions, the golden plates are the sticking point for believers and nonbelievers in the authenticity of Joseph's religion. To the skeptic, they were invented to attract attention in a superstitious society obsessed with treasure hunting. As soon as Joseph mentioned them to his mother, she started calculating how much money could be made from exhibiting this "Golden Bible" at twenty-five cents a time.[40] Fawn Brodie suggests that "perhaps in the beginning Joseph never intended his stories of the golden plates to be taken so seriously, but once the masquerade had begun, there was no point at which he could call a halt."[41] No doubt he brought *something* home in 1827—a brick, a load of sand, a pile of tin plates have all been suggested[42]—and had a box made for it which he allowed some to lift, but none to open. This aroused unbearable curiosity, not least among the financers of his money digging, who expected to share in his profits, and Joseph had to resort to various stratagems to keep the plates from them while sustaining their belief. While he was translating them, a blanket hung between him and the scribe, or the plates were on the table wrapped in a cloth, or even absent from the room.[43] The scribes, Emma Smith, Oliver Cowdery, and Martin Harris, went along more or less grudgingly with these restrictions.

Like the slippery money chests described by Joseph Sr., the miniature vault containing the golden plates showed above ground as a convex stone.[44] The plates themselves moved in and out of physical range, like the Tablets of the Law that reappeared after Moses had smashed them. Moroni confiscated the plates for a while, after Joseph had disobeyed him by lending out and losing his first batch of translation.[45] When Joseph was preparing to leave the Hale farm in Pennsylvania, he packed up the plates so that the angel could transport them safely to the Whitmer home in Fayette.[46] After the eight witnesses had seen them, the angel took them away for good.[47]

The Urim and Thummim or "interpreters" that Joseph found along with the plates were supposedly the objects prescribed in Exodus 28:30 and Leviticus 8:8 among Aaron's priestly regalia, where they are "put in the breastpiece of judgment." Later they were used for divination.[48] Biblical scholars do not know what they looked like. According to Joseph's mother, Lucy, who was allowed to handle the Urim and Thummim through a silk handkerchief, the device consisted of "two smooth three-cornered diamonds set in glass, and the glasses were set in silver bows connected with each other in much the same way that old-fashioned spectacles are made."[49] Martin Harris remembered that "the two stones set in a bow of silver were about two inches in diameter, perfectly round, and about five-eighths of an inch thick at the centre, but not so thick at the edges where they came into the bow. They were joined by a round bar of silver, about three-eighths of an inch in diameter, and about four inches long, which, with the two stones, would make eight inches. The stones were white, like polished marble, with a few gray streaks."[50] Joseph's brother William, on the other hand, called them "two small stones of a chocolate color, nearly egg shape, and perfectly smooth, but not transparent."[51] Moreover, they were attached to a breastplate complete with waist and shoulder straps, which Lucy Smith described as "concave on one side and convex on the other, and extended from the neck downwards as far as the center of the stomach of a man of extraordinary size."[52] The spectacles were joined to it "by a rod which was fastened at the outer shoulder edge of the breastplate and to the edge of the silver bow."[53] Although there are early stories of Joseph detecting danger through the Urim and Thummim, none of the witnesses saw him using this contraption for its stated purpose of translating the golden plates. The scribes bore witness that Joseph habitually translated with a seer stone held in his hat, and Mormon commentators accept, with visible misgiving, that one method was as good as the other.[54]

Brodie's term "masquerade" also seems to fit the performance in the woods before the three witnesses, for whose benefit the angel set out on a table the golden plates, the Urim and Thummim with the breastplate, the Sword of Laban, and the Liahona. The Book of Mormon's early chapters tell the stories behind the last two objects. Laban's sword was a magnificent weapon with a pure golden hilt and a steel blade (I Nephi 4:9). Nephi found its owner drunk and, instructed by the Lord, cut off his head with it. The Liahona simply appeared at Lehi's tent door one morning. It was "a round ball of curious workmanship; and it was of fine brass. And within the ball were two spindles; and the one pointed the way whither we should go into the wilderness" (I Nephi 16:10). Later it is told that the Lord made it himself (Alma 37:38).

Before the three witnesses viewed these objects, Joseph pronounced one of his increasingly frequent "revelations":

> *Revelation given through Joseph, the Seer, to Oliver Cowdery, David Whitmer, and Martin Harris, in Fayette, Seneca County, New York, June, 1829, given previous to their viewing the plates containing the Book of Mormon.*
>
> 1. Behold, I say unto you, that you must rely upon my word, which if you do, with full purpose of heart, you shall have a view of the plates, and also of the breastplate, the sword of Laban, the Urim and Thummim, which were given to the brother of Jared upon the mount, when he talked with the Lord face to face, and the miraculous directors which were given to Lehi while in the wilderness, on the borders of the Red Sea;
> 2. And it is by your faith that you shall obtain a view of them, even by that faith which was had by the prophets of old.
> 3. And after that you have obtained faith, and have seen them with your eyes, you shall testify of them, by the power of God;
> 4. And this you shall do that my servant Joseph Smith, jun., may not be destroyed, that I may bring about my righteous purposes unto the children of men in this work.
> 5. And ye shall testify that you have seen them, even as my servant Joseph Smith, jun., has seen them, for it is by my power that he has seen them, and it is because he had faith;
> 6. And he has translated the book, even that part which I have commanded him, and as your Lord and your God liveth it is true.
> 7. Wherefore you have received the same power, and the same faith, and the same gift like unto him;
> 8. And if you do these last commandments of mine, which I have given you, the gates of hell shall not prevail against you; for my grace is sufficient for you, and you shall be lifted up at the last day.

> 9. And I, Jesus Christ, your Lord and your God, have spoken it unto you, that I might bring about my righteous purposes unto the children of men. Amen.[55]

Given their belief that Jesus Christ was addressing them personally, it is not surprising that signs, wonders, and obedience ensued. Although all of the three witnesses and several of the eight later fell out with Joseph and were excommunicated, none ever went back on his affidavit.[56] Brodie, here venturing into what I have called the middle ground, admits, "Joseph had more than 'second sight,' which is commonplace among professional magicians. At an early age he had what only the most gifted revivalist preachers could boast of—the talent for making men see visions."[57] Support for this comes from later statements by Martin Harris, e.g., "While praying I passed into a state of entrancement, and in that state I saw the angel and the plates," and, "I saw them with the eye of faith, I saw them just as distinctly as I see any thing around me, though at the time they were covered over with a cloth."[58] Likewise, David Whitmer modified his testimony with the words, "Of course we were in the spirit when we had the view. . . . A bright light enveloped us where we were, that filled at noon day, and there in a *vision*, or in the *spirit*, we saw and heard just as it is stated in my testimony in the Book of Mormon."[59]

By all accounts (Joseph's, Cowdery's, and Harris's), the sentences appeared to Joseph on the seerstone in their Nephite characters, together with an English translation that he read out to the scribe. When correctly written, the words would disappear and the next sentence would take its place.[60] The result was a completely unpunctuated text. Presumably, the compositors at Grandin's Press supplied the lack, and later editors set the text in a two-column format to resemble the Bible.

How Joseph, with his minimal education, managed to dictate this long and coherent scripture without notes or revisions irks the anti-Mormons even more than the golden plates. Every possible avenue has been tried to pin the charge of plagiarism on him, with very little success. To be sure, there is the influence of time and place, and much borrowing from the Bible. The literary and philosophical quality of the Book of Mormon does not bear comparison with the Hebrew scriptures or the New Testament, nor its language with the King James version, which it laboriously imitates. But its revised history of pre-conquest America is consistent enough that Mormons, even some with Ph.Ds., can persuade themselves of its truth. Every summer they reenact it in the Hill Cumorah Pageant (mentioned at the end of chapter 2).

After publishing the Book of Mormon, Joseph continued to build up the doctrinal basis for his church. He fine-tuned it with the 133 "revelations" gathered in *Doctrine and Covenants*, of which the most controversial authorized polygamy and excluded blacks from the ministry. (Current editions suppress such passages.[61]) He set out to correct, revise, and amplify the Bible, completing new versions of the Books of Moses and the Book of Abraham. The story behind the latter illuminates the whole process. In 1835, a dealer in antiquities came to Kirtland, Ohio, offering for sale four Egyptian mummies and a collection of papyri written in hieroglyphs. Joseph examined the papyri, declared that they contained the writings of Abraham and the biblical Joseph, and bought the lot. He and some colleagues then set out to translate them. This was before Champollion had provided the key to reading Egyptian hieroglyphs, and the scantily educated Mormons were floundering. They gave up, except for Joseph, who produced his version through the same gift as had enabled him to translate the Book of Mormon. Or so it was possible to believe, until experts examined the facsimiles of hieroglyphs published with his translation, and, worse, when some of the original papyri were discovered in 1967 in the Metropolitan Museum. These were now easily read, and found to contain standard funerary texts. Embarrassment followed, with some believers feebly protesting that these were not the right papyri. Richard Bushman, to his credit, faces the issue head-on:

> What was going on while Joseph "translated" the papyri and dictated text to a scribe? Obviously, he was not interpreting the hieroglyphics like an ordinary scholar. As Joseph saw it, he was working by inspiration—that had been clear from the beginning. When he "translated" the *Book of Mormon*, he did not read from the gold plates; he looked into the crystals of the Urim and Thummim or gazed at the seerstone. The words came by inspiration, not by reading the characters on the plates. By analogy, it seemed likely that the papyri had been an occasion for receiving a revelation rather than a word-for-word interpretation of the hieroglyphs as in ordinary translation.[62]

This comes close to admitting that the golden plates, like the papyri, were only props for a process that could have taken place independently of them. Whether real, faked, or imaginary, they served as the catalyst for words to appear in the seerstones. The Book of Mormon then takes its place within two familiar traditions, one of angelic communications through crystals or magic mirrors, and the other of literary works obtained through mediumship or channeling.

A famous instance of the first tradition is the angelic conversations of John Dee (1527–1609) and Edward Kelley (1555–1597). In this, as in most cases of crystallomancy, the roles were the reverse of those of Joseph and his scribes. The learned Dee directed the operation with suitable magical rites and asked the questions, and Kelley reported what he saw and heard from the spirits that appeared to him. Just as Joseph's plates contained an unknown language and script, of which he transcribed a small sample, so Dee's angels revealed a magical language with its own alphabet, called Enochian after the antediluvian patriarch.[63]

The tradition of crystallomancy persisted in England through the age of Enlightenment, just as its rural version did with the peepstone men of New England. In the early nineteenth century it became a popular pursuit in English society, as well as the chosen vehicle for magical researches, of which I have written elsewhere.[64] Here one example will suffice. One of the key figures in the English occult revival, Frederick Hockley (1808–1885), was given a crystal in 1824 and used it throughout his life in a piously Christian but scientific spirit. Like Dee, he was not clairvoyant himself, but employed seers, usually young uneducated women, who would gaze into the crystal and report what they saw. His main communicator was called the "Crowned Angel of the Seventh Sphere," who produced both visions and writings in which each letter, as seen in the crystal, was composed of blue and white dots with a red border. Hockley filled thirty volumes with the information thus gained. Lord Stanhope (the fourth Earl Stanhope, 1781–1855), who shared experiments, crystals, and seers with Hockley, concluded that the communications could not be attributed to fakery on the part of the seer, nor to telepathic reading of the controller's mind, though their information was often false. Stanhope's conclusions are pertinent to the present case: "The Visions and Writings seen in Crystals are however important[,] as they prove to persons who might not otherwise be convinced the existence of a Spiritual World, though the Answers which are received may be undeserving of credit."[65] Likewise, it is possible to accept the Book of Mormon as originating from a "spiritual world" without crediting a word of it.

Turning to historical and cosmological works originating in mediumship, there is a contemporary parallel to the historical revisionism of the Book of Mormon in the *Philosophical History of the Human Race*, by the French esotericist Fabre d'Olivet (1767–1825).[66] Published in 1822, it resembles Smith's account in its improbable story of human races, their conflicts, migrations, and successive spiritual leaders, all presented as fact. Fabre d'Olivet never revealed his methods or sources, but probably used his wife as a mesmerized medium. Later there would be mediumistic revelations such *Oahspe: A Kosmon Bible*, whose thousand pages were typed in 1880–81 by John Ballou Newbrough (1828–1891), a New York dentist; and the twice as long *Urantia Book* (written in the 1920s, published 1955). Both books pretend to unveil the nature of God, the cosmos, and the prehistory of earth and humanity, as well as the true nature and history of Jesus Christ. Unsurprisingly, no two such sources agree. Rival versions appear in *The Gospel of the Holy Twelve* (published 1901), written by the Rev. Gideon Jasper Richard Ouseley from nighttime visions of manuscripts on a revolv-

ILLUSTRATION 6.2. Peter Whitmer's log home (reconstruction), near Waterloo. Here in 1829 Joseph Smith took refuge and translated a large portion of the Book of Mormon, and in 1830 the Mormon Church was first organized. *Author's photograph.*

ing lectern;[67] and *The Aquarian Gospel of Jesus the Christ* (published 1909), transcribed from the "Akashic records" by Levi H. Dowling (1844–1911).[68] Channelers continue to disgorge such material up to the present day.

The question of where channeled material originates is not easily answered, except by those with fixed opinions at the extremes of belief and disbelief. True believers take at face value whatever their chosen revelation says of its source. Skeptics attribute it to the medium's unconscious mind, probably dissociated through some form of multiple personality disorder. Intermediate hypotheses may include telepathic or clairvoyant input, again without the medium being conscious of the process. For those who entertain the possibility of an outside source (modified, even polluted, by the medium's mind, beliefs, language, and psychology), the sources may include God or one of the gods, angels, demons, extraterrestrials, the spirits of dead humans, elemental beings, the collective energies called "egregores," and living humans with paranormal powers. Then there is the question of their motives and agendas.

In the end, what is most impressive about Joseph Smith is not his visions, as many people had those, nor his writing of the Book of Mormon—there are better and worse books of its kind. It is his genius for organization, which started the Mormon Church going and has served it to this day. Of all the cults and movements described in this book, Mormonism alone continues to flourish and increase worldwide. Whether this is due to its inherent truth, to human gullibility and the will to believe, to some occult power, or simply to the law of chance, I leave the reader to consider.

ILLUSTRATION 7.1. Mordecai Manuel Noah, playwright, diplomat, politician, and proposer of the New Zion. From *Cyclopaedia of American Literature*, ed. E. A. and G. L. Duyckinck, New York: Charles Scribner, 1866, Vol. II, p. 74. *Courtesy of Special Collections, Hamilton College Library.*

CHAPTER 7

The Square and Compass

I had been on a visit to a singular people called Shakers, at New Lebanon, about seven miles from my aunt Van Cott's, and was returning that distance, on foot, on a beautiful evening of September. The sky was without a cloud; the stars shone out beautifully, and all nature seemed reposing in quiet, as I pursued my solitary way, wrapt in deep meditations on the predictions of the holy prophets; the signs of the times; the approaching advent of the Messiah, to reign on the earth, and the important revelations of the Book of Mormon; my heart filled with gratitude to God that He had opened the eyes of my understanding to receive the truth, and with sorrow for the blindness of those who lightly rejected the same, when my attention was aroused by a sudden appearance of a brilliant light which shone around me, above the brightness of the sun. I cast my eyes upward to inquire from whence the light came, when I perceived a long chain of light extended in the heavens, very bright, and of a deep fiery red. It at first stood stationary in a horizontal position; at length bending in the center, the two ends approached each other with a rapid movement, so as to form an exact square. In this position it again remained stationary for some time, perhaps a minute, and then again the ends approached each other with the same rapidity, and again ceased to move, remaining stationary, for perhaps a minute, in the form of a compass; it then commenced a third movement in the same manner, and closed like the closing of a compass, the whole forming a straight line like a chain doubled. It again remained stationary for a minute, and then faded away.

I fell upon my knees in the street, and thanked the Lord for so marvelous a sign of the coming of the Son of Man.

Some persons may smile at this, and say that all these exact movements were by chance; but, for my part, I could as soon believe that the letters of the alphabet would be formed by chance, and be placed so as to spell my name, as to believe that these signs (known only to the wise) could be formed and shown forth by chance.

Renewed in spirit and filled with joy I now pursued my way, and arrived at my aunt Van Cott's, not weary, but refreshed with a long walk, and deep communion with myself and God.[1]

Parley Pratt's vision of 1830, from his Autobiography

Parley Parker Pratt (1807–1857) was born in Burlington, Otsego County, the son of a farmer. He grew up with the typical pioneer blend of physical toughness and sporadic concern for his soul, barely educated and guided only by the Bible. After an early marriage, he and his wife, Thankful, moved to the virgin forests west of Cleveland, Ohio, where land could be had on credit, to be paid off after it had been cleared and crops established. They soon hacked a small paradise out of the wilderness, with Thankful running the district's first school, until Parley, in his own words, "began to understand the things which were coming on the earth, the restoration of Israel, the coming of the Messiah, and the glory that should follow." So certain did he become that he decided to give up homesteading and rely only on "letters of credit" from the Lord.

Pratt was fond of an aunt who lived in Canaan, Columbia County, and his first goal was to visit her. The Pratts sailed from Cleveland to Buffalo, Parley earning their passage by steering the sailboat, then continued by barge on the Erie Canal. On reaching Newark, Parley felt the urge to leave the boat. Sending Thankful on ahead, he took to the road to meet his destiny.

Unknowingly, Pratt had stumbled into the cradle of Mormonism. By the time he rejoined Thankful at his aunt's house, he had been baptized by Oliver Cowdery in Seneca Lake, had met Hyrum Smith (he would meet Joseph on the return journey), owned a copy of the Book of Mormon, hot off the press, and had already made converts through his inspired preaching of the new faith. His visit to the New Lebanon Shakers, mentioned in the quotation above, was doubtless made with that intention. We will not follow the Pratts' adventures any further, except to note Parley's status as one of the church's twelve apostles and his untimely death at an assassin's hand. Instead, I call attention to this vision as a symbolic keystone of Mormon history.

The words of Jacques Vallee, quoted in the previous chapter, spring to mind. Here is another case of the transformation of an "ordinary farmboy" in a context of strange things seen in the sky. The lights take the successive forms of a chain or horizontal line, a square, and a compass, signs "known only to the wise" but actually to every Freemason and to many outside the order. Put simply, the "chain of union" symbolizes the friendship between Masons; the square (an L-shaped drawing instrument) and the compass are the essential tools of geometry, hence of architecture and all the symbolism that Freemasonry attaches to that. If in this vision it seems more like a four-sided figure, it could represent the dressed stone or "perfect ashlar" ready to be incorporated in the temple, symbolizing the perfected human being within a universal brotherhood.

In 1830, at the reported time of Parley Pratt's vision, Freemasonry was in bad odor in New York State. Four years earlier, a stonemason or bricklayer named William Morgan (1774–1826?) had applied to the masonic lodge of Batavia and been turned down. In revenge, he declared that he would publish the secrets of Freemasonry. Before he could do so he was kidnapped and was never seen again, alive or dead. The incident resonated with popular suspicions of Freemasonry as a secret, anti-democratic order with sinister powers, and the political fallout was severe. In New York State, Masons resigned in the thousands, and hundreds of lodges were dissolved. The movement quickly became a conduit for opposition to President (and Freemason) Andrew Jackson. It spawned the first of America's "third parties": the Anti-Masonic Party, which held its first convention in Utica in August 1828, and later contested the presidential election of 1832.

This, then, was hardly a propitious moment to give the Masonic imprimatur to a new religion. However, Parley Pratt's vision, like Joseph Smith's first visitation, was only made known long after the event (in Pratt's case, after his death), so there might have been some adjustment to the record or memory. While historians detect Masonic influences from the very beginnings of Mormonism, it was not until 1842–43 and in Ohio that Smith, Pratt, and other leading Mormons were initiated into the third degree (Master) of Freemasonry. Thereafter the craft and the church blatantly shared symbols, rites, and, to an extent, ideology. For example, the square, compass, and horizontal line are the very symbols emblazoned on the "temple garments," worn to this day and familiarly known as "Mormon underwear." Both institutions cultivate an aura of mystery and secrecy, with information only imparted as a person rises up the grades, but in fact, what really happens is no longer secret. The Mormon endowments, like the Scottish Rite initiations (see below), consist mainly of passively watching a performance, formerly played by actors, now as a motion picture. Their liturgy reads like a parody of Masonic initiations, complete with the throat cutting and disembowelment promised to apostates.[2] Michael Homer's research lays bare the historical connections between the two institutions and the uneasy mix of pro- and anti-Masonry in the early years of Mormonism.[3] The Mormon temples, as oddly eclectic in style as Masonic lodges, display the cosmic symbols characteristic of Freemasonry: the sun, the moon, and the five-pointed star. None of this should surprise when one realizes that both institutions have roots in esoteric traditions.[4]

The restoration of Israel and the coming of the Messiah, which Parley Pratt's study of the Bible had led him to expect, took on another meaning in the imagination of Mordecai Manuel Noah (1785–1851).[5] This fascinating character descended from Jews of Mannheim[6] who had settled in Charleston, South Carolina, a city equally prominent in both Jewish and Masonic history. Dale R. Broadhurst, the historian of Mormonism, chronicles Noah's family connections with influential Jewish members of the Charleston lodge, and his status in the York Rite (a system of higher degrees beyond that of Master Mason).[7] His biographer, Jonathan D. Sarna, calls him a highly significant figure on the American scene, a leader of the American Jewish community, and the "first man in history to grapple with the tensions between these roles."[8]

Noah's career started modestly enough as an office boy, then as an apprentice to a wood-carver, whose wares he peddled in Albany.[9] His breakthrough came with the War of 1812, when he served in the Philadelphia militia, gaining the rank and title of major, and wrote patriotic newspaper articles. Later he wrote under a pseudonym on ladies' fashion (which he despised), servants (mostly unnecessary), dinner parties (a gross waste of money), slavery (incredible in a civilized nation), etc.[10] He had been a passionate theatergoer from boyhood, and as an adult acted in an amateur troupe and wrote plays for both amateurs and professionals. His dramatic comedy *She Would Be a Soldier* (1819) held the stage for nearly thirty years. For a while, Mordecai Noah was mentioned in the same breath as the literary giants James Fenimore Cooper and Washington Irving.[11] Somewhere along the way he also qualified as a lawyer, sheriff, and judge.[12]

In 1813 President Madison appointed this promising young man consul-general in Tunis. The post was no diplomatic sinecure but a "secret low-budget rescue mission"[13] to ransom American seamen who had been captured and enslaved by the Barbary pirates. Given the slowness of communications from North Africa, Noah had to make snap decisions about large sums of money, which he could only hope would be honored by the U.S. government.[14] In fact, he was shamefully dishonored, for the government recalled him on the grounds that it was not appropriate to have a Jew in this position. At least he got home, unlike the ransomed sailors who all died at sea on the way.[15] He wrote a travelogue describing and justifying his actions, then headed into the political forum. As editor of several New York newspapers, Noah had the power of the press at his hands. Historians agree that he became the most prominent and politically influential Jew of the Jacksonian era.

In 1820 Noah petitioned the New York legislature to survey, value, and sell to him Grand Island, an island of some seventeen thousand acres that divides the Niagara River in two. The state had bought it from the Iroquois for a paltry sum, and investors had their eye on its fine growth of timber and its potential for division and resale. The petition was rejected, but one of Noah's agents managed to acquire a good part of the island. Noah then staged the performance on which his fame mostly rests.

On September 15, 1825, the crowds that had gathered in Buffalo to celebrate the completion of the Erie Canal heard cannons at dawn, and at ten o'clock saw a procession that started from the Masonic lodge. First came a band, a deputation of citizens, and assorted military and civil officers. Next followed a Masonic contingent in their regalia. Stewards bore corn, wine, and oil; the "principal architect" carried the square, level, and plumb; others the compass, the terrestrial and celestial globes, and the Bible. There followed "a man of large muscular frame, rotund person, a benignant face, and most portly bearing."[16] This was Major Noah, who had come from New York City with a theatrical costume in his baggage. Presenting himself as "the Judge of Israel," he was clothed "in black, wearing the judicial robes of crimson silk, trimmed with ermine and a richly embossed golden medal suspended from the neck."[17] High-degree Masons (Royal Arch and Knights Templar) brought up the rear. The official report omits to mention that Red Jacket, the famous Seneca chief and nephew of Handsome Lake, was also present.[18]

Into St. Paul's Episcopal Church they went, with the band playing Handel's march from *Judas Maccabeus*. On the communion table lay a three-hundred-pound stone inscribed in Hebrew and English: "ARARAT, A City of Refuge for the Jews, founded by Mordecai Manuel Noah, in the month Tizri, Sept. 1825 & in the 50th year of American Independence." The rector read the morning service with its psalms and lessons from the Old Testament; the Judge of Israel declaimed a "Proclamation to the Jews." The brand-new organ played and a hymn was sung. After a Hebrew psalm and benediction, the procession returned to the lodge, accompanied by patriotic airs from the band and a salute of twenty-four guns, then continued on to refreshments at the Eagle Tavern.

It had not gone quite as intended, for the new Ararat was supposed to be on Grand Island, not on the east side of the river in Buffalo. But not enough boats could be found to ferry the crowd across, and the Episcopal church saved the day by hosting this Jewish-Masonic ceremony. Dale Broadhurst remarks that Noah must have had the support not only of the rector but of his bishop, Henry Hobart, "almost certainly an advanced degree Freemason" and "a very influential person in pre-Jacksonian New York State and in the City."[19]

Noah's Proclamation read, in part:

> I, Mordecai Manuel Noah, Citizen of the United States of America, late Consul of said States for the City and Kingdom of Tunis, High Sheriff of New York, Counselor at Law, and, by the grace of God, Governor and Judge of Israel, have issued this my Proclamation, announcing to the Jews throughout the world, that an asylum is prepared and hereby offered to them, where they can enjoy that peace, comfort and happiness, which have been denied them through the intolerance and misgovernment of former ages.[20]

He invited to this refuge all Jews, including "the black Jews of India and Africa," those of China and the Malabar Coast, and, significantly, the Native Americans:

> The Indians of the American continent, in their admitted Asiatic origin,—in their worship of one god,—in their dialect and language,—in their sacrifices, marriages, divorces, burials, fastings,

> purifications, punishments, cities of refuge, division of tribes,—in their High Priests,—in their wars and in their victories, being, in all probability, the descendants of the lost tribes of Israel, which were carried captive by the King of Assyria, measures will be adopted to make them sensible of their origin, to cultivate their minds, soften their condition and finally re-unite them with their brethren the chosen people.[21]

Noah was not yet done, and neither was the canal. It was finished on October 26, whereupon a flotilla set out from Buffalo to inaugurate its entire length. Noah outfitted a boat, predictably styled the "Ark" and stocked with animals and Indians, which ran into trouble with the locks and had to turn back. The chiefs of European Jewry, when they read his proclamation, treated it with ribaldry and contempt. Noah continued to picture the Ark on the masthead of his paper, the *New York National Advocate*, but he was saddened. In 1834, hearing that the cornerstone was still standing outside St. Paul's, Noah asked a friend to "place it in some secure spot, as he wished to have it preserved where it would not excite comment; for he had heard quite enough about it."[22] After some wanderings it found a home in the Erie County Historical Society, and a marker was planted on the intended location of the Grand Island refuge.

Noah was a sincere and orthodox Jew. Consequently, the American Ararat could only have been a temporary refuge for his people, pending their return to the Holy Land with its capital, Jerusalem. In 1845 he addressed to the Christians of America a *Discourse on the Restoration of the Jews*, in which he sets out his plan for such a return and weighs its possibilities. The Ottoman Empire was visibly crumbling, which meant that soon not just Grand Island but the whole of Palestine might be for sale. He begs America to obtain permission from the Sultan of Turkey for the Jews to "purchase and hold land; to build houses, and to follow any occupation they may desire, without molestation and in perfect security."[23] The moment such permission is granted, he assures his audience, the whole territory will be occupied by enterprising Jews from Europe and everywhere else. America will have a valuable ally in the region; trade will flourish. But his picture is not entirely rosy. Russia, greedy to seize India from the British and Turkey from the Ottomans, will make the Holy Land the theater of a terrible conflict. "Then will ensue the battle so sublimely described by the prophet: the fire and hailstones; the purification and victory; the advent of the Messiah, and the thousand years of happiness and peace which are to ensue."[24]

Noah might seem to be addressing today's fundamentalist Christians who support the state of Israel with similar sentiments, but that would be anachronistic. He saw America's religious freedom as accelerating a process under way since the Reformation: that of "gradually withdrawing from the great founder of the Christian faith, the divine attributes conceded to him by his disciples and followers."[25] Without any loss of respect for Jesus' "sublime morality," Noah saw enlightened Christians as ridding themselves of what most separated them from both Jews and Muslims: the belief that Jesus Christ is God. If the trend continued, then all would become Unitarians.

With that, we are almost back to Freemasonry with its simple acknowledgment of the "Great Architect of the Universe" acceptable to Jews, Christians, Muslims, Deists, and even polytheists, and its ban on religious discussion within the lodge. As such, it serves as a model for civil society and for the principles of religious freedom and governmental non-interference enshrined in the United States Constitution. However, outside the lodge Noah was anything but a freethinker (see chapter 20), nor did he expect anyone else to be one. He believed in the Old Testament as the revelation of God to the Jews, and the New Testament, properly interpreted (i.e., without the divinity of Christ), as God's revelation to the Christians. Yes, he says, Jesus was the Messiah—for them. That the Jews did not accept him as *their* Messiah was, in Noah's ingenious argument, providential. Note the Enlightenment and Masonic terms that I have italicized here:

> The Jews, my friends, were but the instruments of a higher power, and in rejecting Jesus of Nazareth we have a great and overwhelming evidence of the infinite wisdom of the Almighty. Had they acknowledged him as their Messiah at that fearful crisis, the whole nation would have gradually sunk under the Roman yoke, and we should have had at this day paganism and idolatry, with all their train of terrible evils, and darkness and desolation would have been spread over the face of the earth. But the death of Jesus was the birth of Christianity, the Gentile Church sprang from the ruins which surrounded its primitive existence; its march was onward, beset with darkness and difficulties, with oppression and persecution, until the *sun of the Reformation* rose upon it, dissipating the clouds of darkness which had obscured its beauties, and it shone forth with a *liberal and tolerant brightness*, such as the *Great Master* had originally *designed* it.[26]

Almost all the movements chronicled in this book took an evolutionary view of sacred history, with themselves as its inevitable and God-willed outcome. Each adopted its own exemplary form of social life, but they differed in their attitude toward those outside their walls. The Shakers, Millerites, and, to a lesser extent, Jemima Wilkinson's disciples, chose salvation through separation and left the rest of humanity more or less complacently to its fate. Handsome Lake's religion was more like Mordecai Noah's: both taught that God has given different revelations and rules to different peoples, and that their mission was for their own. With this inclusive attitude they were natural allies of the Universalists, for whom no soul is beyond salvation. The Mormons went further: theirs is a revelation for all of humanity, hence their worldwide missionary efforts and their retrospective baptism of the dead, whether Mormon or not.

By the 1840s, the Morgan affair had blown over, the Anti-Masonic Party had been absorbed by the Whigs, and Freemasonry was becoming acceptable again. The next eighty years saw a craze for orders that conferred higher initiations on men who had already passed the three "Blue" degrees of standard Masonry: Entered Apprentice, Fellow Craft, and Master Mason. One was the York Rite, which includes the Royal Arch degree and the Knights Templar, a specifically Christian and pseudo-military order. Another was the Scottish Rite, conferring the famous "33 Degrees" with their esoteric symbolism. Somewhat later (1872) came the Ancient Arabic Order of Nobles of the Mystic Shrine (the "Shriners," with their fezzes and circuses). All three were active in New York State, holding their rites and exercises in the Masonic temples found in almost every town and village.[27]

We might well call these orders eccentric spiritual movements, but their origins, like that of Freemasonry itself, lie far outside New York State. Here I will only mention three Masonic curiosities in the Upstate region. First is the Scottish Rite Cathedral in Corning, Steuben County. William Moore calls it "the only example of a building erected solely and specifically for Scottish Rite purposes in New York," and describes its style charitably as "eclectic romantic."[28] It was built in 1921, when Scottish Rite membership was nearing its zenith. In theory, the Rite comprises thirty-two progressive initiations (the 33rd Degree is only conferred as a special honor), each with its title, its ritual, and an erudite lecture on comparative religion and esoteric symbolism that introduces the Mason into an intellectual world barely suspected by the rank and file.[29] In practice it was nothing of the kind. The higher degrees were conferred wholesale, by payment of fees and attendance at theatrical ceremonies. The candidates watched as the doctrines and legends behind the degrees were dramatized with scenery, lighting, and music, and emerged "initiated." Moore reports that in 1930 there were 37,000 holders of the 32nd Degree among New York State's 346,000 Masons.[30]

A second monument, which the traveler is less likely to come across, is on the heights of Utica's New Forest Cemetery. Lavish in scale and original in design, it commemorates a Utica native, Justus Henry Rathbone (1839–1889), founder of the Knights of Pythias. In 1864, with the end of the Civil War in sight, Rathbone decided to found a fraternal order that would not require Masonic status, and would help to heal Amercia's wounds.

ILLUSTRATION 7.2A. Masonic symbol of square, compass, and the letter G.

ILLUSTRATION 7.2B. Symbol of the Mystic Order of Veiled Prophets of the Enchanted Realm (the "Grotto") at the former Masonic lodge, Hamilton. *Author's photographs.*

His inspiration was the friendship of Damon and Pythias, two members of the Pythagorean brotherhood (fifth century B.C.) who had been willing to give their lives for each other. In its heyday (1921) there were 908,000 Knights of Pythias nationwide,[31] a large proportion being workers or artisans who could not afford the fees of Freemasonry, much less the exorbitant expenses of the high grades.[32] The Emerys explain in their book on the Oddfellows, another fraternal order, that these orders provided a social safety net, caring for their members in sickness and for their eventual widows and orphans. Rathbone's monument, erected in 1899, is triangular in plan, like the Pythians' chief symbol: a shield or triangle with the letters F, C, and B. Its three pillars carry bronze statues of Damon and Pythias (for friendship), a woman with children (for charity), and a Knight in Pythian uniform (for benevolence). The pillars unite to support the crowning statue of Rathbone, and at the base is his hopeful saying: "If fraternal love held all men bound, how beautiful this world would be." Of those treated later in this book, both James Peebles and Dr. E. C. Dunn (see chapter 21) held high office in the Knights of Pythias, as well as in the Freemasons, the Knights Templar, the Order of Good Templars, and the Oddfellows.[33]

Lastly, outside the former Masonic lodge of Hamilton, Madison County, are two bronze bas-reliefs. One is the familiar square and compass enclosing the letter G (for *geometria*, the indispensable science of architect and

Platonist alike). The other is a turbaned Moor's head within a yoke. Until recently, a plaque beneath explained that here, in 1890, was founded the "Mystic Order of Veiled Prophets of the Enchanted Realm," also known as "the Grotto." As a resident of Hamilton, I was curious about such a high-sounding order, and discovered that it had played an important function in a town once dominated by teetotal Baptists. Only Master Masons are eligible, but beyond that the Grotto prides itself on being "primarily an organization for good wholesome fun and frolic."[34] For the M.O.V.P.E.R.'s mysticism I cannot vouch, but its rambling rituals based on ancient Persian mythology have an air of the "serious jest" about them, while the order's work for charitable causes, like that of the outwardly clownish Shriners, can only command respect.[35]

Freemasonry in the United States is at a low ebb today, for reasons not hard to seek. Like the other fraternal orders, it has an aging membership. Gender politics frowns on exclusively masculine institutions; ritual and hierarchy are out of fashion. Catholics, though not averse to the latter, are forbidden to join. As for the pseudo-Islamic orders, they bring problems unimagined by their founders. The history of Freemasonry and its esoteric symbolism seem to be of more interest to outsiders than to its members. The glimpses given in this chapter show how differently it was seen in the nineteenth century, and how vital a part it played in American society.

ILLUSTRATION 8.1. William Miller, biblical interpreter and founder of the Adventist movement. From *Harper's New Monthly Magazine*, Vol. 60 (Jan. 1880), p. 184. *Courtesy of Special Collections, Hamilton College Library.*

CHAPTER 8

Not the End of the World

> OUR WORK—is one of unutterable magnitude. It is a mission and an enterprise, unlike, in some respects, anything that has ever awakened the energies of man. It is not a subserviency to human institutions.—It is not a conflict on a political arena.—It is not the operation of a distinct religious sect. But it is an *alarm*, and a CRY, uttered by those who, from among all Protestant sects, as watchmen standing upon the walls of the moral world, believe the WORLD'S CRISIS IS COME—and who, under the influence of this faith, are united in proclaiming to the world, 'Behold the Bridegroom cometh, go ye out to meet Him!' It is an enterprise that swallows up all the petty peculiarities of sectarism [*sic*], and unites us upon an elevation so far above those mercenary undulations, that they are utterly lost to our view below.[1]
>
> *William Miller on his mission, 1842*

William Miller (1782–1849) was born in Pittsfield, Massachusetts,[2] a few years before his parents joined the post-Revolutionary emigration to New

York State. In 1786 they started a farm near what is now Low Hampton, just across the Vermont border, and there they raised William and fifteen younger siblings. William's biographers tell no stories of teenage illuminations, no connections with money-diggers or itinerant mesmerists. The only thing that distinguished him from other hardy farm lads was his passion for reading anything he could get his hands on—which was not much.

Following a predictable path, at twenty-one William married Lucy Smith of Poultney, Vermont, and moved there to start a farm of his own. In Poultney he found a well-stocked village library, from which he supplemented his sketchy education. As the couple's ten children began to arrive, William climbed the ladder of local influence, becoming a constable, then a sheriff, and also a Master Mason. In 1811 he joined the Vermont State Volunteers at the rank of lieutenant, and when the War of 1812 broke out, Miller was glad to be in the thick of it. Promoted to captain in the national army, he proved a fearless leader and a ruthless disciplinarian. In one letter to his wife, he describes with relish the salutary effects of "picketing," a sort of crucifixion inflicted on insubordinate soldiers. On September 11, 1814, he witnessed the defeat of the British at the Battle of Plattsburgh, and the next day wrote Lucy a dramatic report, culminating thus:

> A naval and land engagement, within the compass of a mile or two, and fifteen or twenty thousand engaged at one and the same time, is superior to anything my eyes ever beheld before. How grand! how noble, yet how awful! The roaring of cannon, the bursting of bombs, the whizzing of balls, the popping of small arms, the cracking of timbers, the shrieks of the dying, the groans of the wounded, the commands of the officers, the swearing of soldier, the smoke, the fire;—everything conspires to make the scene of a battle both awful and grand![3]

These are the words of someone who might welcome the Battle of Armageddon, so long as he was on the winning side.

Miller's reading in the Poultney library had opened up a new philosophical world to him: that of the freethinkers of the French Enlightenment, such as Voltaire and Count Volney, and America's own infidel, Thomas Paine. For about a dozen years Miller identified himself as a Deist, amusing his like-minded friends (but not his wife) by mimicking his grandfather and uncle, who were both Baptist ministers. The war seems to have been the catalyst for his return to the Christian fold. A few weeks after the Battle of Plattsburgh, he writes of a comrade's death:

> But a short time, and, like Spencer, I shall be no more. It is a solemn thought. Yet, could I be sure of one other life, there would

> be nothing terrific; but to go out like an extinguished taper, is insupportable—the thought is doleful. No! rather let me cling to that hope which warrants a never-ending existence; a future spring, where troubles shall cease, and tears find no conveyance; where never-ending spring shall flourish, and love, pure as the driven snow, rest in every breast.[4]

In 1815 the Millers moved back to Low Hampton and built a handsome new house on a farm of two hundred acres. Still tormented by doubts about his after-death state, William turned to the only source he could trust and began a punctilious study of the Bible.

Miller was no scholar but a careful reader, armed with *Cruden's Concordance* and the common Protestant conviction that both Old and New Testaments form a single sacred book, of which every word is a revelation from God. Useful as the concordance is, it lets one suppose that the same word has the same meaning wherever it occurs. Since the Bible is in fact a compilation from various authors, periods, languages, and genres, it is no wonder that it contains contradictions and, when taken literally, many absurdities. Believers in its unitary and divine authorship have much to excuse or explain away, and the more deficient their scholarship, the greater their confidence.

The revelation that most concerned Miller was that of the world's end and the Second Coming of Christ. His learned opponents were quick to point out that in the phrase "end of the world," found seven times in the New Testament, the Greek word that the King James version renders as "world" is not *kosmos* but *aion*, which means "age."[5] Ages come and go; the world remains! None of this mattered to William Miller, as his hobby blossomed into an apocalyptic obsession. "Give me time," he said, "and I will harmonize all those apparent contradictions to my own satisfaction, or I will be a Deist still."[6] As mentioned, anything visionary or mystical was foreign to his character: he worked by comparison and calculation alone. The one exception was a long dream of November 4–5, 1826, which he wrote down two years later, and in which, after many surreal adventures, he seemed to be promised a place in heaven.[7] To a Calvinistic Baptist, this was the clincher.

By the 1830s Miller had solidified his prophetic scheme. His main authorities were two prophecies in the Book of Daniel. In the first, Daniel overhears a conversation of angels in which "2,300 evenings and mornings" are given as the time before the restoration of the sanctuary (Daniel 8:13–14). In the second, the angel Gabriel gives "seventy weeks of years" dating from the command to rebuild Jerusalem until its end in flood, war, and desolation (Daniel 9:24–27). Assuming that these point to the same event, and calculating their starting points on the basis of "the best historians," Miller concluded that the Second Coming of Christ would occur in about A.D. 1843. He found corroborative evidence in the last chapter of Daniel, in the books of Jeremiah, Ezekiel, Matthew, and Revelation. Every way he added up the biblical figures, they pointed to A.D. 1843 as the end of the world.

To Miller, this meant that Jesus would return to earth in that year and judge mankind. The righteous would ascend to heaven with him, and the wicked would be given over to eternal torment in hell. Miller was insistent on this point and vigorously opposed the Universalists' belief in universal salvation, and any scheme that showed God as merciful to unbelievers.

Miller was now torn between the compulsion to give his message to the world and his feeling of inadequacy to the task. He was nearly fifty years old, had no degrees in divinity, and no experience in preaching. But like every prophet the world ever heard of, he gave in, and in August 1831 made his debut in Dresden, Washington County.[8] His first lecture was so well received that invitations followed from churches all over the region. One reason must have been the force of Miller's personality; another, his success in bringing about the public repentances and conversions that were the goal of every Protestant denomination. On September 14, 1833, the Baptist church of Hampton and Whitehall gave him a license to preach, and soon after that nature itself seemed to confirm that the end times were at hand. On the night of November 13–14, 1833, the Leonid meteor shower arrived in the most vivid display in modern times. The heavens seemed to fall as the night sky was thick as a blizzard with shooting stars.[9]

Miller's diaries record eight hundred lectures given between October 1, 1834 and June 9, 1839.[10] He spoke only on invitation, received no fees, and paid his own expenses, traveling by coach, canal, or train with no letup in the winter months. He might have remained a regional phenomenon had not some ministers in Boston become curious, even worried, about what this farmer-preacher was up to. In November 1839, Joshua V. Himes (1805–1895), pastor of the newly built Chardon Street Chapel, invited Miller as a guest in his house and church. After listening to a week of lectures, Himes declared himself converted, and promised to open doors for the wider proclamation of the "midnight cry."

Himes was as good as his word. He remained Miller's chief promoter, publicist, traveling companion, and defender. By March 1840, Miller was addressing fifteen hundred to two thousand people in the city hall of Hartford, Connecticut. He made eight further visits to Boston and gave lecture courses in New York City, Philadelphia, Pittsburgh, Baltimore, Washington, Newark, Providence, Rochester, Buffalo, Cleveland, Akron, and Cincinnati. On the western circuit, meetings were held in a custom-made tent of record dimensions, whose arrival and erection caused all the excitement of a circus coming to town.

Miller's grueling schedule was interrupted by a bout of typhoid fever and a severe attack of boils—twenty-two of them, from the size of a grape to that of a walnut, which he described with good-humored reference to Job and his comforters.[11] His hosts were surprised to find the celebrity plainly dressed, plainly spoken, and in appearance "an old man, shaking with the palsy."[12] But he had stamina: his standard course was sixteen lectures, two a day lasting upwards of two hours each. He enlivened them with large posters showing the statue of Nebuchadnezzar's dream (Daniel 2:31–35) and the beasts of Daniel's visions, together with the biblical chronologies that all culminated in the year 1843. A lithographed version was made for the many preachers who were now promoting the "Millerite" doctrine.[13]

There were anti-Millerites, too. The movement was fine fodder for the newspapers, which printed satirical articles with cartoons of apocalyptic monsters and the tent whisked up to heaven with the Millerites clinging to it. They spread the rumor that the believers had made "ascension robes" like long nightdresses, so as to be properly attired for the occasion. The tent and camp meetings attracted rowdies who threw eggs and stones, and in some places mobs assaulted the believers and prevented the assemblies. Some churches refused to host Miller's lectures, and many ministers preached against his doctrines. Biblical scholars disputed his chronologies and principles, but although their erudition gave them the advantage, they avoided personal slurs and demeaning comments, perhaps fearing—since they too were strict biblical believers—the slimmest possibility that Miller might be right. The Catholic Church, already cast by Protestants as the Whore of Babylon, ignored it, as did the transcendentalists. An anecdote supposedly confirmed by Ralph Waldo Emerson tells that on the "last day" a Millerite met Emerson and Theodore Parker walking calmly near Concord and felt it his duty to inform them: "Gentlemen!—do you know—do you *realize* that the world is coming to an end today?" Parker replied, "It does not concern *me*, for I live in Boston," and Emerson, "The end of the world does not affect me; I can get along without it."[14]

Miller himself never set an exact date for the Second Coming. His calculations simply placed it somewhere during the Jewish year that began at the spring equinox and ran from March 21, 1843 to March 21, 1844. This allowed for a full year's crescendo of anticipation, to which nature again contributed. The brightest comet of the century appeared in February 1843, and by March was easily visible by day.[15] By the end of the period, according to the Methodist Millerite pastor Josiah Litch, the doctrine was being preached by ministers of the following churches: "Protestant Episcopal, Methodist Episcopal, Methodist Protestant, Primitive Methodist, Wesleyan Methodist, Close Communion Baptist, Open Communion Baptist, Calvinistic and Arminian Baptists, Presbyterians, Old and New School Congregationalists, Old and New School Lutheran, Dutch Reformed, etc., etc."[16]

Between February 20 and March 2, 1844, Miller, Himes, and Litch lectured in Washington, D.C., where members of both houses of Congress were among their audiences. They returned via Baltimore, Newark, New

York City, and Brooklyn, and by March 14, Miller was back in Low Hampton with thirty-two hundred lectures behind him,[17] quietly awaiting the fulfillment of his labors.

The "First Disappointment" did surprisingly little to discourage the movement, perhaps because Miller had always admitted the possibility of minor errors in his calculations. Now some Millerites thought they had detected the error, and decided that the correct date should have been the tenth day of the seventh month of the current Jewish year. That translated to October 22, 1844, allowing them another glorious summer of tent meetings. Miller, to his credit, reproved the overenthusiastic disciples who thought it not worth planting crops, or who gave up their jobs or their property as the day approached, and he loathed the flamboyant emotionalism of the revivals. But his message of the imminent return of Christ remained intact. In July 1844, Miller set out with his son George and his faithful lieutenant Himes to lecture in western New York and Ohio. The Cincinnati Millerites had built a brick chapel eighty feet square, and visitors from Michigan and Wisconsin urged Miller to visit their states, too. But enough was enough, and the party returned up the Ohio River to Pittsburgh, then to Harrisburg, Philadelphia, New York City, and home. Miller was by now convinced that October 22 was indeed the correct date, and wrote to Himes: "I cannot refrain from congratulating you daily on the glorious prospect we have of soon entering the gates of the beloved city, and of soon harping on the golden harps the everlasting song of hallelujah to the Lamb."[18]

The "Great Disappointment" of Christ's failure to appear as scheduled brought mass exodus and trauma to the Millerites, ribaldry in the press, and complacency among the public. The surviving believers turned to various explanations:[19]

- That it was all God's plan.
- That the whole thing was a Satanic plot to mislead Christians.
- That there was still some error in Miller's calculations.
- That although the prediction was wrong, God had helped the Millerites because they brought thousands of people to salvation through repentance and study of the Bible.[20]
- That the October 22 excitement was a purely human phenomenon, the result of "mesmerism" or crowd psychology.[21]
- That on the appointed date God "shut the door," and no more sinners would be admitted. So there was no point in preaching the Gospel any more.[22]

- That on the appointed date Christ entered the "heavenly sanctuary" to prepare for his Second Coming. This interpretation, which had the most lasting success, derived from the "cornfield prophecy" of Hiram Edson (1802 or 1806–1882). On October 23, 1844, the day after the Great Disappointment, some Millerites were on their way to visit other believers near Clifton Spring. Edson writes:

> We started, and while passing through a large field I was stopped about midway of the field. Heaven seemed opened to my view, and I saw distinctly and clearly that instead of our High Priest coming out of the Most Holy of the heavenly sanctuary to come to this earth on the tenth day of the seventh month, at the end of the 2300 days, He for the first time entered on that day the second apartment of that sanctuary; and that He had a work to perform in the Most Holy Place before coming to the earth.[23]

At the end of the year the loyal leaders held a conference in Low Hampton and gave up any further attempt to correct the chronology. In January 1845, the local Baptist church excluded William Miller and his followers, which left it with almost no congregation. The Millerites, who had hitherto worshiped as members of the various Protestant sects, began to feel that they had a separate identity and to call themselves "Adventists."

On April 29, 1845, William Miller chaired a conference in Albany, which produced a set of doctrines and resolutions for the new sect. The most important doctrine defined the millennium. According to Revelation 20:2–8, Satan will be bound and the righteous will reign with Christ for a thousand years preceding the Last Judgment. During the nineteenth century the opinion had gained ground, supported by the optimism of the Enlightenment, that the human race could perfect itself. "The essence of this view," writes the Adventist scholar Francis Nichol, "is that the whole world—or virtually so—will be converted, that the change from a wicked world to a righteous one will be gradual, and that the advent of Christ is the coming of His Spirit in mighty power to this earth to win the battle for righteousness in men's hearts."[24] He adds that this is generally coupled with the doctrine of the conversion of the Jews and their return to Palestine.

Miller strongly opposed this interpretation, firstly because the scriptures depict the church "in a state of warfare and suffering" and the good and wicked coexisting on earth until Christ comes, and secondly because such a doctrine makes people complacent, putting off their repentance to a future date and making them unprepared for the sudden and imminent coming. He also emphasized that Christianity makes no distinction between Jew and Gentile, only between believers who are baptized and saved, and unbelievers who are damned.[25] In the terms of modern eschatology, Miller was a Premillennialist, expecting the world to get worse and worse until Christ appears "like a thief in the night," and condemning the Postmillennialist doctrine that expects the world to get better and better until it is fit for Christ's return. Biblical fundamentalists continue the argument to this day.

As for the interpretation of Daniel's prophecy of the twenty-three hundred days, the scholarly consensus is even more literal than Miller's. He had excused Daniel's calling of the twenty-three hundred years "days" as God's strategy for keeping people on their toes, for if they knew how far in the future the world would end, they would not pay attention to prophecy.[26] Given what is now known about the Book of Daniel, there is no need for such a ruse. The editors of the Revised Standard Version of the Bible write: "The author was a pious Jew living under the persecution of Antiochus Epiphanes, 167–164 B.C. To encourage his suffering fellow-believers he tells six stories, set in earlier days in Babylon." The twenty-three hundred "days and nights" (the proper translation) are just that: the 1,150 days, or about three years, before Antiochus's fall and the restoration of the sanctuary.[27]

The most direct and lasting result of Millerism was the Seventh-Day Adventist Church, founded in 1863 under the influence of Ellen Gould White (1827–1915), a former Millerite and visionary living in Maine. (Their title refers to their observance of the Sabbath on Saturday rather than Sunday.) Hiram Edson's vision of Jesus entering the heavenly sanctuary in 1844, in preparation for his return to earth, became a pillar of their theology. Another stream began with Miller and Himes's close colleague George Storrs (1796–1879) and the Adventist pastor George Stetson (1814–1879). Their personal and doctrinal example led Charles Taze Russell (1852–1916) to his own Bible studies, from which he predicted that the Rapture of the Saints would occur in 1878. Russell founded the Watch Tower Bible and Tract Society, which changed its name in 1931 to Jehovah's Witnesses. Thus two of today's most populous and active Adventist sects, together with their offshoots, can trace their roots to the farmhouse that still stands in Low Hampton.

William Miller's was not the only apocalyptic warning to issue from that corner of New York squeezed between the Hudson River and the Vermont border. His near contemporary Robert Matthews (1788–1841) had no lasting influence, but his rise and fall in the early 1830s connects with almost all the characters and movements mentioned so far. His story is elegantly told in *The Kingdom of Matthias* by Paul E. Johnson and Sean Wilentz, the only scholars to have paid much attention to him. Their hero, or villain, was born in a colony of strictly Calvinist Scots near Cambridge, Washington County. A carpenter by trade, a wife-beater by recreation, and all but illiterate, Matthews succeeded in attracting three wealthy disciples, and one ex-slave whose future fame would eclipse them all.

Matthews's theology was delivered in ranting sermons that were recalled later by his disciples. It was never systematic, but is interesting for its variations on themes such as a gendered theology, the Fall of Man, the historic role of Jesus Christ, the corrupt nature of the Christian era, the divine mission of a living man or woman, and the imminent apocalypse, judgment, and millennium. But whereas many of our characters sought to honor or even incarnate the feminine aspect of God, Matthews was a "masculinist" through and through. He declared that the Spirit of Truth, which is God, is male and that it incarnates in many forms. It created Adam and dwelt in him. Later it manifested in Abraham, in Jesus, and after the Crucifixion in St. Matthias (the apostle who was elected to take the place of Judas Iscariot). St. Matthias made a deal with the devil, which is the female power, the principle of chaos and disobedience to the Father, and the root of all evil. He handed the world over to female domination for eighteen hundred years, during which the "Christians" made havoc in it. Forget about praying to the Son, said Matthews: The Father is coming back to claim His Kingdom!

The great event began on June 20, 1830, in Argyle, New York. After Matthews burst into a local church meeting, he was arrested and confined in Albany for two weeks as an insane pauper. In his eschatology he called this episode the "Declaration of Judgment." In two years' time, he promised, he would purge the world of its disobedience to the Father, its prophesying women, and its submission to female rule. He would continue preaching until 1836, when the door would be shut and all who had not entered the Father's Kingdom by then would be damned. There would follow fifteen years of Christian confusion, then in 1851 the whole Gentile world would burn up, leaving the elect to enjoy an eternity of paternal rule. Every father would be lord in his own domain, women would know and love their subservient place, money would be abolished, grandiose temples would be built, and in the grandest of all of them Robert Matthews, now named Matthias, would perch on a stupendous throne, flanked by Sylvester Mills and Elijah Pierson.

The last named were New York City businessmen, widowers with strong, even fanatical religious convictions. They were members of a group of Christian perfectionists (see chapter 10) given to prayer, fasting, abuse of the mainstream churches, and the reformation of prostitutes. On that selfsame June 20, 1830, Pierson had been possessed by the spirit of the prophet

Elijah while riding on an omnibus. When his wife died, he tried hard, but failed, to emulate Elijah's feat by raising her from the dead. Nonetheless, his few associates, including his black servant Isabella Van Wagenen (c. 1797–1883), accepted him at face value. When Matthias came to his door two years later, Elijah Pierson played his role to the full. Told that he was no longer Elijah but John the Baptist, he acknowledged one greater still and never preached again.[28]

A third disciple was Benjamin Folger, who commuted between his office on Pearl Street and his riverside estate, Heartt Place, in Osinning.[29] Matthias was soon installed there as "Father," enjoying comforts hitherto unknown to him, and dressing the part. He favored a military-style green frock coat with pink silk or tartan lining, adorned with brass buttons, gold braid and frogging, silver sun and stars, lace ruffles at wrist and throat, a red sash with twelve tassels for the twelve tribes of Israel, and pantaloons of various colors tucked into high Wellington boots. He carried a gold watch (bought him by Mr. Folger), a heavy chain and key (to lock up Satan in the bottomless pit), an iron rule (for measuring the temple), a two-edged sword, and topped it all with a giant three-cornered or conical hat. He was about the only man in New York to grow his beard.

ILLUSTRATION 8.2. The Miller farm, Low Hampton. Home of William Miller from 1815 until his death in 1849, where he devised his system of biblical interpretation and millennial expectation. *Author's photograph.*

Before his transformation, Matthias had been an admirer of Mordecai Noah. Beside this parody of Noah's ceremonial dress, he imagined his community as being the true Jews, who of course had always worshiped God the Father, not the Son. Since the Father now dwelt among them, there was no need for prayer or Bible study at Heartt Place, now renamed Mount Zion. Perfection consisted in obedience to His laws, however capricious or discomfiting. Not surprisingly, it soon became more of a Venusberg. Like John Humphrey Noyes (see chapter 10), Matthias dictated the pairings of his disciples, following his doctrine of "match souls." His own wife had already thrown him out. He convinced Benjamin's wife, Ann Folger, that as he was Father of the Kingdom, she was to be its Mother, and married her in a homemade ceremony. He consoled Benjamin by marrying him to his (Matthias's) own daughter Isabella, who had temporarily left her own husband in Albany and joined the Kingdom. When she left, after several beatings from her father, Benjamin was re-matched to Catherine Galloway, a servant. Poor Elijah Pierson was too ailing to take part in this roundabout. Weakened by years of self-denial, he died in 1834, the suspected victim of poisoning.

The outside world had been suspicious of Mount Zion all along. In 1834 it hit the news as nothing had since William Morgan's abduction. Charges were brought against Matthias for assault against his daughter Isabella, and against both him and Van Wagenen for the suspected murder of Elijah Pierson. It was a nasty business all around. Pierson's corpse was exhumed, its stomach extracted and pored over by experts. Matthias was held for several months preceding his trial in 1835, then sentenced to three months on the assault charge; the murder was unproven. Benjamin Folger accused Van Wagenen of trying to poison him, too; she sued him for slander and won. Pocketing her $125 damages, she accompanied Matthias on his release from jail. He tried to move in with his wife in Albany, but Mrs. Matthews would have none of it. Matthias headed west and turned up in Kirtland, Ohio, on the doorstep of Joseph Smith, himself an exile. Smith received Matthias courteously and let him address the Mormons, but soon saw what he was dealing with and "cast out the devil." No one knows for certain how Matthias lived and died after that. It all ended like *Don Giovanni:* Benjamin and Ann Folger kissed and made up. Sylvester Mills, after a short recuperation at the Bloomingdale Lunatic Asylum, remarried, and he and the Folgers resumed their profitable businesses. Isabella Van Wagenen left to find a better master. Soon she would be a major force in the abolitionist and women's rights movements, under her new name of Sojourner Truth.

ALBERT BRISBANE.

At the age of thirty.

ILLUSTRATION 9.1. Albert Brisbane, the American disciple of Charles Fourier. From *Albert Brisbane, a Mental Biography with a Character Study*, Boston: Arena Publishing Co., 1893. *Courtesy of Special Collections, Hamilton College Library.*

CHAPTER 9

Brief Utopias

This chapter introduces three contrasting utopian communities that began in 1843–44 and lasted from two to about ten years. Religion was central to all of them in one way or another. The German Inspirationists of Buffalo Creek were intensely pious; the Skaneateles Community was militantly anti-religious; the Fourierist Phalanx of Sodus Bay imploded because it could not decide whether to be religious or not. These were the same years in which William Miller was preaching the end of the world, and the renewal of prophecy among the Shakers was at its height. For all their differences, each of these movements was driven by the determination to opt out of American society and create a more sacred or natural state.

The Inspirationists of Buffalo Creek

> I the LORD, your God, speak a word for your times. If you have faith, keep it and be mindful henceforth that I do not lie, but will hold to what I say and promise. So hearken: It has been my premeditated counsel and will to assign you this place, through my wondrous and secret direction, as the future portion for you and your children; and as it has so prospered hitherto, behold what more I would and shall do. I have promised you my help and support, and I will fulfill it according to my trust, and you shall know that

> I am your God who can help you out of all the troubles through which I have guided you and shall yet guide you.[1]
>
> *Inspiration through Christian Metz, Buffalo, November 27, 1842*

In September 1842, a group of German Pietists set sail for New York. Pietism was a movement within the Lutheran Church that sought a more intense and emotional involvement with Christ and the Christian life. This particular group, called the Community of True Inspiration, also believed that the Lord had chosen them for his special work. The community had long occupied a castle and a disused monastery in the Grand Duchy of Hessen, which was more permissive than many German states. But the Inspirationists crossed the line by refusing military service (in obedience to the Sixth Commandment), the taking of oaths (prohibited by the Third Commandment), and public schooling, and their lives were made intolerable.[2] Like the Pilgrims and other religious dissidents, they decided to make a fresh start in the New World.

The Inspirationists' utopian vision was rooted in a German mystical tradition that began with the fourteenth-century Rhineland mystics (Meister Eckhart, Johannes Tauler, Heinrich Suso) and revived after the Reformation with Jacob Boehme and Pietism's founder, Philipp Jacob Spener (1635–1705). Other branches in America included the Ephrata Cloister in Pennsylvania, the Harmony Society in Indiana and Pennsylvania, and the Society of Separatists of Zoar, Ohio. These are not part of our study, but it is no surprise that some of these religious refugees came to western New York at the time of its maximum expansion, and, like others in the region, conducted their affairs via a direct line to God.

Since their foundation in 1714, the Lord had inspired the community through select members called the *Werkzeuge*, a German word meaning "tools." In America the community had two Werkzeuge. Christian Metz (1794–1867), a former carpenter who led the community for more than fifty years, spoke directly when the spirit was upon him, and his testimonies were taken down in shorthand. Barbara Heinemann (1795–1883), a former servant maid, testified through writing, once she had learned to write.[3] No others were accepted. Even Heinemann was excluded for years on account of her marriage, and after her death the communications ceased altogether. Like the *Doctrines and Covenants* spoken by Joseph Smith or the Shakers' *Sacred and Divine Roll*, the Werkzeuge's sayings were revered as a secondary scripture, and the Inspirationists preserved them in fifty volumes, printed in German *Fraktur* type. Their theology was basically Lutheran but with a Universalist tinge, for it taught that while the pious have better places in heaven, hell is not eternal. As sin had a beginning, so it will have an end, and "after many eternities" the damned will return to God.[4]

The vanguard party sailed from Bremerhaven and suffered a perilous, thirty-seven-day voyage before docking in New York on October 26, 1842. A week later Metz and three companions took the steamship up the Hudson to Albany, then followed the Erie Canal all the way to Buffalo. For nine days they shared a small cabin with seven Irishmen and two Americans, "not without dispute and the exercise of patience,"[5] and it was a relief to put up at a Buffalo inn kept by a friendly German.[6] On November 14 the innkeeper went with them to look at a nearby tract, where an Indian chief rowed them across the river in a dugout canoe. Before leaving Europe, however, they had determined on a tract at French Creek, near Chautauqua, and insisted on seeing it. All the omens were bad. The steamship that took them along the Lake Erie shore nearly sank in a storm. After viewing the tract, which they did not like, it seemed safer to return to Buffalo by the land route, so they took the post coach—which capsized. The Lord, speaking through Metz (see specimen above), led them back to the first property: Buffalo Creek, a former reservation that the Seneca Indians had sold to the Ogden Land Company.[7] After a second visit in the deep snow of December, the Inspirationists decided to buy the ten-thousand-acre tract and to summon their brethren from Germany.[8]

Their troubles were far from over. For months Metz ran to and fro, first to Geneva then to New York City, to negotiate with the land company in his inadequate English. There were delays, difficulties over boundaries, and costly legal obstacles. The Lord, speaking through Metz, expressed his displeasure at the details of the sale,[9] and approved the purchase of only five thousand acres at a price of ten dollars an acre.[10] Once in possession, the Inspirationists were dismayed to find the Indians still there, and very reluctant to leave for the southern reservations assigned to them. It took three years of passive aggression on the Indians' part, appeals to the federal government on the Inspirationists' part, and various payoffs before the community had the land and buildings to itself.[11]

Meanwhile more than eight hundred men, women, and children had arrived from Germany. Cabins were hastily thrown up, and the settlement was named Ebenezer, "The Stone of Help," after the incident in I Samuel 7:12. In time it spawned four villages: Middle Ebenezer, Upper Ebenezer, Lower Ebenezer, and New Ebenezer, to which members were assigned "according to their degree of faith."[12] A large tract across the Canadian border housed some Pennsylvania Dutch who had chosen to join the community.[13]

The Inspirationists were not communists: the richer members received shares in proportion to their contributions, and held mortgages on the property as security. They would not vote in elections or fight in the Civil War, but readily paid the three-hundred-dollar substitute fee and donated clothes and food to the Northern cause. Their way of life was austere. There was no card playing at Ebenezer; nor any music, parties, or social get-togethers. No pictures, newspapers, or magazines were allowed. Meals were held in silence, but beer and wine were drunk. Women dressed so as to hide all lines of grace and beauty; men shaved their moustaches (thought to be a badge of worldliness). Young people who wished to marry had to spend a year in separation, and everyone slept in single beds.[14] Remarriage after the death of a spouse was frowned on. The compulsory daily services were without bells, pews, symbolic objects, or celebrations of Christmas or Easter: there were just chant-like hymns, silent prayers, readings from the Bible and the Werkzeuge, and addresses by the elders. Everyone underwent a yearly examination to determine their piety and assign them to the various "orders."[15] Worst of all, the Werkzeuge often addressed members by name, usually reproving them for their sins, and these personal messages became part of the printed, canonical record.

Frank J. Lankes makes the point that in Germany, the Inspirationists had lived, when not under religious persecution, certainly under economic oppression. For survival's sake, they had submitted to a very regimented existence. In America the pressures were lifted. Poorer members no longer lived on the charity of the richer ones, but could take jobs in Buffalo for higher wages. The city's secular German immigrants, initially an asset to the community, were now thought a bad influence on the young people.[16] For all that, the Inspirationists' work ethic and craft expertise made them one of the most successful intentional communities, building houses, mills, and factories and trading with the worldly inhabitants of a booming region. The New York State Assembly certified their incorporation; President Millard Fillmore, living in retirement in Buffalo, gave them his recommendation.

It was the Inspirationists' very success that forced them to leave New York. By the 1850s they needed more land, but the growth of Buffalo had made it too expensive. The Lord told them to look west, and as a result they bought eighteen thousand acres in Iowa, calling their new settlement Amana.[17] It took them ten years to complete the move and the sale of Buffalo Creek, which they managed without financial loss.[18] The Buffalo suburb of West Seneca absorbed the Ebenezer villages, where a number of the Inspirationist houses remain.

The community in Amana dissolved itself in 1935, separating its commercial enterprises from its religious basis. The settlement's buildings, like the various Shaker sites, have become tourist attractions. According to Peter Hoehnle, the Amana Church Society continues with about four hundred members,[19] and its services still use some five hundred testimonies of the Werkzeuge, translated into English.

The Sodus Bay Phalanx

> We already know that God relies solely upon the force of attraction in guiding the movements of the planets and the suns, which are creatures immensely greater than ourselves, and in guiding the insects, creatures far inferior to us. Could man alone be deprived of the fortune of bring guided toward social good by attraction? Why should there be a break in the chain of the system of the universe? Attraction is the divine guide of the stars and the animals and it suffices to place them in harmony. Why should it not be equally sufficient for man, whose place in the universe is midway between the planets and the animals? Where is the unity of the divine system if the mainspring of the general harmony, attraction, is not just as applicable to human societies as it is to the stars and the animals, if attraction cannot be applied to the agricultural and manufacturing industries which are the pivot of the social mechanism?[20]
>
> *Charles Fourier on the principle of attraction*

It is quite a leap from these devout worker bees to the disciples of the French philosopher Charles Fourier (1772–1837). The Inspirationists would have agreed with him that so-called "civilization" is a corrupt state from which the human race needs to escape. But Fourier also believed that God intends humans to enjoy life to the fullest, that our "passions" are fundamentally good, and should be indulged. His solution was a complete overhaul of social and economic behavior, aiming at a state he called Harmony.

Fourier could see the dehumanizing effects of the Industrial Revolution, and preferred a society based on agriculture. But it must be agriculture done for fun, more like gardening. Everyone in Fourier's utopia chooses the work that satisfies his or her passions. No one is fettered to a single breadwinning job, but in the course of the day moves through several different activities, all done in association with like-minded people. As a single example, garbage disposal is done by a corps of young boys mounted on miniature ponies. Boys, Fourier thought, positively enjoy getting dirty, and in Harmony they are specially honored for their efficiency and devotion to this essential work.

The passions in the Frenchman's list naturally include *amour,* in other words, sex. Fourier's tolerance was absolute: in Harmony, anyone may enjoy sex with anyone else of compatible passions. This included homosexuals—a notion much too radical for its time—but not the typical marriage of the "civilized" state, in which the man regarded the woman as his economic and sexual property. Fourier never married, but spun his fantasies in solitude. He wrote many delightful pages describing life in Harmony where friendly competition takes the place of war, children grow up with no sense of distinction between work and play, and everyone is honored for his or her unique contribution. Fourier predicted that once the human race has made progress in this direction, the earth's axis will shift and the whole solar system will begin to rearrange itself in a more harmonious pattern. This gives a glimpse of the extreme range and strangeness of his thought.

Though he counts as a pioneer of socialism, Fourier was not against private property. After all, some people's passion is to acquire things, and if it deprives nobody, they are welcome to it. Nor was he against religion, though his attitude was far more pagan than Christian. Harmonians may practice any religion or none, but may not force it on anyone else. Fourier believed in a benevolent God, and in reincarnation, whereby humans evolve along with the earth. Though he acknowledged no influences and accepted no authority, his scheme of microcosm and macrocosm following the same laws of "passional attraction" revives the Hermetic doctrine of the correspondence of the Above with the Below, with Love as the motive force of the cosmos.

In the 1840s, America was half ripe for Fourier's ideas. Their prophet was Albert Brisbane (1809–1890), the son of a wealthy Batavia family. He had discovered Fourier during a long educational journey to Europe and Constantinople, and his visits and enthusiasm had cheered the neglected philosopher. After his return, Brisbane wrote a digest of Fourierism called *Social Destiny of Man: or, Association and Reorganization of Industry* (1840).[21] Its ideals aligned him with the most progressive trends of the time, such as women's rights:

> In Association, let a moral code come from woman,—for woman free and independent—who has no favors to ask of men, who does not live upon his industry; and then for the first time we shall see truth and dignity established in the intercourse of the sexes, or in the two passions, love and paternity,—then we shall see these branches of the harmonies of human nature developed with purity and elevation.[22]

Brisbane followed up his book by promoting Fourierism in innumerable newspaper articles, at first paying for the space. During 1842–43 he contributed a regular column to Horace Greeley's newly founded *New York Tribune*.[23] These took instant fire in the mind of a young teacher from Cattaraugus,[24] Theron C. Leland (1821–1885), who spent 1843 lecturing on Fourier to anyone who would listen. And listen they did, in Buffalo and at least twenty other places, with Rochester as the center of gravity for the new craze. August 1843 saw a Fourierist convention there and the foundation of a North American "Phalanx"—Fourier's term for his communities. Noyes calls the surrounding region "the volcanic district,"[25] as phalanges, or plans for them, erupted everywhere. Of those that actually happened, the most important were the Clarkson Phalanx in North Hamlin (Orleans County), the Ontario Union in Littleville (Ontario County), the Bloomfield Association at the intersection of Monroe, Livingston, and Ontario counties, and the Sodus Bay Phalanx in Wayne County. [26] During the spring and summer of 1844, at least a thousand men, women, and children moved into these four communities—and those were the hard-core Fourierists, a small proportion of the many sympathizers.[27]

The Sodus Bay Phalanx is the best documented and, at two years, the longest lived of these experiments. It started with the advantage of land already settled and farmed by the Shakers, who had bought the tract in 1826. It comprised some fourteen hundred to fifteen hundred acres, including Thornton Point and Nicholas Point, and may have held a special geophysical significance in the Shaker cosmos.[28] For it so happened that the Preemption Line of 1796 (dividing the claims on Indian lands by New York and Massachusetts) ran through it, and, as mentioned in chapter 1, is the exact meridian of Washington, D.C. When a new canal was projected to link the Erie Canal at Montezuma with Lake Ontario at Sodus Bay, the Shakers took advantage of the sudden rise in the value of their site and sold it. The buyers were not so lucky, for after the economic crisis of 1837 the canal plan was scrapped. They were desperate to unload the property, and the Fourierists had it at a bargain price to be paid in two years.[29] The Shakers had left them about six large barns, seven houses, various shops, mills, and a tannery;[30] an inventory listed sixty-four rooms for accommodation. The trouble was that within a year eighty-two families had joined the phalanx, totaling 260 people or more.[31]

Overcrowding led to inharmonious behavior. In July 1844 members started sequestering communal property, such as horses, for their private use. There were fines, expulsions, quitters, and arguments about how much the latter should be reimbursed. Fourier's principles of association, with their careful calibration of groups based on passions and attractions, did not stand a chance. Although these principles included complete religious freedom, the phalanx soon split into a religious faction and a secular or liberal one. Each feared domination by the other, and, as always, the situation favored extremists on both sides. The liberals pulled their children out of the religiously run school, while the religious party, in obedience to the Fourth Commandment, forbade all Sunday work. A public trial ended in defeat for the Sabbatarians, who then appealed to the North American Phalanx.[32] Arthur Bestor puts it succinctly: there was an irreconcilable difference between Fourier's theory of passions and a Christian ethic based on sin.[33]

Even more worrying to the Sodus Bay leaders were the overhanging debt and the inability of the phalanx to run at a profit or even to sustain itself. Noyes writes its obituary thus:

> After laboring a year or two under these difficulties, there was a hasty and disorderly retreat. It is said that each individual helped himself to the movable property, and that some decamped in the night, leaving the remains of the Phalanx to be disposed of in any way which the last men might choose. The fact that mankind do not like to have their faults and failings made public, will probably account for the difficulty in obtaining particulars of such experiments as the Sodus Bay Phalanx.[34]

The other phalanges in western New York seem to have vanished into thin air, but they left a lot of angry, disillusioned souls. When two emissaries of the Brook Farm Phalanx in Massachusetts visited the region in 1847, they found "more wealth, refinement, freedom of thought, general intelligence, here, than among either our village or farming population in New England."[35] But the reception of their lectures on association worsened as they went west. In Syracuse they found keen reform movements, especially antislavery, but interest in Fourier was dead. In Rochester and the western counties they scarcely dared to mention his name, so deeply was the public mind poisoned by the collapse of the phalanges.

The Skaneateles Community

> We repudiate all creeds, sects, and parties, in whatever shape or form they may present themselves. Our principles are as broad as the universe, and as liberal as the elements that surround us. They forbid the adoption and maintenance of any creed, constitution, rules of faith, declarations of belief and disbelief, touching any or all subjects; leaving each individual free to think, believe and disbelieve, as he or she may be moved by knowledge, habit, or spontaneous impulses. Belief and disbelief are founded upon some kind

> of evidence, which may be satisfactory to the individual to-day, but which other or better evidence may change to-morrow. We estimate the man by his acts rather than by his peculiar belief. We say to all, Believe what you may, but act as well as you can.[36]
>
> *Principles of the Skaneateles Community, 1843*

If religious controversy spelled the death of Fourierist phalanges, one solution was to do without religion altogether. This was the goal of the Skaneateles Community (1844–46), which stands out as the only explicitly secular movement in our whole collection. I leave others to judge whether it was still a "spiritual" movement; there is no doubt that it was eccentric. The founder was John A. Collins (1810–1900), who was employed as the paid general agent of the Massachusetts Anti-slavery Society and had superintended the one hundred national conventions ordered by the society in 1843.[37] After a trip to England, Collins changed direction, to the distress of his abolitionist colleagues. Frederick Douglass, who attended the Syracuse convention, wrote:

> Our general agent, John A. Collins, had recently returned from England full of communistic ideas, which ideas would do away with individual property, and have all things in common. He had arranged a corps of speakers of his communistic persuasion, consisting of John O. Wattles, Nathaniel Whiting and John Orvis to follow our anti-slavery conventions, and while our meeting was in progress in Syracuse, a meeting, as the reader will observe, obtained under much difficulty, Mr. Collins came in with his new friends and doctrines, and proposed to adjourn our anti-slavery discussions and take up the subject of communism. To this I ventured to object. I held that it was imposing an additional burden of unpopularity on our cause, and an act of bad faith with the people, who paid the salary of Mr. Collins, and were responsible for these hundred conventions.[38]

To Collins's credit (according to Noyes), he afterward declined his salary. But he certainly knew how to annoy people. The following spring he spoke at the convention of the New England Social Reform Society, which had voted to establish a community in Skaneateles, Onondaga County. It would be a community, Collins said, "whose government is based not upon physical force, but reason and moral suasion; unencumbered by organized churches, sectarian priests, and the authority of all books and creeds."[39] There was worse to come. "We have had religion, some say 6,000, but I say 60,000 years, and what better are we for it? Religion is essential to darkness. She cheats man into his present suffering, and cheats him out of present enjoyment."[40] After a vigorous debate, he proposed that the convention pass a resolution: "That we regard the organized Church as adapted to produce strife and contention rather than love of peace—the Bible as no authority, the priesthood an imposition, miracles as unphilosophical and absurd, and salvation for sin, or punishment in a future world through a crucified god, as a remnant of heathenism."[41]

Collins's speech set the convention in an uproar. The Universalists, Unitarians, and Quakers all felt insulted, and they had plenty to say about it. At last someone asked outright: "Does Mr. Collins believe in God?" He ducked the question, saying that if the clergy succeeded in pinning the label of infidel or atheist on the movement, they would "drown the cries of the poor."[42] Back in Skaneateles, his community was thriving. Of its three hundred acres, seventy were in timber, forty in wheat, 130 in corn. There were apple orchards and nurseries, and a sawmill powered by the stream.[43] The ninety members lived in a stone house and adjacent buildings, and all seemed, from visitors' reports and their own newspaper, to be diligent and happy. Their principles were as follows:

1. Denial of revealed religion and of the authority of the church and the Bible
2. Denial of the right of any government to use force to enforce its laws; hence members would not vote, pay taxes, petition, serve on juries, do military duty, or testify in court.
3. All goods would be held in common; the right of individual property holding was denied.
4. As marriage was designed for happiness, same should be dissolved when members had "outlived their affections" and "new alliances" should then be made.
5. Use of meat, narcotics, and alcohol was prohibited.[44]

This libertarian, secular Eden harbored a serpent in the form of Quincy A. Johnson, a lawyer from Syracuse. Collins had made the same mistake as Jemima Wilkinson: out of disdain for personal ownership he had put Johnson's name on the deed as joint owner of the property. Quincy and his wife did not share Collins's ideals, and they almost wrecked the enterprise before Collins could buy him out.[45]

No one is sure why, after weathering this trauma, the Skaneateles Community suddenly came to an end in May 1846. One reason may have been the vote of the New York state legislature denying its request for incorporation, on the grounds that it would "confer privileges prejudicial to the best interest of society."[46] In other words, its infidelity, loose concept of marriage, and general radicalism were more threatening than the God-fearing Inspirationists, who had succeeded in a similar appeal. Collins himself had come to realize that the experiment was premature. He had already had to compromise his principles on several fronts, and had found that nonresistance was no protection against troublemakers or exploiters. He surrendered his share to the community, and since the property had meanwhile doubled in value,[47] no one else was the loser when it was sold back into private ownership. Collins moved to California, where he left a tenuous paper trail. He ran unsuccessfully as a Whig Party candidate for the state senate,[48] edited a Sacramento newspaper,[49] and was friends with leaders of the women's suffrage movement.[50]

Most of the movements with which this book is concerned were in some sense utopian, and some of them were far from brief, notably the Shakers, the Oneida Community, and the Koreshan Unity, which lasted for decades. If all people followed their principles, they seemed to say, what a paradise this earth would be! But of course, most people will not do so, because those communities, seen from the outside, seem anything but paradisiacal. Obedience to the leader, a weird theology, and strict rules of diet and sex have limited appeal. Moreover, the history of utopian and communal movements shows that every rose contains the worm of its destruction, in the shape of plain, cussed human nature that would rather turn on its neighbors than unite with them against a common enemy.

Illustration 9.2. House built by the Community of True Inspiration in the former village of Ebenezer, now West Seneca, after 1842. *Author's photograph.*

ILLUSTRATION 10.1. John Humphrey Noyes, founder of the Oneida Community. From Noyes's *Home-Talks*, Vol. I, Oneida: Oneida Community, 1875. *Courtesy of Special Collections, Hamilton College Library.*

CHAPTER 10

Perfection in This Life

If the spirit of Christ and of the unbelieving world are as hostile to each other now as ever, (which is certainly true,) it is clear that the cross of Christ, must have a development in the dispensation of the fullness of times, as offensive to the Gentile world, as its nullification of the Sinai law was to the Jewish world. Where then shall we look for the present 'offense of the cross?' How shall the gospel of death to the world by the death of Christ, protrude itself in a practical form, as it did in the apostolic age, and attack the central life of the Gentile world? The offense cannot come on the same point as it did in the primitive church; for the special ordinances of Judaism have passed away. . . . Where then shall the death-blow of the flesh fall on the Gentile world? We answer—on marriage. That is a civil as well as religious ordinance, performed by clergymen and magistrates, defended by religion and law, common to all sects, and universal in the world. On that point the 'offense of the cross' will be just what it was in the apostolic age on the ordinances of Judaism.[1]

John Humphrey Noyes on the abolition of marriage

Among Madison County's few claims to fame, the name of Oneida ranks high. In the twentieth century it spelled silver-plated tableware, manufactured in Sherrill by Oneida Ltd. To the social historian, it denotes the utopian experiment of the Oneida Community (1848–1880) with its practices of "complex marriage," in which every male member was, in theory, wedded to every female, and of "male continence," which prevented unwanted pregnancies. This unorthodox venture found voice in a truckload of diaries, journals, letters, and records, which came into the hands of George Wallingford Noyes (1870–1941). A serious scholar as well as a child of the community, he used it as the basis for his three-volume history.[2] But the two Oneidas were not happy bedfellows. After World War II, Oneida Ltd. was planning an advertising campaign to persuade the G.I. brides to welcome their victorious menfolk with sparkling silverware. It would not do to link the Oneida brand name with sexual deviance, as might happen if outsiders got into the archive. So in 1947, to prevent any leakage, the company's directors emptied George Noyes's walk-in safe and burned the lot.

This might have left future historians bereft, had not George Noyes, foreseeing something of the kind, copied the most essential documents onto twenty-two hundred typed pages. Despite the company's Herodian efforts to seek out and destroy every carbon copy, two survived, one in private hands and the other now in the Syracuse University Library. Since 1993, when all restrictions on scholarly access to it were lifted, there is little mystery left about George's famous uncle, John Humphrey Noyes (1811–1886), and how his community began, functioned, and died. Nor, sadly, is the neo-Tudor factory of Oneida Ltd. the fount of local prosperity that it once was.[3]

As often in these pages, we begin in New England and with the crisis of early-nineteenth-century Protestantism, as earnest young men like John Noyes kicked against the dogmas and wondered whether they had damned themselves in the process. Noyes's family was a prominent one. His father rose from teaching to store-keeping to representing Vermont in the U.S. Congress; his mother was an aunt of U.S. President Rutherford Hayes. But this was Vermont, not Boston or Virginia. The Noyes "mansion" in Putney was but a farmhouse,[4] and the family believed in plain living and high thinking. John was destined for the Congregationalist ministry and sent to his father's college of Dartmouth, then to Andover, and finally to Yale.

A ministerial training in the early 1830s was an intense business, coinciding as it did with the Second Great Awakening (see chapter 2). Tall and sandy-haired like Charles Grandison Finney himself, Noyes started as a revivalist; on receiving his license to preach in 1833, he served his first pastorate in North Salem, New York, fifteen miles east of Peekskill.[5] His private devotions involved self-punishment, deprivation of food and sleep, and the eating of cayenne pepper. They led to a "spiritual crucifixion" in which he identified himself with Christ's death.[6] There followed a resurrection, with mystical experiences of "unutterable bliss" in which he "truly entered the secret place of the Most High."[7] In consequence, on February 20, 1834—a date celebrated by the Oneida Community as their spiritual New Year's Day—the young preacher became permanently exempt from sin, and convinced that he would not die until the coming of the Kingdom of God.[8] As he later remarked, "God gave plenty of evidence in 1834, that he had appointed me foreman of his church."[9] Noyes's claim of irreversible perfection following his spiritual catharsis got him dismissed from Yale and destroyed any prospects for the normal ministry, but it left him free to develop a theology all his own, which I now summarize.

The Gospels give the impression that Jesus expected the world to end quite soon, even within the lifetime of some of the apostles (Matt. 24; Mark 13; John 21:22), yet eighteen hundred years later Christians were still awaiting the Second Coming, the Last Judgment, and the apocalyptic events predicted in the Book of Revelation. Noyes's originality was to deny all this. In his version of sacred history, Jesus made no mistake. His Second Coming and the Judgment occurred as prophesied, in A.D. 70, when the Romans destroyed the Temple of Jerusalem, but they took place in the spiritual, not the natural world. As the Jews were the first people on earth to have become spiritually ripe, theirs was the first harvest or judgment, which concluded their cycle of about two thousand years.[10] The next cycle belongs to the Gentiles and will end with their judgment.

Noyes reckoned that many prophecies of Revelation had already been fulfilled. He interpreted the millennium during which Satan was bound (Rev. 20:1–3) as the suppression of idolatry from the Christian emperors (fourth century) through the Middle Ages (fourteenth century). The bottomless pit where Satan was confined was the idolatrous Eastern world, against which Islam formed a temporary barrier. Satan and his idolatry (for Noyes, the worst of all sins against God) returned when Muslim power waned, navigation and trade opened the way to the East, and the Renaissance revived Greco-Roman paganism.[11]

This concept of the millennium as past, not future, needed to be squared with the prophecies of Daniel, already the focus of William Miller's preaching. Noyes's solution was to count "seventy weeks of years" (Dan. 9:24) back from the destruction of Jerusalem to 420 B.C., then to add twenty-three hundred years (Dan. 8:14). This put A.D. 1880 as the year when the sanctuary would be cleansed, the Jews' desolation cease, and the final Judgment occur.[12] Thus Noyes joined the long list of those who were predicting that the world, or at least this aeon, would end somewhere between 1879 and 1881.[13]

The forty years from Jesus' ministry to A.D. 70 were crucial to Noyes's concept of perfection. The Apostles, including St. Paul, were the first humans to achieve perfect freedom from sin, which brought with it freedom from death. Whereas all former humans, upon death, had entered the twilight zone of Hades, the 144,000 early Christians rose with Jesus and formed the "Primitive Church" in the heavens. Now, with the Gentile cycle approaching its end, the corresponding group was Noyes's own. Through him, the Oneida Community was guided by the Primitive Church, whose members had eighteen hundred years' more experience of the sinless life and could therefore advise and judge those below.[14]

The presence of sin and evil has always troubled those who imagine God as the creator of all and infinitely good. Noyes believed otherwise. In his theology, the ultimate cause of all evil is an uncreated evil being (Satan), just as the ultimate cause of all good is an uncreated good being (God). Satan has existed from all eternity, and it's not his fault that he is bad! Nor is it God's fault that some people are incorrigible sinners, joining Satan's side and suffering eternal reprobation.[15] Noyes hastens to explain that his doctrine is not that of the Manicheans, Magians, and Gnostics, who attributed the creation of the material world to the evil power. On the contrary, Noyes's God created the universe as a theater of action for uncreated good and evil to come to a decisive conflict.[16]

Noyes's outlook for the great battle was optimistic. The nations would be brought to Christ one by one: first the leading nations of today's world, i.e., the Gentiles, then the Jews, who already accept the Old Testament; next the Muslims, who at least acknowledge one God and more or less accept the Old Testament; and finally the whole of the heathen world.[17] Then no one will die and go to Hades any more: all will live on earth in a state of perfection. A hint by George Noyes suggests that they might meanwhile be reincarnated, and that by selective breeding evil souls would eventually find no suitable bodies to inhabit,[18] but this may have been his own idea.

Given this theological system, John Humphrey Noyes had limited sympathy for the social reform movements of his time. Although at Yale he had helped to found an abolitionist society, he came to see the reformers as contributing to infidelity, because they all chipped away at the authority of the Bible. The temperance movement was embarrassed by the biblical acceptance of wine, so it bent the text to suit itself. The antislavery movement had to pretend that biblical slavery was not really slavery. The women's rights movement was in point-blank antagonism to St. Paul, who makes women subservient to men. The nonresistance movement could not stomach the wars of Moses and Joshua, although they acted on orders from God. In short, when scripture failed to support reformist agendas, it was scripture that had to go.[19] Noyes could dispense with ministers, services, creeds, and sacraments, but none was more zealous in devotion to every word of God (as interpreted by himself).

After this doctrinal summary, we return to Noyes's mundane activities and the events that led him to Oneida. After dropping out of formal ministry, Noyes worked hard to spread the perfectionist doctrine among the New York reformers. In 1837, convinced that the second resurrection and judgment were at the door,[20] he made overtures to the abolitionists Gerrit Smith and William Lloyd Garrison, who both lent a sympathetic ear. Forty years later, Noyes attributed momentous consequences to his meeting with Garrison. Through his mediumship, he said, God had animated the abolitionists, and his inspiration afterward "became epidemic and brought on the war that freed the negroes."[21] In the same year he toured central New York, which he called "the birth-place of many of the mightiest moral and political movements of the times in which we live."[22] Almost penniless, he tramped through Kingston, Middletown, Delhi (a perfectionist center), Walton, Unadilla, and Genoa, ending in Ithaca, "a most celestial village,"[23] where his ulterior motive resided in the shape of Abigail Merwin, his first love. There he lived for a while and issued *The Witness*, the first of his many periodicals.

Spurned by Abigail, Noyes returned to Putney and married Harriet Holton (1808–1895), the well-dowried granddaughter of a lieutenant-governor and congressman. We might regard their sex life as a private matter, had it not given Noyes the second pillar of the future Oneida Community's practice. As he explains it, he "lived in the usual routine" of married life until 1846. Within six years, Harriet went through the agonies of five births, four of them premature and resulting in stillbirths. After the last one he pledged never again to expose her to fruitless suffering. Having discovered the possibility of male continence (intercourse without ejaculation), his married life became happy as never before.[24] In the phrenological terms that he favored, he had succeeded in separating the *amative* function of sex (love and pleasure) from the *philoprogenitive* (reproduction).[25]

Anthony Wonderley has explained how two influences played on the young man during this period. One was the Millerite agitation (see chapter 8), the other the Fourierist movement (see chapter 9).[26] Like the former, Noyes was convinced that the millennium was at hand, though he disagreed with Miller's biblical interpretation. The American Fourierists wanted to free the passions from civilization's false restraints, though with a tinge of French infidelity that Noyes deplored. Putting these together with his perfectionist theology, we can understand his motivation in creating a core group to prepare for the end of the Gentile cycle. It would replicate the previous moment of perfection: those years before A.D. 70 when Paul and the other disciples lived in secure freedom from sin, before their translation to the heavens.

The parallel also explains Noyes's sexual doctrines, as follows. The perfectionists of the apostolic era asserted their freedom from sin by abnegating the Mosaic Law. As Jesus implied and Paul taught, Christians are no longer bound by Sabbath observance, dietary laws, circumcision, etc. What law should present-day perfectionists abnegate in their turn? Jesus gave a hint by saying plainly that there is no marriage in heaven,[27] and Noyes spelled out the conclusion (see the quotation at the head of this chapter). But this did not imply celibacy, as the Shakers thought: quite the contrary. As in Fourier's ideal of association according to "passional attraction," each perfectionist may enjoy sinless, consensual intercourse with any other of the opposite sex.

During the 1840s Noyes watched Miller's predictions fail and the Fourierist wave rise and crash. Perfectionism survived, and if the progressive sects had little to offer it, the reverse was not the case. By declaring that perfection was achievable here and now, rather than arriving gradually in the future, it opened a way for Garrison to call for the immediate abolition of slavery; for Henry Wright and Bronson Alcott to practice nonresistance; for Brook Farm and Adin Ballou's Hopedale to follow communitarian ways.[28] But the world feared it for its antinomian tendencies and sexual irregularities,[29] real or imagined. The Putney community attracted such a reputation, especially after 1846 when Noyes and his wife inaugurated complex marriage with John and Mary Cragin. Local antagonism rose to the point where a lawsuit for adultery was brought against Noyes. Spurred by this, but even more by fear of a lynch mob, he left Putney on November 26, 1847.

The year 1847 had been crucial in other respects. By June, Noyes had published *The Berean*, a 513-page summation of his theological and social teachings. His disciple George Cragin took fifteen copies to distribute in East Hamilton (now Hubbardsville), where three families were planning a semi-communistic experiment.[30] Noyes himself, armed with his impressive book, attended two perfectionist conventions in New York State: one in Lairdsville (near Clinton) on September 3–5, the other in Genoa (near Moravia) on September 17–19.[31] These groups welcomed Noyes's teachings and called for a perfectionist community to be formed in central New York. The only question was where it should be.

Among the enthusiasts was Jonathan Burt from Chittenango, who had recently bought a sawmill and timber lot on former Oneida Indian territory and built a house there.[32] It had the advantage of being near Oneida Depot, where New York Central's trains were obliged to stop for ten minutes "for refreshments" (a shrewd bargain struck by the landowner[33]), as well as on a feeder for the Erie Canal. On the day that Noyes left Putney, November 26, the Hubbardsville trio moved to Oneida to begin communal living on Burt's property.[34] Noyes visited them in January, and in February decided to summon the Putney community, by then numbering thirty-one adults and fourteen children.[35] They began arriving by train on March 1, 1848, and by Christmas had put up the first "mansion house,"[36] a three-story frame building. Perfectionists from central New York and New England swelled the original group, and by year's end the community was eighty-seven strong.[37] Satellite communities formed in Putney and Cambridge, Vermont; Newark, New Jersey; Wallingford, Connecticut; and Brooklyn Heights, New York.

The Oneida Community was communistic in the sense that members, on acceptance, contributed all their goods. In return they received the promise of lifelong maintenance. Consequently, in October 1849 the association owned property worth $53,000, with another $10,000 available.[38] By 1857, members had invested almost $108,000.[39] But the community still needed a cash flow, and it tried various amateurish means of supporting itself. One was to send members out as peddlers of useful wares and trinkets. Another was growing fruit, a favorite activity in Fourier's imaginary communities. It might have worked in the French climate, but in New York it was a disaster. The money problem was solved in a way no one could have predicted when a member, Samuel Newhouse, invented a new design for animal traps. He started turning them out from his forge, but such was the demand that production rose to industrial level, employing all three hundred perfectionists and even some outside hands. In 1864 alone the community made and sold 275,000 traps of all sizes.[40] I have never seen a word of regret that Oneida's prosperity rested on the sufferings of animals, most of them trapped for their fur.

The community got along well with the Oneida Indians, whom they would invite for festivals of strawberries and song,[41] but the outside world was of little interest to them. During the Civil War, a bureaucratic mix-up spared their young men from the draft, and the war only increased demand for their products.[42] In 1861 they broke ground for a new mansion house, this time of brick with stone trimmings and combining French and Italianate influences. In 1869 a new wing was added to house all those still living in the old building, and in 1878 a third wing, bringing the house to the state in which we see it today.[43]

The Mansion House's outward magnificence belies the simplicity of life within. Besides living without sin, the perfectionists lived without newspapers, liquor, or money. Pierrepont Noyes points out that they lacked three major motives for the pursuit of wealth: to provide for one's children, to gain power and status, and for men to attract women.[44] The women defied contemporary fashion by not wearing corsets, cutting their hair short, and wearing regulation pants with mid-length skirts. The children, in a memorable holocaust, burned all their dolls.[45] The adults, including John Noyes, no less painfully quit chewing and smoking tobacco.[46] They lived a sacralized life without ministers, church services, or public devotions, replacing these with Noyes's chats, music, self-improving study, and the dreaded rite of Mutual Criticism. For the most part, they were free of doctors and diseases, but when someone fell sick, the cure was often a dose of Mutual Criticism.[47] Nor did the Oneidans get emotionally involved in progressive causes, having leap-frogged over them to attack the greatest evil of all. In his first annual report, Noyes counted the four necessary stages of redemption:

1. The breach with God, cured by holiness;
2. The disruption of the sexes and curse on woman, cured by free love;
3. The curse of oppressive labor, cured by association;
4. The curse of death.[48]

The community had already achieved the first three stages. "If Christ is going to be elected we must have Death out of the way," said Noyes in 1852. There was no use in going to Hades if one had to come back so soon.[49]

Noyes's view of sex was the antithesis of the Victorian attitude, which associated it with shame, concealment, and unmentionable filth. For him it was a sacrament. "If the Primitive Church could discern the Lord's body in the meat and drink of the Lord's Supper, how much more naturally can we discern the Lord's body in each other, and in all our interviews [sexual intercourse] receive each other as members of Christ!"[50] Given full rein, he would have elevated the act to a public ritual: "We shall never have heaven till we can conquer shame, and have a beautiful exhibition on the stage."[51] However, he was realistic enough to add that the least spiritual are apt to be the most sexually active, and that the young are the most attractive. Every effort was made to crush budding love affairs between young Oneidans, and since interviews were only granted by permission of Noyes or some older deputy, the general rule was that the young must mingle with the old. The mundane reason was obvious: it took practice and maturity for a man to master and learn the pleasures of male continence. Teenage boys were willy-nilly initiated by post-menopausal women, so that their mistakes would be inconsequential. The corollary, which gives critics of Oneida their firmest ground, was that girls were initiated the moment they reached puberty by older and experienced men, usually Noyes himself. Hence most Oneidans, instead of rutting like rabbits as they were pruriently imagined, had far less frequent intercourse than the average married couple.[52] Noyes wielded a powerful weapon over his flock by giving or withholding sexual privileges.

Three things brought the Oneida adventure to a close. One was the growing resentment at the older men's monopolizing of the attractive women, while forbidding genuine love matches. The second was Noyes's attempt to hand over the direction to his son Theodore, a neurotic, Harvard-educated M.D. with serious doubts about the existence of God. The third was the invasion of spiritualism (see chapter 12). Noyes had always discouraged ouija boards, table rappings, and trance circles on the grounds that the messages came from low souls in Hades rather than from the Primitive Church. But he recommended that Theodore investigate spiritualism in order to counteract his scientific materialism, and soon the whole community was addicted to it. In 1878 Noyes himself had joined in, holding daily séances in his room.[53] That the Judgment of the Gentiles was due in a year or two seems to have been forgotten.

Noyes was no foe to science, and was willing to reconcile the Bible with Darwin and the geologists. For instance, he wondered if humans might have descended not from apes but from the intelligent serpentine race already present in the Garden of Eden. As the new science gave an immensely longer estimate of earth's age than the biblical six thousand years, God appeared to be in less of a hurry, and the resurrection perhaps far off.[54] This was the rationale for "stirpiculture" (from Latin *stirps*, a sprout, root, or race): a plan started in 1869 for breeding the optimum human vehicles for the future. Suitable couples were carefully selected, usually by Noyes, and he himself fathered nine of the fifty-eight babies thus conceived.[55]

The death whimper of the Oneida Community began on the night of June 22, 1879, when Noyes secretly slipped out of his room. Beside the decay of his ideals as practiced in the community, he was in danger of arrest under the infamous Comstock Laws (see chapter 20). Taking a deceptive route, he made his way by carriage, train, and ferry to Canada, and never returned. Within two years the Oneida Community had dissolved, reconstituting itself as a joint stock company with its assets divided among the members. Oneida Ltd. was born, but its infant years were hard ones. The

ILLUSTRATION 10.2. Mansion House of the Oneida Community, Kenwood, 1861–69. *Author's photograph.*

old perfectionists were quite inept at handling money matters and doing business on the world's terms. Attempts to get advice from the spirit of Noyes did not help.

Rescue came from the return of the stirpicults. One of Noyes's sons, Pierrepont Burt Noyes, saw the company nearing bankruptcy and decided to take action. In 1904 he summoned his half brothers and sisters to Oneida and applied modern methods to the faltering silverware business. In the words of Dorothy Rainwater, "A complete change in advertising methods in high-priced, large-circulation magazines proved enormously effective. It was the first 'pretty girl' advertising in America and it not only affected the sales of their silver, it also had a profound effect on the whole advertising business."[56] How fitting that Oneida Ltd. should have found its salvation in sex appeal!

Ann Lee, Jemima Wilkinson, Joseph Smith, William Miller, and John Humphrey Noyes all built their movements on the foundation of absolute faith in Christ and the Bible. Even Mordecai Noah and Handsome Lake, though not Christians, acknowledged Jesus as divinely inspired. The next chapters tell of a different brand of leaders and movements, and of the tension generated by two seemingly contrary influences: the rejection of biblical authority in the face of science, leading to free thought and atheism, and the thirst for experience of higher realities, manifesting through spiritualism and the occult.

ILLUSTRATION 11.1. Andrew Jackson Davis, the "Poughkeepsie Seer." From Davis, *The Great Harmonia*, Rochester, N.Y.: Austin Publishing Co., 1909. *Courtesy of Special Collections, Hamilton College Library.*

CHAPTER II

The Poughkeepsie Seer

1. God, as much Mother as Father, is the Cause—manifested as immutable laws.

2. Matter, containing all forms and forces, is the Effect—manifested and known as the universe.

3. Spirit, covered by both body and soul, is the ultimate—*man*, spiritually individualized forever.

4. The Human spirit is individualized—drawn from the infinite spiritual ocean,—about two hundred days after conception, or ten weeks before birth.

5. A perfectly organized human mind is crowned with a dome of moral and spiritual powers—a keystone to two sides of the phrenological arch, known as cerebrum and cerebellum combined.

6. The earth is a man-bearing planet—a manufactory, so to speak, wherein fish, reptiles, birds, marsupials, quadromants, bimants, &c., operate as broad and narrow gauge lines from the elemental, mineral, and

vegetable resources to their grand final destination,—the evolution of the human race.

7. Man, having the perfect and final form, is an "heir apparent" of immortality; but when crowned with spirit, he is an heir absolute to all the riches of eternal life. "Survival of the fittest" is an immutable law. The first sign of the existence of spirit in man is *superstition*. The next superior evidence is self-consciousness, and self-determining *will*; also a comprehension of truth, justice, love, and a voluntary living for others; and, lastly, a conception of eternal principles, which means and guarantees a corresponding eternal personal career.

8. Death is a screening process,—a chemical purification as by fire,—removing the causes of appetites and habits, but entailing the *effects* thereof upon and within the spiritual body, which can be overcome by the desires and efforts of the individual after death; so that every man is measurably responsible for the *future* duration of his pains and punishments.

9. Death, physically speaking, is a backward and downward movement by which the spirit is enabled to leap into the Summer-Land.

10. Life in the next world is substantially the same as is life in our present existence.[1]

Credo of Andrew Jackson Davis

During the earlier nineteenth century, two powerful ghosts made their presence felt in the New World. One was Franz Anton Mesmer (1734–1815), practitioner of animal magnetism or "mesmerism"; the other was Emanuel Swedenborg (1688–1772), who revealed a system of multiple worlds and spoke with their inhabitants. In this chapter we will see how their influences blended to turn a cobbler's apprentice into a patriarch of the spiritualist movement.

Mesmer's theories and healing methods assumed that the universe is permeated by an imponderable "magnetic fluid" that can be harnessed either by metallic magnets or by the human organism. A committee of the French Academy of Sciences, including Benjamin Franklin, examined Mesmer's theories and healing methods in 1784. Because no materialistic theory could explain them, and under pressure from established medicine, the committee declared them null and void. This was a hard blow to Mesmer, who had enjoyed a glamorous and profitable public reputation, but it did not stop the movement or discourage his disciples. One of these, the Marquis de Puységur (1751–1825), was already following his own path of research. He dispensed with Mesmer's apparatus of iron magnets, rods, and tubs, soft lighting and music, and did not try to induce the physical and emotional crisis that Mesmer thought essential for a cure. While Mesmer's Society of Harmony attracted high society, Puységur worked with the peasants on his estate, holding sessions beneath a venerated elm tree. Through hand motions, eye-to-eye contact, and an act of will, the marquis put his subjects into a state of somnambulism or "magnetic sleep," with unexpected consequences. The somnambulists seemed to enter a state of lucidity far surpassing their normal consciousness, in which they could answer questions, diagnose their own ailments, and prescribe cures.

In Germany, the new phenomena were noticed by the *Naturphilosophen*, "natural philosophers," or scientists with a leaning toward mysticism. No case was more remarkable than that of Frederica Hauffe (1801–1829), known as the Seeress of Prevorst.[2] This pious forester's wife manifested many of the same symptoms as Ann Lee, the Shakers, and the sleeping preachers. Up to the birth of her second child, Hauffe's life was a tale of fevers, spasms, phobias, and periods of catalepsy in which she seemed to be dead. The doctors called to her bedside tried every cure, including magnetism, to which she responded with a deep somnambulistic state. While entranced she gave discourses, sometimes in verse, sometimes in High German (instead of her usual dialect) or some unknown tongue. She drew elaborate diagrams of cosmic and human principles, brought messages from the dead, sang songs, ran around in circles, and diagnosed people's ailments by seeing into their bodies. Her visitors testified to her powers of mind reading, precognition, and spiritual healing, and to the rapping sounds and poltergeist phenomena around her. The poet Justinus Kerner (1786–1862) fascinated European readers with his digest of the three thousand sessions he spent with Hauffe. It was published in 1829 as *Die Seherin von Prevorst*, and in 1845 in an English translation, *The Seeress of Prevorst*.

On the other side of the Atlantic, George Washington bought a set of the "metallic tractors" for magnetic treatment patented in 1796 by Elisha Perkins (1740–1799), a physician from Plainfield, Connecticut. At twenty-five dollars a pair, Perkins made a fortune selling pen-like rods, one brass and one iron, to be held in the operator's left and right hands. But aspiring magnetizers soon found that anything similar would work just as well.[3] Thomas Jefferson and Benjamin Franklin were no friends of mesmeric practices,[4] Jefferson being influenced by the French Academy's warning that they were dangerous to women. It was not until the 1830s, amid the psychic turmoil of the Second Great Awakening, that animal magnetism caught on in the United States. American magnetists began finding cases of clairvoyance, extrasensory perception, and preternatural knowledge that challenged materialists and theologians alike.[5] Public interest took both the high and the low road. A wave of new publications from Britain gave the highbrows much to think about,[6] while the populace enjoyed the sort of comic and humiliating displays that stage hypnotists still thrive on.

Charles Poyen Saint-Sauveur, the son of West Indian planters, took the middle road with his lectures and demonstrations of animal magnetism in Boston and Providence during 1836, described in his *Progress of Animal Magnetism in New England* (1837). The book is chatty and personable, full of accounts of magnetic techniques, their amazing results, the poking and prodding of his female subjects by the professors of Brown University, and testimonials from worthy citizens from all over New England. With Poyen, magnetism escapes all definition and theory but enters a new stage, for he found that manual passes were not needed. It was enough to give his instructions mentally, even from the next room or from miles away. Nor was his power unique. Others found that they could command his somnambulists by force of will, and they would respond. Poyen's best subject, Miss Cynthia Gleason, developed as a successful medical clairvoyant, diagnosing either directly or in absentia through a lock of the patient's hair. She often recommended lancing a part of the body from which a mass of purulent matter would ooze out, discomfiting the doctors whose chief "cure" was bloodletting. Poyen writes of Gleason's X-ray vision (though of course he does not use that term), "Miss G. has several times described accurately various articles of food and drink contained in my stomach, although I had not told her a word about it!"[7]

This sets the scene for Dr. James Stanley Grimes (1807–1903), itinerant mesmerizer and later professor of medical jurisprudence at Vermont's first medical college in Castleton. Grimes was skeptical of the mesmeric fluid and all pseudo-physical theories. His frame of reference was phrenology, the science that associated psychological tendencies and functions with parts of the brain and areas of the skull. Using phrenological jargon, Grimes writes that after some failed experiments,

> I did, at length, succeed in discovering, first, that the principal, if not the only, active agent, in almost all cases, is the language

> of the operator; second, that the susceptibility of the subject is of such a nature that it may properly be classed among diseases; third, that the principal effect is upon the conforming social organs, Submissiveness, Kindness, Imitativeness, and Credenciveness, upon the upper part of the head. . . . I was busily engaged in preparing a work on the subject, which I afterwards published, when I gave the course of lectures and experiments in Poughkeepsie.

Among the auditors at these lectures was seventeen-year-old Andrew Jackson Davis (1826–1910), the son of an impoverished part-weaver, part-shoemaker with a weakness for drink. Davis was born in Blooming Grove, a hamlet on the west side of the Hudson, and spent his childhood years across the river in Hyde Park. In 1839, when he was about thirteen, he had a mystical experience of a melodious voice that suggested he might wish to travel, adding "to Pough-keep-sie."[8] Somehow the boy persuaded his father to find work and settle in that riverside city, and Davis would forever remain the "Poughkeepsie Seer."

When Davis attended Grimes's lectures in 1843, he knew nothing of mesmerism, and had only gone for entertainment. Some of the youths present succumbed to the magnetizer's suggestions; Davis did not. Grimes describes what happened next:

> Another individual who attended the lectures, and became interested in the subject, was Mr. Wm. Levingston, a merchant tailor. One day, during the time that the course of lectures were proceeding, Davis went into Levingston's shop, and proposed to try the experiment which I had described. Levingston consented, and proceeded to the trial. In a few minutes, Davis declared, that he could see through the back of his head, and Mr. Levingston has assured me, that Davis actually read a newspaper which was held up behind him, while his eyes were closed, as readily as if he had been looking at it with his eyes. The rumor, that young Davis was an extraordinary clairvoyant, soon spread through the town, and naturally created a great sensation. Hundreds flocked to Levingston's store, to test the wonderful powers of the clairvoyant, and Levingston soon learned to make medical prescriptions, and to charge a fee for each.[9]

At the time of writing the above, Grimes was denouncing spiritualism, as he had denounced the theories of the mesmerists. But he also boasted of the part he had played in its origins:

> Of course, there could be no sympathy between the clairvoyant practitioners and myself, after a public declaration of such sentiments; and, *though my lectures in Poughkeepsie gave birth to modern spiritualism, and first caused A. J. Davis to come into notice*, I distinctly protested at the time, and always since, against the principles and the practices which grew thus illegitimately out of my labors, and finally resulted in producing a motley brood of pretended spirit mediums.[10]

Two Universalist ministers had a strong influence on the budding seer. Poughkeepsie's Universalist pastor, Abner Rogers Bartlett, took Davis under his wing and became his mentor. Bartlett's successor in 1844–45 was Gibson Smith, who was a student of the mesmerist John Bovee Dods. Smith collaborated with Levingston to send the mesmerized youth out on astral tours to report on planets, comets, and the inhabitants of Saturn. Buescher attributes to Bartlett the Universalist flavor of Davis's early messages, and to Gibson Smith the glittering, mystical visions in which he was guided by spirits of the dead.[11]

Levingston magnetized Davis daily, beginning on or around December 1, 1843. To judge from a report from Albany, the tailor-pharmacist and the pastor had a good scheme going.[12] The Rev. Smith would give a lecture or sermon, the tailor would mesmerize Davis, who would display his clairvoyant powers and give diagnoses, and Levingston would then sell remedies. Outwardly, the youth seemed a freak of nature, performing all the tricks and tests that gawping visitors expected. But his inner experience was very different. Describing what he saw as he looked at the people around him, he wrote:

> I could see all the organs and their functions—the liver, the spleen, the heart, the lungs, the brain—all with the greatest possible ease. The whole body was transparent as a sheet of glass! It was invested with a strange, rich, spiritual beauty. It looked illuminated as a city. Every separate organ had several *centres* of light, besides being enveloped by a general sphere peculiar to itself. And I did not see the physical organ only, but its form, aspect, and color also, simply by observing the peculiar emanations surrounding it. For example: I saw the heart—surrounded by one general combination of living colors—with special points of illumination interspersed. The auricles and ventricles, together with their orifices, gave out distinct *flames* of light; and the pericardium was a garment of magnetic life, surrounding and protecting the heart while in the performance of its functions. The pulmonary or respitorial [*sic*] department was also illuminated with beautiful flames, but of different magnitude and color. The various air-chambers seemed like so many chemical laboratories.[13]

Davis wrote this in his autobiography, thirteen years after the event. He says that at the time of these early visions, he would wake with no remembrance of them. Only later was he able to revisit the experience. This raises important doubts. Is he giving here an accurate account of a forgotten experience, now resurfacing as a memory in full photographic detail? In that case, it resembles the memories retrieved under hypnosis in modern times, some of which have given rise to the myths of abduction by aliens and satanic child abuse, and which many psychologists dismiss as figments of the unconscious mind. Alternatively, is this an imaginative reconstruction of general impressions, improved in the light of further education? In that case, the original experience is inaccessible, and we can only read his later interpretation of it. From there it is a small step to regard the whole thing as a literary exercise.

These questions aside, Davis is a rare case of a medical clairvoyant with enough self-awareness to describe how he saw the human body, with instinctive grasp of its functions. After the experience related above he found himself outside the room, looking down on the earth:

> The properties and essences of plants were distinctly visible. Every fibre of the wild flower, or atom of the mountain-violet, was radiant with its own peculiar life. . . . I saw the living elements and essences flow and play through these simple forms of matter; and in the same manner I saw the many and various trees of the forests, fields, and hills, all filled with life and vitality of different hues and degrees of refinement. . . . But my perceptions still flowed on! The broad surface of the earth, for many hundred miles before the sweep of my vision—describing nearly a semicircle—became transparent as the purest water. The deep alluvial and diluvial depositions were distinguishable from the deeper stratifications of stone and earth, but the comparative and superior brilliancy of the ingredients of the former. Earth gave off one particular color, stones another, and minerals still another. When first I discerned a bed of minerals—it was a vein of iron-ore—I remember how I started and shivered with a sensation of fright. *It seemed that the earth was on fire!* . . . Innumerable beds of *zinc*, *copper*, *silver*, *limestone*, and *gold* next arrested my attention; and each, like the different organs in the human body, gave off diverse kinds of luminous atmospheres. All these breathing emanations were more or less bright, variegated, and beautiful. Everything had a glory of its own! Crystalline bodies emitted soft, brilliant, azure and crimson emanations.

One thinks of poets like Thomas Traherne, Wordsworth, Blake, and the Romantic feeling of intimacy with nature, but this is more than feeling.

Like Goethe studying the morphology of plants or bones, Davis ha a quasi-scientific understanding of how the vegetable and mineral worlds function. He sees the subtle bodies of the minerals in gorgeous colors, like the alchemists who personified their substances as crow, eagle, or peacock. In both cases, nature is alive and active right down to its lowest subterranean elements. In conformity with the Hermetic dictum "as above, so below," every element has its correspondence in man:

> In this mystic vision, gentle reader, I saw everything just as you will—with the penetrating senses of the spirit—after you pass away from the visible body at physical death. It was very, very beautiful to see everything clothed with an atmosphere! Every little grain of salt or sand; every minute plant, flower, and herb, every tendril of the loftiest trees—their largest and minutest leaves; the weighty mineral and ponderous animal forms, existing in the broad fields before me—each and all were clothed with dark, or brown, or gray, or red, blue, green, yellow, or white atmosphere—divided and subdivided into an almost infinite variety of degrees of intensity, brilliancy, and refinement. And—mark the fact!—in each mineral, vegetable, and animal I SAW SOMETHING OF MAN! In truth, the whole system of creation seemed to me like *the fragments of future human beings!* In the beaver I saw, in embryo, one faculty of the human mind; in the fox, another; in the wolf, another; in the horse, another; in the lion, another: yea, verily, throughout the vast concentric circles of mineral, vegetable, and animal life, I could discern certain relationships to, and embryological indications of, Man!

This excerpt is still richer in associations. In a few words it contains a theory of the afterlife contrary to that of the churches, though not to that of Socrates, who taught that the philosopher must practice "dying" while still alive. Davis describes everything as enveloped by what later occultists would call an aura or etheric body. It is not just a fuzzy shape or glow, but an entity with its own anatomy, fully as complex as the physical body. (I am reminded here of Alex Grey's paintings.) He glimpses the evolutionary process in which every lower creature has prepared a part of future man, and *is* a part of us. That the animals anticipate powers of the human soul refers indirectly to the twin sciences of phrenology, which classified those powers for Davis's era, and physiognomy, in which animal characteristics were deduced from human faces. Lastly, there is a hint of the Kabbalistic teaching of an anthropomorphic cosmos, a "Grand Man" created, like the human body, in the image of the Body of God.

The next spring Davis had a momentous experience of a different kind. On March 6, 1844, he was teleported in his sleep from Levingston's house to Catskill, forty miles away.[14] As he hiked back to Poughkeepsie he kept falling into the somnambulistic state, and thus, in a graveyard, he met two spirits. One was the Greek physician Galen, who handed Davis the magic staff from which his autobiography took its title.[15] It was a mechanical device that sprang open like an umbrella to reveal a central silver rod and an assemblage of blocks. On these all humanity's diseases were written in an unknown script, which Davis nonetheless could read, and inside the blocks were the substances that cured them. Galen explained that the staff symbolized the principle of divine truth sustaining all of creation, and promised that Davis should have it. But as the youth climbed out of the graveyard he caught his coat on a rail. He handed the staff to Galen while he freed himself, embarrassed at his clumsiness before these sublime visitors, then in a fit of anger broke the rail in two. After he landed on the other side he asked for the staff, but the sage would not give it back. Instead he received a moral lecture and the promise: "In a due season thou shalt return, and then it shall be thine."[16]

One can hardly miss the parallel with Joseph Smith's first discovery of the golden plates on Cumorah Hill, when the guardian spirit prevented him from taking them and told him to return in a year's time. The "magic staff" is also reminiscent of Smith's "magic spectacles," the Urim and Thummim, with their silver frames and their ability to unlock hidden knowledge and read ancient scripts. The next day Davis staggered into the Levingstons' house, ravenously hungry, to find the company planning to send out a search party. With a new seriousness of purpose he announced that he would no longer give mesmeric displays to the curious but would henceforth devote his gift to healing.[17]

Some of the medicine he prescribed in the trance state was "alternative," to say the least. To a deaf person, Davis recommended: "He must catch thirty-two weasels, take off their hind legs at the middle joint, and boil out *that oil* which Nature has deposited in the feet and the parts adjacent thereto; and this preparation, being an oleaginous and penetrative liquid, must be dropped (one drop at a time) in each ear, twice a day, till the whole is gone—when you will be nearly cured!"[18] Only *nearly?!*

Now we must turn to the other graveyard spirit: a tall and noble figure identified as Swedenborg, who promised Davis that he would soon receive instruction that would make him a new light to mankind. Swedenborg's teachings about the spirit world, human destiny, and the true meaning of the Scriptures had reached Philadelphia in 1784. Their bearer and expositor was James Glen (1750? –1814), a Scotsman who owned a plantation in British Guiana and had been a member of the Swedenborgian New Church in London. Other groups formed in Baltimore, and a German-speaking one in Lancaster,

Pennsylvania. In 1821 Charles Doughty (1784–1844), an attorney of Quaker background, built a temple for the sect on Pearl Street in New York City.[19]

New York State was unique for the spread of the new sect independently of the major centers. Dr. Louis Beers (1768–1849), a Unitarian minister and physician in Danby, Tompkins County, joined after reading a Swedenborgian magazine. He was ordained to the New Church ministry in 1816 and founded societies in the villages of Danby and Spencer (Tioga County), and in Ithaca.[20] The other Swedenborgian church in the Upstate region was founded in 1817 in Plattekill (or Platikill), Ulster County.[21] This seems significant, for Plattekill lies only a few miles from Poughkeepsie. Acquaintance with its members may account for the young Davis's undeniable familiarity with Swedenborg's personality and writings.

Levingston and Davis were plying their medical clairvoyance in Bridgeport, Connecticut, where they were noticed by a local doctor, Silas Smith Lyon, and two Universalist ministers, William Fishbough and Samuel Byron Brittan.[22] Dr. Lyon was about to move his medical practice to New York City, and saw Davis as a valuable adjunct to it.[23] Soon Davis was out of Levingston's hands and under the influence of this more ambitious trio. During 1844 and 1845, magnetized several times a day by Lyon and with Fishbough as scribe, Davis delivered a series of 157 trance lectures. His future wife, Catherine Wolf Dodge,[24] paid for their publication in 1847 as *The Principles of Nature, Her Divine Revelation, and a Voice to Mankind, By and Through Andrew Jackson Davis, the "Poughkeepsie Seer": and "Clairvoyant."*

Among the audience at these lectures were America's foremost Fourierist, Albert Brisbane (see chapter 9), and its most prestigious Swedenborgian, George Bush, professor of Asian languages at New York University. Some noticed that the entranced lecturer leaned toward Fourierism when Brisbane and his friends were present, toward Swedenborg in the presence of Bush & Co.; when both groups were there the two systems were "jumbled in liberal and extraordinary confusion."[25] It was a syndrome already familiar in continental mesmerism: that mediums were subject to telepathic influence and would mirror the expectations of those present.

George Bush was delighted, and quickly added an appendix to his book, *Mesmer and Swedenborg* (1847), in which he showed how Davis's lectures were full of parallels and quotations from Swedenborg's *Arcana Caelestia* and *The Earths in the Universe*. Most extraordinary was a paper written in calligraphic script that Davis had found, clutched in his hand, after a solitary trance in a cave near Poughkeepsie. It quoted *Arcana Caelestia* verbatim, complete with the paragraph numbers. Bush wrote:

> Here then stands the astounding fact, that a young man of the utmost simplicity and truthfulness of character—of fair natural parts, but of exceedingly limited intellectual culture—who had

> never read a page of Swedenborg's writings—is prompted, while in a preternatural state, to indite a long communication made up from beginning to end of a series of quotations from one of these works, embodying a train of profound philosophical thought, such as he is utterly incapable of entertaining or expressing in his normal condition! Indeed I am myself satisfied that even if he had had the book before him, he would be utterly incapable of framing from it such an article as we have here presented to us.[26]

There was a snag, though. *The Principles of Nature* was not a verbatim transcript of Davis's words. Fishbough confessed that he had struck out a few sentences and supplied others "according to direction," corrected the grammar, pruned out redundancies, and clarified some obscure sentences. The reviewer in the London *Athenaeum* was highly suspicious and made the point, "That a seer 'commercing' with the Mysteries of Nature should have *needed* an editor in this technical sense is remarkable enough. It might have been supposed that the Revelation which brought to an uneducated man the secrets of Science might have brought him grammar, too, to express them in."[27]

James Grimes, looking back on the phenomenon some years later, writes of the controversy raised by this work and its origin:

> There are two views taken of this matter, which are hostile, and utterly irreconcilable with each other: one is that A. J. Davis was assisted by unearthly spirits to compose the book entitled "Divine Revelations," that the spirits furnished the ideas, and Davis and Fishbough the language, while Lyon sustained Davis by his magnetic influence, and Brittain [*sic*] aided and assisted in the work, witnessed its growth, attested its genuineness, and advocated its doctrines. The other theory is, that Davis was a mere dupe, and mesmeric mouthpiece of Lyon, & Co.; that Lyon privately mesmerized Davis, and while in the mesmeric condition, Davis was taught certain lessons, which when afterwards publicly mesmerized, he could repeat, to the astonishment of the uninformed witnesses, though, in his ordinary state, he, possibly, knew nothing upon the subject; that Davis was inspired by those who employed him, mesmerized him, and paid his expenses, and by no one else; that the pretence, that he was assisted by disembodied spirits, was merely designed to excite an interest in the minds of the weak and credulous, and create a sale for the forthcoming book.[28]

The reader may have other and subtler explanations than this simplistic either-or choice. In any case *The Principles of Nature*, which went through thirty-four editions, had a momentous effect. In Phillip Charles Lucas's pithy summary, "it became the first of an important genre of esoteric treatise—purportedly received in a trance state or from spirit beings . . . and its ideas helped provide a philosophical and theological underpinning for the nascent Spiritualist movement of the 19th century."[29]

After *The Principles of Nature* was published, Davis found that he no longer needed a mesmerizer to put him into the clairvoyant state, and became an oracle on his own account. His philosophy attracted many Universalist clergy, including Thomas Lake Harris (see chapter 16). In 1847 Davis started *The Univercoelum*[30] (pronounced univer-*see*-lum), the first of several periodicals that would chronicle the spiritual issues of the day alongside his own ideas. He began writing the series of books, almost as weighty as Swedenborg's own, expounding his "Harmonial Philosophy." As the name suggests, this was essentially optimistic and holistic. It begins with an impersonal Power or spiritual Sun akin to Plato's "One," from which emanate, like the Platonic Forms, Wisdom, Goodness, Justice, Mercy, and Truth. Following the doctrine of correspondences, all of nature reflects these forms, both in the spiritual and the material worlds. The human being follows the same harmonious laws and is inherently perfect in body and soul. It is our task to realize this perfection. To this end, Davis supported all the progres-

VIEW OF LAKE "MORNIA," IN THE SUMMER LAND.

ILLUSTRATION 11.2. *View of Lake "Mornia," in the Summer Land.* From Andrew Jackson Davis, A *Stellar Key to the Summer Land*, Rochester, N.Y.: Austin Publishing Co., 1909, p. 132. *Courtesy of Special Collections, Hamilton College Library.*

sive movements of his day including the abolition of slavery, the rights of women within marriage and without, the education of children as souls to be nurtured rather than as creatures to be disciplined, temperance, and various alternative and natural therapies. He never set himself up as a cult leader.

As for human destiny, Davis foresaw progress both in this world, thanks to the movements mentioned, and in the next. The spirit world simply continues our education as we move up through our heavens surrounding the earth. Blending Swedenborgian celestial geography with modern astronomy, he recasts the Hermetic ascent (described in the *Poimandres*, the first treatise of the Corpus Hermeticum) in which the soul ascends through the planetary spheres, progressively losing its negative tendencies. Of these multiple heavens, the one closest to the earth is sometimes accessible to us, and that is how he accounts for the spirit communications.

Davis calls this proximate heaven the "Summer Land," doing away at a stroke with the horrific Dantean images that haunted the Christian imagination. He goes not only beyond the Calvinists, the Methodists, and the Unitarians but even beyond the Universalists, for whom Christ and the Bible remained central. To Davis, the Bible is a noble but outdated document, and Jesus an admirable moral teacher and no more. Thomas Lake Harris and the Swedenborgians soon realized that he was not one of them.[31]

When the spiritualist craze took off in the 1850s, Davis was dismayed by its obsession with phenomena and the banality of most spirit communications. While dissociating himself from the movement, he claimed he had known about it all along, for on the morning of March 31, 1848, the date of the first communication with the Fox sisters, "a voice, tender and yet peculiarly strong" had whispered in his ear: "Brother! The good work has begun—behold, a living demonstration is born!"[32] Thereafter he lived by his lectures, magazines, and books until interest in them tailed off in the 1870s. In 1880 the New York medical profession managed to get a law passed that prohibited healing mediums, clairvoyant physicians, and magnetists.[33] Davis was already a trustee of the United States Medical College in the city, and had helped to found a new chair of psychological science and magnetic therapeutics. He immediately enrolled as a student of the college and obtained an orthodox medical diploma. With this degree under his belt he could practice medicine, magnetic or otherwise, as he pleased. He moved to the Boston area and worked as a much-loved physician until his death.

Davis's importance as the metaphysician of the spiritualist movement can hardly be overestimated.[34] If spiritualism had had a creed, it would have been very like the one quoted at the head of this chapter. The dual-gendered God, the lifting of the threat of hell and the fear of death, the evolution of bodies and souls to an unimaginably glorious destiny: these survived the decline of spiritualism to become pillars of New Thought, and remain as promises of the New Age.

ILLUSTRATION 12.1. Kate Fox, initiator of the "spiritual telegraph" between the living and the dead. From Emma Hardinge Britten, *Modern American Spiritualism*, New York: William Britten, 1870.

CHAPTER 12

Rapping Spirits

My husband had gone to bed when we first heard the noise on this evening. I had just laid down. It commenced as usual. I knew it from all other noises I had ever heard in the house. The girls, who slept in the other bed, in the room, heard the noise, and tried to make a similar noise by snapping their fingers. The youngest girl [Kate] is about twelve years old; she is the only one who made her hand go. As fast as she made the noise with her hands or fingers, the sound was followed up in the room. It did not sound different at that time, only it made the same number of noises that the girl did. When she stopped, the sound itself stopped for a short time.

The other girl [Maggie], who is in her fifteenth year, then spoke in sport and said, "Now[1] do this just as I do. Count one, two three, four," etc., striking one hand in the other at the same time. The blows which she made were repeated as before. It appeared to answer her by repeating every blow that she made. She only did so once. She then began to be startled; and then I spoke and said to

> the noise, "Count ten," and it made ten strokes or noises. Then I asked the ages of my different children successively, and it gave the number of raps, corresponding to the ages of the children.
>
> I then asked if it was a human being that was making the noise? and if it was, to manifest it by the same noise. There was no noise. I then asked if it was a spirit? and if it was, to manifest by two sounds. I heard two sounds as soon as the words were spoken. I then asked if it was an injured spirit? to give me the sound, and I heard the rapping distinctly.[2]
>
> *Statement of Mrs. Margaret Fox, 1848*

As many readers know, modern American spiritualism started in Hydesville, a hamlet not far from Rochester, on March 31, 1848, through the agency of the Fox sisters: Kate (Catharine, 1836–1892) and Maggie (Margaretta, 1833–1893). It is a great story, but told so often that there is no need to repeat it all here. I will use this chapter, instead, to clarify the circumstances around the Hydesville phenomena, to introduce the most intelligent contemporary commentator, and then to present a theory that is seldom discussed by historians.

Villagers swarmed round the Fox family's cottage on All Fool's Day (April 1) and the succeeding days. They got the thrill of their lives, as leading questions put to the phantom rapper revealed that it was the spirit of a peddler. He had been murdered in the house and buried right there, in the cellar. No time was lost in grubbing for his corpse and accusing the former tenants of murder, all of which dissolved into farce. But spirit rapping became contagious. The next summer, Kate brought the virus to Auburn, where the antislavery journalist Eliab Wilkinson Capron and a group of ex-Millerites hosted her. Soon, Auburn had fifty mediums rapping away, tipping tables, or writing automatically. By March 1850, Capron could draw up a long list of places where people had witnessed the phenomena. Besides Auburn and Rochester he named Fleming, Kellogsville, Skaneateles, New York City, Brooklyn, Buffalo, Troy, Syracuse, Scipio, Cortland, Greece, Port Byron, Waterloo, Macedon, Ithaca, and Salina.[3]

While spiritualists celebrate the Hydesville rappings as a breakthrough in relations with the other world, the consensus view dismisses them as a practical joke played by the Fox sisters.[4] Superficial historians are content to cite the secondhand exposé of 1851, when Kate Fox is said to have confessed to cracking her toes and employing a Dutch servant girl as accomplice,[5] and Maggie's public recantation of 1888, when she said that she and Kate had faked the raps in that way. On that occasion the aging, alcoholic medium stood on a table, lifted her skirt, and showed the assembled experts how she did it, while Kate sat in the audience mutely assenting.[6] For a year after her exposé, Maggie made a little money giving lecture-demonstrations of fraudulent raps. Then in 1889 she recanted, blaming the "strong psychological influence of persons who were opposed to [spiritualism]."[7] Considering the lifelong pressures on the sisters, nothing they said carries much conviction one way or the other. Perhaps once they were working as professional mediums the raps did not respond and they had (sometimes?) faked them. But the Hydesville phenomena had begun before the sisters were in any way involved. The families that had rented the cottage before the Foxes had been bothered by them, too.

Within days of the Fox incident, with no idea of the exponential growth that would soon come of it, several local people gave testimonies.[8] In the winter of 1843–44, Mrs. Bell, her lodger Lucretia Pulver, and some young companions of Lucretia's had heard frequent knockings and the sound of a man heavily walking around when none was present. Michael Weekman, the next tenant, had heard and felt unexplained raps on the door, and his wife, Hannah, was often scared by strange noises in and around the house. One night their eight-year-old daughter screamed because something cold was moving over her head and face. Jane Lape, their lodger or servant, saw the apparition of a man.

The raps resumed soon after the Foxes' arrival as tenants of the Hydesville cottage. After the tumultuous weeks of spring 1848, they behaved more like poltergeists than hauntings, being attached to persons rather than to places. The noises followed Maggie when her elder brother David sheltered her in his nearby farmhouse, and they accompanied Kate when her elder sister Leah Fish (1813–1890)[9] took her to Rochester. What went on at Leah's house is typical of poltergeist phenomena: objects were hurled and furniture shoved around, doors opened and shut by themselves, footsteps were heard climbing the stairs and stamping, cold hands and slaps were felt in the night, and a large man appeared to be lying on the sisters' bed.[10]

To dismiss all poltergeist phenomena as the tricks of the child or adolescent who is usually present is to make him or her a virtuoso in stage magic, and all the investigators gullible idiots. This is simply not the case. Credulity in the opposite direction attributes the phenomena to the spirits of dead humans, and that was what gave birth to modern spiritualism. We will pass over the attribution of them to the devil, though even a careful chronicler like Henry Spicer resorts to it in the end.[11] In the aftermath of the Hydesville event, some progressive minds tried to reconcile the phenomena with a physics and a biology that were, at the time, still in the formative stages. E. C. Rogers, a mesmeric physician,[12] starts from the premise that there was nothing *spiritual* about the phenomena, and that to think otherwise was sheer superstition. Rogers was no dogmatic materialist in the modern sense. He was familiar with electricity and mesmerism, with Reichenbach's theory about a subtle matter called "odyle," and with the practice of dowsing, as well as with the history of poltergeists. These provided a context for the possible relation "of matter to matter connected by an imponderable agent."[13] Rogers writes:

> For it cannot be doubted, that if a mundane agent emanating from the earth, with sufficient power, when passing through the organism, to twist a stick held in the hand of a sensitive person, or to cause its rotary motion when simply resting on the thumb and finger, the same mundane force, under other circumstances of the organism, on passing through and emanating from it, may move a table or a chair in contact with a sensitive person,—ay, may more than that even without contact, as in the case of Angelique Cottin [a medium].[14]

Certain places, Rogers adds, seemed to favor this relation, western New York among them. Hydesville, in particular, had the conditions required for a "nervous epidemic."[15] So much for the possibility of the physical phenomena. But whence comes the *intelligence* that raps or moves a table in response to questions, or makes a medium's hand write ten times faster than normal, without the conscious effort of any mortal present?[16] Rogers sees two possibilities: (1) another identity takes possession of the medium; (2) another part of the medium acts like a second personality, but has none of its own. In both cases, it acts independently of the medium's real personality.[17]

Spiritualists chose the first alternative, believing the "other identity" to be a spirit that had survived physical death. Rogers, even though living long before the concept of multiple personality disorder, prefers the second. He reminds his readers that there is no reason to believe that the spirits are who and what they claim to be. His hypothesis is that the intelligence in question resides in the medium's brain, acting independently of the conscious mind. This is why drugs, alcohol, or mesmerism are known to favor the condition: they suppress conscious control. It also explains two puzzling aspects of mediumistic behavior: the bad spelling of some spirit messages, and the speaking of others in languages the medium has never learned.[18]

Without using the term "cryptomnesia," Rogers knew that the brain stores memories that normally never resurface. The textbook example is of hearing a foreign language spoken in childhood, then reproducing the words years later, while entranced.

Rogers's treatise is admirably rational and open-minded. He does not pretend to explain what he does not understand, namely the "imponderable agent" by which matter affects matter. This question would continue to tease some of the best scientific minds until the early twentieth century.

I turn now to the hypothesis that some historians know as the "Hidden Hand." It suggests that the Hydesville phenomena were neither spontaneous nor faked, but caused by living persons, with no lesser intent than changing the worldview of Western civilization.[19] The first to suggest such a thing was Col. Henry Steel Olcott (1832–1907), cofounder of the Theosophical Society. He was a conventional spiritualist until he met the other future founder, Helena Petrovna Blavatsky (1831–1891). At séances in Chittenden, Vermont, and in Philadelphia, he witnessed how the phenomena became much more powerful and bizarre when Blavatsky was present, and attributed this to her own psychic powers. Toward the end of the book in which he describes these experiences, *People of the Other World*, Olcott drops a hint: "After knowing this remarkable lady . . . I am almost tempted to believe that the stories of Eastern fables are but simple narratives of fact; and that this very American outbreak of spiritualistic phenomena is under the control of an Order, which while depending for its results upon unseen agents, has its existence upon Earth among men."[20]

As for the unseen agents, the early Theosophists were preoccupied with elementals—half-personified spirits of the intermediate realm—and with ways to make them visible and obedient. Olcott probably had the idea that an accomplished adept could summon an elemental through ceremonial magic or in a crystal, and dispatch it to a distant place to produce phenomena there. Alternatively, he may have had in mind the process described in the anonymous narrative called *Ghost Land*, published in 1872 by Emma Hardinge Britten (1823–1899), a fellow spiritualist and, for a while, a Theosophist. The early chapters of the book recount the experiences of Louis, the narrator, around the 1830s as child medium for a Berlin circle of occultists, "the German branch of a very ancient secret society." One of their experiments involved the deliberate causing of poltergeist-type disturbances.

> On one occasion, the society having thrown me into a profound sleep by the aid of vital magnetism, and the vapors of nitrous oxide gas, they directed my "atmospheric spirit" to proceed, in

> company with two other lucid subjects, to a certain castle in Bohemia, where friends of their resided, and then and there to make disturbances by throwing stones, moving ponderable bodies, shrieking, groaning, and tramping heavily, etc., etc. I here state emphatically, and upon the honor of one devoted only to the interest of truth, that these disturbances were made, and made by the spirits of myself and two other yet living beings, a girl and a boy who were subjects of the society; and though we, in our own individualities, remembered nothing whatever of our performance, we were shortly afterwards shown a long and startling newspaper account of the hauntings in the castle of Baron von L—-, of which we were the authors.[21]

The author depicts the members of this Berlin circle as disbelievers in the immortality of the soul. Motivated solely by scientific curiosity, they were as indifferent to the effects of such experiments on the witnesses as on their young mediums. Whether fact or fiction, *Ghost Land* takes its place within a long tradition of using children in magical practices, especially for clairvoyance or scrying.

The idea of a deliberate provocation of the Hydesville phenomena fell dormant for almost twenty years. Early in 1893 a Christian esotericist, Charles G. Harrison, (1855–?) revived it in a course of lectures in London. He explains the origins of spiritualism as follows. By about 1840, modern Europe had reached the "point of physical intellectuality" in its evolutionary cycle, involving it in gross materialism. Occultists debated as to whether they should counteract this by revealing that there is an unseen world around us, as real as the world of sense; and if so, how it could be done safely. Experiments were made with mediums, first in America, then in France and Britain. "But the whole thing was a failure. The mediums, one and all, declared that they were controlled by spirits who had departed from the earth."[22] Realizing that they had created a Frankenstein's monster, the occultists withdrew from the experiment, but the mischief was done. "The door had been opened to extra-mundane influences, and could not be reclosed." The mediums were thereupon manipulated for political or temporal advantage by the less scrupulous occultists whom Harrison calls the "Brothers of the Left," while the more conservative ones strove to throw discredit on the whole movement.

The Theosophists were quick to notice and appropriate this theory. Alfred Percy Sinnett (1840–1921), in a lecture given on November 21, 1894, to the London lodge of the Theosophical Society, said that he had received information from persons whom he believed in a position to know, to the effect that:

> in the beginning the development of modern spiritualism was earnestly promoted by a school of living occultists,—not the school to which the Theosophical development has been due, but a school of which I should never think without great respect. . . . I am fully prepared to believe that spiritualism has thus had, from the first, a certain amount of Adept support. Without this, Theosophists will feel pretty sure, a great many of its developments in the beginning would have been impossible. Now, however, the whole system has acquired such momentum, that it has, I venture to think, entirely outrun the original design in one way; though in another—in reference to the effort to show mankind at large, that forces independent of the physical plane are at work around us—it has attained a very imperfect success.[23]

What was this "school of living occultists"? None but a self-described occultist could answer, and none more readily than the up-and-coming Theosophist Charles Webster Leadbeater (1854–1934). In his book *The Astral Plane* (1895), Leadbeater identified the order behind spiritualism as a lodge of Atlantean adepts that had persisted in America for thousands of years. This is how they went about their work:

> The method adopted was to take some ordinary person after death, arouse him thoroughly upon the astral plane, instruct him to a certain extent in the powers and possibilities belonging to it, and then put him in charge of a spiritualistic circle. He in his turn "developed" other departed personalities along the same line, they all acted upon those who sat at their *séances*, and "developed" them as mediums; and so spiritualism grew and flourished. No doubt living members of the original lodge occasionally manifested themselves in astral form at some of the circles—perhaps they may do so even now; but in most cases they simply gave such direction and guidance as they considered necessary to the persons they had put in charge. There is little doubt that the movement increased so much more rapidly than they had expected that it soon got quite beyond their control, so that, as has been said, for many of the later developments they can only be held indirectly responsible.[24]

Further light on the Atlantean adepts came from Countess Constance Wachtmeister (1838–1910), a lady of Franco-English parentage, Swedish nobility (by marriage), and a loyal friend of Madame Blavatsky. On July 23, 1897, in an address to a spiritualist camp meeting near San Francisco, she retold the story more or less in Sinnett's words but added that these adepts were "living men, great souls from Atlantis incarnated into the bodies of North American Indians."[25] So in this version it was the Indians who had taken the momentous decision to rescue Western humanity from materialism, and used their occult powers to start the rappings in Hydesville and make intelligent responses to the Fox sisters' questions.

None of the Theosophists seems to have followed this logical chain of argument. Perhaps the impoverished remnants of the Iroquois tribes seemed unequal to the task. Annie Besant (1847–1933), leader of the Theosophical Society after Blavatsky's death and a close collaborator with Leadbeater, attributed both spiritualism and Theosophy to living adepts who can pass at will into the invisible world and communicate with the dead.[26] During World War I she gave a series of talks in India that contain the fullest account yet, from which I extract the most relevant parts:

> Many of you may perhaps know that the impulse which originated the Spiritualistic movement came from the White Lodge itself, and was passed through certain Initiates and Disciples of the Fourth Race; and it is that which gave it its peculiar character. Most of you have doubtless heard of the Brotherhood of Yucatan, in Mexico, an exceedingly remarkable group of Occultists, who came down by definite succession in Fourth Race bodies, maintaining the Fourth Race methods of occult progress. . . .
>
> Their methods have always been—as were Fourth Race methods of the past—those which dealt with the advance of mankind through what is now called "the lower psychism"; that is, through a number of occult phenomena connected with the physical plane and tangible, so that, on the physical plane, proofs might be afforded of the reality of the hidden worlds. . . .
>
> Hence, when it was seen that the Fifth Race was drifting into materialism in its most advanced members, the scientific world, and that knowledge was progressing much faster than the social conscience and moral evolution, it was thought necessary to start a movement which would appeal to those who were materialistically-minded, and would afford them a certain amount of proof, tangible on the physical plane, of the reality of the superphysical, of the unseen, though not of the spiritual, worlds. Hence the Spiritualist Movement. . . .
>
> The Yucatan Brotherhood, accustomed to the use of that method [of materialization], handed down from ancient days, took up the guidance of this rescue movement. . . .

> But when [the sensitives], in a time of ignorance of Occultism, came into the world, and were exposed to all its difficulties without any kind of outer protection, they became the ordinary mediums of the last century, who could not protect themselves at all. They were open to every influence which came from the astral world and from the higher regions of the physical world. Hence they were mostly in touch with the less developed human beings who had passed on, the crowds of average people who throng the lower reaches of the astral world.[27]

In Besant's version, the Atlantean agents are under the direct guidance of the brotherhood of masters known in Theosophy as the White Lodge. Sinnett agreed when he returned, in a lecture of 1920, to the old theme of spiritualist-Theosophical rivalry. He urges fraternal respect between the two movements:

> Some of us know now, and all should see how reasonably they may believe, that the Masters of the Divine Hierarchy who instituted the Theosophical movement were equally concerned at a previous date, in setting the Spiritualist movement on foot. It was urgently needed at the time to combat Materialism, and did magnificent work in that direction. If all had gone well it would also have proved a broad highway leading up to its sequel—the Theosophical movement. . . .
>
> There are various lines of activity in which the great Masters specialize, to use our familiar phrase, and thus, while two of whom readers of Theosophical books have most often heard, do truly concern themselves especially with the progress of Theosophy, another especially watches over and sympathetically promotes the progress of Spiritualism, as he has done from the beginning of that grand development designed to arrest the poisonous growth of disbelief in any future life beyond the delusive finality of physical death.[28]

These later Theosophists were effectively taking credit, on behalf of their masters, for launching the spiritualist movement in 1848 as a prelude to their own. As an alternative to their claims, I turn to the views of René Guénon (1886–1951), a founder of the Traditionalist or Perennialist current in modern esotericism, who accepted the Hidden Hand theory but attributed it very differently. In his first book, *L'erreur spirite* (The spiritualist error), Guénon writes that the Hydesville phenomena were caused by people

ILLUSTRATION 12.2A. Greek Revival house in Auburn. A rare survivor of the many houses where séances were held during the heyday of Auburn's spiritualist activity in the 1850s. *Author's photograph.*

ILLUSTRATION 12.2B. Hydesville Memorial Park, Hydesville. The recent building covers the foundations of the Fox family's cottage, where modern spiritualism began in 1848. *Author's photograph.*

acting at a distance, by means only known to a few initiates, members of the "Inner Circle of the H[ermetic] B[rotherhood] of L[uxor]."[29] He offers some alternative explanations for how it happened: (1) the H. B. of L. provoked the Hydesville phenomena by using the favorable conditions they found there; (2) they imparted a certain direction to phenomena which had already begun; (3) the H. B. of L., or another agency, profited by what was going on in Hydesville by acting on the inhabitants and visitors through suggestion. Without this minimum contribution, Guénon says, there is no way to explain why modern spiritualism began then and there, rather than at the many other places where strange phenomena have happened.

Guénon adds that since the beginning of the nineteenth century there were secret societies distinct from Freemasonry, which worked with magical evocations and magnetism; as a source, he refers to none other than *Ghost Land*. He says that the H. B. of L., or whatever preceded it, was in contact with certain of these German organizations.[30] Despite his aversion to Theosophy (on which he wrote another polemical book), Guénon shared Blavatsky's critique of spiritualist belief, namely that whatever is contacted in séances, it is certainly not the spirits of dead humans. That was what the secularists and materialists had said all along, but without pretending to know what *was* behind the phenomena.

In this brief survey of the Hidden Hand theory, the Hydesville rappings have been attributed to (1) the masters behind the Theosophical Society; (2) North American Indians; (3) a secret order in Mexico using Atlantean methods; (4) scientists experimenting with the paranormal; (5) a fraternity of occultists worried by humanity's plunge into materialism; and (6) the "Inner Circle of the Hermetic Brotherhood of Luxor." I find the theory intriguing, but being of a practical frame of mind, I cannot imagine a plausible working method. One thing we can agree on is that Rochester and its environs provided what Guénon calls "favorable conditions," both geographically and in the collective psyche.

ILLUSTRATION 13.1. Gerrit Smith, landowner, abolitionist, and supporter of progressive causes. From *The Phrenological Journal,* vol. 60, no. 3 (Mar. 1875), p. 145. *Courtesy of Special Collections, Hamilton College Library.*

CHAPTER 13

The Progressives Take Notice

My neighbors, we are all aware that a low place in the ecclesiastical world is assigned to Peterboro. For many, many years, we have been giving great offense to the clergy and the churches. And yet, I must think, that this little village probably the only spot in the State to which the Anti-Slavery Society, that was mobbed out of Utica nearly a quarter of a century ago, could retreat in safety—is, in respect to a sound and rational religion, greatly in advance of almost every other place in the land. Our families with certainly very few exceptions dwell together in peace and love; and in this there is no little proof that the religion of Jesus prevails among us. No little proof also of this is there in the fact that a great many years have passed away since intoxicating drinks were openly sold among us: and no little proof too in the fact that the filthy vice of snuffing, chewing, and smoking tobacco is held by a large share of our people to be disgraceful and sinful. And where I ask most emphatically is there a place in all our broad land so free as this from the spirit of caste? Whose table is there here

> to which a black man is not as welcome as a white one? When I heard the other day that our respectable youth of white faces and black faces had mingled together freely in a public dance, I confess (although I am not the advocate of public as I am of private dances) that I felt proud of my village. Where else in our country has the religion of Jesus achieved a conquest so beautiful, so decisive, and so much needed?[1]
>
> *Gerrit Smith, on his home village of Peterboro*

In the previous chapter we learned that after the Hydesville rappings, Leah Fish took her younger sisters, Maggie and Kate, from their weak-willed parents and gave them a new home in Rochester. Mr. Fish was long gone and Leah passed as a widow, earning her living as indicated in the *Rochester City Directory* of 1849: "Fish, Mrs. Ann L. Music teacher, h[ouse] 31 Troup." Soon Leah was producing raps in turn, and some joker in the city office composed her 1851 entry as "Fish, Anna L. Mrs. Mysterious knocker, h. 59 S[outh] Sophia."[2] While intended satirically, it was correct as a business description, for with Leah, the profession of medium was born.

Sophia Street (now Plymouth Avenue) had more going on than mysterious knocking. Leah's apartment building had a hiding place[3] that was probably used to conceal runaway slaves. Down the street at no. 36 lived Isaac Post (1798–1872) and his second wife, Amy (1802–1889), who managed one of the most active depots on the Underground Railroad. Both houses have been demolished now. A historical marker outside the Hochstein Music School commemorates the Posts and their work for abolition, but does not mention that modern spiritualism would never have got off the ground without their assistance.

The Posts stemmed from long-standing Quaker settlements in Queens (now Nassau) County, Long Island.[4] Isaac and his first wife, Hannah Kirby, came Upstate in 1823 to farm in Scipio, Cayuga County. After Hannah's early death in 1827, Isaac married Amy Kirby, who had come to Scipio to care for her ailing sister. The couple moved to Rochester in 1836, where Isaac set up as a pharmacist and did well in that trade. The Posts' Quakerism was of the most radical kind: both politically, in demanding immediate freedom for slaves and equality for women, and spiritually, in reaction to the complacent urban Quakers who paid little attention to the Inner Light. They naturally went along with the breakaway movement of Elias Hicks in

1827 (the same year as slavery was abolished in New York State). But even that was not radical enough for the Posts, for the Hicksites would not collaborate with non-Quaker abolitionists. In June 1848 the Posts were among the founders of an even more liberal group in Waterloo, Seneca County, called the Congregational Friends. According to the historian of spiritualism Ann Braude, they believed in an unbroken chain of communication between the Infinite and all beings,[5] making them ripe for the events to come.

During the 1840s the Posts' home became the informal headquarters of the Western New York Anti-Slavery Society, founded in 1842. Fugitive slaves arrived by the dozen on their doorstep, and were fed and sheltered before being shipped on to Canada and freedom. The most famous of them all, Frederick Douglass (c. 1818–1895), called the Posts "two people of all-abounding benevolence, the truest and best of Long Island and Elias Hicks Quakers."[6] Douglass stayed in Rochester and, with their support, started his antislavery newspaper, the *North Star*, which ran from 1847 to 1851.

Women's rights were equally important to the Posts. On July 19–20, 1848, Amy attended the women's rights convention at Seneca Falls. Already a confident speaker, thanks to the Quaker custom of allowing women to testify, she addressed the audience and signed the Declaration of Sentiments.[7] Quakers were prominent among the three hundred participants, as was Douglass, being the sole African American present. In a stirring speech he swayed the company to approve the motion for women's suffrage, not just "rights." Historians have remarked on the closeness of this epochal event to the Hydesville rappings, less than three months before and twenty-five miles away. The connection is closer than that. Not only had the Fox family lived in Rochester before moving to the Hydesville cottage, but in a house belonging to the Posts. This appears from a letter from Isaac to his brother and sister-in-law, in which he refers to Maggie and Kate as "Girls of 12 & 14 years who used to live in our house at Cornhill and with whom we always had good understanding."[8]

Maggie and Kate had hated rural life in the cramped Hydesville cottage and were glad to be back in Rochester. Once installed with their sister Leah on Troup Street, they were anxious for the Posts to "enjoy what they did there."[9] Isaac invited them to his home, watched their demonstrations of spirit communication, and admitted, in the same letter, that he was impressed. This alone might not have convinced the Posts to accept the "spiritual telegraph" and all that it implied about the afterlife. But there was one more piece to complete the puzzle, and a tragic one. Isaac's first wife, as mentioned, had died four years after their marriage, and their son Edmund was killed at the age of five in a threshing accident. Isaac and Amy had three sons and one daughter, Matilda: she too had died at age five, in 1845.

The bereaved couple lost no time in trying to reach the spirits of their children.[10] The young mediums assured them, through raps, that Matilda was in the spirit world and was happy there. Sometimes Isaac magnetized them, after the example of Andrew Jackson Davis, who spoke from a mesmeric trance and seemed inspired by the Inner Light. Then Leah found that being magnetized not only cured her headaches, but made a medium of her, too. She gave many communications from Edmund, Matilda, and Hannah, Isaac's first wife. The Posts were now convinced of the genuineness of the phenomena, and, encouraged by the spirits, decided to display the young mediums to the world. Isaac and his cousin George Willets rented Rochester's new Corinthian Hall for three evenings, beginning on November 14, 1849. At seventy-five cents a ticket, it was a sell-out. From that moment on, Maggie and Kate Fox were celebrities, with all the glory and misery that that would entail.

Isaac had done his part: the genie was out of the bottle. Now it was his turn to develop mediumship. (Amy never did, though she was a believer.[11]) His mother's spirit explained to him that a reformation was going on in the spirit world, and that its inhabitants were seeking the company of honest men on earth. She prompted him to try automatic writing, a quicker method than rapping or the alphabet board. Isaac soon found the cream of the spirit world eager for his company. Quaker dignitaries came—George Fox, William Penn, and Elias Hicks—and so did Emanuel Swedenborg. George Washington and Thomas Jefferson had their say. Benjamin Franklin was a favorite communicator on account of his experiments with electricity (often thought, by the scientifically minded, to have something to do with the process). Margaret Fuller and Mrs. Franklin represented the women, along with Sarah Sharp, a murder victim. John Caldwell Calhoun (1772–1850), the former U.S. vice president and a defender of slavery, came with his tail between his legs to confess his error and join the other spirits in applauding the Posts' principles. All these and many others contributed messages to Isaac's book of 1852, *Voices from the Spirit World*, for which the spirit of Franklin obligingly wrote an introduction.

Frederick Douglass loved the Posts but could not share their beliefs. Being around them in the 1850s, he could not avoid their spirit circles, which tried his patience. After one of these he wrote to Amy Post to apologize for having used the word "atrocious": it didn't refer to the company, he explained, but to the rapping when the spirit refused to answer the only question that would have tested its intelligence.[12] Very different was the attitude of William Cooper Nell (1816–1874), who had come to Rochester in the fall of 1847 to work with Douglass on the *North Star*. Unlike Douglass, who was not safe from arrest until his supporters had paid off his ex-owner, Nell was from a free black family in Boston with a strong abolitionist tradition. He lodged with the Posts and enthusiastically joined the Rochester circle. His experiences there stayed with him all his life. After returning to Boston in 1851 to pursue his career as a publicist, he wrote regularly to Amy Post about his other life as a spiritualist. John Murray Spear (see chapter 17) suggested that Nell should write about his Rochester experiences, but he was too busy with journalism, speaking, and running for office. In his free time he met rapping, trance, writing, and medical mediums, sat in spirit circles, made a temporary believer of his colleague William Lloyd Garrison, and watched the rapid growth of the movement in New England. He told Amy that he could fill a volume with his Boston experiences. If he had done so, we might know more about the "spirit circle among some colored friends, some of whom enjoy these sittings under protest from their pastors"[13]—an under-documented spiritualist subculture.

The abolitionist William Lloyd Garrison (1805–1879) was a believer only in the sense of accepting the reality of the phenomena. Pestered by requests for his opinion, he wrote in his newspaper, the *Liberator,* of a séance in New York City in 1854 with the eldest Fox sister.[14] Six gentlemen and four ladies sat around a large table and felt phantom hands grab their garments and their own hands, watched a bell ring by itself and a walking stick slither, snakelike, around their feet. A pocketknife vanished and reappeared; names were scrawled on a piece of paper. The raps, responding to calling out the alphabet, told the sitters to hold onto Leah's own feet. One spirit identified itself as Jesse Hutchinson, member of a popular abolitionist singing group, and banged out the rhythm as the company sang his hit song, *The Old Granite State*. Another spirit said it was Isaac T. Hopper (whose daughter was present): he was a Hicksite Quaker and a founder of the Underground Railroad. Both spirits said they were very happy.

Garrison had a strong spiritualist contingent among his supporters. He had to be tactful as well as truthful about phenomena that were as inexplicable as they were trivial. This is his conclusion:

> How shall demonstrations like these be accounted for, except on the hypothesis of spirit-agency? If we cannot positively affirm that Isaac Hopper and Jesse Hutchinson were present on that occasion, we are at least prepared to declare, as our own conviction, as well as that of the entire company, we believe, that invisible spirits, not of this mundane sphere, performed the phenomena we have thus briefly narrated to our readers.[15]

Garrison's cautious reaction was typical of those already committed to reform (temperance, abolition, or women's rights) when they encountered spiritualism. They tended to be Universalists or ex-Universalists with a dusting of transcendentalism, or else they were Quakers, open to the divine influx and the physical effects that had given the sect its name. Having already dared to challenge consensus politics and the Protestant mainstream, they had little to lose in going a step further. Something mysterious seemed to be happening, but how important was it? The rank and file could divide their attention between social activism and the new craze, but the leaders of the progressive movements held back.

Gerrit Smith (1797–1874) is an example. Born in Utica and loaded with inherited land, he chose to live in obscure Peterboro, Madison County (see quotation at the head of this chapter). From a diminutive land office he sold off his vast holdings to fund his philanthropy. Donna Burdick, the Smithfield town historian, describes how reformers and spiritualists alike thronged the Smith mansion and the healing springs in nearby Siloam.[16] It had not escaped Smith that the two concerns often went together, and that spiritualists almost always voted with the progressives.

Like the Posts, Gerrit and Ann Smith had lost children, and in 1852 Ann used a medium to try to get in touch with them. The name of her son, Fitzhugh, was rapped out on her foot, and a short message assured her that he was watching over his father. Such evidence satisfied her, as it did thousands of others. Smith's first biographer, Octavius Brooks Frothingham, writes:

> Mr. Smith was not a spiritualist. His wife was, and in company with her, he visited mediums and attended circles. But the "manifestations" did not convince him. It is probably that his absorbing interest in human affairs made him indifferent to the problem of the hereafter. This he confessed. It is probably also, that the moral confidence in God that was habitual with him, made him incurious in regard to details of evidence. Certain it is, that the subject presented to his mind little attraction, though his deep respect and affection for his wife forbade other than playful criticism of it.[17]

A recent and more comprehensive biography does not even broach the subject, but does clarify Smith's spiritual position. His was a religion of nature and reason, science and progress. He believed man to be morally good and capable of righting the world without theological assistance. He disliked the forced belief and conformity of the established sects, reinforced as it was with threats of hellfire. In an essay for Horace Greeley's *New York Tribune*, Smith wrote: "Fifty or a hundred people in Peterboro or Cazenovia, however much alike in their views and spirit, should no more be required to adopt a common religious creed than to shorten or stretch out their bodies to a common length."[18] Moreover, the new science, even before Darwin, had expanded his imaginative horizons and made him an evolutionist: "Why is it unreasonable to believe that the races of men millions of years hence will surpass what they are now, quite as much as the most finely organized and the most beautiful specimens of animals in this age of the earth surpass the trilobites and other fauna of the Silurian period?"[19] This brought down to earth what Andrew Jackson Davis was teaching about evolution in the higher spheres.

In 1843, to the vexation of the local Presbyterian minister, Gerrit Smith started a Free Church with himself as pastor, adding in 1847 the building that still stands on the Peterboro green. Burdick names some of those who came to speak there, including Davis, Paschal Beverly Randolph (see chapter 15), the suffragist and phrenologist Elizabeth Oakes Smith, and the trance medium Laura de Force Gordon (later to become one of the first woman attorneys in California). Larger waves were made by one of the minor interests of the Peterboro circle: dress reform. Mid-century bourgeois fashion was squeezing women into corsets and hampering them with yards of floor-length petticoats and skirts, to the great profit of the whalebone and fabric industries. Smith's daughter Elizabeth Smith Miller and her friend Amelia Bloomer tried out a new, practical costume of a shortish skirt and baggy trousers. But "bloomers" were much too far in advance of their time, and the costume only encouraged male ribaldry.

In the *History of Woman Suffrage*, the authors draw up a roll call of the "first wave" of the women's rights movement, before the Civil War, that underlines the centrality of the Upstate region:

> At Rochester, were William H. Channing,[20] Frederick Douglass, the Anthonys,[21] the Posts, the Hallowells,[22] the Stebbins,[23] some grand Quaker families in Farmington, and Waterloo[24]; Mrs. Bloomer and her sprightly weekly called The Lily, at Seneca Falls; Mrs. Wright, Mrs. Worden, Mrs. Seward,[25] at Auburn; Gerrit Smith's family at Peterboro; Beriah Green's[26] at Whitesboro, with the Sedgwicks[27] and Mays,[28] and Matilda Joslyn Gage at Syracuse.[29]

In the rest of this chapter we will look at some of these pioneers. They all knew spiritualism by repute if not directly, but it did not necessarily make spiritualists of them—or for that matter anti-spiritualists. George Willets wrote to Isaac Post about the people who had heard the raps, independently of the Fox sisters. He named Mary Ann M'Clintock, Elizabeth Smith Miller, and Elizabeth Cady Stanton, who heard them when visiting Mrs. Miller.[30] "If it is Humbug it seems to spread fast," Willets added. Mention of Mary Ann M'Clintock (1800–1882) brings us to the mythic beginnings of the movement, for she was one of the four women who issued the unsigned call for the Seneca Falls Convention.[31] It also puts us among the "grand Quaker families of Waterloo," their grandeur expressed in the Federalist and Greek Revival homes that line the broad streets of the region's towns.

Thomas and Mary Ann M'Clintock were Hicksite Quakers; he was a pharmacist, like Isaac Post, and also ran a school. They rented a house from some wealthier Quakers, Richard and Jane Hunt, famous for hosting the tea party at which a women's rights convention was first mooted.[32] Following that, Elizabeth Cady Stanton ((1815–1902) from Seneca Falls, Martha Coffin Wright (1806–1875) from Auburn, and Martha's sister Lucretia Coffin Mott (1793–1880), who was visiting from Pennsylvania, gathered at the M'Clintocks' on July 16, 1848, for another tea party. There they wrote the historic Declaration of Sentiments, based on the Declaration of Independence, as the platform of their movement.[33] The M'Clintocks' mahogany tea table (now in the Smithsonian) had already witnessed the organization of the Quaker breakaway group, the Congregation of Friends, and on both occasions, legend has it that approving raps were heard from it.[34]

Lucretia Mott, who was there, was not impressed. She wrote to her sister Martha that "your knockings are probably a humbug," perceptively associating the spirit messages with mesmeric phenomena. What passes in the mind of the client, she said, is conveyed to the clairvoyant, who gives it forth; it is all according to natural laws, if you only know what they are.[35] Her husband James Mott attended a séance during ten weeks over the winter of 1851–52, but Lucretia found a "grossness" about the spiritualist communications, hardly suited to the state of spirits "just made perfect." She worried about the effects they were having on Isaac Post's mind, and mentioned that a Mrs. Taft had gone insane from such a cause.[36]

Lucretia Mott had come to the area from Philadelphia to stay with the Wrights in Auburn and to attend the organizational meeting of the Congregational Friends. She was surprised to find Elizabeth Cady Stanton there, whom she had last seen in London at the antislavery convention of 1840. Both the Motts and the Stantons were already active abolitionists. Elizabeth Cady, a native of Johnstown, had met her husband-to-be, Henry Stanton, at Gerrit Smith's in Peterboro. They now lived in Seneca Falls, having moved there to escape the sickly air of Boston, and raised seven children before Elizabeth could devote all her energy and genius to the women's rights movement. While she doubtless heard raps and much else, her biographers agree that Stanton was not a spiritualist, but a freethinker—which does not mean an atheist or even a skeptic, as we will see when we come to treat her *Woman's Bible* in the next chapter.

Susan Brownell Anthony (1820–1906), who became the icon of the entire movement, entered the scene after the Seneca Falls Convention.

She was the daughter of a Massachusetts mill owner who lost his fortune, obliging her either to marry or earn her own living. Choosing the latter course, she taught at the Academy in Canajoharie, then in 1849 moved to Gates, Monroe County (now a western suburb of Rochester), to manage a small family farm. The Anthonys became friendly with the Posts, Frederick Douglass, and the other Rochester abolitionists. Susan's parents and her sister Mary attended the 1848 convention, but Susan was more absorbed in the temperance cause. In spring 1851 she went to Seneca Falls for a meeting—some say abolitionist,[37] others temperance[38]—as a guest of Amelia Bloomer, and there met Elizabeth Cady Stanton. The two women immediately hit it off, and began a collaboration that would last, with ups and downs, for more than half a century.

Living where she did, and among the people mentioned, Susan Anthony could not avoid knowing a lot about spiritualism. Initially a nervous speaker, she envied the ease with which trance speakers could hold forth in public,[39] but when she wrote to Stanton that she had "prayed to be made a speaking medium for a whole week," I sense a sardonic tone of voice. Anthony approved of spiritualists only because they supported women's rights. She had no inhibitions about using their platforms—she spoke annually at Lily Dale—but her mission concerned this world alone. From beginning to end she concentrated on a single goal: the right of women to vote. All other considerations were a distraction from this imperative, which she, like many secular progressives, obeyed with quasi-religious zeal. Later in life she wrote: "The truth is, I can no more see through Theosophy than I can through Christian Science, Spiritualism, Calvinism or any other of the theories, so I shall have to go on knocking away to remove the obstructions in the road of us mortals while in these bodies and on this planet; and leave Madam Besant and you and all who have entered into the higher spheres, to revel in things unknown to me. . . ."[40]

Matilda Joslyn Gage (1826–1898), speaker, organizer, protester, and historian, was born in Cicero, Onondaga County, and educated first by her father, then at the Clinton Liberal Institute. She also missed the 1848 convention, and joined the movement in 1852. In chapter 20 we will examine her incendiary treatise, *Women, Church and State*. Of the first wave of leaders she comes closest to being a spiritualist, for she did consult mediums and willingly attended séances, especially after the death of her granddaughter, but found a more congenial home in Theosophy.

The authoritative *History of Woman Suffrage*, coauthored by Stanton, Anthony, and Gage, ignored spiritualism. By 1881, when the first volume was published, the two movements had parted company, and it was not politic to emphasize their former alliance. Only when the authors write that there was "Quite a magnetic circle of reformers in Central New York," some

ILLUSTRATION 13.2A. The Hunt House, Waterloo. Residence of Richard and Jane Hunt, where on July 9, 1848, it was decided to hold a women's rights convention. *Author's photograph.*

ILLUSTRATION 13.2B. The M'Clintock House, Waterloo. Residence of Thomas and Mary Ann M'Clintock, at which Elizabeth Cady Stanton, Lucretia Mott, and Elizabeth Smith Miller planned the first women's rights convention and drafted the Declaration of Sentiments, July 16, 1848. *Author's photograph.*

readers knew exactly what that meant. The omission set the trend for a century of historiography. To the modernist frame of mind, women's rights and abolition were good and progressive movements, while spiritualism and Theosophy were irrational and regressive, hence bad. It was forgotten how closely they were once entwined, especially among the rank and file. Scholars began to realize this after the appearance of Ann Braude's *Radical Spirits* in 1989. By now it is obvious that both the political and the spiritual movements grew from the same fertile soil of central New York, and that they drew on similar energies to those that had fueled the earlier religious revivals. Anyone involved in one had to be aware of the other, and both demanded choices that challenged one's inmost ethical and metaphysical principles.

Illustration 14.1. Paschal Beverly Randolph, medium, occultist, and Rosicrucian. From *Beyond the Veil: Posthumous Work of Paschal Beverly Randolph*. New York: D. M. Bennett, 1878.

CHAPTER 14

Sex, Drugs, and Mirrors

Dear Brother:

After finishing my labors in Jordan,—which by the way, I found to be an *exceedingly easy* road to travel, for the opposition was so extremely weak, that there was nothing particular to struggle against or contend with,—I reached Syracuse again, and delivered two lectures. The first was on "The origin of Evil and the Nativity of the Devil," and the second was on the "Spirit-World."

The last lecture was delivered before the largest audience I ever spoke to. The hall was literally *packed* with human beings, and there was hardly standing room for the mass of people, so that large numbers were obliged to go away, being unable to get a place within the hall. Mr. J. Stanly Grimes, whilom a lecturer on Phrenology, but now crusading against Spiritualism, was in the hall. I endeavored to call him out, but without success. He will not be called out. Well, let him go on his way, for you know that some portions of the race like to be humbugged, and it strikes me that Mr. G. is just the man to lay it on thick. He seems to call the attention of the people to subject, consequently he does *some* good be it ever so little.

Some few persons came quite a distance to the lectures, and one gentleman and his lady all the way from Utica. I scarce remember to have heard a similar fact, when other creeds were the attraction. Next day I went to the last named city, and found a party of ladies and gentlemen, who were going to Koontown or rather Edmeston, a village 24 miles from Utica, where we were to be met by another party from Earlville, including several very powerful and remarkable mediums. The sleighing being excellent, we all arrived in good time. After tea, the Circle was formed, and there were eight mediums present, including Mrs. Loomis, of Saquoit, a rapping and moving medium of wonderful powers. In her presence, from three to five persons have stood on a large table, and by their utmost leverage power, their shoulders being braced against the ceiling, have attempted to keep the table still, but it *wouldn't stay put*, for in spite of the enormous weight, (something over 3000 pounds) the table moved around as if it was made of cork. I have seen a man weighing 225 pounds, try his best to keep the table still, but he might as well have tried to stop the west winds. It would hop round in spite of him. The man was H.H. Phelps, Superintendent of Syracuse and Utica Rail Road at that time. Mrs. W. of Earlville, and her two sons aged 12 and 14 years, were there, and another lady medium, whose name I forget. After sitting a few minutes, the Spirits seized some bells provided for the purpose, and also a tamborine, and played them to a *charm*, making such good music that I was completely astonished. These boys have a variety of manifestations, but the most singular is, that from the table at which they sit, in a darkened room, will arise phosphorescent lights from the size of a pea to that of an acorn. These lights will dance about the room in all directions, and arrange themselves in the form of a crown, and settle over the heads of some one or more of the party. In the same place is a Miss W., in whose presence there occurs a phenomenon that throws the performances at the "Miracle Circles" in Ohio and New York entirely in the shade. It is nothing less than the creation of matter. For the Spirits will spin from her finger ends what looks like fine steel wire, perfectly visible and palpable, for it can be handled. This substance is about as fine as horse hair generally, and has a kind of steelish look. It is soft to the touch like velvet, and when held in the flame of a candle, it turns and twists as if it *felt* the flame. Some of it was placed in a book and kept several hours, but finally exhaled. I do not feel competent to account for this startling phenomena. It is one of those facts which are extremely valuable, *as it may furnish the key* to that vast problem, the formation of the universe. I trust some who are *competent*, will go to Earville [sic], and investigate the subject.

I shall go from here to Troy, where all letters should be sent up to March 10th; to the 15th at Utica or Syracuse; to April 1st at Buffalo, New York. Trusting in truth and working for wisdom,

I am, sir, for justice,
P. B. Randolph
Utica, Feb. 23d, 1855.[1]

Letter from Paschal Beverly Randolph
on séance phenomena, 1855

Paschal Beverly Randolph (1825–1875) is one of the unsung heroes of Black American history. Respectable neither in life nor in death, he was forgotten by all but a miniscule sect of self-styled Rosicrucians. That changed with John Patrick Deveney's biography, provocatively subtitled *A Nineteenth-Century Black American Spiritualist, Rosicrucian, and Sex Magician* (1997) and essential reading for anyone hoping to understand modern occultism. Once again, its roots are in central New York.

Randolph's version of his life story varied according to his needs or whims.[2] It seems certain, at least, that he was born in New York City, and that he was illegitimate, motherless from childhood, and kicked around at the bottom of the social barrel. He mentions having been a bootblack on the city streets before going to sea for further humiliation as a cabin boy and teenage sailor. Whether or not he thrice circled the world, as he later boasted, at about the age of twenty an injury ended his sailing days. He settled in Portland, Maine, working in two of the few trades open to free blacks, those of barber and dyer. Lacking any formal education, he would become one of the most readable, original, and entertaining of all writers on occultism.

By the time of the Hydesville rappings in 1848, Randolph was already interested in psychic phenomena and the development of his own mediumship. He writes that when spiritualism first appeared, he went to investigate the knockings in Litchfield, Michigan.[3] He also stayed three weeks with Andrew Jackson Davis and his wife in Hartford, where he experienced an illumination not unlike Davis's own, in which he seemed to see the universal fire in all objects and to gain omniscience thereby.[4] This was about the year that Randolph settled in Madison County, probably thanks to the abolitionist Gerrit Smith who was giving farmland to free blacks. Despite their common interests, their relationship was later to turn very sour.[5] In 1851 we find Randolph writing from Stockbridge, a village five miles from Smith's residence in Peterboro, where he had a smallholding of about four acres.[6] Randolph's first wife, Mary Jane, was probably of mixed race, as he was: he claimed descent from the royal house of Madagascar and the slave-holding Randolphs of Virginia. Although both were at pains to conceal or deny any "negro blood,"[7] it is more fitting today to honor Paschal as one of the most brilliant and original men of his race, and Mary Jane as one of its countless long-suffering women.

Randolph soon turned his sights on Utica, the nearest city, where his reputation quickly rose from "barber-orator" in 1852 to "clairvoyant physician and psycho-phrenologist" in 1853. He also did automatic writing and shared his effusions with the *Spiritual Telegraph*, Partridge and Brittan's New York City magazine. They were the typical mixture of messages from loved ones and from the great ones of the past. In one, his mother warned him to resist the influx of lower spirits, lest he be driven to "vice, folly, superstition, and, perchance, to worse."[8] In another, the Persian sage Zoroaster confessed that he should have taught the worship of the true God of Nature, not Ormuzd and Ahriman.[9] Randolph also received visible spirit guides. Zoroaster came to see him in July 1853, bringing Blaise Pascal and one Eben el Teleki, and inspired Randolph to write that God "manifested himself first, by rays of love, in seven modes, forms, or degrees; and when it had performed its first office (for there are still six more), matter was ushered into being; man, the *animus*, was born, and love manifested itself in him in the form of desire, which is the first of all actions."[10] This seeming gibberish contains hints of Andrew Jackson Davis's cosmology, the Fourierist psychology of the passions, Randolph's later sexual theory, and the sevenfold cycles and rays of Theosophy.

In January 1854, the Davises organized a Harmonial convention in Auburn, where utopian spiritualists could meet "without distinction of color, sex or money."[11] Randolph was among the speakers, and when his turn came he became clairvoyant and gave a resounding discourse on the non-existence of evil. After a break for lunch he resumed, urging that in the land of liberty and the age of free inquiry we should read the Book of Nature, instead of following theological systems that fail to satisfy the human mind. Davis, in his own speech, was vocal about the right to criticize the Bible. Randolph later referred to this as the "whack Moses" brand of spiritualism.[12]

Just as had happened with the young Davis (see chapter 10), the fringes of the medical profession were eager to exploit Randolph's gift. In summer 1854 the *Spiritual Telegraph* reported:

> Mr. Randolph, the Clairvoyant and Psychometrist, is now in this city, and intends to devote himself to the examination of disease, and to giving delineations of character. Mr. Randolph is now magnetized by Dr. Bergevin, of Paris, one of the most skillful and scientific physicians in the country; being a graduate of the Medical School of Paris, Member of the Philosophical Institute of France, Director of the Société Magnétique, and assistant of the Baron Dupotet and M. Cahagnet. At a secret trial of Mr. Randolph's powers, Professor Toutain, of France, expressed his belief that as a seer Mr. Randolph is superior to Alexis, of Paris, the world-renowned somnambulist. This is a high recommendation, coming, as it does, from such a source.[13]

The French connection would in time yield fruit, but for now Randolph was working for various doctors in New York City, seeing fifty patients a day.[14] Presumably, Mary Jane was keeping the Stockbridge farm going.

The letter quoted at the head of this chapter gives a rich impression of Randolph's life on his return Upstate. Anyone knowing the region will be struck by the ease with which he could get around in February, and plan a lecture tour from Troy to Buffalo. During winter, people were if anything more mobile, for once the snow had fallen, the abominable roads and the snail's pace of the canal boats gave way to sleighs. On the day mentioned above, Randolph thought nothing of sledding from Utica to Edmeston, located on a tributary of the Unadilla River. There his party joined another from Earlville, twenty miles across the eastern hills, which included the redoubtable Mrs. Wright and seven other mediums. This rare account of an assembly in a remote village bears witness to a rural spiritualist activity that has left barely a trace in the printed record.

As for the phenomena, levitating tables, even pianos, were the stock-in-trade of antebellum mediums. But Mrs. Wright's production was of a different and almost unique order. Randolph was sufficiently impressed to mention it in another communication, where he writes:

> Mrs. Wright has been a medium three years, and on several occasions there has in broad daylight been seen to spin from her hands large quantities of what may be likened to silver hair. This substance could be taken hold of by another person and stretched across an entire room. It could be cut in two, but both ends would instantly unite. It has been kept several hours, and in the night looks like a wire of light. Enormous quantities of this substance could be pulled from her person.[15]

This was not the "ectoplasm" commonly exuded by later mediums. That came out of their mouths or other orifices, only appeared in darkness, and looked gauze-like or viscid—hence was often faked. Mrs. Wright's substance was more like the "angel hair" familiar to readers of the UFO literature, which falls from the sky and usually dissolves in a few hours.[16] Since the "key to the formation of the universe" still remains to be found, I simply offer Randolph's accounts as a contribution to the literature of unexplained phenomena.

Spontaneous as it is, Randolph's letter shows that when not channeling, he was a born writer as well as a riveting speaker. In 1855 John Murray Spear (see next chapter) chose him to deliver a message at Robert Owen's World Convention to Inaugurate the Commencement of the Millennium. Although kept from the platform, for which he never forgave Owen, Randolph mingled to advantage with the British spiritualists, mesmerists, and researchers into crystal vision. He then crossed to France, where his introductions from the New York experiments gave him entry to Dupotet's and Cahagnet's circles. The French were more interested in clairvoyance than in messages from the dead, and Randolph impressed with his ability to read and play chess while blindfolded. At some point—maybe in his seafaring youth—he seems to have become fluent in the language.

On both sides of the English Channel there was a lively interest in the potential of drugs for enhancing clairvoyance. They were all legal. Opium, taken in the liquid form of laudanum, was a popular remedy for many ills; there were also belladonna and henbane, toxic in quantity but consciousness-altering in careful doses; and above all there was *cannabis sattiva*, usually ingested as a pill or potion of hashish rather than smoked. The discovery of hashish was epochal for Randolph, enabling him to escape from passive spirit control and to exercise clairvoyance on his own account.

On returning from this first transatlantic trip, Randolph resumed his trance lecturing in the major centers, from Boston to Cleveland and Canada. By early 1857 he had gone back to England and France, where he probably did give sittings, as he claimed, for the Emperor Napoleon III and Empress Eugénie, who were known patrons of spiritualism. His performances in high society earned him enough to continue his travels through Turkey, Syria, Palestine, and Egypt (at this time all parts of the Ottoman Empire). Everywhere he sought out the holders of occult knowledge and their secret brotherhoods, and he returned to America no longer a spiritualist but a "Rosicrucian," at least in his own imagination.[17] The legendary founder of the Order of the Rosy Cross, Christian Rosenkreutz (1378–1484) had likewise learned his wisdom during travels in the Middle East, and Randolph now cast himself in that role.

By March 1858 Randolph was back in Stockbridge with his neglected family, and picking up the threads of his connections in progressive circles. From September 10–12, Andrew Jackson Davis held a Philanthropic convention in Utica, at which Randolph again stole the show. This time it was not through the force of his trance speaking, but through loudly renouncing spiritualism and returning to the Christian fold. Not content with this rebuff to Davis, Randolph also alienated his friends in the abolitionist movement. He declared the integrity of the Union to be the supreme value, which offended William Lloyd Garrison's principle of "no union with slave-holders," all the while bragging about his Virginian ancestry. Consternation followed, and Randolph briefly capitalized on it by repeating his recantation speech before large audiences in Boston and New York City. He also started flaunting the title of "doctor."

Randolph would later admit that he had "squander[ed] in world-roving a sum more than sufficient to have rendered my family comfortable for life."[18] Instead, as the offended spiritualists closed their doors to him he was reduced to subsistence farming. In a pathetic letter to Gerrit Smith he writes of the need to sell his watch to buy pigs, a cow, and feed.[19] The situation in Stockbridge became desperate. Already heavily in debt, the Randolphs discovered that they did not, in fact, own their little farm, but only held it as agents for Smith. During this period, their daughter Winnie died of hunger, and possibly their son Jacob died too. Of Mary Jane's children, only Cora, born about 1854 and always referred to as a cripple, would survive to a destitute adulthood.[20] Among the pleas and recriminations that Smith seems to have stolidly ignored, one fact stands out: On April 11, 1860, the Randolphs sold their Stockbridge farm to Rensselaer Coe—for one dollar.[21]

After a brief period in Boston, the Randolphs came back to Utica,[22] where Mary Jane worked as a healer and dispenser of Native American remedies.[23] She also acted as Paschal's agent, distributor, and publisher, for during this blighted period he had managed to complete a two-volume novel (*The Wonderful Story of Ravalette*), his first major doctrinal work (*Dealings with the Dead*), and many smaller pamphlets. I do not believe that anyone has noticed this passage in *Dealings with the Dead* (published 1862), and wondered whether Thomas Edison, the sometime Theosophist, had noticed it, too, before inventing the phonographic cylinder in 1877:

> Memory is but the photography of soul. Everything that strikes the eye, or the senses in anyway [sic], leaves an exact image of itself upon the cylinder of Retention, which cylinder winds and unwinds, according as it takes on or gives off the impression, whatever it may be. Thus the image of a tone, a sound, a peculiar trill, as well as of material things, can be, and are photographed upon the soul.[24]

It was not long before Mary Jane's restless husband took off again, arriving in San Francisco in September 1861 for ten weeks of lecturing in California. There he published his first work on sexual science, *The Grand Secret, or, Physical Love in Health and Disease*, and founded a Rosicrucian Supreme Grand Lodge.[25] Then he took ship back to New York and by his own account visited (in some order) England, Ireland, Scotland, France, Malta, Greece, Turkey, Syria, Egypt, the Sudan, Arabia, and maybe Persia.[26] This second trip to the East lasted nearly a year. Coming back to Utica, he settled at no. 7 South Street[27] and wrote *Pre-Adamite Man*, an astonishingly learned work for a self-educated man. It is a contribution to the then current debate over human origins.

One of the objects of Randolph's travels had been to visit sites such as the megalithic temples of Malta and the Egyptian pyramids, which cast doubt on the biblical version of prehistory. *Pre-Adamite Man* draws on these experiences and on contemporary earth sciences, astronomy, paleontology, and the Enlightenment mythographers such as Godfrey Higgins. One of its conclusions is that humanity is not unitary, but that the different races have separate (though unexplained) origins. Framing it is a macro-historical scheme in which the planet between Mars and Jupiter collapsed or exploded around 58,600 years ago, knocking the earth's axis off kilter and causing the Great Flood.[28] In the near future, he added, the sun will melt the polar ice caps, the earth will swing around again to its proper position, new continents will arise, and a millennial era will begin.[29] When Randolph revised *Dealings with the Dead* as *After Death*, he predicted that the latter event would probably happen in more than eighty years' time, but certainly within the next two hundred years.[30]

On January 22, 1864, Mary Jane divorced him.[31] Randolph left the Upstate region and threw his energies into the Unionist cause. He was in Syracuse briefly in October for the National Convention of Colored Men, at which Frederick Douglass was elected president and Randolph's oratory was much admired. At the war's end this unschooled man was principal of a school for freedmen in New Orleans, which soon failed for lack of funds. His life thereafter continued its seesaw from triumph to despair and back, until its squalid end by suicide in Toledo, Ohio.

During his Upstate period, Randolph established the three pillars of his practical occultism. The first, already mentioned, was hashish. According to Deveney, Randolph was probably the largest importer of it into the United States before the Civil War,[32] though like all his commercial endeavors, it did not solve his perennial money problems. In his privately sold pamphlets he gave the recipes for extracting it from Indian hemp. Like other users of the drug, he vacillated between ecstatic praise of its powers and disgust at the dependency that it encouraged.

The second pillar was sex, on which he had both an exoteric and an esoteric point of view. As to the former, Randolph's privately distributed writings disclosed what was news to the average American male: that women might also take pleasure in sex, but that it was the man's responsibility to ensure that it was equally satisfying to both. Only then would it contribute to the physical and mental vitality of both partners. Typically, he contradicted this sound advice with his unreasoned opposition to any form of birth control. For a while he taught (for a price) the male continence practiced by the Oneida Community, but later insisted that the male and female fluids must be mingled, or "ruin" would ensue. That was the code word for the debility, blindness, insanity, and early death consequent on onanism (*coitus interruptus*), masturbation, and even excessive wet dreams. For all their progressive ideas, Randolph and Davis shared the superstitious Victorian terror of seminal waste. Unfortunately, their method threatened women, supposedly liberated from selfish male desire, with perpetual pregnancy. Randolph himself fathered at least three more children whom he was incompetent to raise.[33]

To aspiring initiates, Randolph disclosed his more secret doctrines on the uses of properly conducted sexual intercourse. It was these that the

ILLUSTRATION 14.2. House near Stockbridge, residence of Paschal and Mary Jane Randolph from 1851–1860. *Author's photograph.*

Hermetic Brotherhood of Luxor (see chapters 12 and 18) would sell to their members under oath of secrecy. One of their Randolph-derived manuscripts, "Mysteries of Eros," lists seven planes or benefits of magical sex:

I. For purposes of increasing the brain and organic force of an unborn child.

II. For influencing one's wife or husband; directing their internal thoughts, and magnetically controlling them.

III. Regaining youthful beauty, energy, vivacity and the affectional and magnetic powers.

IV. For prolonging the life of either the subject or the operator, or both, at will.

V. For the attainment of supreme command in the realms of white magic and evolving the supreme will.

VI. For the furtherance of financial schemes and worldly prosperity and success.

VII. For the attainment of the loftiest insight of nature's mysteries.[34]

The third pillar of Randolph's occultism, and probably the safest, was the magic mirror, which he came to prefer above the crystal balls used by most English scryers. He was an importer and manufacturer of a wide variety of mirrors, the luxury models being "consecrated" probably through containing sexual excretions or hashish between their two layers.[35] Mirror-gazing came to be the royal road in his program for developing the will, concentration, clairvoyant vision, astral travel, and, ultimately, contact with beings on higher planes—at which point its "safety" becomes questionable.

All of these techniques offered and demanded more than common spiritualism, which was essentially a passive activity. Séances might give the comfort of communing with the departed and the thrill of phenomena, but they required no effort of will and did not transform either sitters or mediums. Charismatic cult leaders from Ann Lee to Cyrus Teed sucked their disciples into their own orbit, some for better, others for worse. Randolph's occultism, on the other hand, meant taking responsibility for one's own evolution, and training the higher faculties as an athlete trains the physical body. He won it at the price of comfort, security, love, money, respect, and ego gratification—in short, everything that we desire in life. Therein lies his tragedy, and his immortality.

ILLUSTRATION 15.1. *Last House at Spiritualists' Springs, Kianton,* [sic] N.Y., sketch by Viola G. Cushman. *Courtesy of Special Collections, Daniel A. Reed Library, State University of New York, Fredonia.*

CHAPTER 15

Chautauqua Follies

Many centuries antecedent to the discovery of this continent by Columbus, the Valley of the Kiautone, [sic] together with an extensive fertile country surrounding it, was densely populated by a refined and highly cultivated people. They lived a pure and harmonious democracy; with them, "Reform" had done its perfect work; so that evil was wholly unknown. With them, disease, physical or moral, was never named, for they were as exempt from it as were out first parents ere they were seduced by the forbidden fruit in the Garden of Eden. They had no written Constitution—no laws—no iron customs—but were righteously governed by the impulses of their own pure and holy hearts. The marriage institution had no existance [sic] with this holy and happy people. Unrestrained Free Love was the law of the affections. Man and woman were guided by the whisperings of their attendant guardians, and met by divine opportunity. They gazed on each other with a holy pleasure—spake, always uttering the unfettered words of affection; grew rapturously happy in each other's

> society; lingered till their hearts beat ecstatic response, their hands involuntarily joined, their lips, freighted with the honey of pure love, met with a holy concussion; their spirits united and their souls' essence melted and blended as the vapors melt and blend in transparent ether—thus completing harmonial and holy wedlock.[1]
>
> *Account of the early inhabitants of Kiantone*

We have already mentioned Chautauqua County in connection with Thomas Lake Harris, who founded a vineyard at Brocton, on the shores of Lake Erie. Now we turn to the extreme south of the county, to the village of Kiantone (pronounced *Kye*-an-tone) and the extraordinary follies that went on there.

The story begins with John Chase, a blacksmith turned farmer, who owned property straddling the Pennsylvania border.[2] In 1837 or 1838, a fortuneteller had told his wife that there was a great treasure on his land, but nothing came of it; Chase tried repeatedly to sell it, and failed. Around 1850, William Brittingham (1824–1900)[3], a neighbor of Chase and a "magnetizer," learned from a clairvoyant of the treasure and also of a salt spring. Early in 1852 Brittingham took a clairvoyant to pinpoint the spot, and Chase bargained with him to dig there during the summer. The situation recalls that of Isaac Hale, who in 1825 employed Joseph Smith to dig for a Spanish silver mine reputed to be on his property (see chapter 6). But there was a large cultural shift between the "peepstone man," a fixture in rural life since Colonial times, and the use of Mesmer's technique for enhancing extrasensory perception.

This time, it worked. Brittingham and his team dug a well twenty-five or thirty feet deep at the base of a hill on the north margin of Kiantone Creek, and hit not one but two different springs, giving forth water with a slight smell of sulphur.[4] Thaddeus Sylvester Sheldon (1817/18–1868), a wealthy neighbor who lived a dozen miles away in Randolph, took an interest, and brought samples of the spring water to New York City for analysis.[5] One of those who heard his account of the Kiantone spring was James P. Greaves, a medical doctor from Milwaukee. Greaves was sufficiently intrigued to stop at Kiantone on his homeward journey late in 1852, where he gathered the information that I have summarized and made it known to the spiritualist community. He also credited reports that since September 1852, drinking or bathing in the waters has been effective in "various kinds of fevers, dyspepsia, pneumonia, rheumatism, inflammations of the thoat, burns and scalds, erysipelas, scarlatina, etc.," and urged further research.[6]

The clairvoyant who guided Chase and Brittingham worked through automatic writing, producing hieroglyphics that presumably he or she was able to translate.[7] The communicators were a race of "Celtic Red-Skins" who had inhabited the region a thousand or fifteen hundred years ago. (Compare Joseph Smith's golden tablets, likewise written in an ancient script and deposited around A.D. 500 by tribes originating in the Old World; also the Atlantean Indians said to have caused the Hydesville rappings.) The Celtic Indians said that they had covered up their spring during the invasion of barbaric hordes from the north. As to its properties, they added that since all diseases are either positive or negative in character, cure comes through the contrary qualities, negative and positive, of the twin springs. The cynical reporter in the Jamestown newspaper advised his readers just to take soap.

More details on Kiantone's beginnings appeared in Horace Greeley's *New York Tribune* in 1858, when the free love agitation was attracting national attention. The reporter tells that in spring 1853, John Chase's wife and daughter became trance mediums themselves. They revealed the courting habits of Kiantone's aboriginal inhabitants, as given at the head of this chapter. But the world they unveiled was no rustic paradise. Kiantone, they declared, had once been the site of a magnificent capital city with the benefits of advanced technology.

> The prevailing style of its architecture was copied from Nature. Every building, public or private, had a circular ground plan, and internally it was vaulted and painted blue in imitation of the ethereal canopy. Windows were not in use. Every building was lighted during the day by a gorgeous and dazzling bright solar light, and in the night by a pale lunar lamp, together with almost innumerable stellar lights bespangling the whole cerulean vaulted roof and walls of the edifice. Externally, the city was incomparably grand and magnificent. It was profusely adorned with lofty domes, turrets, spires, colonnades and battlements, all of which were wrought in a style of ornate beauty and splendor never before nor since known to architectural skill. The city was also beautified with walks, leisure grounds and gardens, wherein the hand of cultivation had brought forth the greenest and softest of swards, the most symmetrical shrubs and trees, and the rarest and richest of flowers that ever gladdened the vision of mortal man.[8]

Unfortunately, this blessed race became infected by the seeds of evil, and followed the downward path that destroys almost all nations. Among other forms of vice and immorality, according to this revelation, they instituted marriage, "bringing in its train physical and moral disease." Quarrels, bloodshed, invasions, and wars followed, until the earth took matters into her own hands. "A deep dark chasm yawned like the jaws of a hideous monster, then closed again, and the city—WAS GONE! The magnetic Springs were swallowed up. Thousands of people were buried deep in the bowels of the earth!" It is Plato's Atlantis myth all over again, and the first of many channeled or mediumistic versions, such as those of William Juvenal Colville ("The Lost Continent of Atlantis," 1884), William Scott-Elliot (*Atlantis: A Geographical, Historical, and Ethnological Sketch*, 1896), William P. Phelon (*Our Story of Atlantis*, 1905), and Frederick S. Oliver (*A Dweller on Two Planets*, 1905).[9]

John Murray Spear (1804–1884) now enters the picture. Until middle age he had served as a Universalist minister and worked tirelessly for abolition, temperance, repeal of the death penalty, and especially prison reform. In 1851 he came under the ubiquitous influence of Andrew Jackson Davis, who urged him to open himself to the spirits. Within a year Spear had become a trance medium and handed his whole life over to spirit direction. Just before coming to Kiantone, he had become the agent and communicator for an especially important group of spirits called the "Association of Beneficents."[10] They included Thomas Jefferson, Benjamin Franklin, Benjamin Rush, and John Murray (see chapter 2), the founder of Universalism who had baptized Spear and after whom he was named.[11] These august beings had decided to make an epochal push to reform humanity and usher in the millennium. To this end, they subdivided into six further associations: those of Electricizers (with Franklin at the head), Elementizers, Educationizers, Healthfulizers, Agriculturalizers, and Governmentizers. Spear's spirits liked making up new words—or was it a puckish side of his own unconscious mind?

In the heat of this commission, while preaching in Cleveland, Spear heard about the springs in Chautauqua County, and on April 14, 1853, joined a party of investigators. Urged by the Association of Beneficents, especially Rush who, as a medical doctor, knew about such things, Spear and Sheldon tried to form a consortium to exploit the medicinal waters for the benefit of humanity. But when Chase and Brittingham glimpsed the possibilities of profit, they refused to share. Not to be put off, Spear's wealthy Cleveland followers bought an adjacent farm of 173 acres with its own spring and dedicated it to his cause.[12] Spear returned to the site in June, but that was as far as it went for the time being. The spirits had more urgent priorities. Beginning in July 1853, the Association of Electricizers started giving Spear instructions for building a "New Motor."

It was an affair stranger than any fiction.[13] Spear and his dedicated team of men and women labored for nearly a year making this contraption, of which unfortunately no plans or images exist. They moved for the purpose to Lynn, Massachusetts, a town familiar to Spear, for Frederick Douglass (see chapter 13), a companion in his abolitionist efforts, had lived there before coming to Rochester. Jesse Hutchinson, a singer and spiritualist, had built a house (High Rock Cottage) and a tower where, in John Buescher's words, "he watched the skies for advancing storms, falling comets, breaching sea serpents, and other prodigies."[14] The Beneficents found the place ideal for vivifying the New Motor. It was to be both a perpetual motion machine, destined to save humanity from physical toil, and a living being infused with the life force that fills the universe. The plan was that eventually other towers would be built, one of them on Thaddeus Sheldon's property in Randolph.[15] Telepathic communication by mediums seated in them, wearing metallic garments, would eliminate the clumsy physical telegraph. Looking at today's landscape dotted with cell phone towers, one wonders whether such hare-brained schemes had a prophetic element.

The New Motor had to be brought to life through what the spirits called a "wombonic process," that is, a woman artificially suffered the pangs of childbirth in its presence. It was said that after this, some parts of the machine did actually move. But it needed a further push, which, if we read between the lines of Spear's account, involved sexual intercourse with a specially qualified man. Buescher suspects that the man in question was none other than Paschal Beverly Randolph (see chapter 14).[16]

Word of the goings-on at High Rock Tower leaked out to the inhabitants of Lynn, and in 1854 Spear's group found it prudent to leave town. Dismantling the device and stowing it in a wagon, they moved five hundred miles to Randolph and reassembled it in a shed, "where it began pulsating again, no more and no less than it had been doing before."[17] Alas, their radical notions were no more welcome there. In August a mob broke in and destroyed the Living Motor. Spear's spirit guides turned their attention to other inventions, such as a furnace for producing perpetual heat, a flying vehicle, an electric ship, and a sewing machine. The last of these really did work, but Isaac Singer turned out to have invented an even better model, and Spear's hopes for making millions came to nothing.

Meanwhile in Kiantone the magnetic springs had delivered neither a fortune to Chase and Brittingham, nor the universal benefit to humanity for which Sheldon and Spear had hoped. Chase tried to promote the spring by building a boardinghouse, but as the location was too remote it was not a success. It needed something else to lure visitors. In 1854, Spear's association directed that a utopian community be founded on the land that his followers had bought, to be called "Harmonia" or "the Domain." In June they instructed his fellow Universalist Simon Hewitt to design buildings like those of the ancient capital city: circular, domed, and painted either in pastel shades or in all the colors of the rainbow.

With their rounded contours, the houses of Harmonia were designed to correspond to the human body. Spear's writings describe how in the ideal house the domed roof corresponds to the intellect, the living room to the lungs, the dining room to the stomach, the kitchen to the intestines, the central spiral staircase to the spine, and the wiring, water pipes, etc., to the veins and nerves.[18] Hewitt, on spirit instructions, obtained a human skeleton, or rather pieced one together from various bones, in order to comprehend the plan. He slept with the blueprints under his pillow, and in the morning, "lying awake in his bed, he had electrical flashes of circles, which taught him that his rooms must be either circular or oval."[19] We will see a parallel later in the revelation of Timothy Brown's Spirit House.

Such ideas were already in the air, and in the region. In 1848 Orson Squire Fowler (1809–1887), a native of Cohocton in Steuben County, had published his influential book *The Octagon House: A Home for All.* Some thousands of American houses, large and small, followed his principles, of which hundreds survive. In 1853 Fowler finished building his own octagonal mansion at Fishkill on the Hudson, financed by his phrenology practice and publications, and everyone had heard of it. Phrenology itself rests on the same traditional doctrine of correspondences as inspired the Harmonial architecture, for it associates psychological tendencies with areas of the skull and brain. Even the titles of Spear's spiritual bureaucracy seem to be from the same awkward vocabulary as the phrenological terms: Amativeness, Philoprogenitiveness, Concentrativeness, Alimentiveness, and so on.

The Domain eventually comprised ten or twelve houses, round, oval, or octagonal and one story high.[20] Some give their diameters as sixteen to thirty feet; others, ten to fourteen feet.[21] At least one house was mounted on glass bottles or cylinders, so that it could be rotated to face the sun. Another sheltered the wreck of the New Motor.[22] After the community's demise the houses became wrecks themselves. The last oval house served until the end of the century as the summer home of an eccentric lady, and in 1907 was sketched by Viola Cushman before farmers tore it down for firewood.[23] Nothing of them now remains.

In 1855, as mentioned in the chapter 14, the Welsh reformer and industrial magnate Robert Owen organized a world conference in London to inaugurate the millennium. Owen had been converted to spiritualism by Maria Hayden, a Boston medium whom Spear's group had sent as a missionary to London two years previously, to resounding success. Now the group, hearing of Owen's plans, called Paschal Beverly Randolph from his

Stockbridge farm and Utica consulting room, and sent him to carry a message to the conference from the General Assembly of Spirits. Although a failure from Spear's point of view, it launched Randolph on his quest through society séances through Syrian hashish to Jesus and back again.[24]

By 1857, Spear's sights were again trained on western New York. In March, he organized a convention in Buffalo, followed by two in Ohio, whose theme as popularly imagined was free love, but whose esoteric significance was eugenic responsibility. The idea, which would later be a pillar of Randolph's teaching, was that sexual intercourse by consent between two loving partners would attract the higher sort of souls into incarnation, and a proper conduct of life during pregnancy would enhance the situation, for the betterment of the human race. To achieve this, women needed happiness, health, and free choice—all of which were denied them by their status as sex slaves, baby factories, and victims of unwholesome diet and dress. In short, they should choose their breeding partners, rejecting unsuitable ones even if those were their husbands, and if necessary experimenting to discover the right ones.[25] This prospect implied the use of contraception of one kind or another, which, with masturbation and homosexuality, formed the unholy trinity of the Victorian imagination. Not even the freest of free lovers had any tolerance for the latter pair.

In their wilder moments, Spear and his associates were sure that a crisis of cosmic dimensions was imminent. It was all mixed up with eugenics, for it would involve the birth of a new planet from the sun and the creation of a new human race that would unite matter and spirit. They saw their movement as educating the progenitors of this race. All this, and much more, was given to the public in Spear's great anthology of his spirit teachings, *The Educator* (1857). It seems almost banal to record that he now left his wife and children, built an octagon cottage at the Domain, and cohabited from spring 1858 with a divorced woman, Caroline Hinckley. She was soon pregnant with a miraculous child, a first harbinger of the new age.

With the New Motor a thing of the past, the Harmonial community now threw its energies into excavating a tunnel, penetrating deep into the hillside beside their spring. There was some occult connection with Caroline's pregnancy, and also with Kiantone's foundational myth. This did not begin with the Celtic Indians, who had been latecomers to the region. In the words of one early historian of Chautauqua County: "Those who dug the hole were assured by the spirits that they would find the fossil remains of a web-footed specimen of the human race, a sort of prehistoric lake dweller."[26] Another historian writes, "at a specified depth they would discover relics of a web-footed prehistoric race of human beings."[27] Half a century later, the autodidact thinker Jean-Pierre Brisset (1837–1919) would demonstrate, to the delight of the surrealists, that humans were indeed descended from frogs.[28]

The tunnel was an engineering project far beyond the community's unaided power. Sheldon and another wealthy supporter, John Montgomery Sterling, bore the cost of about twenty thousand dollars (which could have kept Spear, always on the brink of poverty, in comfort for life). It sloped steeply down and, not surprisingly, kept filling with water that had to be pumped out. The spirits promised incredible treasures just ahead, for which the women of the Domain prepared a velvet-lined casket. After penetrating about 150 feet the work was abandoned, and in time the tunnel was sealed up and forgotten. Since early descriptions are contradictory and unreliable, we take up the tale in summer 1933, when the then owner, Gerald G. Staples, rediscovered the entrance. It was closed by a massive plank door and led to a passage only four and a half feet high by three feet wide, walled with logs that were notched into the logs lining the roof and floor. The tunnel was not straight, but included steps and sharp turns to the left and right. Staples descended about fifty feet until the water level stopped him. Honoring the tunnel's creators, he held a séance at which the spirits urged him to continue, promising that he would find a chamber big enough to hold two hundred people. He declined, and instead ringed the entrance with a concrete reservoir and allowed the tunnel to refill with water.[29]

The tunnel of Harmonia reminds me of the passages of the Great Pyramid of Giza, with their steep slopes and excruciatingly low ceilings leading to chambers of unknown use. Maybe an archetype was making itself felt, and the Harmonials were swept up in it. The following year (1859) saw John Taylor's *The Great Pyramid: Why Was It Built and Who Built It*, and in 1865 Piazzi Smith, Royal Astronomer for Scotland, tested Taylor's theories through careful measurement on site. Smith was an adherent of the British Israelite movement and, like Spear, a millennialist. He staked his scientific reputation on his proof that the pyramid's passages chart the history of the world from the Creation until the Second Coming of Christ and the Millennium, which was due in 1882.

From September 15–17, 1858, Spear's group held a convention at Kiantone. Horace Greeley, beside his personal interest in spiritualism, saw the opportunity for good copy and sent a reporter for the *New York Tribune*. He and his readers were not disappointed. The long article told the history of the Domain, somewhat muddied by the passing of time. It described with sickly delicacy the lovemaking of the ancient (but not web-footed) inhabitants, and the splendor of their ancient city, as quoted above. Then the reporter moved on to the real meat of the convention. He tells how a "pale, haggard-looking woman" defied the band of five hundred rowdies to declare her own views on free love, "using disgusting, obscene language and descending to vulgar and filthy expressions." More alluring was the young woman from Cattaraugus:

> She exhibited awful contortions of her pretty face when sinking into the "trance" condition. She commenced speaking by "twitches" and "jerks," but her tongue very soon escaped from its fetters, and then, mercy on us! how it "went"! Free Love was the theme, and never did I listen to a more vehement speech. The "medium" rocked to and fro, her bosom rose and receded like the swells of the ocean. Her voice, which waxed strong and clear, rang through the elm woods and reverberated between hill and hill, her countenance, at first flushed with excitement, became as white as porcelain and almost as translucent as the morning vapor, and her whole frame quivered with intense emotion, as she screamed, "Free love! free love! it is God's law, it is Heaven's command; let not man presume to chain and imprison the heart, lead captive the young affections, and quench the divine scintillations of holy love." The young lady was evidently a little too rapturous to suit the older heads, and this fact was made known by several sharp jerks upon her dress. For a moment she exhibited signs of a "struggle within"; then she threw her head spasmodically backward, gave a loud nasal sound, like the snort of a terrified swine, opened her eyes, emerged from the trance condition, and after a few more quivers and deep-drawn sighs, subsided into her seat—and there was a calm.[30]

Upright spiritualists like Emma Hardinge Britten were terribly shocked.[31] To tar the whole spiritualist movement with the brush of free love threatened the livelihood of professional mediums. Nor did free love do any good for the women's emancipation movement: it radicalized one wing of it, which led to a conservative reaction and the passing of the Comstock Laws in 1872 (see chapter 20). Spear somehow scraped through, leaving the Domain and New York State as he embarked on yet other quixotic missions, which the interested reader can pursue in John Buescher's most readable work.

The other spiritualist movement that arose in Chautauqua County sounds staid by comparison, but its history both precedes the Hydesville rappings and continues to this day. This is the Lily Dale Assembly, a summer resort for spiritualists on the shores of Cassadaga Lake. It began in Laona, a hamlet five miles to the north that was a hotbed of liberal thought.[32] The intellectual leader there was William Johnson, who was in revolt against his father, an orthodox minister with extreme views. In the winter of 1844–45, a Dr. Moran from Vermont visited Laona and gave a course of lectures in animal magnetism and mesmerism. After Moran's departure, Johnson experimented himself, using as mesmeric subject Jeremiah F. Carter, a workman who had been given up by the physicians as sure to die of consumption. As a result, Carter was not only cured—he lived to a ripe old age—but gained clairvoyant powers. Like Andrew Jackson Davis, he could find lost objects, diagnose illnesses and prescribe cures, and discourse on physiology and medicine, of which he knew nothing in the waking state. Again like Davis, he found that he did not need to be magnetized, but could put himself into a trance state, though on awakening he remembered nothing of what he had said.

This all began two months after Davis's illumination, making Carter the second known spiritualist medium in America and predating the Hydesville phenomena by three years. Other Laonians developed clairvoyance, and the village formed its own society, first called the Laona Free Association,[33] then in 1855 the Religious Society of Free Thinkers. Twenty men paid twenty dollars each to provide a place for speakers of any creed, race, sex, or color. All the stars came, including William Denton, Paschal Beverly Randolph, Andrew Jackson Davis and his wife, Mary Fenn Davis, Samuel Brittan, John Murray Spear, and Cora Richmond. In 1870 the society took over a Universalist church for its meetings.

The move from Laona to Cassadaga Lake happened in a suitably mysterious way, Whereas Davis's revelations came from his own clairvoyance, Jeremiah Carter, like Spear, was a mouthpiece for the spirits. Carter's special control identified itself as Dr. Hedges, a physician who had practiced in Chautauqua County early in the nineteenth century. Amanda Jones (see chapter 17) wrote of them:

> Jeremiah Carter was a worthy man, a tailor, very ignorant. Some said he could not read. More awkward English, more desolate of Grammar, than his common talk, could hardly be imagined. His manners, not offensive, were wholly without polish.
>
> Dr. Hedges was a gentleman. Courteous in deportment, scholarly in language, technical when speaking of diseases (which he seemed to read as one might read a primer) choosing botanic remedies, and carefully explaining to all his patients all their properties, seeing past and present, yes, and future also within certain limits!—such, and more, appeared this Dr. Hedges.[34]

When a journalist visited the still sprightly Carter in 1895, the old man said that he had always charged fifty cents for a sitting, no more; that the physicians of Chautauqua and Cattaraugus counties were among his warmest friends; and that since Dr. Hedges came to him, his brain had enlarged by two inches. Carter then obligingly went into trance and the interview continued with Hedges.

The late doctor had strong views on contemporary spiritualism. Asked about physical manifestations, he echoed the views of Randolph, Blavatsky, and other occultists by blaming them on mischievous, silly, unevolved spirits, adding: "As long as men and women are anxious to form a magnetic circle in the dark and hear bells ring and horns toot and have musical instruments hit them over their heads, very likely the elementals will find a medium through which their wishes can be brought to pass." As to his own history, Hedges explained that he had been a social type, and after leaving the body he wanted to continue with practical work. On first entering spirit life, he had joined a band of philanthropists who were trying to form an electric battery in order to communicate with humans. Once they had mastered thought transference between the spiritual and material worlds, he saw that the time was ripe for the world to become spiritually educated. For that purpose he chose a site on Cassadaga Lake, because it had been his favorite hunting, fishing, and roving ground while he was on earth. Hedges said that he had visited every spiritualist summer assembly in the world, and found none better.

The Cassadaga site (now the area around the Leolyn Hotel and woods) belonged to a sympathetic landowner, Willard Alden. The Laona spiritualists had long used it for picnics, and they consecrated it on June 15, 1873. For three summers starting in 1877, they held large-scale camp meetings there.[35] In 1879, after Alden's death, the spiritualists bought the present twenty-acre plot next door and named it the Cassadaga Lake Free Association. This is the present Lily Dale, which has functioned ever since as a summer resort for spiritualists and a place where mediumship is a normal condition. Many have built small houses on the assembly's land, and a few live there year round. The public spaces include an auditorium, a hotel, two libraries, an assembly hall, a healing temple and a forest temple, the Andrew Jackson Davis Lyceum for children, a shop, a maze, a museum, a firehouse, the "Assembly Stump" (commemorating the first meetings) and a fairy trail in the woods. The one thing missing is the Fox cottage. Here is Arthur Myers's account of it:

> B. F. Bartlett, for many years a resident of Lily Dale, purchased the building in 1915. Since the ground on which the cottage

> stood could not be purchased, Mr. Bartlett decided to transport it to Lily Dale and make the cottage a shrine to Spiritualism. The cottage was taken down in sections, carried over country roads to the Erie Canal, placed on a barge and floated to Buffalo, N.Y. From there it was trucked to Lily Dale. The cottage was then reassembled and restored to its original appearance when it was occupied by the Fox family. It was dedicated as a shrine to Spiritualism during the summer of 1916.[36]

On February 21, 1955, the cottage burned to the ground in a fire of undetermined origin. But only the historically aware mourn its loss today, for the assembly's horizons have broadened with the times. The summer sessions now include astrology, sweat lodges, Tibetan mandalas, animal communication, dowsing, crystal healing, astral travel, spoon-bending—the whole New Age spectrum.[37]

Lily Dale feels like a miniature, even a parody, of the more solemn Chautauqua Institution, which sits beside a larger lake and has bigger houses, hotels, auditoriums, churches, and an orchestra. Chautauqua began in 1874 as a summer camp for Methodist ministers and grew into a nationwide program for adult education. Thousands come each summer to hear lectures by the big names in the liberal Christian and democratic traditions, and

ILLUSTRATION 15.2. Houses at Lily Dale, Cassadaga Lake. *Author's photograph.*

generally to improve themselves. There is no folly about Chautauqua, except in the architectural sense of a charming or eccentric landscape feature. Lily Dale has its fairy houses; Chautauqua, true to its evangelical roots, has a scale model of the Holy Land. It is near the lakeside tower, easily overlooked but well maintained. You can clamber up Mount Horeb and look down on the puddle of the Dead Sea and the trickle of the Jordan. From a God's-eye view you can contemplate the white city of Jerusalem, the size of a chessboard, with little Bethlehem a pace or two away.

Illustration 16.1. Thomas Lake Harris, founder of the Brotherhood of the New Life. From Harris, *God's Breath in Man and in Human Society*, London: E. W. Allen, 1892.

CHAPTER 16

Open Breathing

Borne down with gloomy terrors imbibed from Calvinistic dogmas, sick at heart with the doctrine of an angry and vindictive Deity, and recoiling also from the opposite extreme of disbelief in the Christian Revelation; just entering on an untried life, and almost on the verge of recklessness and perhaps ruin, we were made the subject of a heavenly visitation. Unable to sleep, pondering over the awful life-questions with heavy heart, the room which we occupied grew suddenly bright, apparently to the natural vision. It was about midnight. In the middle of the room stood a spirit, defined apparently to the external senses, clothed in spotless white, and with a golden cincture to the waist. She floated, upborne in her own radiancy. Drawing near, she laid her hand upon the aching head, and whispered words of heavenly comfort. It was the spirit of a departed mother who had lived and died in the Lord. I was only able to receive from her two great truths; but they were enough to mark the beginning of a new existence: those truths were the Fatherhood of God, and the universal

> brotherhood of man; nor could any external agency remove the fixed impression from the mind. This led us into Liberal Christianity as a substitute for the old church.[1]
>
> *Vision of Thomas Lake Harris, 1840*

If Thomas Lake Harris (1823–1906) had not written so much soporific poetry and impenetrable prose, scholars might have tried harder to make sense of him. It is a daunting task. We have Schneider and Lawton's 1942 dual biography of Harris and Laurence Oliphant, with its hundreds of quotations from them and their friends, but Harris has yet to find his Buescher or his Deveney, whose books opened up the strange worlds of Spear and Randolph to our curiosity and delight. Here I will merely lift a corner of the shroud that has kept the apostle of the "Two-in-One," the Pivotal Man, in virtual oblivion.

Harris was born in Fenny Stratford, Buckinghamshire, England. His parents immigrated to the United States when he was five years old and made their way to Utica, where his father kept a store.[2] His mother died in 1832 and was replaced by an unkind stepmother, but she later returned to comfort her son in the memorable vision recorded above. Sean Guerin, in his thesis on Harris, wonders whether it was the vision that brought about the conversion to liberal Christianity, or vice versa.[3] We cannot be sure, but often in our casebook it has taken the shock of a mystical experience to lift the angry God from a young man's shoulders.

Utica's Universalist ministers befriended the unhappy teenager, gave him an alternative home, and steered his intense religiosity into training for the ministry. In 1845 he married Mary Van Arnum and moved to New York City to take up his first pastorate. This was at the Fourth Universalist Society on Elizabeth Street,[4] where Horace Greeley, the great patron of progressive causes, sometimes attended services. For a time, Harris was just one of the city's socially active clergy, leaning at one moment to Greeley's current favorite, Fourier, and at the next to Swedenborg. A year later he learned of Andrew Jackson Davis's revelations (see chapter 11) and became an ardent, if temporary, disciple of the Poughkeepsie Seer. Harris announced that he was going to Europe to restore his health, and instead headed west on a lecture tour, promoting Davis's doctrines.[5] From New Orleans he wrote to ask Davis to use his clairvoyant powers to advise him where to go next.[6] Their relationship continued, but it never warmed. Davis recorded on November 25, 1847, that he had "entered clairvoyance to discover the location and present condition of hard-working Brother Harris." He found him growing very nervous and "susceptible to the psychological play of spirits," pursuing a very painful and unprofitable form of mediumship, and likely to mislead many. It would soon be impossible to help him, Davis concluded.[7]

Harris's judgment of Davis is equally sour. According to his disciple Arthur Cuthbert (probably repeating what Harris had told him), Davis was no devil and was doubtless sincere, but was no master of himself, thanks to Grimes's and Levingston's hypnotizing. Harris too had felt the temptation: he had visited other mediums, and gone forth as Davis's missionary to preach that the spirits of the dead are communicating with us. Then he saw that he must either adopt the rule of the spirits, or break off occult relations with them altogether. He found that he could only avoid obsession and assault by them by prayer to Jesus Christ.[8]

This decision marked a change, but not an end to Harris's mediumship. Davis, still in his early twenties, was going through a similar process, freeing himself of his controllers and managing his own clairvoyance. Both were wary of the spiritualist craze that had followed the Hydesville rappings, with its greed for phenomena, its lack of metaphysical depth, and the pathetic longings of the bereaved. Harris's next recorded experience put him in touch with a better class of communicators. Samuel Brittan, the Universalist minister who switched his allegiance from Davis to Harris, records that in March 1850, certain spirits visited Harris's house on Second Street. They were "members of a society in a poets' heaven," no less. One of them put him into a trance and showed him a book with seven seals. Harris could glimpse only a few pages, each one like a portal into another dimension. He remembered one that showed a landscape that was actually a cosmic diagram, and there were also hieroglyphs pregnant with profound meaning. The spirit promised that in four years this volume would be opened to him. That is how the spirits described the event when, four years later, Brittan asked them about it (presumably with Harris as medium).[9]

This is our third example, after Joseph Smith's golden plates (see chapter 6) and Andrew Jackson Davis's silver staff, of a young man shown a magical object and told he must wait before he could examine or possess it. We seem to be in the realm of fairytales. In fact, Harris would enjoy a lifelong relationship not just with dead poets and angels but with fairies. It is one of his few endearing characteristics.

Later in 1850, Harris's wife, Mary, died. We do not know who cared for the two infant sons, but Harris fell in with a rascally Seventh-Day Baptist, James Leander Scott,[10] and with the spiritualists of Auburn. Ever since Kate Fox's visit (see chapter 12), the city on Cayuga Lake had been sizzling with spiritualist fervor, and Scott took over one of the many groups there. It was called the Apostolic Circle because its medium, Elizabeth Benedict, rapped out communications from Saint Paul. The spirits summoned first

Scott, then Harris, and the pair uttered messages from assorted prophets, apostles, and even from the Lord himself. Emma Hardinge Britten writes that "Pope Harris" and "Cardinal Scott" managed to absorb and control nearly all the spiritualism in Auburn before disillusion set in and the city returned to (spiritualist) normality.[11]

Scott then received apocalyptic warnings and the command to lead his followers to a refuge from the wrath to come. The chosen place was Mountain Cove, Virginia,[12] where they arrived in October 1851. According to John Humphrey Noyes's informants, a number of perfectionists from Oneida and Madison Counties were among the group. The reason given for going so far away was that the Virginia location had been the original Garden of Eden, and had remained uninhabited and undisturbed by nature's convulsions ever since Adam and Eve had left it.[13]

Harris joined them in May 1852, and for the rest of the year he and Scott recorded their revelations in the *Mountain Cove Journal,* a weekly newssheet. Despite the proximity of higher worlds, despite Harris's hearing "The Throne Melodies of Planetary Orbs" and beholding the majestic planetary spirits seated upon their glorious thrones,[14] the community sank into a morass of shady property deals and fleecing of the flock.[15] The leaders insisted that they were the "Lord's chosen vessels," the "two perfect mediums," and the "two witnesses" mentioned in the Book of Revelation 11:3–11, but to no avail.[16] By late 1853 Harris was back in New York City, lecturing to spiritualists and running an independent Swedenborgian church.[17] It was called the Church of the Good Shepherd, and the sheep obliged. Horace Greeley came over to it, as did George Waring, who managed Greeley's farm in Chappaqua, and his sister Jane Lee Waring (1830–1916), heiress to a fortune of between a quarter and a half million dollars.[18] She became Harris's close companion and, in 1892, his third wife.[19]

Now a new phase of his career began. Harris had a talent for verse improvisation—not so rare in an era when poetry was much appreciated, even by readers of the popular press—and he dictated his first original work, *An Epic of the Starry Heaven.* According to Samuel Brittan, who was with him day and night, Harris was busy at the time with a new mechanical invention and preparing to move to the South, and had no preconceived plan for the work.[20] Brittan recorded all the times and places of the process: it took a total of twenty-six hours and sixteen minutes, in daily sessions from November 24 to December 8, to deliver the 150-page poem. The verses just rolled off Harris's tongue in all their variety of metrical and rhyming schemes, all their thematic originality and coherence, and with a poetic quality that critics extolled—until they learned of the source.

Samuel Brittan explained the phenomenon. Harris, he said, was permitted to receive impressions from societies of spirits who meditate deeply upon the science of forms, numbers, degrees, and their correlatives. On the poetic side, Harris was in rapport with lyric angels, introduced to them by none less than Dante himself. As for the *Epic of the Starry Heavens*, "It is given through the agency of a circle of Mediaeval Spirits who inhabit a classic domain in an ultimate dependency of the Heaven of Spirits, which corresponds in many of its features to lower Italy."[21]

The heavens and stars of this epic poem are formed around sevenfold systems of correspondence and a hierarchy of worlds. There is some kinship with Andrew Jackson Davis's cosmology, especially in the blending of physical planets with spiritual dwellings, and, as Harris's disciples were later to claim, much anticipation of theosophical ideas.[22] Musical imagery is frequent, as in Harris's poetry in general. There is a "lyre of Nature," the suns and planets are "keys of a great organ," and Christ is called the "revelation of the harmonic man." He has harsh words for abuses both social (e.g., slavery) and religious (e.g., the "great beasts of Calvinism and Rome"). The tone is apocalyptic—Harris never stopped expecting the end of the world[23]—and millennial. There are descriptions of a new, electric island like a white dome that will rise in the Pacific Ocean, and of "radiant moving shapes" floating UFO-like above the spires and streets, with millions gathering and calling to them in "pure celestial songs."[24] As in Fourier's eschatology (see chapter 11), the solar system will be transformed along with future humanity; as in Universalism, "all men to God return"; as in Mormonism, humans are potential gods ("all men kings, each on a globe"). Here is an excerpt describing the future state of the earth in terms of mid-nineteenth-century science fiction. A hundred years later, it might have substituted the word "atomic" for "electric":

> Thy world again shall wonders see—
> New creation yet to be.
> Electric steeds shall paw the air,
> Electric chariots angels bear;
> Electric ships outsail from heaven,
> By an interior will-power driven.
> Electric cannon yet shall pour
> Their fiery charge, and change the fate
> Of lands predestined to a great
> Free destiny of yore.
> Electric lions, beautiful,
> Shall seek on lower earth their kind,
> And magnetize with power of mind
> Their earthly mates, till they fulfill
> The ancient prophecy, grow mild
> And dally with the unweaned child.[25]

Harris produced two further works in a partial state of trance,[26] both book-length poems. In 1855 he published *A Lyric of the Morning Land*; in 1856, *A Lyric of the Golden Age*, dictated at Schroon Lake by the spirits of Byron, Keats, Shelley, Coleridge, and Robert Pollok,[27] with contributions by Jean-Jacques Rousseau and the god Indra. The rest of his work was written in the waking state, though this did not preclude dictation and the visible (to him) presence of angels, fairies, and demons. In March 1857 he suffered an attack from evil spirits, including the demon Joseph Balsamo,[28] who had planned a subtle scheme for his physical destruction.[29] The wily spirits impersonated great poets and dictated lively, cynical, and often humorous verse. Harris unmasked them by publishing it as *The Song of Satan: a Series of Poems, Originating with a Society of Infernal Spirits, and Received, During Temptation-Combats*. Alongside these came prose works, poems, and periodical writings too numerous to name.

Harris begins to sound slightly unhinged, but he is full of surprises. In *The Wisdom of Angels* (1857), an angel gives a new twist to the "solar myth" theory of religious origins: it tells that the most ancient peoples knew that God was a Divine Man, but so brilliant and overwhelming that they took the sun as his representative or symbol. Then comes an astonishing passage:

> They discovered that there was a difference between the idea of God impressed upon the right chamber of the brain, and the idea of God impressed upon the left chamber of the brain . . . receiving impressions from God in his Divine Love through the right lobe of the brain, and consequently through the passive, feminine or perceptive organization. . . . The most ancient peoples conceived of God in his Divine Truth through the left chambers of the brain; through the lungs, because the lungs corresponded to understanding. . . .[30]

Harris published this four years before Paul Broca's experiments with the localization of brain functions (1861), and long before it was known that the left hemisphere of the brain controls speech, logic, and analytical thinking ("Divine Truth"), and the right hemisphere imagination, creativity, and holistic thinking ("Divine Love"). There is no point in trying to establish scientific priority for Harris, but it is interesting to find some true if useless insights lurking among the psychic detritus.

In 1859 Harris took leave of his city congregation for a preaching tour of England, in which he reputedly described American spiritualists as pantheists, disbelievers in God and the Scriptures, gross sensualists, and immoral livers.[31] For part of the time he lived pleasantly in the Yorkshire

Dales, but was shocked by the poverty and squalor that he saw as the fallout from modern industry.[32] This was one factor that decided him to start another rural utopia, after the failed Mountain Cove experiment. The other was that by the time he returned to America, the Civil War was imminent. The Harrises decided to sit it out with a small group of disciples in a remote corner of Dutchess County. They started in autumn 1861 with a farm in Wassaic, then sold it and bought a farm and gristmill in nearby Amenia. Harris's followers in general were called the Brotherhood of the New Life; this center was known as "the Use." Members were assigned names by Harris, who was known as "Faithful"; Miss Waring was called "Dovie," and Mrs. Harris was "Aunt Emily," though she called herself "Lady Pink-Ears."[33]

At this point the brethren did not surrender their possessions, but submitted to Harris's spiritual instruction, which could entail humiliating or laborious tasks. The chief means of spiritual advancement was "open breathing" or "internal respiration." Harris may have found the idea in Swedenborg, who wrote quite detailed descriptions of the process, tracing its development and loss to Adamic and antediluvian times.[34] That probably set him experimenting with it and discovering some of the phenomena of *pranayama*, the yogic science of breath. Winchell Wallace, in his study of Harris's mysticism, considers internal respiration closer to raja yoga than to kundalini yoga, but adds that it owed nothing to Eastern practices. Harris, like Blavatsky, warned that hatha yoga is harmful to Westerners.[35] His disciples practiced a gentle in-and-out breath that quieted the mind and induced visions, especially when practiced for twenty minutes before sleep.[36] The theory is that with every breath one takes in not only air but influences and energies from higher planes, thereby regaining the Adamic state. Harris claimed, in all modesty, that he was the first human since the Fall to have attained perfect internal respiration, conceding that George Fox (the Quaker leader) and Swedenborg had achieved it to a very limited degree.[37] It gave him a unique status in sacred history.

Portentous events followed this discovery of the 1850s. One, which cannot be described in all its bizarre detail, was the descent of the "Lily Queen," Harris's heavenly female counterpart. By inspired improvisation on the "best piano available," he brought down her "electro-vital form" in full substantial embodiment. Lady Lily had once been human (naturally "from one of the most ancient and illustrious of the reigning families of Europe"), but had died while still a child, so as to become a queen in the spirit kingdom.[38]

The second phenomenon was the establishment in Harris of the "Two-in-One." Like many others studied here, he held that God is both male and female: two-in-one, as opposed to the three-in-one of trinitarian doctrine. Since the human being is made in the image of God, it too is a dual being. Such was Eve-Adam, says Harris, and so was Jesus, whose indwelling feminine counterpart was called Yessa. Since the Fall, however, the rest of us have lost that condition. We need to replace the animal soul, and the gross sexuality that goes along with it, with a divine soul or feminine counterpart, like Lily.

What this means for women is unclear, but that is hardly surprising since most occult instruction on sexuality is addressed exclusively to males. It may be a joke when in one of Harris's later books the militantly celibate Ann Lee appears, and the Lord promises her a man as counterpart.[39] Here is the angel Issadona, speaking his/her mind on the subject: "Woman, on the civilised earth, is a form of disease: she will so remain, till her sex enters into its form of pleasure: she carries occultly in her sex that, which if it were once made divinely operative, would enable the just man to pass bodily out of age to youth for the rounds of eternal life."[40] In other words, woman is only a vehicle for men to achieve immortality. We have heard that tale before.

No one is certain what exactly the Brotherhood of the New Life practiced. There were of course allegations of sexual irregularity, but the party line was that physical sex must cede to spiritual nuptials. Harris's true wife was not Mrs. Harris, with whom he may have had no sexual intercourse, but the immortal, golden-haired Lily Queen, with whom . . . well, one wonders.

The Wassaic-Amenia community was very different from the utopian efforts described in chapter 9. It began with Harris, his wife, his two sons, John Hampden and Thomas Lake, Jr., and about twelve chosen and invited persons.[41] They were joined by some southern landowners fleeing the war, and a group of Japanese samurai, of whom four became permanent disciples. Then there were the Oliphants. Lady (Maria) Oliphant (1809–1881) was the widow of Sir Anthony, chief justice of Ceylon and founder of that island's tea industry. Her son Laurence (1829–1888) was a globe-trotting diplomat, travel writer, novelist, barrister, war correspondent, member of Parliament, man about town, and pal of the Prince of Wales. The besotted devotion of the pair to Harris, and the high-handed ingratitude with which he treated them, stand out in the history of cults and cult leaders.[42]

While Harris relieved the wealthy Oliphants of many thousands of pounds, he was already coining money on his own. On moving to Amenia in 1863, he noticed that the fledgling community lacked a bank. He started the First National Bank of Amenia as a counter and a safe inside a one-room house. Farmers would linger there, chat, and deposit their money, to be lent out tenfold or more. Within two years Harris replaced it with the sturdy, mansard-roofed stone bank that remains today.

In 1867, irked by criticism, Harris ceased publishing his books. Thereafter his writings were privately printed for the Brotherhood of the New Life.[43] In the same year he sold the Amenia property and bought sixteen hundred acres of land in Brocton, at the other end of the state. The *New York Sun* reported that he bought half with his own money, the other half with funds from his associates.[44] For all his weirdness, he was every inch the businessman when dealing with the world. In 1867, when Harris had acquired about twenty separate pieces of property, Laurence Oliphant wrote, "Faithful received a wonderful special influx to enable him to come out from his internal states into ultimates for a time. When in this condition he has great power over external people, so that even though they may not want to sell, they cannot resist his influence when he proposes to them to do so."[45]

Vine Cliff, a beautiful farm on the shores of Lake Erie, would be the brotherhood's next center and the beginning of a new commercial venture.[46] It comprised two thousand acres, including houses for the sixty or so members, a hotel, a restaurant, a store, and above all, vineyards. By all accounts, the members slaved away at whatever tasks Harris assigned them, and thought themselves fortunate to get any personal attention from him. High-born disciples like the Oliphants were treated especially harshly, forbidden to associate with their loved ones and given humiliating tasks to stamp out their pride. When Laurence Oliphant went back to London to take his seat in the House of Commons, it was under Harris's orders not to speak; so to the general amazement this brilliant and loquacious man sat in Parliament from 1865 to 1868 without saying a word. But Harris, to give him his due, was not a mere parasite. Besides being the brains behind a large commercial operation, he was not above working at farm chores, woodwork, and helping to slaughter the cows and hogs. We read this in the 1871 diary of Kanaye Nagasawa (1856–1934), one of the samurai disciples. He dwells on Harris's intense physical and spiritual suffering, not only on behalf of the brotherhood but also for public figures (Emerson and Fowler are mentioned). For recreation, Harris would go fishing, but not in the spiritual world, where no harm is done to the fish.[47] More portentously, Harris reported on March 27, 1871 a "great encounter with the Napoleonic sphere," declaring that it had broken and that Napoleon's power would decline.[48]

The Brocton estate ran successfully enough, but Harris was still restless. In 1875 he took Lady Oliphant and other select members to a property she had bought him in California's Sonoma Valley. There he stayed for

ILLUSTRATION 16.2A. The First National Bank of Amenia, founded and built by Thomas Lake Harris, 1865; now M&T Bank. *Author's photograph.*

ILLUSTRATION 16.2B. Barn at "Vine Cliff," Brocton. Home of Thomas Lake Harris from 1867–1875, where the Brotherhood of the New Life started their first vineyard. *Author's photograph.*

seventeen years in a Georgian-style mansion, surrounded by vineyards and by those disciples who could still revere him. For those who did not, Harris had not only disinterest but malice. After the disenchanted Oliphant died in England in 1888, Harris kept muttering, "I was in at the death; I watched him die and heard him talk. *I* did it."[49]

Upon his marriage to Miss Waring in 1892, Harris moved to a luxurious apartment in New York City and spent the winters in Florida. His death in 1906 greatly disappointed those who were convinced of his immortality, and the body was cremated without more ado. His only known memorial is Thomas Lake Harris Drive in Fountain Grove, Santa Rosa.[50] But the Santa Rosa vineyard continued. Even through Prohibition, it sold grape juice and stockpiled its wares under the direction of Nagasawa, Harris's right-hand man in viniculture and eventually the sole owner of the property.[51] Before he died, Nagasawa donated 117 acres to the city of Santa Rosa for the Sonoma County Airport—now named not for Thomas L. Harris, but for the creator of the comic strip *Peanuts*, Charles M. Schulz.

ILLUSTRATION 17.1. Amanda Theodosia Jones, medium and inventor of the vacuum method of preserving fruits and vegetables. Amanda T. Jones, 1874. From *Poems 1854–1906* (New York: Alden Bros., 1906).

CHAPTER 17

Practical Spirits

He had been occasionally impressed, as he thought, by spirits from the higher life. Awaking from a peaceful sleep in his new home, and lying on his bed thinking how to build a house, he had presented before him several buildings standing out clearly in the air, as though he was to select from them. The model he adopted was thus presented at different times, and so made clear and lasting in his mind. All this, he felt, was from a favorite sister Mary. He once asked: "If this is Mary let her open the bedroom door," which swung to of its own weight usually, but which then gently opened as he laid [sic] on his bed. He once saw a luminous mist, which broke away and revealed—as if lying or floating on the air—a beautiful woman, who soon faded from his sight.

Along with this was borne in upon him the conviction that *this house must be built*, and consecrated to Spiritualism and to free speech in the service of humanity.[1]

Vision of Timothy Brown, 1860s

Timothy G. Brown (1807–1885), builder of the Spirit House in Georgetown, was a prosperous farmer and sawmill owner in Newbury, Vermont.[2] In middle life he decided to move to Madison County, maybe because Sarah, his wife, had relatives there. Starting in 1845 he cashed in his Vermont properties, bought a hundred acres north of Georgetown, flipped them for a profit, then settled on 145 acres beside the plank road to Otselic. Since the Browns had only one child (Edmund, born in 1839), Sarah was free to follow a trade of her own, and she worked at cheese making. The Browns were not rich by city standards, but at the 1860 census their worth of five thousand dollars was among the highest in the township.

Nominally a farmer, Brown could turn his hand to anything. The 1868 business directory calls him also carpenter, painter, and mason, and he almost certainly built his own farmhouse in the 1850s. He chose the newly fashionable Gothic Cottage style, but instead of decorating the steep gables with the usual pierced bargeboards, he lined them with a double row of stalactites ending in green balls.[3] It is a cheerful design that I have seen nowhere else, and a harbinger of what was to come.

Cheese making was a major industry in an area newly cleared and ideal for cows, but lacking refrigeration, and it had its own technology. In 1856 Timothy Brown filed two patents with the U.S. Patent Office: one for a metallic alloy for making "cheese hoops (essential apparatus for squeezing out the whey), and the other for a mold for casting such hoops. Through experiment, he had found the exact proportions of zinc, tin, copper, and antimony that would resist corrosion from lactic acid. It was no small thing to obtain the raw metals, smelt them with furnace and crucible, test various alloys, cast them in a mold of his own design, and make technical drawings for his patent application. Resourceful as he was, I wonder whether he had some help from the Morse factory in nearby Eaton, a prime manufacturer of steam engines.

In 1864 Timothy Brown bought a three-quarter-acre site next to Georgetown's Baptist church, and Sarah added on her own account an adjacent three acres. There Timothy built a house in obedience to the vision described at the head of this chapter. It is basically a foursquare, three-bayed, two-story frame house, whose outlines and proportions follow the Italianate style of the mid-century. But there are two unique features. Giant pilasters bulge on the corners and between the bays, carved all over with a scalloped pattern. The thousands of scallops, crisp and entirely regular, repeat on a smaller scale around the doorjambs and in the interior moldings. Above looms an oversize cornice with three rows of pendants, each one turned like a chair leg and flanked by a pair of curly brackets. Constance Noyes Robertson, a descendant of the Oneida Community, likened it to "a tiered petticoat of stiff wooden lace";[4] locals call it the Wedding-Cake House. In an era when provincial architects improvised freely on Greek, Gothic, French, and Italian themes, Brown's house wins a prize for sheer effrontery. As for the purported origin of its design, there is at least one precedent from the previous decade. Edmonds and Dexter's *Spiritualism* tells of a medium who asked his spirit friends to show him scenes and buildings actually existing in the spirit world. "In every instance the scenes were unlike anything I have ever seen, or could have imagined, for though they corresponded in general to things upon earth, yet in all cases they were distinctly different, embodying to me new and strange ideas."[5] One of them was a square dwelling house, apparently of wood, whose four sides inclined so that the windows of the three stories were flush at their bottom sills, then stood out at the top like dormers.

Local legend, and the journalists who parrot it, have long painted Timothy Brown as an inspired rustic who had never picked up a hammer, but simply let the spirits guide his every stroke. This is obviously nonsense. Architectural historians who have examined the Georgetown house note how solidly it is built, and how ingeniously the concave roof funneled rain down a central pipe into the cellar. They can tell that Brown used machine tools: a lathe, a band saw, and probably some device for gouging the scallops, perhaps driven by one of Morse's portable steam engines. But this is not to debunk the story of the house's origin. True to his mission, Brown planned the interior with a single upper room, thirty-five feet square, and called it Brown's Free Hall. For thirty years it served Georgetown and the neighboring villages as a place for assemblies, town meetings, trials, plays, dances, sugar festivals, temperance lectures, and not least for spiritualist séances. The Central New York Association of Spiritualists held their annual picnic there into the twentieth century. By 1874 the space was proving too small, so Brown bought a disused Presbyterian church, moved it down the street, and joined it to the back of the house, thus doubling the size of his assembly room.

Since the Browns' time, the Free Hall has had its ups and downs, and its preservation is a matter of local concern. Generally known as the Spirit House, it is one of Madison County's noted landmarks, but it is more than that. Brown's consecration "to Spiritualism and to free speech in the service of humanity" is a reminder of the alliance between spiritualism and the progressive movements of his time. There are very few standing monuments to that suppressed episode in the political and spiritual history of the nation. Moreover, now that the circular houses of Kiantone are gone, the Georgetown Spirit House is the only building in New York State—and perhaps beyond—whose design is directly credited to "spirits." It matters not what *we* think they are. To Timothy Brown the experience was real, and the result is architecturally unique.

Amanda Theodocia Jones (1835–1914)

Some one drew near and swept my eyelids down so that my soul could see. There was a blaze of softened light that filled all space around; and on the lift of land—Southward, between the swamp and road—I saw an edifice. It seemed an Institution—not a dwelling house—built all of brick, and wide, high, and "set four-square to all the winds that blow." One said:

"This is a home for abandoned women,—a House of Reform."

It disappeared, but still the light remained. Then it returned but in that instant "fifty years" had passed; and all around it lay a peaceful, prosperous village. First the "Home" and after that, so many other homes.

"As it will be! Promise bodily healing and you may save these lost ones!"

Then first I understood, what afterward was proven, that Yuh Heh Springs surpassed all other waters known, in curative effects. I rushed away, and in my private room fell down upon my knees, crying aloud: "My Master, let me be of use. O, give me strength to help!"

"It shall be yours to help!"

Behold at last a work! Behold a chosen and accepted servant! So the new life began.[6]

Amanda Jones's vision of her mission, c. 1870

Inventor, feminist, poet, teacher, psychic, and philanthropist, Amanda Jones was one of the many remarkable women who came out of the spiritualist movement.[7] One of twelve children of an East Bloomfield weaver, Henry Jones, and his wife, Mary Alma Mott, she lived her long life under the perennial threat of consumption and heart disease, and never married. Instead, she qualified as a teacher at East Aurora's academy, and by fifteen or sixteen was running country schoolrooms. But she never settled down. During the 1860s she lived in people's houses in return for teaching music to their children. For a while she did well in the publishing business in Chicago, editing magazines and writing children's material under various aliases. She was also a poetess, widely published and even paid for her work, as poets were in those days.[8] Her earlier verse was marked by the Civil War; later it was more nature oriented. She never had much money, and often none at all, but she had faith, and someone would always notice her plight. Her ambition, if she were ever to grow rich, was to found institutions for the rescue and reform of prostitutes and young offenders.

Though raised a Baptist, Jones naturally gravitated to the Congregational (or Progressive) Friends, the radical Quaker group already noted for its contribution to the women's rights movement (see chapter 13). From childhood, her life was full of psychic and paranormal experiences. In her *Psychic Autobiography* she writes of premonitory dreams and waking visions, especially those predicting a death; of visitations by the recently dead; telepathic messages; and inspired piano playing and dancing. After a visit by the Dentons, authors of the influential book *The Soul of Things*, she discovered her talent for psychometry: holding an object and receiving information about its past history and owners. From the moment she tried table tapping with friends in Buffalo, spiritualism became her philosophy and her faith, but she remained independent. Although she served as a vehicle for what she believed to be the spirits of the dead, she insisted that she was not a medium, had never been hypnotized or drugged, and was certainly not hysterical,[9] but rather the possessor of two distinct mental states.[10] She was conscious in both of them, but in the secondary state her ego was more an observer than an actor, and other entities could use her voice and mind, either through direct speech or automatic writing.

Jones had met Jerry Carter of Fredonia and heard his guide, Dr. Hedges, speak through him (her impressions of the séance were quoted in chapter 17). In time she acquired two guides of her own: Dr. Jonathan Andrews, who said he was a Boston physician of some eighty years ago, and J. R. Evelyn, formerly a judge in Liverpool (presumably the one near Syracuse, rather than the English city).

Dr. Andrews appeared to Jones only once.[11] It was at a séance where everyone was feeling sick and rather glum. She saw him dimly as a well-built, white-haired gentleman of fifty, who said in matter-of-fact tones: "My friend [i.e., Jones herself] was very sick some months ago. Her brother called on me for aid. Now I have taken her in charge; I have her life to save." And so he did. For five years Dr. Andrews took Jones under his wing, watching over her fragile health. The treatment of choice was the "compressed air-cure," a therapy newly imported from Europe and offered at Clifton Springs Sanitarium, near Canandaigua. Jones writes: "There during seven months I spent two hours each day, with others, in a tank lighted with plate-glass windows, breathing and living in a more than doubled atmosphere."[12] Dr. Andrews advised her, gave her energy through spirit-circles, and lectured to the small group that gathered around her. Here are two of his themes as she related them—and, we must remember, as they were spoken with her own voice:

> Once he chose to make us understand that light and music are correlative,—colors and sounds responding, each to each. This has since been demonstrated; but at the time, I half revolted. Not the less when he had finished his discourse, I seemed to be among the morning stars; and lo, they "sang together!"
>
> Once, in effect, he said: "My friend supposes that the marriage-bond on earth, if holy, must involve eternal unity. That is to say: Love's ultimate perfection may exist where all is imperfection! That is not God's way! Marriage is holy when the highest self you recognize assents. Death may dissever even such a bond. I do not say it will."[13]

The question always arises whether such entities are really suppressed parts of the personality, rather than what they declare themselves to be. If so, Amanda Jones belongs with Jane Roberts (see chapter 25) among the most enigmatic instances of multiple personality. For decades, living in full conscious control of her life and a professional writer herself, she also spoke and wrote discourses for which she had no known ability or preparation.

Around 1871 Dr. Andrews told Jones that he would be leaving her. "We hear of wonderful conditions on the planet Mars," he said. "Many spirits have been there and have returned to tell us. We have formed a company to visit Mars and be instructed, before we pass to other worlds—also inhabited."[14] He promised that the spirit of Theodore Parker would take his place. The famous Unitarian made only one intervention, to give a sermon, before Judge Evelyn entered Amanda Jones's life.

It began in May 1872, when she was staying at another healing center called Yuh Heh[15] House. This was in Barre, eight miles from Albion, where Jones had a cousin. The owner was Mrs. Collins, a widow and old acquaintance of Jones's. Her husband, speaking as a spirit, had forbidden her to sell the land, promising that it harbored valuable healing waters, oil, and minerals. She had recently developed it and discovered "magnetic waters," which, according to an advertisement, were a remedy for rheumatism, syphilis, bilious, nervous and kidney afflictions, dyspepsia, catarrh, impurity of the blood, sore eyes, and much else.[16] Jones was at first skeptical: "To tell the simple truth I had but little faith in mineral waters. I believed in blazing suns and blowing winds and double atmospheres and Graham-water gems and grape-juice, you remember."[17] But the Yuh Heh cure worked on her, and she became Mrs. Collins's friend and guest.

There was a problem. Jeremiah Eighmie, another spiritualist, had lent Mrs. Collins the money for a mortgage, and in turn received the oil and mineral rights to the property. Although he had never lent a hand or a dollar to develop it, he was now claiming half of the profits of the Yuh Heh spring. Unable to reach an agreement, Collins and Eighmie asked Jones's spirits to mediate. Thereupon something used her brain and voice and announced with great authority, "I shall adjudicate between this woman and this man. My name is J. R. Evelyn. I was once a Judge in Liverpool. I am competent in law."[18] His opinion was that spring water was not part of the rights in question, and that profits from it belonged to Mrs. Collins alone. Amazingly enough, Eighmie agreed to abide by the verdict. The judge dictated documents in impeccable legalese; they were signed and witnessed, and all remained friends.[19]

Judge Evelyn now started using Jones for his own agenda, ordering her to give a series of discourses on "social jurisprudence." It meant nothing to her as, night after night, he went on about patents, inventions, and marketable grants. He even mentioned canning. In the early summer of 1872, at the house of the Browne family in Shortsville, he dictated a longish text called the *Crusade Documents*. This was a utopian scheme for a sovereign people under the direction of a group calling themselves "Crusaders." Their object was to "rescue the sacred land from selfish monopolies, and once again raising up the standard of the chosen children of God, the Workers." This socialistic plan involved many rules, regulations, and a complex organization with bureaus of appointment, administration, investigation, education, assistance, attraction, publication, employment, and registration. There was no sexual discrimination, but the default pronouns were feminine. Beneath the earnest language I sense a Fourierist influence, and a hint of another celestial bureaucracy, John Murray Spear's Association of Beneficents (see chapter 15). However, Judge Evelyn did not involve any other spirits. Like Jones, he was an independent.

During the spring and early summer of 1872, Jones spent her days in recreation and writing for pay, with no thought of social jurisprudence, then in the evenings, as she says, "another person took my place." As soon as the transcription of the "Crusader Protocol" was complete, her host, William Livingston Browne, sealed it up in a metal cylinder and denied her further access. Before the year was out, he had printed it and registered it at the Library of Congress under his own name, as *The American Crusade*.

Jones learned of this when she happened to meet Victoria Woodhull

ILLUSTRATION 17.2. The Spirit House, or Brown's Free Hall, Georgetown. Built by Timothy Brown in the 1860s following a design received in visions from the spirit world. *Author's photograph.*

at a water cure.[20] Apparently Browne had approached the famous feminist with "his" scheme. Although Jones did not claim authorship, she resented this appropriation, which did not even mention her name or the spirit origin of the document. This led to the intervention of a living lawyer, John W. Edmonds (1816–1874), who was well known for his spiritualist sympathies. The reprint of the document in her autobiography reads: "Debarred from circulation and use by legal interference of Judge Edmonds, of New York, on behalf of the rightful owner, early in 1873."[21]

During this period, Jones's own concern, apart from her perennial plans for a women's home, was the preservation of fruits and vegetables. This was the holy grail of the burgeoning foods industry, and no one had yet figured how it could be done without cooking them first. One day she woke from her air-bath slumber and saw how to do it: "The air must be exhausted from the cells and fluid made to take its place."[22] "No spirit told me this," she added; it was her own invention.

Jones took her idea to a distant cousin, Dr. Leroy C. Cooley of Albany.[23] "These thoughts of yours are plausible," he said. "I'll try and prove them true."[24] Judge Evelyn drew up a contract between them, then in 1873 told Jones that she was henceforth on her own. There followed an arduous process for both Jones and Cooley as they scraped up money for equipment and tested various methods. It was a slow business, because they had to wait weeks to see if each refinement had succeeded in preserving the food. (Oysters were the ultimate test.) As it became clear that the process had industrial potential, Jones insisted that it should be a *women's* affair: women should own and run the business, and should work in it for a fair share of the profits.

By 1892 she had succeeded, up to a point. The *New York Press* reported: "There is a woman in Chicago who can keep a secret, and her name is Miss Amanda Jones. She is president of the Woman's Canning and Preserving Company, which conducts a business on a financial basis of $1,000,000. Miss Jones keeps locked up somewhere the secret for canning uncooked fruits, which has been the means of making her business venture a tremendous success."[25] That was not exactly how Jones saw it. Her autobiography tells of how "men slithered in." One group ran a scam to get sympathizers to buy twenty-five-dollar shares, kept the money, and were eventually arrested by the district attorney.[26] Within three years she was squeezed out of the company, which survived until 1921.

After the debacle of the Women's Canning Company, Jones's attention turned to crude oil. A visit to western Pennsylvania had woken her up to the value of petroleum, and the lack of a safe system for burning it in home furnaces. Here her autobiography is anything but psychic, for it goes into every detail of the feed valves that she invented and patented.[27] In her old age she could admit that, "I stand today with both hands full of patent values five-fold greater than at first."[28] But the longed-for women's home was never built. All she could chalk up was the rescue of a dozen women and a number of smaller acts of charity.

As for the question of spirit inspiration, Jones did not doubt that Dr. Andrews and Judge Evelyn were real people who had once lived on earth. About her inventions she was not so sure, coming as they had in the hypnagogic state (like Timothy Brown's), rather than through possession of her voice or writing. She wrote near the end of her autobiography: "Whether the things I saw were etchings traced upon the brain or pictured in the air by spirit-hands—my very own (the lower self submerged from consciousness), or other spirit hands, is not for me to say. I saw no spirit, heard no voice, received no telepathic word . . ."[29] In this she joins the more philosophical psychics such as Eileen Garrett and Jane Roberts (see chapter 25), who admit that they do not know whether what speaks through them is their own higher self or an independent entity; nor, if the latter is the case, what its nature might be. At all events, we can celebrate Amanda Jones as one of America's inventors—no need to insert the condescending "woman"—who made a lasting contribution to our lives.

PORTRAIT OF MADAME BLAVATSKY
Taken by Beardsley, of Ithaca, N.Y., in 1875, at the time of the Ithaca visit.

ILLUSTRATION 18.1. Helena Petrovna Blavatsky, photographed by Beardsley of Ithaca, 1875. From *Some Unpublished Letters of Helena Petrovna Blavatsky, with an Introduction and Commentary by Eugene Rollin Corson*, London: Rider, 1929.

CHAPTER 18

Theosophy, from Ithaca to Halcyon

Spiritualism is an experimental science. Its development, which is the aim of the Theosophical Society, will make it possible at long last to find the foundation of a true philosophy. Truth is one and is higher than all else! Theosophy is bound to wipe out such meaningless expressions, as "miracle" or the "supernatural"! . . . Everything in nature is natural, but not everything is known. And there is nothing more wonderful than its powers, whether hidden or revealed. Spiritualism—i.e., the spiritual powers of humanity and a deeper knowledge of the psychical aspects of being, which we Theosophists teach, will cure the centuries-old evils of religious strifes, owing to which the faith of men in the sacred and immemorial truths of immortality and the reward for merit is disappearing. [Alfred Russel] Wallace speaks the truth when he says that spiritualism will deserve the sympathy of moralists, philosophers, and even politicians, and of everyone who desires the perfecting of our society and our life.[1]

H. P. Blavatsky to her sister Vera de Zhelihovsky,
late 1875 or early 1876

Around September 17, 1875, Madame Blavatsky (hereafter H.P.B.) arrived in Ithaca, Tompkins County. She came as guest of Hiram Corson (1828–1911), professor of Anglo-Saxon and English literature, and his French wife, Caroline Rollin, a linguist and translator, to stay for three weeks in their house on Heustis Street.[2] It was Hiram's involvement with spiritualism that had brought about this unlikely meeting. Of course any Shakespeare scholar, as Corson was, is familiar with ghosts, fairies, and sprites, but this order of things had recently become all too real to him. In July 1874 his only daughter, Pauline, died at the age of sixteen after a long illness. Like many others, Corson reached out to mediums for comfort and reassurance. Within a week of Pauline's death he had found his way to Moravia, a village at the southern end of Owasco Lake. There lived Mary Andrews, a medium famous for materializations and for having been visited in February 1872 by Mary Todd Lincoln.[3] Mrs. Andrews's manifestations of Pauline's shape, voice, and presence convinced Corson. He became a firm believer in spiritualism and published an article to that effect in the *Cornell Review*.[4] It must have surprised students and colleagues who knew him as a model of professorial authority, scholarship, and rhetoric, but Cornell University, true to its freethinking principles, never gave him any trouble over it.

Corson had appreciated H.P.B.'s early writings, and it was he who opened the correspondence between them.[5] In reply, she made the oft-quoted statement: "I am here, in this country sent by my Lodge, on behalf of *Truth* in modern Spiritualism, and it is my most sacred duty to *unveil what is*, and expose *what is not*."[6] In the same letter she dropped the names of Raymond Lull, Pico della Mirandola, Cornelius Agrippa, Robert Fludd, Henry More, and the Kabbalistic terms *Ain Soph*, *Sephiroth*, and *Macroprosopus*, and flippantly dismissed the famous spiritualists Allan Kardec, Camille Flammarion, Andrew Jackson Davis, and Judge Edmonds as "school boys just trying to spell their *A B C* and sorely blundering sometimes." How could Corson resist so bold and flamboyant a character? He invited her to join his family during their summer vacation at Cascade,[7] a resort at the southern end of Owasco Lake, where Mrs. Andrews and her husband had bought a hotel and leased it to a clairvoyant physician.[8]

H.P.B. did not take vacations, and anyway in January 1875 she had badly injured her leg while moving a heavy bedstead in her Philadelphia apartment. By June her knee had turned black and the doctors were reluctantly getting out their bone saws. Having already warned the respectable Corsons about her Russian manners, her pug nose, her poor English, and her chain-smoking, she now threatened to come to Ithaca with a wooden leg. But willpower or her masters saw her through, and she recovered almost overnight.

The leg injury had not slowed down this indefatigable woman. Since it occurred she had married a younger man of Georgian origin, Michael Betanelly, and after a brief cohabitation deserted him. She had translated Buckle's *History of Civilization* and Darwin's *Origin of Species* into Russian. She had been to Long Island to deal with, and win, a lawsuit over some land in which she had invested her patrimony. She had delivered messages to her future colleague Henry Olcott from entities called Serapis, Tuitit Bey, and a Brotherhood of Luxor: the first appearance of the masters who would become so contentious within and without the Theosophical Society. In addition to writing for newspapers and spiritualist magazines, she had published her first doctrinal article, "A Few Questions to 'Hiraf,'" which, in Olcott's words, "laid open the whole field of thought since ploughed up by the members, friends, and adversaries of the Theosophical Society."[9] She had moved house from Philadelphia to Irving Place in New York City, and held meetings in her apartment at which the Theosophical Society was planned and named.[10] And she had decided to write "a great work treating of theology, ancient beliefs and the secrets of the occult sciences."[11] It was with this intention that in mid-September she set out on the boat to Albany, then continued her journey by train.

Once in Ithaca, H.P.B. showed little interest in its gorges, cascades, and fall foliage, and still less in meeting Cornell University's president Andrew Dickson White (see chapter 20) and his distinguished faculty. Nor did she fulfill Corson's hopes for séances and phenomena. Her one concession to domestic ritual was playing the piano, one of many accomplishments that seemed to come effortlessly to her. Otherwise she kept to her room all day and much of the night, starting what would become *Isis Unveiled*. A quarter of a century later, Hiram Corson recalled that "she would write in bed, from nine o'clock in the morning, smoking innumerable cigarettes, quoting long verbatim paragraphs from dozens of books of which I am perfectly certain there were no copies at that time in America, translating easily from several languages, and occasionally calling out to me, in my study, to know how to turn some old-world idiom into literary English . . ."[12]

With time, Corson's attitude mellowed, but he must have found H.P.B. a difficult guest. Several biographers have retold with delight how he persuaded her to go for a carriage ride to see the sights. Since propriety forbade her to be seen with him smoking, she got down and sat on a stone by the side of the road to indulge her two-hundred-a-day habit, saying, "If the country people take me for a gypsy why not, what harm would it do?" while horses, coachman, and professor waited on her.[13] That Corson thought her "a great Russian bear" was fair enough, but if she seemed to him "ignorant of all the graces and amenities of life,"[14] this scion of Russian, French, and German nobility must have been putting on an act.[15]

A happier outing was to an Ithaca photographer, with results that greatly pleased H.P.B. She ordered five dozen large prints, probably of the photograph reproduced here rather than the one with cigarette in hand, to send to her European friends and relations. As for the major preoccupation of these three weeks,[16] H.P.B. confided to her sister Vera in Russia: "All that I shall write will not be my own; I shall be nothing more than the pen, the head which will think for me will be that of one who knows all."[17] From eye witnesses we know that much of *Isis Unveiled* was produced with dissociation of her waking personality, as clairvoyant dictation or automatic writing. Eugene Corson (who missed her visit) states that she had only his father's library to hand, which contained no relevant books, and that she seldom asked his advice. Yet she told an English correspondent that in Ithaca she was "busy in the university library,"[18] and after leaving the Corsons she wrote that she had been fortunate to find at another friend's "some very precious rare works" like Godfrey Higgins's *Anacalypsis*.[19] Olcott records a letter she sent him during her visit:

> She wrote me that it was to be a book on the history and philosophy of the Eastern Schools and their relations with those of our own times. She said she was writing about things she had never studied and making quotations from books she had never read in all her life: that, to test her accuracy, Prof. Corson had compared her quotations with classical works in the University Library, and had found her to be right.[20]

On the eve of her departure, Hiram Corson found by his bedside a spirit portrait of his daughter Pauline on a sheet of special paper that, he knew, could only have come from President White's study (where H.P.B. had never been). H.P.B. attributed it to her familiar spirit of the time, John King, who had mischievously added some grinning faces in the background. When Caroline Corson saw it, she exclaimed that it was the work of the devil, burst into tears, and threw the paper into the fire.[21] H.P.B. was mortified at having upset her hostess, and soon afterward "John King" disappeared from her entourage.[22]

The awkwardness with her host was of a different nature. The inaugural address of the Theosophical Society, delivered by Olcott on November 17, 1875, in Mott Memorial Hall in New York City, ridiculed the beliefs of most spiritualists and made extravagant promises of occult phenomena that would change the world. Corson was outraged when he read the transcript, to be told that the precious contact with his daughter was probably just a trick by an elemental spirit, and that nine out of ten spirit phenomena were faked.[23] The professor wrote a long, angry letter to the *Banner of Light*.[24] H.P.B. tried to mollify him, then learned that he had referred to her as an "impostor," and penned an earnest complaint to his wife (in perfect French).[25] In time, things were patched up between them, so that by August 1878 Caroline Corson, who was planning a trip to Heidelberg, could ask H.P.B. for a letter of introduction to her friend and publisher Alexander Aksakof, to which H.P.B. warmly responded.[26]

Hiram Corson maintained his firm faith in spiritualism alongside his international reputation as a Shakespeare, Chaucer, and Browning scholar. In the last months of his life he held a series of sittings with a Boston medium, Minnie Meserve Soule. He wanted to get coherent messages from a "Band" that his wife had gathered in the spirit world after her death in 1901. Mrs. Soule was able to speak for them at dictation pace, so that Corson could record their messages verbatim. The Band included literary lions whom Corson had known, or who at least had known of him: Walt Whitman, Henry Longfellow, Nathaniel Hawthorne, Alfred Tennyson, Robert and Elizabeth Browning. From England there were Prime Minister Gladstone and the psychical researcher F. W. H. Myers. Beside his wife, Carrie, and Pauline, there were two sons who had died as babies, now all grown up and reunited in the spirit world. A band of Indian spirits, appropriately brought by Longfellow,[27] did service keeping away low-grade intruders.

The messages from these exalted spirits are coherent, beautifully phrased, and, as usual, void of any original ideas or information not already in the questioner's mind or memory. They depict a utopia in which everyone works harmoniously with their social and intellectual peers for ethical development, refined culture, and the good of the less fortunate earthlings. One might call it the Platonic form of the university, or the pipe dream of a venerable Cornell professor.

Corson never forgot H.P.B. (who had died in 1891), and on September 24, 1910, during a conversation with Pauline through Mrs. Soule, he asked after her. Here is the reply:

> She is not here, today, but she asked me to give you her kindest regards, and tell you that she never forgot your kindness to her, which she never adequately expressed her appreciation of, while she was in the body. Mamma laughs, and with a funny little smile, says, 'I had all I wanted of her. She was more than enough for one household to take care of, and I thought she would never go. She liked our home so much. I was glad when I saw the

> last of her, and yet she was fascinating in the extreme, at times. She was a wonderful medium, and was controlled to do a great work, and she had to do it in the way her spirit could be used.'[28]

H.P.B. left Ithaca for New York City on October 6, 1875.[29] On October 17 the Theosophical Society was officially organized in Emma Hardinge Britten's apartment, with Olcott as president and H.P.B. as corresponding secretary. It was at first a metropolitan affair with little resonance Upstate. After the initial burst of publicity and opposition from spiritualists, it became quite exclusive and secretive. H.P.B. herself was never out of the limelight, especially when the 1,320-page *Isis Unveiled* was published in September 1877. As Olcott put it, "she made the epoch with her book."[30] Its great theme, for those who could see the wood for the trees, was not the war between science and religion, but their reconciliation through occultism.

If "spiritualism" had been the watchword of advanced thinkers for the past thirty years, that word now was "occultism." It was about discovering the latent potentials of the human being, not just in theory but in oneself. The early Theosophists were all either involved in practical occultism, or wanted to be. Most of all they hoped to achieve "astral projection," or the separation of consciousness from the physical body.[31] Therein lay their frustration, for *Isis Unveiled* was rich in promises of the extraordinary feats of adepts, yet neither within its pages nor from any accessible teacher could aspiring occultists actually learn what to *do*.

As H.P.B.'s vision shifted eastward, the Theosophical Society ceased its regular meetings, and when she and Olcott sailed for India in December 1878, they left it in suspended animation, taking the membership list with them. Olcott appointed General Abner Doubleday (1819–1893) as president pro tempore. Doubleday was a native of Ballston Spa, a Civil War hero, and long interested in spiritualism.[32] However, he was not the person to keep Theosophy in the public eye, being content to wait indefinitely expecting instructions from India on the rites, grips, and passwords that would restart the society on a pseudo-masonic basis.[33] Consequently, almost nothing happened for the next four years.

Once again, the wake-up call came from Rochester. In 1882, Josephine Cables (1843–1917)[34] applied to form a branch of the Theosophical Society in that city. The parent society in Bombay consented, with a caveat that reflects the Rochester group's desire for practical instruction:

> I am now directed to request that you will use your discretion, as Col. Olcott's representative, as to the sending of a suitable person to Rochester to organize the Branch. You had better impress upon

> their minds the fact that the secret of occult phenomena is to be sought with the help of magnetism, the crystallic researches of von Reichenbach, the Psychometry of Buchanan and Denton, and the phenomena of mediumism. But to learn it fully one must, of course, add to all these a higher mode of research under teachers who are only accessible to the few who know where to look for them and how to reach them. If this had but been realized from the first, much disappointment felt by our members would have been avoided. The above named branches of investigation are the several steps on the flight which lead up to the higher level upon which the Adepts stand.[35]

This was the first American branch to be chartered since the parent society was founded in 1875. Doubleday asked Blavatsky's old associate Albert Leighton Rawson (1828–1902) to go to Rochester and supervise the project. Rawson found an admirably serious group. He appointed W. B. Shelley as their president, "a gentleman of very respectable social position," and as secretary Mrs. Cables, "a lady who possesses certain strange psychical powers, which she accounts for by a rational interpretation of natural law."[36] As the only active branch in America, it attracted special privileges from the society's leaders. In May 1884, Olcott decreed a "Board of Control for America" to include Cables and Shelley, empowered to admit members and grant temporary charters for new branches without requiring permission from the parent society. William Quan Judge, as Olcott's deputy, wrote Cables to say that since there was now no recording secretary in America, she was practically in charge.[37] When the board met in September, it elected Cables corresponding secretary, the post that H.P.B. herself had held in the original society.

A less friendly source described Josephine Cables as "a Christian Spiritualist, afflicted with psychic tendencies," and her journal, the *Occult Word*, as "a curious mixture of Christianity, Spiritualism, Mysticism, personal vagaries on diet, 'Asceticism,' and 'Occultism.'" The anonymous writer goes on: "Mrs. Cables gave frequent talks before the Rochester T. S., held séances, and endeavored by every means in her power to 'open up communication' with the Mahatmas."[38] These were the masters Koot Hoomi and Morya, who had been writing to the journalist A. P. Sinnett since 1880, and whose correspondence became public knowledge with the latter's *Esoteric Buddhism* (1883).

On July 4–6, 1886, the American Theosophical Society held its convention at Cables's home at 40 Ambrose Street. The whole board of control converged on Rochester, including Professor Elliott Coues of the Smithsonian, Professor Jirah Dewey Buck (a native of Fredonia) from Cincinnati, Elliott

B. Page from St. Louis, Mordecai Evans from Philadelphia, General Abner Doubleday from New Jersey, and Thomas M. Johnson from Osceola, Minnesota, editor of the *Platonist*. There were also Thomas H. Parsons of the *New York Tribune*, William Q. Judge, editor of the *Path* from New York City, Dr. William P. Phelon from Chicago, Hollis B. Page and Charles and Arthur Kendall from Boston.[39] During the meeting, a private session took place whose proceedings were leaked to the press. One does not have to swallow the following account whole in order to see what interested the Rochester group.

> The Theosophists at this session, according to the reporter's informant, produced phenomena disproving the prevalent impression that so-called supernatural manifestations have ceased since Madame Blavatsky's departure from America. . . . These incidents included cosmic and theosophic phenomena which would be startling to those unacquainted with the strange events which are said to occur when "adepts" are alone [illegible word] their powers. It was learned that one of the telegrams received from abroad during the conventions was of a doubtful character and for this reason the Theosophists determined to bring the convention into psychic communion with the party rendering it. After barring the doors, the "psychic telephone" was operated by one of the members present. The peculiar tones of Madame Blavatski [sic] were soon heard and she said: "Ha, ha! you thought I could not come here when I chose: you mistook my telegram," and then she corrected the telegram. On the occasion of sending of some telegrams abroad, the strange figure of a Hindoo, with the blazing star of India upon his breast, was visible in the "achazic [sic] light" to several persons with exalted vision. He was clearly recognized as one of the Mahamic [sic] Brotherhood, which has charge of this movement in America. So distinct are his features said to have been that a pencil portrait was drawn of him before he melted away, the outline of his face and beard being taken.
>
> One of the members, wishing some information from New York, undertook the difficult and dangerous experiment of the "projection of the double," or the sending of his astral body to New York. On recovering, he had lost all recollections of what he had done, but his presence there, declared the reporter's informant, had so impressed the person he had visited, that a telegram was received conveying the news desired. One of the gentlemen present was suffering from a severe attack of sick

> headache, and one of the ladies undertook his cure. As both were clairvoyants the operation was brought about with perfect success. The person who was cured saw the astral fluid falling upon the head of the operator, then passing out through her hands and effecting impact upon the patient's head.[40]

Rochester seemed for a while to be spearheading America's occult revival. Toward the end of the same month, Cables hosted a public meeting at her house. There was a talk on reincarnation, and Cables spoke on "The Inner Life of Man." Judge's journal, the *Path*, reported, "This is really the first public Theosophical meeting we have had in America, and marks an era. Strangely too, it occurred in Rochester, where the spiritual rappings first were heard."[41]

There was trouble in the air, though. Cables was now calling her group the Rochester Theosophical Brotherhood,[42] preparatory to severing links with the parent society. In the *Occult Word* for October–November 1886, Cables and her colleague William T. Brown published a scathing article on "The Theosophical Mahatmas." They complained that members had greatly desired to be put in communication with them, but that having received no response, they were now giving up on Eastern masters and returning to the "Essenian Master," i.e., Jesus Christ.[43]

H.P.B. had no patience with such whining. She wrote a long counter-complaint, asking if the complainers had even knocked at the right door. "Do you feel certain that you have not lost your way by stopping so often on your journey at strange doors, behind which lie in wait the fiercest enemies of those you were searching for?"[44] She mentions the need for a seven-year probation, during which the candidate must remain unswervingly faithful to the chosen master and the society he helped to found. With her typical dry humor, H.P.B. adds that the society and its founders have never offered the masters as a "*chromo-premium*[45] to the best behaved"! Finally she quotes from a message of the Maha-Chohan, chief of all the masters, which read in full: "Rather perish the T[heosophical] S[ociety] with both its hapless founders than that we should permit it to become no better than an academy of magic, a hall of occultism."[46]

H.P.B. had good cause to worry, for not only Josephine Cables but a majority of the American board of control had already joined the enemy, in the shape of the Hermetic Brotherhood of Luxor (hereafter H. B. of L., mentioned in chapter 11 in connection with the Hydesville rappings). "Academy of magic" is too grand a name for this "Ancient and Noble Order" that only started in 1884: it gave initiation by mail order. But the documents and rituals it sold, under oath of secrecy, were largely based on the teachings of Paschal Beverly Randolph (see chapter 14),[47] and they offered the instruction in practical occultism for which many Theosophists hungered. While outwardly promoting Theosophy, Cables was quietly heading one of the two American lodges of the H. B. of L.[48] In 1885 she brought to Rochester a son of Peter Davidson, the grand master of the order, to make magic mirrors for her circle's use.[49] Her combination of practical methods of spiritual development with esoteric Christianity became a major alternative to Blavatsky's Buddhism and its myth of the masters.

THE RICHARDSON COTTAGE
Temporarily occupied by Professor Corson in 1875, at the time of H. P. B.'s visit.
(*Reproduced by permission of Spence Spencer, University Book Store.*)

ILLUSTRATION 18.2. The Richardson Cottage, Ithaca, where H. P. Blavatsky stayed with Hiram and Caroline Corson in 1875 and began writing *Isis Unveiled*. Now demolished. From *Some Unpublished Letters of Helena Petrovna Blavatsky, with an Introduction and Commentary by Eugene Rollin Corson*, London: Rider, 1929.

As soon as Josephine Cables detached her group from the Theosophical Society there came the hammer blow of the "Hodgson Report" from the Society for Psychical Research, branding H.P.B. as an impostor and a Russian spy. Many members resigned, but Judge and the Americans in general remained loyal to her. After H.P.B.'s death in 1891, the Theosophy movement split apart, or in a more positive view it ramified, as one group after another sprouted off to follow its independent path.

One of these was the Syracuse branch, organized on August 30, 1893, at the home of Dr. F. G. Barnes on Cortland Avenue, with twenty-two members. They included G. W. Gerhardt as president, Dr. George J. Gladman as vice president, Dr. William H. Dower as secretary, and Mrs. G. B. Clark and Dr. F. G. Barnes as librarians.[50] For a while they held lectures, invited prospective members, etc., having allegiance to Judge and the American society. However, after Judge died in 1896, many members could not accept his successor, Katherine Tingley of Point Loma, California.[51] In Syracuse, it was Dower (1866–1937) who filled the void. Like Josephine Cables, he was not satisfied with a secondhand connection with the mahatmas, and got in touch with them, as he believed, through the medium Francia A. LaDue (1849–1922). Their chief contact was called Hilarion, a master rarely mentioned by H.P.B., hence ripe for development. (Similar instances arose later with another obscure master, Djwal Kul, channeled through Alice A. Bailey, and with the master Saint-Germain, channeled by Elizabeth Clare Prophet and others.)

In 1898, Dower and other breakaway Theosophists formed the Temple of the People, still active today, though not in Syracuse. In 1903, on the master's instructions, the group moved to California to form a utopian community at Halcyon, in San Luis Obispo County. Unlike most such groups with their dictatorial leaders, Dower's seems to have been an innocently philanthropic enterprise. He started a sanatorium that specialized in tuberculosis and addiction cure, and built a hotel beside it. The master Hilarion dictated a weighty volume called *Theogenesis*, which purported to be the completion of H.P.B.'s *Secret Doctrine*.[52] Among the members who had joined in Syracuse was the Irish poet John Varian, who also worked as a chiropractor and healer. He organized pageants with themes from Irish mythology, for which the modernist composer Henry Cowell (1897–1965) wrote music. The community's buildings include a triangular temple and a "University of Halcyon," which Harold Forgostein (1906–1990), the fourth guardian, decorated with twenty-four paintings of the legend of Hiawatha.[53] In honoring the chief who founded the Iroquois Confederacy, the Temple of the People thus recalled its Onondagan roots.

ILLUSTRATION 19.1. Cyrus R. Teed, founder of Koreshanity and revealer of the Cellular Cosmology. From Koresh, *The Cellular Cosmology*, 1898. *Courtesy of Special Collections, Hamilton College Library.*

CHAPTER 19

The Hollow Earth

It would be utterly impossible to describe the form of beauty, which was so unlike in perfectness of form, vivacity, and grace, anything I had ever witnessed. It was impersonation of Life itself. After the manifestation of the face, there appeared the neck, shoulders, and arms, equally exquisite in every detail of formation, to the very finer extremes, adorned with the most delicate, matchless, consummate finger nails, so framed as to challenge admiration.

Gracefully pendant from the head, and falling in golden tresses of profusely luxuriant growth over her shoulders, her hair added to the adornment of her personal attractiveness. Supported by the shoulders and falling into a long train was a gold and purple colored robe. Her feet rested upon a silvery crescent; in her hand, and resting upon this crescent, was Mercury's Caduceus. Suddenly she disappeared, and the twelve diamonds stood before me as twelve representative men. For a moment, all was again lost to my vision; then the Motherhood stood alone in my presence, I still invisible to myself. I addressed her,

> bowing low, or felt the consciousness of such an act, yet I saw not my own form. I only seemed to feel the impulse and motion of my mind and obeyed it.
>
> 'Most August Motherhood, I feel the sanctity of thy sacred presence. I have desired from my early childhood to know the Voice of God, and have sought for power to raise me from the thraldom of sin, and sanctify me for my heavenly Father's will. I was not cultured to know of the Divine Motherhood, only as she had an imaginary existence in the mind of the mythical. I find myself face to face with thy pure presence, and in this chastity I revel so delectably that I prefer to dwell forever in this holy ecstacy and sanctuary of my newly-acquired delight.'
>
> 'Offspring of my most potential desire,' she responded, 'thou art chosen to redeem the race.'[1]
>
> *Vision of Cyrus Teed, October 1869*

Cyrus Reed Teed (1839–1908), prophet of Koreshanity, holds an honored place among American eccentrics. What many find hilarious is his doctrine that the earth is a hollow sphere, and that we live not on the surface but on the inside, like mites in a Swiss cheese. Not only did Teed believe this, he proved it through scientific experiment, and he founded a community, the Koreshan Unity, that outlasted him by half a century.

Teed was not born to rural poverty but to a rising clan of mill owners, inventors, and professional people. His grandfather, Jesse Teed, Sr., had worked in iron foundries in Utica, and set up his own mills and foundry in Moravia. His other grandfather was the Rev. Oliver Tuttle, minister of the Baptist church at Meredith Square.[2] His uncle, Samuel F. Teed, Jr., was a medical doctor in Utica. His father, Jesse Sears Teed, invented water turbines and smaller "water motors" that produced an electric current from a natural or faucet flow. His mother, Sarah Ann Tuttle, is said[3] to have been a cousin of Emma Hale, wife of Joseph Smith, Jr., though I cannot trace the connection in the Mormon genealogies.

Cyrus was born during his parents' short residence in the booming sawmill town of Teedsville, now called Trout Creek in Delaware County.

The family may have moved to Guilford, for Cyrus's obituary says that he was from there,[4] and the Guilford Iron Works used a waterwheel of Jesse's invention.[5] They then settled in New Hartford, where Cyrus received a minimum of schooling and at the age of eleven was sent to work on the Erie Canal. That is the official story, though hard to reconcile with the family's intention that he should enter the Baptist ministry.

Cyrus chose instead to study medicine with his uncle Samuel, and chemistry on his own. He also had some early religious experience that he does not mention in his own writings. His uncle recalled that one day the youth came home and announced: "I am Jesus Christ! I see the whole world. It is opened before me."[6] At age twenty, Cyrus married Fidelia M. Rowe, a second cousin, and fathered one child, Douglas Arthur Teed (1860–1929), who became an artist of some reputation.[7] When the Civil War began, Cyrus joined the Union army but was soon invalided out. He moved to New York City to study at the Eclectic Medical College, and graduated M.D. in February 1868. By the next year we find him in the Utica city directory, prominently listed as physician and surgeon in partnership with his uncle.[8]

Eclectic medicine was a mildly antiestablishment movement that favored natural and botanical remedies, some of them derived from Native American usage, instead of the dominant practice of bloodletting, purging, and dosing with extracts of mercury, lead, antimony, and arsenic. Outside the Teeds' practice in Utica hung a sign in foot-high letters: "He who deals out poison, deals out death," referring to the druggist down the street.

In his spare time Teed studied alchemy, bringing modern electrical techniques to bear on its ancient mysteries. One day in autumn 1869, looking at his material through a microscope, he saw "minute molecules of golden dust as they fell in showers through the lucid electro-alchemical fluid."[9] He had no doubt that he had achieved transmutation, the philosophers' stone. There followed his first great vision of God in female form, of which the extract above is a short sample. It is more classical than Christian: she carries the Hermetic caduceus and calls him Horos, "offspring of Isis and Osiris." Other attributes and the general style recall the epiphany of the goddess Isis in Apuleius's *Metamorphoses, or The Golden Ass*, a Neoplatonic novel well known in the nineteenth century, which may have influenced the imaginal form that Teed's experience took, and its later literary expression.

Several weeks of intense revelations followed. The first to notice the change in the young doctor were his cousins, the Myrons. Baldwin Myron, working on a construction site, saw Cyrus approaching bathed in a halo of light. When the two men entered Baldwin's house together, his wife saw the same light enveloping them both. Already that day she had clairvoyantly perceived two cherubim perched on the wall brackets. These anecdotes come from Claude J. Rahn, one of the very last members of Teed's community.[10]

The illuminations marked the decline of Teed's medical practice and the end of normal family life, for his wife, already consumptive, took Douglas with her to her sister's house in Binghamton. It was not a violent breakup, for they remained friends, but now Teed was looking for another kind of family. He still worked as a physician, but in a sporadic and unsettled way. According to Lyn Millner's researches, he first tried Binghamton, then practiced in Trout Creek, Deposit, Cannonsville, Rock Royal, Bartlett Hollow, Apex, Equinunk (Pennsylvania), and Sandy Creek.[11] During this restless decade he visited the Harmony Society in Economy, Pennsylvania, a successful communal society with German roots. Like the Shakers, they were hardworking and celibate, and a potential field for Teed's revealed doctrine that the human race, in order to evolve, must start by giving up tobacco, alcohol, and sex.

Apropos the latter, Teed reckoned that most children are born "illegitimate," by which he meant not engendered deliberately, but the accidents of lustful intercourse. The vileness of the average male, soaked in nicotine and alcohol, passes through the sperm cells to infect the next generation, and woman has every right to protect herself against him.[12] Once celibacy becomes the rule, a remarkable evolution will take place in her: "The material elimination will be metamorphosed to psychic energy and directed to their focal point, through which these will proceed to the formation of the new immortal flesh."[13] Indeed, the goal of continence is nothing less than the alchemical transmutation of the mortal to an immortal body. No man or woman has achieved it since Jesus, whose immortal flesh and blood were due to his parthenogenetic birth (which, incidentally, shows that God has other ways to populate the earth). Jesus was able to dissolve his body, convert it to Holy Spirit, and communicate this holy substance to his twelve Apostles.[14] Our potential destiny, after many reincarnations have refined us, is no less.

Fortified by these beliefs, Teed moved to Moravia and joined his parents in running a mop-making business.[15] There he formed his first community, consisting mainly of his own relatives. The town was already a spiritualist hotbed, thanks to the Keeler family and the medium Mary Andrews (see chapter 18), but it did not take kindly to the new prophet and soon he was on his way again. His next port of call was Syracuse, where he joined his brother Oliver, another eclectic physician, in running the Syracuse Institute of Progressive Medicine (with a special department of medical electricity) from one of the best locations in the city.[16] In 1884 there came the first of several lawsuits brought by disenchanted followers or husbands whose wives had left them for Teed's community,[17] and he found it politic to leave Syracuse. With a much diminished group—Peter Hicks names four ladies, including a sister and a cousin—he now spent two years in New York City in a state of near destitution.

Salvation came in 1886 from Mrs. Thankful Hale, a patrician lady from Chicago who invited Teed to come at her expense and address the convention of the National Association of Mental Science. A full course of paid lectures followed, then another, and Teed decided that Chicago would be a more fertile field for his endeavors than New York. According to Peter Hicks, his personal magnetism attracted well-to-do, educated women of progressive principles, and his fortunes reversed accordingly. In 1891 he adopted the name of Koresh (the Persian original of Cyrus) and styled his community the Society Arch-Triumphant of the Koreshan Unity. There was a threefold hierarchy of members: investigative (sympathizers and contributors of funds); marital (couples who believed in intercourse for procreation only); and celibate-communal, who surrendered their worldly goods and lived together. By the early 1890s they occupied Beth Ophrah, a mansion in Washington Heights with seven cottages and a huge barn to serve as printing office.[18] They dated their publications, such as the weekly news magazine the *Flaming Sword,* both in the Christian and the Koreshan calendar: A.D. 1892 was A.K. 53, and so on.

Teed's Chicago period coincided with the excitement of the World's Fair (1893), which brought visitors from all over the world. It was a time for Americans to question who they were and where their country was going in the next century. From the *Flaming Sword* we can compile a list of what Koresh was for, and what he was against. In the public forum he was against money, especially gold; capitalism; millionaires; war; capital punishment; discrimination against blacks; police harassment of vagrants and tramps; immigrants who won't assimilate; the connivance of church and state; the Christian churches, especially the Catholic; the pope; belief in hell; and the doctrine that the British are the true Israelites. Among spiritual leaders and groups he was tolerant of Swedenborg, Thomas Lake Harris, Christian Science, spiritualism, and Theosophy, but considered them a total failure. A new system was essential, and that could only be Koreshanity.[19] On the positive side, Koresh and the disciples who compiled and wrote much of the magazine were in favor of a moneyless society based on credit for honest work; the humbling of the rich and mighty; the nationalization of the telegraph and telephone systems; woman suffrage; woman's rights over her body; and the Sunday opening of the World's Fair. All these topics, especially the economic ones, supplied inexhaustible rants to sustain the weekly magazine. There was also the stock-in-trade of the nineteenth-century press: articles and cuttings from other papers, anecdotes, jokes, advice to women, and advertisements. More valuable to the historian are its expositions of Koresh's own doctrines, reprinted from his earlier, unfindable periodicals the *Herald* and the *Herald of the New Covenant* (1879) and the *Guiding Star* (1880s).

We come now to the doctrine of the cellular cosmogony, which was part of the Utica revelations of winter 1869–70. Teed's expositions are pompous, verbose, neologistic, and anything but lucid. In the summary that follows, I may be projecting more sense into them than they deserve. The basic premise is that the entire universe is contained in a concave sphere or shell, which has existed from all eternity. What, if anything, is beyond that cannot possibly concern us: God and man alike are all inside. The sphere is about a hundred miles thick and has seventeen layers. Counting from the outside are seven shells made from the noble metals, the outermost being pure gold. Then come five mineral strata and five geologic strata, the inner one being the surface of the earth on which we live. It lines a concavity of about eight thousand miles in diameter, with continents and oceans just as on our globes, only curving the opposite way. Proceeding inward are three atmospheres, the first of oxygen and nitrogen, the next of pure hydrogen, the inmost of a finer substance called "aboron." Occupying the same space but in a second dimension are seven spheres of "physical spirit." In the center is the (real) sun and stellar center, a "great compound magneto-electrical battery," which generates six primary energies: "Light & Heat; Electricity & Magnetism; Levity & Gravity."

Everything in the cosmos is in motion, the chief movements being that of matter toward the center and of spirit toward the circumference. The six primary energies exist at the center in a spiritual state; as they radiate outward through the spheres they become more materialized. After reaching the earth plane they continue through the strata to the seven metallic shells, which are their ultimate, pure material deposits. Reciprocally, all waste products of the earth, animal, vegetable, and mineral rise toward the center, accumulating on the seven planetary spheres. In the process they break down into finer and finer vibrating particles until they reach the limit of physicality and enter the metaphysical condition. Thence they return, as described. So there is a perpetual alchemical dissolution and coagulation that takes place between the center and the circumference of the cosmic vessel.

It may be objected that this does not fit cosmic appearances as we know them. Koresh had answers for all this, which I will summarize. "That which we call the sun is the projected form of the occult or hidden solar center."[20] When the energies radiating from the center meet the limits of our visible atmosphere, they produce images of the sun and stars. The center also generates, by its perpetual motion, positive and negative faces that radiate heat and cold. These, reflected onto our atmosphere, cause day and night. The planets are reflections too, but from the other extreme of the system. There between the metallic shells are seven "mercurial discs" in perpetual spiral motion, which reflect on our heavens as the images of Mercury, Venus, Mars, Jupiter, Saturn, Uranus, and Neptune. The moons and rings around some of the planets reflect secondary discs moving between the shells. Our moon is situated between the first two atmospheres, where it serves as the reservoir or "terminal of the seven planetary oozings." Teed calls it "the queen of the psychic realm as the sun is king of the pneumic spheres."[21] The markings we see on it are simply the reflection of the earth's lands and oceans.

Thus Koresh accounts for the main features of our visible cosmos. Humanity is coextensive with it.[22] There are seven types of men and peoples corresponding to the seven planets. "All people, when death comes to the body, pass over into the remaining humanity, retaining consciousness in the spiritual world. Their bodies, when they pass to dissolution, pass out on the alchemico-organic energies to the physical stars, and their substances are given back to 'successive embodiments.'"[23] Reincarnation is the core of Koreshan anthropology, separating him from the spiritualists and all believers in heavens or hells, whether eternal or temporary. This, with prevalence of sevens and the doctrine of correspondence, brings him closer to the Theosophists, although his system, if it was revealed early in 1870, predates Blavatsky's.

Koresh's system seems to me more of a throwback to classical antiquity. For example, Aristotle, as well as the Stoics and Epicureans, had an uncreated, eternal cosmos energized by the constant up-and-down movement of finer and grosser elements. Pythagoras's principles of reality are pairs of opposites. Plutarch contested the doctrine—evidently current in his day—that the moon mirrors earth's oceans and continents. The Neoplatonists, notably Emperor Julian, taught that the sun we see is only the material reflection of a higher solar divinity. They also taught the return of souls to new bodies. The Hermetic writings describe the posthumous ascent through the seven planetary spheres, at each of which the former human deposits part of what was accumulated during life, before either achieving immortality or returning for another incarnation. Koresh holds that the only man to have achieved immortality in the present cycle was Jesus, for reasons mentioned above; but his Christology is too complex to summarize here. Nor can I dwell on his biblical exegesis. As we know, even the devil can quote scripture to his own advantage, and so could Koresh.

The Koreshan doctrine of cycles is also classical in flavor. Since earth and humanity are eternal, it is not troubled by the questions of their creation and age that vexed Christians and Darwinists alike. The Koreshan inner sun performs motions in a twenty-four-thousand-year cycle that divides in three ways: (1) into the twelve astrological ages of two thousand years each; (2) into seven "days," each with a night and day of about seventeen hundred years; (3) into Gold, Silver, Brass, and Iron ages of six thousand years apiece. The twenty-four-thousand-year cycle itself is one day of a week of seven such ages, ending with a sabbath and comprising a full series of creation.[24]

Koresh did not date these cycles exactly, but understood his time to be on the cusp between the Age of Pisces and the Age of Aquarius, and also near the end of the Iron Age, awaiting the next Golden Age. It was his mission to prepare for the new age by revealing the way to immortality: by performing the alchemical transmutation in the vessel of the human body, sublimating sexual into spiritual energy.

This principle made Koresh a natural ally of the Shakers. Christian Goodwillie has traced his relationship with the North Family of Shakers at Mount Lebanon (see chapter 3). The seed may have been sown in 1879 by D. M. Bennett (see chapter 20), a former Shaker who recommended Teed to his community.[25] It was not until December 1891 that Koresh, having failed in his attempt to infiltrate the Harmony Society, visited Mount Lebanon, whereupon his rise was meteoric. On July 3, 1892, the Shaker leader Frederick W. Evans confirmed the election of Koresh's close disciple Annie G. Ordway and appointed her "Shepherdess of the Gynecato of the Koreshan Unity." Soon Koresh was its Shepherd, too.[26] In a letter to him, Evans admitted that the Shakers had been a little hesitant to accept the pair, but that their doubt was cleared by the wonderful document that Koresh had sent them, plainly showing that he was a Christian and "not intending to build himself up."[27]

How wrong they were! Koresh was soon explaining in the *Flaming Sword* that Ann Lee had been an incomplete incarnation of the Motherhood, not possessing the full science of transformation which is "in the hand of the Shepherd of Koreshanity, installed such by the Shaker body."[28] Statements like that worried the Shakers, as did Koresh's urging them to open industrial plants and compete with the world's corporations. His doctrines of reincarnation and immortality jarred with Ann Lee's teachings about heaven and hell. The more Koresh bragged about the high office to which the Shakers had appointed him, the more unhappy they became. As his real beliefs and ambitions dawned on them, they regretted the whole connection, and Koresh, with characteristic hauteur, dropped them.[29]

That was the end of Koresh's New York connections. In 1894 he set his sights on Florida, and the first Koreshans began moving to Estero, twelve miles south of Fort Myers. Over the next seven years the Florida branch grew to house about two hundred members, the final seal being the move of the printing machinery from Chicago.[30] This bold venture into almost virgin territory proved remarkably successful. Koresh lived until his death among his disciples, some of whom had been with him ever since the Moravia days. Following the cellular cosmology, the central building was called the Planetary Court, which housed an inner group of seven women who managed the community's affairs.[31]

During 1896 and 1897 the Koreshans organized experiments to ascertain that the surface of the earth curves not down, but upward. They started on July 25, 1896 with telescopic sightings on a five-mile stretch of the Old Illinois Drainage Canal.[32] Over several months in early 1897 they erected an apparatus called the "Rectilineator" on the beach of Naples, Florida.[33] This was a series of twelve-foot posts projecting a perfectly straight "air line." The line began 128 inches above the sand. After four and one-eighth miles, it reached sea level, marked by a tide staff. Koresh calculated that if the earth's surface were convex, as most people believed, the line would have ended twenty-two feet *above* the water. The English polymath John Michell, in his description of the Rectilineator experiment, asks how such a meticulously planned and executed experiment could have yielded the results that it did. His answer has been a beacon to me in these studies: "Perhaps the answer lies in the malleable, obliging nature of the universe, which reflects every image projected upon it and gives every experiment a tendency to gratify the experimenter."[34]

The Koreshan community lasted another half century, until in 1961 its last four members deeded the property to the state of Florida. It is now the Koreshan State Historic Site, part of Florida's state park system, which maintains it for the pleasure of campers and outdoor recreations, and the buildings for visitors with historical interests. There one can admire the Planetary Court with its late-Victorian furnishings, a monster dynamo that powered the site, the Art Hall with its model of the hollow earth, the map of the ideal city that Koresh imagined for Estero's future, paintings by his son Douglas, musical instruments, and other mementos of the community's cultured life. While their celibacy and community of property linked them to the Shakers, they had more middle-class interests and, once the physical hazards had been overcome, prepared for their next incarnations by lifelong education.

Koresh's last years were shadowed by the hostility of the outside community and an assault by local thugs. He died in 1908, and after it became

ILLUSTRATION 19.2A. Cyrus Teed's model of the earth as a concave sphere, Koreshan State Park, Estero, Florida. A working model of the cosmological scheme revealed in Utica, 1869. *Author's photograph.*

ILLUSTRATION 19.2B. The Planetary Court in the Koreshan settlement, Koreshan State Park, Estero, Florida, built c. 1904. Here Koresh (Cyrus R. Teed) lived with seven celibate women disciples until his death in 1910. *Author's photograph.*

clear that he had not achieved physical immortality, was buried in a mausoleum that was washed out to sea in 1921. On a visit in January 2012, I was charmed by the atmosphere of the place, under the friendly and informed guidance of the museum curator, Andy Tetlow. Thanks to the visibility of this site and the acquisition of Koreshan materials by the Florida State Archives and Hamilton College Library, research on Teed's later years is blossoming, yet much remains to be discovered about his Upstate beginnings.

Illustration 20.1. Ernestine Rose, freethinker and women's rights leader. From Susan B. Anthony, *History of Woman Suffrage*, Rochester, S. B. Anthony, 1887.

CHAPTER 20

Freethought

We have all been taught by the church that nothing is so well calculated to excite the ire of the Deity as to express a doubt as to his existence, and that to deny it is an unpardonable sin. Numerous well-attested instances are referred to of atheists being struck dead for denying the existence of God. According to these religious people, God is infinitely above us in every respect, infinitely merciful, and yet he cannot bear to hear a poor finite man honestly question his existence. Knowing, as he does, that his children are groping in darkness and struggling with doubt and fear; knowing that he could enlighten them if he would, he still holds the expression of a sincere doubt as to his existence, the most infamous of crimes. According to orthodox logic, God having furnished us with imperfect minds, has a right to demand a perfect result.

Suppose Mr. Smith should overhear a couple of small bugs holding a discussion of the existence of Mr. Smith, and suppose one should have the temerity to declare, upon the honor of a bug, that he had examined the whole question

> to the best of his ability, including the argument based upon design, and had come to the conclusion that no man by the name of Smith had ever lived. Think then of Mr. Smith flying into an ecstasy of rage, crushing the atheist bug beneath his iron heel, while he exclaimed, "I will teach you, blasphemous wretch, that Smith is a diabolical fact!" What then can we think of a God who would open the artillery of heaven upon one of his own children for simply expressing his honest thought?[1]
>
> *From Robert Ingersoll's essay on "Individuality"*

Not only a cradle for mystical sects and charismatic leaders, the Upstate region also nurtured freethinkers. In one respect, the two types were equally eccentric, for they both rejected the established churches. Otherwise they were as different as could be. The freethinker, once emancipated from church, clergy, and Bible, was not about to submit to Shakerdom, believe the Book of Mormon, or take secondhand orders from spirits. This chapter treats Robert Ingersoll, the "great agnostic"; D. M. Bennett, editor of the *Truth Seeker*; and Andrew Dickson White, cofounder of Cornell University. Then we return to three women's rights leaders, Ernestine Rose, Elizabeth Cady Stanton, and Matilda Joslyn Gage.

Robert Green Ingersoll (1833–1899) was born on the shores of Seneca Lake in Dresden, Yates County, the son of a Presbyterian minister. Although his family left Dresden when he was still a baby, his birthplace there has become a small museum dedicated to his memory and principles. Alice Hubbard included his sayings in her *American Bible*, placing Ingersoll between Whitman and Emerson, which some might consider excessive tribute. It did not seem so at the time, for none was more famous as a freethinker, agnostic, secularist, infidel, atheist, or blasphemer—depending on who was speaking about him. Ingersoll's name was a byword for resistance to the Christian sects and their social, psychological, and political control. Naturally he was in favor of abolition, women's rights, tolerance of differences, and a nonpunitive attitude to children. In short, he set out the principles by which half the nation, whatever their faith, now aspires to live.

De Robigne Mortimer Bennett (1818–1882), who preferred to go by his initials, was born in Springfield, Otsego County, and received about four years of schooling in Cooperstown.[2] At fifteen he decided to join the Shakers and witnessed the "era of manifestations" in New Lebanon, where he had become the chief medical officer. In 1846 he shocked the community by leaving to marry a Shakeress, Mary Wicks, and started a new life among the world's people. The reading of Thomas Paine's *Age of Reason* decided Bennett against Christianity and for a secular humanist philosophy, and for the rest of his life he worked for progressive causes. In 1873 he founded a newspaper, the *Truth Seeker*, which is still running today; he served as vice president of the National Liberal League, and hoped in vain that Ingersoll would run for U.S. president.

From August 22 to 25, 1878, the New York Freethinkers' Association held its first convention at Watkins (now Watkins Glen), Schuyler County.[3] Bennett was a prominent supporter of the venture, and his *Truth Seeker* was to publish its proceedings. For the thousand or more participants it promised to be a pleasant outing among the beauties of the Finger Lakes and the natural wonders of the glen.[4] Many of them came by the overnight train from New York City. The speakers included the Theosophists Albert L. Rawson and James M. Peebles, some clergy who boldly defied the prevailing atmosphere, at least one Shaker (Elder Evans), and a few women, notably Matilda Joslyn Gage making her first appearance on the freethought platform.

All was soon to turn sour. A notorious free-love pamphlet called *Cupid's Yokes* was displayed for sale, and Bennett and two colleagues, Josephine Tilton and W. H. Bell, sold copies to buyers who had been put up to it by the local clergy. The police (also put up to it) immediately arrested the three for selling indecent material, in contravention of New York's recent anti-obscenity or "Comstock" law.[5] They were hauled before the local judge and released on bail of a thousand dollars each. Amy Post and Gerrit Smith's daughter Elizabeth Smith Miller posted bail for them, though the latter reneged once she had read the pamphlet.

The case seems never to have been tried, but in the following year, 1879, Bennett was arrested for sending *Cupid's Yokes* through the mail. The Comstock faction was determined to make an example of him. Ingersoll and other freethinkers lobbied desperately to persuade President Hayes to pardon him, but they failed. Bennett was condemned to thirteen months in the Albany State Penitentiary.

On his release, Bennett was either a martyr to freethought or an embarrassment, depending on how one stood on the sex question. He restored his fortunes by lecture tours, promoting his anticlerical and freethinking philosophy. This brought him ready allies in the Theosophical Society, whose founders shared his antipathy toward churches and missionaries. In the 1870s Bennett had reported on Olcott's investigations of spiritualist phenomena, and was friends with other founding members of the society. He knew the socialist book dealer Charles Sotheran, and in 1880 toured Europe with Rawson. When Bennett's lecturing took him to Bombay in 1882, he not only found a ready welcome from Olcott and Blavatsky but his arrival was announced by the Mahatma Koot Hoomi. Drop your anti-American prejudice, wrote the mahatma to A. P. Sinnett, and look out for "one of our agents (unknown to himself) to carry out the scheme for the enfranchisement of Western thoughts from superstitious creeds."[6] Bennett would probably not have welcomed the compliment, for he acknowledged no master and cast a doubtful eye on all occult claims, but he knew who his friends were.

Andrew Dickson White (1832–1918) was born in the pleasant village of Homer, Cortland County. His grandfather had emigrated from Massachusetts to become a successful farmer; his father had risen to be a banker and the richest man in the county. White's own career continued the trajectory. From Geneva College[7] and Yale to Washington and the embassies of Europe, it was brilliant from beginning to end. Yet like many such bright stars, White's would have been long forgotten had he not joined an Ithaca telegraph magnate in founding Cornell University in 1865 and becoming its first president.

Ezra Cornell (1807–1874), another Quaker turned freethinker, was born in Westchester and grew up in De Ruyter, Madison County. The university that he and White designed was unique in having no religious foundation, and in admitting women almost from its beginnings. Not everyone approved of this.[8] When the New York State Senate debated giving Cornell a land grant, nearly all the sectarian colleges sent their agents to Albany to fight the proposal. They included Genesee College (Methodist Episcopal), Hamilton College (Presbyterian), Hobart College (Episcopalian), Madison University (Baptist), Rochester University (Baptist), and Union College (Interdenominational). Ezra Cornell pacified his most persistent opponent, Genesee College, by buying them off for twenty-five thousand dollars.[9]

For all his elite education, White was on the side of the progressives. During his first academic post, at the University of Michigan, he invited Frederick Douglass as a speaker. One of Cornell's trustees was Horace Greeley, whose *New York Tribune* served as mouthpiece for White's first musings on the relationship of religion to science. After many years these matured in his *History of the Warfare of Science with Theology in Christendom* (1896). White signed the introduction in 1894 while he was minister at the U.S. Legation at Saint Petersburg, and dedicated it to Ezra Cornell.

The two volumes of White's history tell of the stupidities, bigotries, and cruelties that have justified themselves through Judeo-Christian doctrine and scripture. They also offer a layman's compendium of scientific knowledge as it stood at the end of the nineteenth century. One of the high points is the treatment of the witch scare, for which White drew on his unrivalled collection of witchcraft literature, now one of the treasures of Cornell's library. As a complacent post-Darwinian, White saw science as rescuing humanity from the slough of ignorance and bad behavior. But he was no atheist, nor even agnostic; his faith in progress applied to religion, too. He writes:

> My conviction is that Science, though it has evidently conquered Dogmatic Theology based on biblical texts and ancient modes of thought, will go hand in hand with Religion; and that, although theological control will continue to diminish, Religion, as seen in the recognition of "a Power in the universe, not ourselves, which makes for righteousness," and in the love of God and of our neighbour, will steadily grow stronger and stronger, not only in the American institutions of learning but in the world at large. Thus may the declaration of Micah as to the requirements of Jehovah,[10] the definition by St. James of "pure religion and undefiled,"[11] and, above all, the precepts and ideals of the blessed Founder of Christianity himself, be brought to bear more and more effectively on mankind.[12]

While the theory of intellectual and social history embodied in White's title seems outdated today, it was at the time the gospel of progressive thought. Stripped of the too indulgent hopes for religion, it survived two world wars as the confidence that humans, without divine interference, would steadily improve their world. White would probably be dumbfounded by today's America, where science's plans for the future are widely mistrusted, and fundamentalism far from conquered.

On a lighter note, White applied his great mind and his sense of humor to a famous hoax of the period, the Cardiff Giant,[13] a ten-and-a-half-foot sculpture of a recumbent, conspicuously male figure that now reposes in the Farmers' Museum of Cooperstown. In October 1869, William Newell, a farmer in Cardiff, Onondaga County, discovered it while supposedly digging a well, and it was instantly identified as the petrified body of an antediluvian giant. To believers, this confirmed the biblical statement, under attack from the Darwinists, that "there were giants on the earth in those days" (Genesis 6:4). White writes:

> A week after my first visit I again went to the place, by invitation. In the crowd on that day were many men of light and leading [sic] from neighboring towns,–among them some who

> made pretensions to scientific knowledge. The figure, lying in its grave, deeply impressed all; and as a party of us came away, a very excellent doctor of divinity, pastor of one of the largest churches in Syracuse, said very impressively, "Is it not strange that any human being, after seeing this wonderfully preserved figure, can deny the evidence of his senses, and refuse to believe, what is so evidently the fact, that we have here a fossilized human being, perhaps one of the giants mentioned in Scripture?"

White could tell at a glance that this was nonsense, and, taking a sample for chemical tests, he discovered that the giant was made from gypsum, a soft rock. He pointed this out to a panel of experts from Albany State University, including the state geologist, but they would not listen. Those who doubted the petrification theory claimed the giant as an ancient sculpture, possibly of Phoenician origin. White, who only wanted to save them from embarrassing themselves, wrote that Schiller's phrase kept coming to mind: "Against stupidity the gods themselves fight in vain."

Within a year the circus magnate P. T. Barnum, having failed to buy the original, was touting a replica of the giant around the country. Witnesses spoke of having spied a large wagon moving by night shortly before the excavation on the Newell farm, and soon everyone realized it was a hoax. In 1898 the perpetrator, now an old man, told the whole story. He was Newell's brother-in-law, George Hull of Iowa. The giant was his ingenious revenge on "the Rev. Mr. Turk of Ackley, Iowa, who by lungpower had worsted him in the argument as to the giants mentioned in Scripture." Hull had commissioned it from Edwin Burckhardt, a gravestone cutter in Chicago,[14] colored it to make it look old and bashed it with needles to simulate pores in the skin. Then he boxed it, shipped it by rail to Binghamton, hauled it to Cardiff at night by wagon, and he and Newell buried it before digging it up again. It seems a lot of trouble and expense, but was amply repaid by the admission fees of the thousands who came to see the giant in Cardiff, Syracuse, and Albany, and by selling it on to a syndicate. Most of all, Hull was rewarded by making the biblical fundamentalists look silly and, as a bonus, the scientific experts.

Of the three women freeethinkers under consideration here, Ernestine Potowski Rose (1810–1892) never settled Upstate, but made her presence and opinions felt there. She was born in Poland, the daughter of a rabbi, and fled her family at the age of seventeen to avoid an arranged marriage. After adventurous wanderings in Europe she made her way into London's socialist and freethinking circles. There she married a jeweler and silversmith called William Ella Rose, and came with him to New York in 1836, fearless and full of reforming zeal.

The Roses were Owenites, that is, disciples of Robert Owen, an English manufacturer and philanthropist who had founded a short-lived community (1825–27) in New Harmony, Indiana. Some of their principles were communal ownership, equality of race and gender, marriage as a secular contract, birth control, and opposition to religious authority. "Get the churches off women's necks!" was one of Ernestine's slogans.[15] In August 1843 she attended the Rochester Fourierist convention, and when she heard of John Collins's secular Skaneateles Community (see chapter 9), she sensed a promising Owenite venture. She returned to New York City and started raising funds for it, then went on to lecture in New England about the communal movement. The next spring she spoke on the three-month lecture series at Amory Hall, Boston. As her biographer, Carol Kolmerton, points out, the fact that the other lecturers included William Lloyd Garrison (the organizer), Adin Ballou, Emerson, Thoreau, and Charles Dana placed her in "powerful company."[16] She was back in Skaneateles for the summer of 1844, but broke with Collins and turned her attention to other radical causes.

During the 1850s, Ernestine Rose was a regular speaker at the radical conventions. Reports noticed her elegant costume (always mentioning the gloves), her Jewish looks, and her foreign accent. Most of all, it was her atheism that set her apart from the majority, and especially from the spiritualism with which many progressives were infatuated. At the Rutland Free Convention of 1858, the spiritualists took over and left the unbelievers only ten minutes to speak,[17] and they also dominated the Utica Philanthropic Convention of the same year (see chapter 14). Rose must have squirmed at the effusions of Andrew Jackson Davis, Paschal Beverly Randolph, and others with whom she shared the platform. Afterward she wrote that she wanted nothing to do with ghosts, and remained an infidel to her dying day.

Ernestine Rose stands at one extreme of the freethinking movement, that of militant atheism. At another extreme, Matilda Joslyn Gage found a spiritual home in Theosophy. The views of Susan B. Anthony and Elizabeth Cady Stanton fell somewhere in between. I have already discussed these women's part in the early radical movements (see chapter 13), and turn now to their later life. Much of their energy went into writing three large works: *History of Woman Suffrage* (vol. I, 1881; vols. II–III, 1882)[18] by Stanton, Susan B. Anthony, and Gage; *Woman, Church, and State* (1893) by Gage alone; and *The Woman's Bible* (vol. I, 1895; vol. II, 1898), by Stanton and a "revising committee." All three are monuments of late-nineteenth-century freethought, and shed light on the dynamics of politics, faith, and rivalry among these leaders.

Susan B. Anthony was the prime mover and publisher of the *History of Woman Suffrage*, while Stanton did most of the writing. Anthony was keen to set the record straight on her single issue—getting women the vote—and after contributing her memories of forty years she destroyed her papers. Gage worked with Stanton on the three volumes and wrote at least the first two chapters[19] and the signed closing essay of volume 1, "Woman, Church, and State." This is where our interest starts, for the essay grew from Gage's speech at the Watkins convention. She spoke for many of the women there, outraged by the clergy's sting operation and, in general, by the contempt of the churches for women's rights:

> Do you know what is the foundation principle of the three great divisions of the Christian Church—Catholic, Protestant, and Greek? The foundation is not upon Christ; not upon Paul; not upon the doctrine of immersion; it is not upon any of these, but the Christian Church is based upon the fact of woman servitude; upon the theory that woman brought sin and death into the world, and that therefore she was punished by being placed in a condition of inferiority to man—a condition of subjection, of subordination.[20]

It was the first salvo of an attack that would occupy the rest of Gage's life. Readers of the *History of Woman Suffrage* could not get beyond the first of its two thousand pages without being told that "'subjection to the powers that be' has been the lesson of both Church and State, throttling science, checking invention, crushing free thought, persecuting and torturing those who have dared to speak or act outside of established authority."[21] The closing essay documented these fighting words with hair-raising examples of clerical and judicial misogyny, contrasted with the (supposedly) honorable and equal status of women in ancient and pagan cultures.

Beset by health, family, and money troubles, it took twelve more years before Gage could amplify this charge to her satisfaction. In the meantime, Elizabeth Cady Stanton had joined her in the indictment not just of the churches but of Christianity itself. In 1883, visiting London as a break from the *History*, Stanton preached at South Place Chapel, asking, "Has the Christian Religion Done Aught for Woman?" and "showed triumphantly it had not." She added, "I felt happy and magnetic, hurling my thunder at our worst enemies."[22]

These were giddy times for Stanton. In London she mixed with Fabian socialists, including Annie Besant (1847–1933), who was still in her atheistic phase.[23] Stanton's friend Frances Lord introduced her to the Theosophical Society and to H. P. Blavatsky's works (Blavatsky herself was in India). Stanton liked the ideas of an impersonal Mind as alternative to God the Father, the identity of all souls with the universal Oversoul, and the promise of reincarnation for all.

On her return she settled down in Geneva with Elizabeth Smith Miller for six weeks to study all this. In Blavatsky's difficult but thrilling *Isis Unveiled,* they found many congenial sentiments, e.g., "If both Church and priest could but pass out of the sight of the world as easily as their names do now from the eye of our reader, it would be a happy day for humanity."[24] They read A. P. Sinnett's *The Occult World,* which told of paranormal experiences around Blavatsky in India; Anna Kingsford's *The Perfect Way,* which blended Theosophy with Gnosticism; and invited Gerald Massey, a theosophical author, to visit and instruct them.[25]

It did not last. Stanton, who had already been through spiritualism, was too much of a positivist to accept the occult teachings of Theosophy, but it gave her sympathy with those who did. When in the 1890s she began serious work on her *Woman's Bible,* several of the contributors were Theosophists or adherents of what was being called "New Thought."

Gage's commitment to Theosophy was more serious. The historian John Algeo has discovered that she joined the Rochester Theosophical Society on March 26, 1885, brought into it by Josephine Cables (see chapter 18). Matilda Joslyn Gage was thus at the nexus of three movements: women's rights, freethought, and Theosophy, all having a main theater of action in central New York.

The full title of Gage's 550-page book, published by Bennett's Truth Seeker Company, is *Woman, Church and State: A Historical Account of the Status of Woman Through the Christian Ages: With Reminiscences of the Matriarchate.* This last word alerts us to an influence from the Swiss jurist and anthropologist Johann Jakob Bachofen (1815–1887), author of *Das Mutterrecht* (Mother-Right). Gage adopted Bachofen's theory that prehistoric humans had lived under a matriarchy or gynocracy as peaceful tillers of the soil, and that the oppressive patriarchal system was a later development. Most readers would have noticed nothing peculiar or esoteric about her narrative, which goes its inexorable way piling up the evidence of man's inhumanity to woman. But Theosophists would have known her as one of theirs. She cites Volney's *Ruins of Empires,* a favorite of freethinkers for its treatment of Christianity as just another ancient cult. She repeatedly footnotes Godfrey Higgins's *Anacalypsis,* a compendium of mythologies written in the same spirit, which supplied freethinkers with ammunition against Christian supremacy and occultists like Blavatsky with ideas about ancient mysteries. Gage knew some Kabbalah, as far as it had been translated into English, and its doctrine of a dual-sexed god. Among modern works she cites *Isis Unveiled,* Kingsford's *The Perfect Way,* Samuel F. Dunlap's *Sod, Son of Man* (on Christian origins), Ignatius Donnelly's *The Great Cryptogram* (asserting that Bacon wrote Shakespeare), Mabel Collins's channeled work *Light on the Path,* and Sanskritist Max Müller's *Chips from a German Workshop.*

Compared with Andrew Dickson White's *History of the Warfare of Science with Theology*, Gage's *Woman, Church and State* is amateurish. Both were ambitious works, written to persuade a general audience, but White had every educational advantage, and the footnotes reflect his professorial care. Gage does not bother to document many of her facts or properly source her quotations: they pour out in emotional rhetoric. While White in his ivory tower sadly smiles at the contemplation of human folly, Gage is angry, and with good reason. She was angrier still when the school board of her own village of Fayetteville, after consultation with Anthony Comstock, refused to put the book in the school library.[26]

The publication of *Woman, Church and State* spurred Elizabeth Cady Stanton to finish her own project, *The Woman's Bible*. In the meantime, the two of them had split with Susan B. Anthony over the merger of two organizations: the National Woman Suffrage Association, to which Stanton, Gage, and the more radical types belonged, and the American Woman Suffrage Association, which included otherwise conservative women. Some of the latter, notably members of the Women's Christian Temperance Union, only wanted the vote so that they could enforce their social agendas. Susan Anthony, single-mindedly focused on the suffrage issue rather than on women's natural rights, saw more opportunities and better funding in the American Association, and worked to absorb the National into it. In 1888 this maneuver prompted Gage to explode to her loyal son: "Our [National] Association has been steered into an orthodox pit-hole by Miss Anthony and her aids—and it needs not only a strong will, but money to put us back. You would scarcely believe that even Mrs. Stanton has been dictated to and outrageously treated by Susan and some of her young aids."

When representatives met at the National's 1889 convention in Washington, Gage was visiting her children in Dakota and could not afford the extra travel. The vote was held near midnight, when many members had left, and as one historian writes, "the remaining group of tired and unsuspecting women approved the new constitution without giving it much thought."[27] To add insult to injury, Anthony proposed Stanton as president of a new "National-American" association. Incredibly, Stanton accepted, though it made no difference to the lifestyle she now enjoyed: one of leisurely visits to her children in Europe and occasional writing on religious questions from the freethinking point of view.[28]

Gage was now alienated from both of her former comrades-in-arms. In 1890 she founded the Woman's National Liberal Union. According to Algeo, it was largely funded by the Aldriches (i.e., by Josephine Cables and the rich husband she had married in 1889), but all the burdens fell on Gage, and it did not last long. Meanwhile, Stanton felt compromised in her alliance with the Christian and prohibitionist wing, and in 1893 she invited her friends in the women's movement to join a revision committee for the projected anti-Bible.

Some of them, not wanting to be associated with such a freethinking project, surprised her by declining. Gage accepted, and contributed more pages than any of the other collaborators, with the understanding that the work would be copyrighted in both Stanton's name and her own. It was not.[29]

Stanton was quite straightforward in stating her beliefs:

> The only points in which I differ from all ecclesiastical teaching is that I do not believe that any man ever saw or talked with God. I do not believe that God inspired the Mosaic code, or told the historians what they say he did about woman, for all the religions on the face of the earth degrade her, and so long as woman accepts the position that they assign her, her emancipation is impossible.[30]

—and her anticlericalism, with its implied wake-up call to women to stop supporting an institution that despises them:

> It is truly pitiful to see the deceptions that have been played upon the people in all ages and countries by the priests in the name of religion. They are omnipresent, ever playing on human credulity, at birth and death, in affliction and at the marriage feast, in the saddest and happiest moments of our lives they are near to administer consolation in our sorrows, and to add blessings to our joys. No other class of teachers have such prestige and power, especially over women.[31]

Stanton, who was now eighty, sometimes forgets that the whole thesis of the book is that the Bible is not to be believed, and excuses it like a liberal-minded Sunday school teacher. How did Elijah ascend to heaven in a chariot of fire? "Probably Elijah knew how to construct a balloon. Much of the ascending and descending of seers, of angels and of prophets which astonished the ignorant was accomplished in balloons—a lost art for many centuries."[32] And whenever some biblical male behaves with unaccustomed courtesy towards women, Stanton is quick to hold him out as an example to modern men.

Some of the revising committee wrote at a higher critical level. Frances Ellen Burr contributed an essay on the Kabbalah, based on McGregor Mathers's recent *Kabbalah Unveiled*,[33] which proved that "man and woman are from the creation co-equal and co-existent, perfectly equal, one with the other."[34] Ursula N. Gestefeld, a future Christian Scientist, valued the Bible as concealing mystical truths. Thus for her, the seven leading characters of Genesis (Adam, Enos, Noah, Abraham, Isaac, Jacob, and Joseph) "represent the seven chief stages of the soul's existence which follow each

ILLUSTRATION 20.2. Matilda Joslyn Gage Home, Fayetteville. Home of the women's rights leader and her husband, Henry Hill Gage, from 1854 to 1898. *Author's photograph.*

other like the notes in the musical scale. It is our own experience that is there portrayed, both present and prospective."[35] Lucinda B. Chandler interprets the temptation of Eve in Neoplatonic fashion as the descent of the soul, the feminine part of man, into the limitations of matter.[36] Gage, like Blavatsky and the Enlightenment mythographers, finds sun- and star-lore: Elijah's chariot of fire is a record of sun worship, and the Queen of Sheba was testing King Solomon with astronomical and astrological questions.[37] All the names of places in the Hebrew holy land are astronomical, and the Seven Churches of Asia of Revelation are the seven planets.[38] Gage honors the Sabeans of Arabia, an "occult body," as the source of Eastern wisdom, "from which it also radiated to the British Isles of Europe at the time of the Celtic Druids." From their descendants, the Spanish Arabs, "Columbus first learned of a world beyond the Pillars of Hercules."[39]

Such esoteric commentary must have been incomprehensible to the average purchaser of *The Woman's Bible*. Gage acknowledged this with her parting shot: "But our present quest is not what the mystic or the spiritual character of the Bible may be; we are investigating its influence upon woman under Judaism and Christianity, and pronounce it evil."[40]

The first volume of *The Woman's Bible* appeared in 1895, containing comments on the Pentateuch.[41] As expected, the clergy did their best to ban it from bookshops and libraries. In their eyes, to dissect and criticize the Bible was bad enough, but that *women* should do so was an outrage. More disappointingly, the book was panned from another side as being a century out of date in its scholarship, harking back to the eighteenth-century Deists and ignoring the Higher Criticism of the German school. Worst of all, it threatened the ancient friendship between Stanton and Anthony, who had no sympathy for New Thought or Besant-led Theosophy. Anthony and her allies thought the book would do the women's suffrage movement more harm than good, by offending its growing Christian contingent.

It did indeed, and the reaction was swift. At the annual convention of the National-American Woman Suffrage Association, held in Washington in January 1896, the resolution was proposed "That this Association is non-sectarian, being composed of persons of all shades of religious opinion, and that it has no official connection with the so-called 'Woman's Bible,' or any theological publication."[42]

Anthony loyally spoke against the motion, but after long and animated discussion it was carried. When the second volume limped into print in 1898, with comments on the books from Joshua to Revelation, Stanton made no secret of the controversy. An appendix of letters and comments aired disagreements between the critics and even within the revising committee. The book closed with the resolution from the 1896 convention and a transcript of Anthony's speech, so that she could not deny that she had once been Stanton's ally.

Susan Anthony lived long enough to elbow Stanton out of the collective memory, in which Ernestine Rose was long erased and from which Gage, too, had been dropped. For a century Anthony was the very image of the women's rights movement. In 1999 Ken Burns and Paul Barnes did Stanton justice in their documentary film *Not for Ourselves Alone: The Story of Elizabeth Cady Stanton and Susan B. Anthony*. The next year, Leslie Brammer's *Excluded from Suffrage History: Matilda Joslyn Gage, Nineteenth-Century American Feminist* did the same for Gage, albeit for a smaller audience. In 2010 Sally Roesch Wagner's long campaign for Gage's recognition succeeded with the opening of her former home to the public. Now each of the trio has her place of pilgrimage: Anthony's Victorian brick house in Rochester, Stanton's frame farmhouse in Seneca Falls, and Gage's Greek Revival home on the main street of Fayetteville.

ILLUSTRATION 21.1. James Martin Peebles, minister, medium, and world traveler. From J. O. Barrett, *The Spiritual Pilgrim: a Biography of James Martin Peebles*, Boston: William White & Co., 1872. *Courtesy of Special Collections, Hamilton College Library.*

CHAPTER 21

Oz and Ends

At the time of which I write, Ozma's best friend and most constant companion was a little Kansas girl named Dorothy, a mortal who had come to the Land of Oz in a very curious manner and had been offered a home in Ozma's palace. Furthermore, Dorothy had been made a Princess of Oz, and was as much at home in the royal palace as was the gentle Ruler. She knew almost every part of the great country and almost all of its numerous inhabitants. Next to Ozma she was loved better than anyone in all Oz, for Dorothy was simple and sweet, seldom became angry and had such a friendly, chummy way that she made friends wherever she wandered. It was she who first brought the Scarecrow and the Tin Woodman and the Cowardly Lion to the Emerald City. Dorothy had also introduced to Ozma the Shaggy Man and the Hungry Tiger, as well as Billina the Yellow Hen, Eureka the Pink Kitten, and many other delightful characters and creatures. Coming as she did from our world, Dorothy was much like many other girls we know; so there were times when she was not so wise as she

> might have been, and other times when she was obstinate and got herself into trouble. But life in a fairy-land had taught the little girl to accept all sorts of surprising things as matters-of-course, for while Dorothy was no fairy—but just as mortal as we are—she had seen more wonders than most mortals ever do.
>
> *From L. Frank Baum,* The Scarecrow of Oz, *chapter 2*

After ending the last chapter with Matilda Joslyn Gage's denunciation of the patriarchy, we turn to her son-in-law, L. Frank Baum (1856–1919), one of the most popular children's authors of all time. Baum was born in Chittenango, a busy service station for the Erie Canal, where his father, Benjamin Baum, manufactured barrels for shipping liquids, butter, etc. After his factory burned in 1860, Benjamin cut his losses and browsed the richer pastures of Syracuse. He became a petroleum and property dealer, the founder of a bank,[1] and owner of theaters both in and out of state. By 1866 he had settled his family on a beautiful estate called Roselawn, to which he added a gentleman's farm of some 160 acres.[2] All of Frank Baum's biographers mention the influence of this idyllic childhood home, and of an early passion for the stage. Like his father, Frank would lurch from wealth to bankruptcy and back again, and he inherited Benjamin Baum's resilience and capacity to make the best of every circumstance.

Although neither the Chittenango log house nor the Syracuse mansion stands today, the quiet canal village is proud of its native son and sports a yellow brick path along its main street. It awakens each summer when thousands of fans arrive for a festival called the Oz-Stravaganza, with processions, costumes, celebrities of stage and screen, and experts on Baum's oeuvre. In Michael O. Riley's words, "The Oz phenomenon can be bewildering to critics and other adults who were not exposed to Baum's stories as children."[3] I am one of those, having grown up in postwar England oblivious of Baum's books and even the 1939 movie with Judy Garland. I suppose they were considered too vulgar and American by those who knew what was good for us.[4] So I have taken the shortcut to Oz, which leads via Matilda Joslyn Gage: Baum's mother-in-law, his support through hard times, and his spiritual awakener.

Frank married Maud Gage in 1882, while he was trying to make a living as an actor. Matilda was not thrilled by this match, but she soon took to her son-in-law and spent months at a time with Frank and Maud in Dakota Territory (where all her children had gone) and Chicago. Her house in Fayetteville became a second home to them, and her blend of feminism, freethought, spiritualism, and Theosophy became the moral and spiritual undercurrents of Baum's fictional world. We will take them one by one.

Strong female figures are as prominent in the Oz mythos as they are absent, say, in Tolkien's *Lord of the Rings*, though like everyone else they are fair game for Baum's sense of parody.[5] Dorothy Gale is America's answer to Lewis Carroll's Alice, though she started out a little younger (the 1900 edition shows her aged about six, Munchkin-sized) and more proactive. Guided by the light of reason and a firm sense of justice, she makes her sure-footed way among a cast of inadequate males. Her mentor is a good witch, and Oz, once the Wizard has departed, is a matriarchy ruled by a sorceress. Just so, Matilda Gage exalted the archaic matriarchal state that was supplanted by the rule of men. She defended the witches who were persecuted and burned because they were too wise and threatening to the patriarchy.[6] This might have been her own fate had she lived before the Age of Enlightenment.

The Freethought Trail, a web-based tourist guide to sites in New York State, includes Baum along with Matilda Gage, Robert Ingersoll, Andrew Dickson White, Mark Twain, the birth-control advocate Margaret Sanger, and other nineteenth-century opponents of religious authority. When Baum was editing the *Aberdeen Saturday Pioneer* in Dakota, he used a comic character called "Our Landlady, Mrs. Bilkins," to mock organized religion and point out how much paganism survived in Christianity.[7] Baum's utopias have no God, ministers, or churches. Instead, there is a sense of a fundamentally good creation in which every being, however lowly or grotesque, deserves respect and the freedom to be itself. The Wizard's unmasking at the climax of *The Wonderful Wizard of Oz* seems to me pure Gnosticism: the doctrine that humanity is kept servile and ignorant by the demiurge, a low-grade god who pretends to be the creator of all. Rebecca Loncraine takes it in a broader, political sense: "Baum's story is a particularly devastating critique of power not only because it attacks false and undeserved authority, but because it shows how easily people who lack belief in themselves can become willing participants in the deceptions practiced by manipulative figures who rule over them."[8]

Baum never expected *The Wonderful Wizard of Oz* to be a best-seller. He published five other books in 1900, and probably had more hopes for *The Art of Decorating Dry Goods Windows and Interiors*.[9] After young readers clamored for more, Oz changed from being a place of disillusion from which Dorothy returns home to Kansas, into a desirable realm in which she eventually becomes a princess. As in Fourier's utopian phalanges, there is no money there; people work half the time and play half the time.[10] As in the Arts and Crafts ideal, to which Baum was also attracted, they enjoy the one as much as the other. Michael Riley writes that if Oz is not a version of heaven, at least it is an earthly paradise, like the utopian visions of William Morris and Edward Bellamy (author of *Looking Backward*).[11]

Baum knew that to paint a world similar to ours but more colorful and richer in possibilities, especially for children, is the recipe for writing successful children's literature. But maybe Oz is not of this world at all. Spiritualism offers a clue. Matilda Gage regularly took part in séances, as did Maud and Frank Baum, at least when Matilda was visiting them.[12] Both the Baum and Gage families had lost a number of infants, and spiritualism offered the consolation that they were living on in what spiritualists since Andrew Jackson Davis (see chapter 11) had called the "Summer Land": a place of beauty and happiness where dead babies and children continue their development in spirit bodies. The quotation at the head of this chapter, whether intended or not, could easily be read in that sense.

The influence of Theosophy on Baum's imagination should have been common knowledge since 1973, when Michael Patrick Hearn devoted several pages to it in *The Annotated Wizard of Oz*.[13] John Algeo, one of the few prominent Theosophists in the academic world, elaborated on it during the 1980s, but it still did not register. Few literary critics, after all, have studied Blavatsky's *Isis Unveiled*, as we know that Frank and Maud Baum did in Dakota during the summer of 1888. Four years later, in Chicago, they joined the Ramayana Lodge of the Theosophical Society, where their sponsors were William P. Phelon (mentioned in chapter 18 in connection with the Syracuse Theosophists) and his wife, M. M. Phelon. In between, Baum used his editorial columns for the enthusiastic promotion of theosophical and kindred ideas.[14] Baum's more recent biographers, to their credit, have begun to investigate what it was about Theosophy that appealed to him. At the other extreme from scholarly neglect are those who interpret Baum's work as theosophical allegory in its every detail: the silver shoes represent the *muladhara chakra*, the golden cap the *sahasrara chakra*, etc. Such ideas circulate on the Internet, as does the contrary interpretation of Baum's work as part of a mind-control plot by the Illuminati.[15] I cannot imagine Baum as either so learned in esotericism, or so meticulous a planner, as to have written the elaborate romans à clef in which these exegetes believe. Instead, I sense a theosophical atmosphere around Oz, as surely as there is a Christian atmosphere around Harry Potter's world or C. S. Lewis's Narnia.

By the end of the century, Theosophists had turned from studying Blavatsky's difficult writings to those of Charles Leadbeater and Annie Besant. Interest shifted from comparative religion to the astral world, clairvoyance, the masters, elemental spirits, and reincarnation—all rich in possibilities for fantasy writing. Meanwhile, the doctrine of reincarnation superseded the spiritualist view of the afterlife. In later theosophical teachings, influenced by Eastern philosophies, the dead after a period of rest come back to earth, perhaps even reborn in their own families. (Frank and Maud were certain that they had known each other in past lives.) As for the phenomena of the séance room, Blavatsky had attributed them either to the cast-off "shells" of the dead or to mischievous elementals: gnomes, undines, sylphs, salamanders, elves, fairies, sprites, *longaevi*, etc. Baum's world is as full of fairies as Thomas Lake Harris's (see chapter 16), and the parallel is not so far-fetched. Katharine Rogers writes: "Baum's fairies and fairyland are so concretely realized because, as a theosophist, he believed they had spiritual or subjective reality. In his imagined world, which is not sharply distinguished from the world in which we live, divine or at least extraordinary presences are all around, many of whom devote themselves to watching over children and other living things."[16] She also mentions the theme of animal rights that runs strongly through Baum's works, a cause dear to the Theosophists for whom every creature is on the evolutionary path to perfection.

Baum, like many artists, felt more like a medium or channel for his stories than as their exclusive creator. Loncraine, with her usual insight, writes of how he lived in a culture preoccupied with access to the spiritual world: "In understanding his creativity as a form of spirit possession, Baum disowned his imagination. He believed in Oz as a semi-real place, as he half believed in the astral plane, his own reincarnation, and in ghosts."[17] This, as we know, was a culture in which whole books like the Book of Mormon, *The Principles of Nature*, or *The Epic of the Starry Heaven* had come down ready-made. Closer to home, when William Phelon sponsored the Baums' membership of the Theosophical Society he had probably written, though not yet published, a book of which he claimed to be merely the mouthpiece. Phelon's *Our Story of Atlantis* told of a land in the distant past with magicians both male and female, mysterious technologies, flying machines, magic mirrors, an emphasis on colors, and the presence of elementals. Like other channeled or clairvoyant accounts of Atlantis, Lemuria, the Summer Land, Devachan, the astral plane, etc., Phelon's book reads like amateur fantasy fiction, rich in color but poor in humor, irony, and character development.[18] From the theosophical point of view, Baum, with his semi-automatic writing and his half-beliefs, was doing something more valuable. He was seeding children's minds so that they might bear fruit later in life—or in later lives.

This chapter concludes with sketches of two other cases of a now familiar syndrome: that of the Universalist minister who feels wider horizons beckoning. The first is James Martin Peebles (1822–1922), who lived to see the rise and fall of most of the movements treated here. His fame too has evaporated, but in his time he could land anywhere in the world and count on being feted and offered a lecture tour. By the end of the century he had visited nearly every state in the Union and circled the globe three and a half times.[19]

Peebles was born in the same Vermont village, Whitingham, as the Mormon leader Brigham Young (1801–1877), and grew up in the same region of Chenango County.[20] The Youngs had settled near Sherburne; the

Peebles in Smithville. James's father had been a Vermont militia officer, and his mother, once her eight children were raised, taught school. Smithville was near the prosperous village of Oxford, on the new Chenango Canal. Peebles was already working as a schoolteacher in Pitcher and Upper Lisle[21] when he enrolled at Oxford Academy, chartered in 1794 as one of only four academies west of the Hudson.[22] He learned Latin and Greek, and set his sights on the ministry. A later outburst reflects the spiritual tension and fears, felt even in these backwaters, which sent him and many others into the Universalist fold:

> I recently saw in a catechism used in the Methodist church questions and answers embodying the most pernicious doctrines. In this the young were taught that they were by nature an enemy of God, heirs of perdition, and that everlasting torment was their portion if they failed to be converted. Contrast with those doctrines the teachings of the lyceum [Universalist school]: that we are heirs of God, ever progressing towards perfection and endless happiness. What infinite difference![23]

Even before he was formally ordained, Peebles started preaching at the Universalist church of McLean, a village in Tompkins County near the future spiritualist center of Freeville. The McLean congregation liked the sensitive, elegant young preacher well enough to reappoint him for five successive years (1842–46). In 1846 he took the pastorate of Kelloggsville (1846–49), with responsibility for the Universalists of Genoa and Mottville as well.[24] He worked in Oswego, where he was remembered for opening his pulpit to Amelia Bloomer (wearing her eponymous outfit), and then in Elmira (1853–55). Greater things seemed in prospect when the Universalist Society of Baltimore invited him to be their pastor, but within a year (1856) he had quit. Peebles's preaching of abolition and distributing Greeley's radical *New York Tribune* were too much for this slave-owning city. Hurt and sickly, Peebles retreated to his wife's town of Canton, New York, to rethink his career.

Anyone as valiant in the causes of abolition, women's rights, temperance, anti-tobacco, prison reform, anti-capital punishment, pacifism, vegetarianism, freethought, and dress reform was sure to encounter spiritualism. In Peebles's last year at Kelloggsville, a fellow Universalist persuaded him to visit Auburn to hear the spirit rappings. The phenomena impressed but did not convince him. It took an all-night session with the Davenport brothers, popular performance mediums who subjected the astonished minister to every trick in their book,[25] to bring about his complete conversion. That was in Cleveland, when Peebles was on his way to Minnesota to join a cousin in the real estate business. By the time he got there, he was ready to turn around and resume preaching. For six years he led the progressive First Free Church of Battle Creek, Michigan, where his flock included Sojourner Truth (the former Isabella van Wagenen; see chapter 8).

Peebles was an inspiring speaker and a fluent writer, but he lacked psychic gifts. For contact with the spirit world he relied on mediums, especially Charlie (Elisha Charles) Dunn (1840/41–1916), a fifteen-year-old runaway whom he discovered in a circus and undertook to reform. Their close relationship raised some eyebrows. Some said that Peebles was traveling with a young woman dressed as a man.[26] Colonel Bundy, scourge of fake spiritualists, mentioned Peebles's "long practice of an unmentionable crime against nature."[27] Once tamed, Dunn turned out to be an excellent medium. The spirits spoke readily through him, and he demonstrated levitation and immunity to fire.[28] During their long sea voyages in 1872–74, Dunn gave Peebles almost daily communion with the other world.[29]

Like Hiram Corson and John Murray Spear (who admired Peebles and named him "the Elucidator"), Peebles had a personal band of spirits, a mixture of family, celebrities, and mysterious strangers. He wore a cross inscribed with their nine names: Lorenzo Peebles (one of James's brothers), Canà (an unidentified "positivist"), James Leonard (unknown), Madame Elizabeth (sister of Louis XVI, 1764–1794), Hosea Ballou (Universalist minister, 1771–1852), Mozart (composer, 1756–1791), Perasee Lendanta (a male, Italian spirit), Aaron Nite (a Yorkshireman, died c. 1600), and John W. Leonard (a disguise for St. John the Divine).[30]

During the Civil War, Peebles took leave from his Michigan flock to support the Union effort in Alabama and Tennessee. He ministered to the wounded and dying, and worked as a clerk in the quartermaster's department, gaining respect for his handling of large sums of money.[31] After the war he was part of the Congressional Indian Peace Commission. In company with five generals and two colonels, he spent the winter of 1867–68 visiting the tribes of California and the Northwest "for the purpose of organizing treaties, stopping the shedding of blood, and befriending them in their natural rights to a living on the American continent."[32] Everywhere he went, Peebles admired and defended native peoples, and after this excursion even General Sherman agreed that the Indians were "cheaper to feed than kill."[33]

On his return, Peebles announced his intention to visit spiritualists in Europe and then to see the Holy Land. A new career in diplomacy loomed when President Grant appointed him United States Consul in Trebizond, a strategic trading city in Turkey. The title had its uses as Peebles passed through England, Scotland, France, Italy, and Greece, always drawn to the centers of spiritualist activity. Once in Turkey, he could not wait to get away. He respected Islam, as he did every religion, but was never comfortable in the Muslim world,[34] and the Black Sea air sickened him. He soon left Trebizond, with his companion Dunn, to traipse at leisure through Sicily, Naples, Rome, and Florence.

In the latter city Peebles cheerfully joined in the Anti-Ecumenical Council or Congregation of Free Thinkers of late 1869, an event staged in opposition to Pius IX's First Vatican Council that was busy declaring papal infallibility. Insofar as he was capable of hatred, Peebles loathed the pope. He was happy among freethinkers (we have already mentioned his speaking at the 1878 Watkins Convention), and comfortable with Theosophists, despite Blavatsky's demeaning comments about the spirits in whom he put his trust. He called her "Blavatsky the irrepressible . . . writing huge volumes of wisdom, of sense, nonsense, and undemonstrated theories heavily seasoned and spiced with ancient Hindoo mythology."[35]

Historians of the Theosophical Society have noticed that he appeared as though on cue at crucial points of its development. While Peebles was in Cairo in 1873, he gathered the only independent testimony for the "Spiritualist Society" that Blavatsky had started there two years before. In 1874 he was attending the Eddy Brothers' séances at Chittenden, Vermont, when Blavatsky and Olcott first met each other there.[36] The Buddhist and Hindu friends whom Peebles made in London in 1870 and on his first trip to Ceylon and India would act as the magnet to draw Blavatsky and Olcott to the East in 1878. He visited Olcott in Adyar in 1897 and, like Blavatsky and the colonel, took Buddhist vows, but never ceased to call himself a Christian.[37]

On returning to the United States, Peebles emulated his friends Andrew Jackson Davis and Albert Rawson by qualifying as a (sort of) M.D. His degree came from the high-sounding Philadelphia University of Medicine and Surgery, an "eclectic" medical school that operated from 1860–75 and was thereafter a diploma mill.[38] In his second half-century he enjoyed security and celebrity, collecting a long list of honors and memberships of learned societies and even a bishopric.[39] Peebles is yet another example of someone raised in the Upstate region with no apparent prospects of fame or fortune. Once exposed to the swirling currents of the day, his native cunning and ambition took fire and led him first to circle the region, then the globe, preaching the dual gospel of spiritual optimism and social reformation.

As for Charlie Dunn, in 1897 he wrote affectionately of Peebles, but said that he had not seen him for twenty years. He had returned from their round-the-world trip with ten thousand dollars in gold, partly earned by speculating in ostrich feathers and cashing them in, to great profit, in Paris. He then enjoyed life to the full, first as a performing medium, then as an M.D. (eclectic, of course), to become one of the chief citizens of Rockford, Illinois. Dunn proved as adept at exploiting the material world as he had been with the world of spirits. Being fined for bribing a utility company made hardly a ripple in his ascent to becoming a city alderman and owning a magnificent house, several automobiles, and a private museum.[40]

Jesse Charles Fremont Grumbine (1861–1938) took a different route, ending in the borderland between occultism and New Thought. He was born in Cincinnati and educated at the University of Cincinnati and St. Lawrence University in Canton, New York (a Universalist foundation).[41] Following ordination, in 1884 he became clerk of the Cayuga Universalist Association,[42] and from September 1, 1885 to February 1, 1888, pastor of the First Universalist Society of Syracuse.[43] Here he fell foul even of this tolerant denomination, becoming a zealous supporter of the antipoverty movement of Henry George (promoter of the Single Tax) and Father Edward McGlynn. The pope had excommunicated McGlynn in July 1887 for his left-wing views; in December the Syracuse church tried to fire their preacher for similar reasons.[44] This took more than one attempt, for "a majority of the congregation declared their adhesion to the eloquent and brainy young minister."[45] All the same, Grumbine had to give his 1888 Easter sermon in the secular Freeman Hall.[46] His next pastorate was in Oneonta. The gossip column of the *Syracuse Daily Courier* wrote in January 1889 that Mrs. Grumbine and family were already settled in that "delightful and go-ahead village,"[47] presumably more friendly to radical preachers, but he lasted less than a year there.[48]

Grumbine now left the Upstate region for Chicago, where he probably came into contact with the Koreshans and metamorphosed from a Universalist preacher to an adept of the occult sciences. Around 1899 he returned to Syracuse for a year or two as president of the College of Psychical Sciences and Unfoldment, also called the College of Divine Sciences and Realization. Its headquarters were at 1718 West Genesee Street (no longer standing). Regular advertisements in Cyrus Teed's *Flaming Sword* explained what it was about:

> It is devoted exclusively to the System of Philosophy concerning Divinity, and is connected with the Order of the White Rose, branch of the Rosicrucians. The secrets and mysteries of Magic and Occultism are revealed. The mystic and potential powers of Divinity, such as Clairvoyance, Psychometry, Inspiration, Psychopathy, Ontology, Hypnotism, Telepathy, and Illumination are taught. Special teachings are arranged for out-of-town students and belong to the college extension department. Development is thus ensured in the student's home for a nominal sum.[49]

By 1900 the College could boast an impressive-sounding faculty. Their disciplines show the direction Grumbine had now taken: a blend of Theosophy, New Thought, and alternative therapies.

ILLUSTRATION 21.2. The Baum-Neal House, Syracuse. Built in 1867, the home of William Neal and Harriet Baum Neal (sister of L. Frank Baum), where Frank Baum met his future wife, Maud Gage, and where his mother died in 1905. It is hoped that the house will be restored as a Baum museum. *Author's photograph.*

- J. C. F. Grumbine, B.D. Chair of Metaphysics, Ontology and Philosophy of Divinity
- Mrs. Benjamin J. Harrett, Chair of Sanskrit Literature and Oriental Philosophy
- Miss Lucy C. McGee, Ph.B., M.A., Chair of the New Psychology and the Philosophy of Color and Color Tones
- Mrs. Etta McK. Mayr, Chair of the Psychology of Music
- W. J. Colville, Chair of Mental Science and Healing
- Dr. Herbert Parkyn, Chair of Suggestive Therapeutics[50]

Colville is a major figure in spiritualist history, and all except Mrs. Harrett have books to their name. But was there anything collegial about it? It seems rather to have followed the model of the Hermetic Brotherhood of Luxor (see chapter 18) in providing distance-learning or mail-order instruction in practical occultism. The Order of the White Rose, also known as the Order of Melchisedek, was held out as its more esoteric circle.

James Peebles was not impressed. He wrote: "It will be noticed that though the White Rose Order is generally designated the Spiritual Movement by Mr. Grumbine, it makes no reference to spirit phenomena, spirit demonstrations of a future life, spirit communications, spirit ministries, mediums, writing mediumship, angel guardianship, trance mediumship, materializations, etherealizations, etc., etc."[51] This was not quite true, because Grumbine believed his enterprise to be inspired by a group of spirits, especially the poet Elizabeth Barrett Browning (1806–1861). But while Peebles's generation was indelibly marked by Hydesville and its repercussions, Grumbine's was looking to the development of one's own higher powers. With or without occultist trappings, that was what New Thought was all about. After the turn of the century, Grumbine left Syracuse for good and for years crisscrossed the nation, running his organization from Boston, Washington, Los Angeles, Cleveland, and finally coming to rest in Portland, Oregon.[52]

The Upstate years of L. Frank Baum, James Peebles, and J. C. F. Grumbine immersed them in the blend of social reform and contact with the spirit world, which has been the central theme of this book. They had all left the region by the next century, by which time spiritualism was out of fashion and the radical movements had partially achieved their goals. Our next chapters deal with three who remained: Elbert Hubbard in East Aurora, Gustav Stickley in Syracuse, and Claude Bragdon in Rochester. Artists rather than preachers, they showed a different path to self-improvement and social reform: through beauty and the consecration of work.

ILLUSTRATION 22.1. Elbert Hubbard, c. 1900. Wikimedia Commons.

CHAPTER 22

The Fra

CREDO

I believe in the Motherhood of God.

I believe in the blessed Trinity of Father, Mother and Child.

I believe that God is here, and that we are as near Him now as we ever shall be.

I do not believe He started the world a-going and went away and left it to run itself.

I believe in the sacredness of the human body, this transient dwelling-place of a living soul, and so I deem it the duty of every man and every woman to keep his or her body beautiful through right thinking and right living.

I believe that the love of man for woman, and the love of woman for man, is holy; and that this love is in all of its promptings as much an emanation of the Divine Spirit, as man's love for God, or the most daring hazards of the human mind.

I believe John Ruskin, William Morris, Henry Thoreau, Walt Whitman and Leo Tolstoy to be Prophets of God, and that they should rank in mental reach and spiritual insight with Elijah, Hosea, Ezekiel and Isaiah.

I believe we are now living in Eternity as much as we ever shall.

I believe that the best way to prepare for a Future Life is to live one day at a time, and do the work you can do the best, doing it as well as you can.

I believe there is no devil but fear.

I believe that no one can harm you but yourself.

I believe that we are all sons of God and it doth not yet appear what we shall be.

I believe in freedom—social, economic, domestic, political, mental, spiritual.

I believe in every man minding his own business.

I believe that men are inspired today as much as men ever were.

I believe in sunshine, fresh air, friendship, calm sleep, beautiful thoughts.

I believe in the paradox of success through failure.

I believe in the purifying process of sorrow and I believe that death is a manifestation of Life.

I believe the Universe is planned for good.

> I believe it possible that I will make other creeds, and change this one, or add to it, from time to time, as new light may come to me.[1]
>
> *Credo of Elbert Hubbard, 1900*

Writers about Elbert Hubbard (1856–1915), a.k.a. Fra Elbertus, Doctor Phil, the Pastor, etc., cannot avoid using the word "flamboyant," but his beginnings were as dull as could be. He grew up in Hudson, Illinois, the son of a poor country doctor. At fifteen he left school and became a door-to-door salesman for Larkin's, a soap firm. Shortly after, the firm built a factory in Buffalo, and Hubbard worked for them for another twenty years. He settled in East Aurora, a village eighteen miles to the east, married his Illinois sweetheart, Bertha Crawford, and fathered three sons.

In his own words, Elbert Hubbard was "born again at 33."[2] While attending the Chautauqua Literary and Scientific Circle of East Aurora, he met and fell in love with Alice Moore, an educated Bostonian who had come there as a schoolteacher.[3] Hubbard's wide reading and way with words, hitherto funneled into advertising copy, found their destiny: what he would sell henceforth was not soap, but the products of his own mind.

The first fruit of his new life was a novel, published in 1891 under the pen name Aspasia Hobbs.[4] It was titled *The Man: A Story of To-Day, With Facts, Fancies and Faults Peculiarly its Own; Containing Certain Truths Heretofore Unpublished Concerning Right Relation of the Sexes, etc., etc.*, and whatever its literary merit, it reveals the paths he was now traveling. The unnamed man of the title is a hermit who lives in a log cabin deep in the woods (but within bicycling distance of Buffalo). He is three hundred years old and still in good health, thanks to mental, physical, and spiritual right living. His mother had grown up in an Italian aristocratic family that lived in London during the late sixteenth century. Among the family servants was a young man from Stratford-upon-Avon who was a part-time actor and aspiring playwright. Inevitably, the young people fell in love, then combined their talents in a literary collaboration. The Italian lady, with her fine classical education, supplied the plots, the man from Stratford the poetry, and the result was the plays of William Shakespeare.

Hubbard's first novel seems to have been spawned by Ignatius Donnelly's *The Great Cryptogram* (1888) out of Bulwer Lytton's *Zanoni* (1842), and incidentally to have godfathered John Uri Lloyd's *Etidorhpa* (1895) with its ageless character "I Am the Man." Donnelly's challenge to the Shakespeare authorship did not convince Hubbard, but it was the talk of the times and frequently alluded to in his writings. As for *Zanoni*, it is famous for its occult and Rosicrucian theme. Lytton's plot hinges on the supreme worth of human love, which redeems Zanoni from his five-thousand-year sojourn on earth. The same doctrine echoes in *The Man*, where the platonic relationship of the Man with an orphan girl from Buffalo gets them prosecuted for the crime of "free love," and indeed it is central to Hubbard's philosophy of life.

Larkin's had done extremely well out of Hubbard's salesmanship, and so had he. In 1892 he quit the firm, demanding his share in cash, about sixty-five thousand dollars (worth at least fifty times as much in today's depreciated dollars), which ensured his freedom to live as he pleased. The first impulse was to catch up on his missing education, and he tried to enroll as a regular undergraduate at Harvard University. Alice Moore's presence in Boston, where she was a postgraduate at the Emerson School of Oratory, had something to do with this; the two of them had a daughter in 1894. Harvard, however, would only accept him as a "special student," and after a single term listening to professors whom he despised, he returned to his large house and family in East Aurora. After this, Bertha, too, gave birth to a daughter.[5]

In the summer of 1893, Hubbard had been to Chicago to see the World Columbian Exhibition, the architectural high point of which was Louis Sullivan's Transportation Building. The next summer he spent two months in England and Ireland. The two experiences frame the path his life was now to take. In London he had visited the Kelmscott Press and met with associates of its founder, William Morris (though almost certainly not with the great man himself). He had seen the beautiful books printed and bound by hand, the fabrics, tiles, wallpapers, ceramics, and tapestries made by Morris & Co., and felt the breath of a new movement for the beautification of life and the sanctification of work. These would henceforth be Hubbard's own ideals. He would be craftsman, writer, and social reformer: America's William Morris.

The Chicago Fair was another matter. To every thoughtful visitor, it posed the question: What next for America? With the whole civilized world's productions on display, were ours good enough? What was to be the true American style, its authentic rather than borrowed architecture? What should be the relation of labor to the capital that was being heaped up as never before? To some, the chief event was the Parliament of Religions, and the stars of the show were Swami Vivekananda, the Hindu, and Anagarika Dharmapala, the Buddhist. The New England Transcendentalists and the Theosophists had already held up Eastern wisdom as equal to Western; here were its living spokesmen.

Having failed to make his mark as novelist, Hubbard now made a fresh, threefold entrance onto the publishing stage. In 1894 he persuaded

G. P. Putnam's Sons in New York to let him complete and continue a series they had started in 1853, called *Homes of American Authors*. There had been eleven of them; now Hubbard would write a twelfth, on Walt Whitman, and from January 1895 would supply Putnam with a new one every month.[6] He would call them *Little Journeys to the Homes of Great Men, Great Women, Great Artists, Great Composers*—the possibilities were endless. Hubbard had met some of the people and seen some of the homes; the rest was culled from encyclopedias and his imagination. These middlebrow booklets sold by the hundreds of thousands, first by subscription, then in bound volumes, then in complete editions with a special bookcase to house them, finally becoming the bane of secondhand booksellers as their cheap suede covers disintegrated.

Hubbard's second enterprise followed a recent fashion for nicely printed "little magazines" that dispensed a monthly dose of literature, poetry, and entertaining chit-chat. With two colleagues, East Aurora printer-journalist Harry C. Taber and Buffalo news editor William McIntosh, he launched in June 1895 the *Philistine: A Periodical of Protest*. The first issue opened with McIntosh's history of protesters, tracing them back to the "Serpent of Eden" or even to the "Sons of the Morning," who rebelled before the world was made.[7] Hubbard's mischievous humor came out in snide remarks about other little magazines, especially *The Chap-Book*, which he called *The Chip-Munk*.[8] The *Philistine* outlasted and outsold its rivals, rising to a plateau of about a hundred thousand subscribers[9] and ceasing only with Hubbard's death.

The third wing of Hubbard's publishing campaign appeared in January 1896, and was aimed at connoisseurs of fine printing. Bertha Hubbard designed it, Taber printed it by hand, and Elbert signed the six hundred copies. The text was *The Song of Songs* from the Apocrypha, prefaced by a long "study" by Hubbard, who wrote: "To me the Song of Songs is simply the purring of a healthy young barbaric chief to a sun-kissed shepherdess, and she, tender-hearted, innocent and loving, purrs back in turn, as sun-kissed shepherdesses ever have and will."[10] Although he mocks those who excuse the book's eroticism as an allegory of "the love of Christ for His Church," sensual love for Hubbard was as sacred as anything we know. *The Song of Songs* was the first of many limited editions, which Hubbard offered with graded options of decoration and binding. He thereby single-handedly created a clientele of middle-class collectors of fine books, while supplying richer ones with illuminated copies in modeled leather bindings.[11]

These first productions were issued by the Roycroft Printing Shop and bore the orb-and-cross symbol that Hubbard would use all his life. Both name and emblem were probably suggested by Harry Taber,[12] who had also instigated the *Little Journeys* and thus relaunched Hubbard's literary career.[13] Thomas Roycroft was a seventeeth-century printer whose name echoes "royalty" and "craft"; the emblem, imitated from early printers' colophons, neatly combines the initials HT and EH. However, Taber was unable to bear the magazine's cost, and in November 1895 Hubbard, flush with Larkin money, bought him out. He thereafter conducted the *Philistine* "for his own amusement," and sometimes wrote the whole thing, including the advertisements.[14] The magazine promoted young poets, including Claude Bragdon[15] (see chapter 24) and, more importantly, Stephen Crane (1871–1900), whose Civil War novel, *The Red Badge of Courage,* earned him lasting fame.

In March 1899, the *Philistine* carried one of Hubbard's typically opinionated "preachments," using his reformed spelling (e.g., "fyseek," "enuf," "abolisht"). It was about a soldier, Andrew Rowan, who had played a crucial role in the recent Spanish-American War by taking a message to the Cuban revolutionary Calixto Garcia. Hubbard disapproved of all wars, but his point was that if everyone behaved with the same readiness and initiative as Captain Rowan, the world would get along much better. There was nothing special about Hubbard's essay, but it was noticed, and before he knew it, the New York Central Railroad had ordered a hundred thousand copies to be printed with their advertisements on the back. This started an avalanche of orders from businesses, clubs, schools, and the military, who all saw the *Message* as motivational material. By the end of the year it had sold a million copies; a year later, ten million, issued in every language, format, and printing quality.[16]

Hubbard's pen had made him richer than Larkin's soap had ever done, but true to his creed, he recycled his wealth into a utopian Arts and Crafts community. The Roycroft Press had already diversified into leatherwork (for bookbinding), and as new buildings went up, they needed metal fixtures and furniture, which might as well be made on site. Soon a blacksmith shop, a copper shop, a pottery, and a furniture shop were hard at work, their products all marked with the orb and double cross. The Roycrofters' payroll, supervised by Alice, grew to several hundred, almost all of them natives of East Aurora or the immediate region.

While William Morris remained Hubbard's lodestar, he also admired Charles Robert Ashbee (1863–1942), who had founded the Guild of Handicrafts in London's East End. The intention there was to rescue boys from poverty and train them to be craftsmen, while educating public taste by elegant and innovative design in metalwork, pottery, furniture, and jewelry. Ashbee had lectured in the United States in 1896, and in 1900 his wife, Janet, visited the Roycrofters. Soon after, the Guild of Handicrafts moved to the rural town of Chipping Campden, Gloucestershire, where it replicated on a smaller scale the Roycroft ideal of a "phalanstery" in a rural village.[17]

Hubbard had a good eye, but unlike Morris, Ashbee, or Gustav Stickley, he was no draftsman, artist, or expert in any craft. There was consequently no Roycroft style but that of the variously gifted designers who were allowed free range. They included William Wallace Denslow (1856–1915), illustrator of L. Frank Baum's *Father Goose: His Book* and *The Wonderful Wizard of Oz*; Dard Hunter (1883–1966), a superb book and poster artist; and Karl Kipp (1881–1954), who brought Viennese Secession and Glasgow Mackintosh influences to the metalwork. After decades of academic disdain for Hubbard himself, the Roycrofters' place in the American Arts and Crafts movement is now appreciated. Here I will turn to Hubbard's philosophical and spiritual character.

Hubbard's second magazine, the *Fra: A Journal of Affirmation*, carried portraits on its covers, to give each issue its leading theme. That of December 1908 featured Jesus, and inside there was a list of the "rebels" who had carried on his good work:[18]

- Moses rebelled from the religion of the Egyptians
- Jesus, from the religion of Moses
- Paul, from Judaism
- Savonarola, against Constantine's composite religion
- Luther, Calvin, and Knox, more successfully against it
- Henry VIII defied the Catholic Church
- Methodism and Congregationalism broke from both Knox and Henry VIII's religion
- Unitarianism revolted against the Congregational Church
- Emerson and Theodore Parker rebelled against Unitarianism

Hubbard was shoulder to shoulder with Matilda Gage, continuing the rebellion by refusing the rights of any church or faith to impose itself on the individual, by threats or cajolement, or on society, through evading taxes and passing faith-based laws. Theology, he had quipped in an earlier number, is "a bum science";[19] Islam and Christianity have a history of murderous deeds; the only cults that have no blood on their hands are the Buddhists, Quakers, Unitarians, and Agnostics.[20] Alice added fuel to the pyre by compiling *An American Bible*, provocatively titled since its scriptures were by Franklin, Jefferson, Paine, Lincoln, Whitman, Ingersoll, Emerson, and Elbert Hubbard.

So far, one can understand Hubbard's oft-expressed admiration for the arch-unbeliever Robert Ingersoll (1833–1899). But as we know from several previous cases, freethinking often went hand in hand with a noninstitutional spirituality. In the same year, 1908, the *Fra* quotes from two leaders of the theosophical movement, Dr. Franz Hartmann (1838–1912) and Katherine

Tingley (1847–1929), as well as carrying an article by Edward Carpenter (1844–1929), a Whitman-like character on the fringes of Theosophy. Aside from their contempt for Christian dogmas and Blavatsky's denial of a personal God, Theosophists believed in occult forces, communications from the Tibetan mahatmas, and reincarnation. Hubbard would have none of that. In the *Philistine* he had written a piece on "Astral Autografs" that skewered all three beliefs:

> My relative applied for Madame Blavatsky's autograf, but an adept answered: "Madam is out. Since she arrived she has really never been all in. Hers was a manifold nature. She is now in part in a Chinese diplomat, a rival of Li Hung Chang; she also fully possesses a Professor of Psychology in Cornell, and what was left over of her, being merely baser elements, went into a rhinoceros in the Amsterdam Zoo."[21]

Yet when it came to the heart of the matter, his metaphysical system was theirs, even if he called it "the Religion of Humanity." In the same spring number of 1908 he writes under that title that, "Man is part and particle of the Divine Energy, that lives in all." The Religion of Humanity, he explains, knows nothing of dogmas, or whether we have an individual life after death. It's essentially monistic, believing that there is but one thing in the world, called Universal Intelligence, the First Principle, or, if you must, God. This has "a million myriad manifestations"; it incarnates itself as primordial gas, matter, vegetation, and animal life. Its highest manifestation is man, but he is still only in process.[22]

As for realizing this principle, Hubbard's path, like Blavatsky's, was not through religion or prayer but through a kind of rational mysticism. In one of his most serious articles, on "Time and Change," he advises us to "get out of self-consciousness" and into a partial trance condition. Then we will be "surprised by the quantity of knowledge and the extent of insight you possess." If we go deeper, we may "feel guided by a spirit not our own, knowing nothing of the miraculous storing up of truth in the cells of subconsciousness." But then comes the danger: "you wither at the top because you rely on the dead."[23]

This is quite mysterious, but it seems to refer to the benefits and hazards of deep meditation. The danger mentioned is in attributing one's own birthright of wisdom to an outside source, such as a dead religious figure or a spiritualistic visitation. "All men," Hubbard adds, "are equally gifted, but some can muster mental legions, others not."

Just as mysterious (in the sense of touching on Mysteries) are Hubbard's words on what he calls the Brotherhood of Consecrated Lives. Though he styled himself "Fra" and sometimes acted the abbot, he was never a joiner and certainly not a Freemason. In an oft-reprinted article he castigates secret societies, first because they have no secrets, and second because they mostly exclude women.[24] Instead, he felt a companionship beyond creed or label:

> To join this Brotherhood of Consecrated Lives requires no particular rites of initiation—no ceremonial—no recommendations. You belong when you are worthy. But do not for a moment imagine you have solved the difficulty when you have once entered. To pride yourself on your entrance is to run the danger of finding yourself outside the pale with password hopelessly forgotten. Within the esoteric lines are circles and inner circles, and no man yet has entered the inmost circle where the Ark of the Covenant is secreted. All is relative.[25]

The Ancient and Mystical Order Rosae Crucis (commonly known by its acronym AMORC) claims that Hubbard was a Rosicrucian, and a close and early associate of its founder, Harvey Spencer Lewis (1883–1939). The AMORC's branch in Dayton, Ohio, is even called the Elbert Hubbard Chapter. The official history of the order states that Hubbard was prominent in Lewis's Rosicrucian Research Society, which operated from 1904–09 under the name of the New York Institute for Psychical Research.[26] Quite apart from my opinion that Hubbard would have found Spencer Lewis and his pretentions good for a two-liner in the *Philistine*, the scholar cannot accept a statement that rests solely on Lewis's testimony, while the existence of any such institute is also uncorroborated. Esoteric orders—the Priory of Sion comes to mind—have a way of enrolling the great ones of the past when they are not around to object.

Whether Hubbard incorporated any esoteric ideas in the symbols and structures built under his supervision remains a more open question. Mason Winfield, in his studies of the mysteries of western New York, considers the possibility of sacred geometry and geomantic siting in the Roycroft campus, as well as hints of Rosicrucian and Illuminati sympathies in Hubbard's writing from *The Man* onwards.[27] Winfield also mentions the stone sculpture *Magna Mater* [The Great Mother] by Katharine Maltwood (1878–1961) that Alice and Elbert commissioned in 1911. One naturally associates it with the first article in Hubbard's Credo, and maybe recognizes the name of the sculptress. She it was who in 1929 beheld a vast zodiac anciently laid out around Britain's sacred site of Glastonbury: a vision that would become a founding myth of the British New Age movement. Like Edward Carpen-

ILLUSTRATION 22.2A. The Roycroft Chapel, East Aurora, 1899. *Author's photograph.*

ILLUSTRATION 22.2B. *Magna Mater*, sculpture by Katherine Maltwood (detail), 1911, at the Hubbard Museum, East Aurora. *Author's photograph.*

ter's writing for the *Fra*, Maltwood's sculpture draws a triangle between Roycroft, the English Arts and Crafts movement, and the esoteric world of the early twentieth century with its blend of influences from Theosophy, spiritualism, and ceremonial magic. Theirs were all "consecrated lives," but I see no trace of the formal, secretive activity that some would love to find under every stone.

Instead there was an overt mystical pantheism, proclaimed in the sentence from the Gnostic Gospel of Thomas carved on the main door of the Big Shop: "Raise the Stone and Thou Shalt Find Me; Cleave the Wood and I Am There."[28] And there was Hubbard's one-liner on the potential divinity of the human being: "We are gods in the chrysalis."[29] Nothing could be plainer.

ILLUSTRATION 23.1. Gustav Stickley, drawn by William (or Wilhelm) Gherhardt. From *Craftsman Homes*, New York: Craftsman Publishing Co., 1909.

CHAPTER 23

The Craftsman

The heart's desire of a man is fulfilled in his work. In some flash of inspiration he sees a vision of his work, his pathway, his home, his way of rendering account of the talent given him. The ecstasy that lifts him into realms never to be forgotten, wonderful though it be, is only of short duration; but the steady pleasure of carrying out the vision never leaves him. It requires Herculean work to manifest our ideal, slow, patient hours when apparently little is being accomplished though so much is intended. It is not at all ecstatic like the joy that accompanied the vision, yet the memory of it stays with us as a dear secret that we are always aware of, like the sweet consciousness of the child that is yet unborn which gladdens a woman's heart.

Work that is so necessary, so absolutely necessary in this world was never intended to be done in the breaking of one's heart, but in the fulfilling of the heart's deepest desire. . . .

Inspiration has been drawn from the fields from time immemorial. The greatest teacher who ever blessed this

> world, who kindled an inextinguishable light, who left a fountain of pure water from which all who thirst may drink, would go to the fields for inspiration, for the parables through which he could reveal eternal truths. Through our love and familiarity with the homely things of everyday life He led us on to understand inner truths; we were led from the outer court of the temple to the inner court, and then in to the holy of holies—when we could bear it.[1]
>
> *Gustav Stickley on work and inspiration, 1911*

To most of us, Stickley and Roycroft products look much alike, both proclaiming "Arts and Crafts, early twentieth century" and maybe "Mission Oak." Experts know better, and remind us that there were five Stickley brothers, each with his own history as a furniture maker. Here I am concerned with Gustav (1858–1942), because he not only made beautiful chairs, tables, bookcases, desks, and so on, not only designed houses and sold everything with which to furnish them, but he also founded, edited, and wrote for the flagship magazine of the Arts and Crafts movement. In addition, he ran a business that, at its zenith, comprised a twelve-story building in New York City, a factory in Syracuse, and a utopian community and farm in New Jersey.

Stickley, like Frank Baum, was of German immigrant stock, though his ancestors arrived much later. He was born Gustave Stoeckel in Osceola, Wisconsin, to a stonemason-farmer even poorer than the Hubbards, and apprenticed in his father's trade. As in Elbert's case (whose sister married a Larkin), Gustav's relatives gave him a leg up. An uncle took the lad on in his chair factory in Brandt, Pennsylvania, where Gustav eagerly absorbed every aspect of the woodworking craft. From then on, he was unstoppable. By 1884 he and his brothers Charles and Albert were running their own factory in nearby Binghamton, where for a while he also ran an electric trolley company. In 1888 Gustav left his brothers for a partnership with Elgin Simonds, a salesman, and in 1890 moved to Auburn to direct manufacturing at the state prison (but did *not*, as sometimes stated, make the first electric chair[2]). In 1892 the partners bought property in Eastwood, now part of Syracuse, and built a new factory there. Gustav and his family moved up the hill to exclusive Walnut Street, now lined with Syracuse University's fraternity and sorority houses.

Stickley & Simonds furniture was in the nineteenth-century style that was really no style at all but an imitation of features from past eras, overstuffed, overdecorated, and overvarnished. This pleased the Waldorf Astoria Hotel in New York, which in 1897 dropped a golden egg on the Syracuse firm, ordering several hundred chairs at every degree of elaborate design.[3] Once the Waldorf job was done, just as Hubbard had levered Taber out of Roycroft, Stickley forcibly bought out Simonds so that he could run the company on his own terms.

Around 1901, Stickley's furniture reached its trademark style: heavy slabs of quarter-sawn oak, faultless joinery and finish, leather cushions, no ornamentation except the ghost of a Gothic arch in some of the vertical members.[4] That same year Stickley began running his company as a guild, United Crafts, in which the workers received dividends on the profits; he adopted an emblem (a carpenter's compass), a motto *Als ik kan* (old German, via Morris, "As [well as] I can"), and started a magazine, the *Craftsman*.

None of this would have happened if Stickley had not met Irene Sargent (1852–1932), an Auburn-born woman who had penetrated the masculine domain of Syracuse University and made herself indispensable to the College of Fine Arts. She had no known higher degrees but had traveled much in Europe, knew five or six languages, and had the histories of art, architecture, literature, and culture at her fingertips. Gustav's relationship with this confirmed spinster was not at all like Elbert Hubbard's with Alice Moore, but it is fair to say that she sparked his rebirth.

Mark Hewitt describes Sargent as the center of a small Arts and Crafts cadre centered in the Yates Hotel in Syracuse, where Sargent lived and in which Stickley had a financial interest. It included the potter Adelaide Robineau (1865–1929) and Bragdon's friend Harvey Ellis (1852–1904).[5] Sargent edited the *Craftsman* for its first five years and wrote much of it, either under her own name, under Stickley's, or translated from other languages. It gave her scope to express herself on any subject in elevated but not academic style, and it gave Stickley a mouthpiece for the mission he had now taken on.

The first two issues of the *Craftsman* honored William Morris and John Ruskin. The next had as their themes the medieval guilds, textiles, factory reform, beautiful books, metalwork, and architecture. The parallel with Roycroft is obvious, but due more to their common roots in the English movement. The *Craftsman* studiously ignored East Aurora, and the silence must have needled Hubbard, for in 1905 he twice bought a full-page advertisement. Quoting the high prices at a recent auction of Colonial and Federal-period furniture, he commented:

> All the furniture here mentioned was made a hundred years ago by men who had the time, talent and inclination to make it well. We think that we are making by far the best furniture in America today. We make furniture that is an endowment investment for you—you use it and can pass it on to your heirs. It does not wear out, and like true friendship, grows better with the passing years. We have the plant, the people, the materials, and the time.[6]

Stickley would not have put it like that, but he certainly thought *he* was making by far the best furniture in America, and many would agree. Their rivalry does not matter now, but Hubbard was quite right: furniture from Roycroft and Stickley alike has soared in value as it has become "period" in its turn.

The *Craftsman*'s mission was to mold its readers' thinking about every facet of art, craft, interior design, and architecture, and as time went on, about gardening, ecology, politics, music, education, literature, and life in foreign parts. Sargent worked from the start on a large canvas. In the second issue, she traces the progress of art all the way from barbarism, through Fetich [*sic*] worship, Egyptian symbolism, polytheism ("from the mixture of races"), luxury and decadence, the "Deep restorative influence of Christianity," the monasteries, the revival of learning and free thought, the "Frank paganism" of the Renaissance, to a "Negative spirit, tyrannous and vain." After that, art was ripe for redemption by the "Two sons of Oxford" [Morris and Ruskin].[7]

According to David Cathers, the Stickleys attended Park Central Presbyterian Church throughout their Syracuse years.[8] The magazine seems to have addressed a liberal-minded Christian public, happy to read the occasional religious verse and friendly to Judaism, Buddhism, and Native American religion. Early on, there were some erudite articles on comparative religion and symbolism. Jessie Kingsley Curtis wrote on the spiritual meanings in oriental rugs;[9] Caryl Coleman, on how the haloes of saints and the Chi-Rho cipher of Christ all go back to sun worship.[10] The solar theory of religious origins was a commonplace theme, thanks to Professor Max Müller (1823–1900), whose collected essays *Chips from a German Workshop* (1867–75) suggested the title for Stickley's regular op-ed column, "Chips from the Craftsman Workshop."

The Arts and Crafts movement always had a strong moralizing backbone. Like Ruskin and Morris, the *Craftsman* preached simplicity and the return to nature. Stickley admired the no-nonsense outdoorsman Theodore Roosevelt, and they both admired Charles Wagner, an Alsatian pastor who had made a stir in sybaritic France with his book *The Simple Life*. When

Roosevelt invited the pastor to America, Stickley organized lectures for him in Syracuse,[11] and for a while, the *Craftsman*'s cover carried the subtitle *An Illustrated Monthly Magazine for the Simplification of Life*. By that time the Craftsman workshops were working at full capacity. Stores in fifty U.S. cities carried their wares, and as many as a hundred advertisers bought space in each issue of the magazine, to sell everything from rifles and silent toilets to motorcars and prep schools. Simplicity sold!

On the negative side, the traditional enemies of the Arts and Crafts movement were ugly, machine-made goods and the soul-destroying labor system. By the 1900s, Irene Sargent spied a subtler danger creeping over from Europe: Art Nouveau. She might have known that in England Arts and Crafts bloomed in uneasy proximity to the decadent movement in art and literature. She wrote that

> . . . the art movement of the present day is a most dangerous and threatening one. For, under pretext of interpreting Nature by an advanced and subtle method, artists of great worth no longer observe the great mother of life. They attempt to subvert and destroy principles which are as permanent as the laws of mathematics. They would have chaos in place of order, and set up the personality, the individual fancy of the designer against the laws of the eternal republic of art. They are blind to all save "the wavy line."[12]

Sargent's weighty sentences contain a perennial philosophy of art: that it reflects the divine order as manifested in nature and its geometry, and that the artist is morally bound to follow that order, rather than his own ego or fantasy, lest chaos supervene. One could argue with her from many points of view, but in this case one would be arguing with Plato.

Although the *Craftsman* had an up-to-date attitude to the "sex question" and was firmly on the feminist side, Sargent warned readers that in art, we must distinguish the "healthy animalism" of a Rubens from "prurient morbid sensuality of [the Italian poet Gabriele] D'Annunzio's type."[13] She deplored the pagan tendencies of the Italian Renaissance, where life in "pleasure palaces" led to degeneration and vice. "No man could exist, faun-like and without being conscious of a soul, as was possible before Christianity had saddened and uplifted the world."[14] Her favorite painter, not surprisingly, was Puvis de Chavannes, with his sexless pastorals and washed-out colors.[15]

After Sargent departed as editor, the *Craftsman* was lumbered with the subtitle *An Illustrated Monthly Magazine Edited and Published by Gustav Stick-*

ley in the Interests of Better Art Better Work and a Better and More Reasonable Way of Living.[16]Art Nouveau was already losing its sting. The new tool of decadence was the Secessionist art of Vienna and Berlin. Stickley, who knew it well since he subscribed to the magazine *Deutsche Kunst und Dekoration*, writes that Secession seeks only the shock of the bizarre; it reflects neither the national spirit nor the spirit of the age, but is a parasite, with no roots in the life of people.[17]

The *Craftsman* had plenty of alternatives to offer. There were, of course, United Crafts' own products, which the magazine promoted at every opportunity. Beyond that, contemporary American sculpture and mural painting were of special interest, for they seemed to express the national aspirations that were such a preoccupation of the age. Californian mission architecture and the art of Native Americans offered an alternative to European models, and among foreign cultures, Japan was a particular favorite. Almost every issue has some news and pictures from abroad. There are photographs of new Spanish paintings, Norwegian log houses, Viennese interiors, Greek folk fabrics, English country houses, ancient Roman silver, Belgian ironwork, and Japanese prints. The articles range over Prince Kropotkin, Gorki, Boecklin, Bakst, Grieg, Vallotton, Gaudi's cathedral, Lalique, Bourdelle, the Armory show, Strauss's *Salome* and *Elektra*, Debussy's *Pelléas et Mélisande*—and those are just some of the famous names. The *Craftsman* staff had its fingers on the pulse of the entire cultural world.

Stickley's business took a conceptual leap in 1904, during the few months when Harvey Ellis worked for United Craftsmen. Ellis brought delicate inlaid ornament and a springier texture to Stickley's furniture, emulating the British Art Nouveau designers Mackintosh, Voysey, and Baillie Scott. Ellis's seductive and imaginative drawings of houses and interiors made readers yearn to build and live in them. Stickley responded by publishing designs and plans for Craftsman houses, ranging from holiday bungalows to mansions. His firm would take on the contracting itself, or sell plans for building one's own. The magazine *Craftsman Homes* published some two hundred designs and had a lasting impact on American domestic architecture. Another frequent contributor, Louis Sullivan, had an even larger impact. He used the magazine for his polemics against American taste in art and habits of life, and for his principle that "form follows function," the very basis of modernist architecture.

In 1905, the *Craftsman* moved from Syracuse to an office and showroom in New York City, at 29 West 34th Street. Stickley's business demanded it, but his heart was elsewhere. Like William Morris he yearned for country life, and wrote that when he died, his chief regret would be that "I failed to enjoy so much of the beauty of this dear earth and sky."[18] In 1907 he gave his editorial page a new header, showing a man in a Stickley chair looking out over roofs and smoking chimneys. Beneath, he wrote about how his thinking had evolved:

> We are not primarily concerned about making beautiful things, but about developing makers of beautiful things; men and women in whose lives rise the fountains of beauty and gladness, who see the soul of beauty in the simplest flower and the farthest, faintest star; workers whose work will be full of grace and beauty because of the indwelling grace and virtue of their lives. . . . Such was the deeper, profounder spiritual significance which the arts and crafts movement developed.[19]

Gustav Stickley's answer was the same as many before him: he would found a rural utopia. The next year he started buying land near Morris, New Jersey, already a commuter town for Manhattan, and pieced together about 650 acres.[20] He called it Craftsman Farms, where workers in the various crafts would lead a healthy life close to nature, building and furnishing their own houses, raising cattle and poultry, growing their own food, and running a school for boys on liberal, idealistic lines. Amazingly enough, he achieved all of it except the school, which never attracted pupils. Here at last Stickley built his own house, illustrating it proudly in the magazine, and lived there with his family for a few idyllic years.

During the Craftsman Farms period, another utopian architect, William Lightfoot Price (1861–1916), wrote in the *Craftsman* a "Confession of Faith" redolent of the platonic ascent from physical to intellectual beauty: "Art is the middle ground lying between the realms of matter and of spirit, glorifying matter in expressing the spirit, carrying its true devotee beyond the power of man to express, building his spirit up until palette and trowel fall idly, in the realization of the impossibility of mere material expression."[21]

Price was a wealthy Quaker who had founded an Arts and Crafts community at Rose Valley, Pennsylvania, based on William Morris's utopian novel *News from Nowhere*. Later that year, Stickley produced a "Message from Craftsman Farms" in the same mystical-philosophical style, heading it with a quotation from St. John of Kronstadt (1829–1908). This is the excerpt quoted at the head of this chapter, which seems to speak of two authentic moments of illumination: one concerning work as worship (what Hinduism calls karma yoga) and the other in ecstatic communion with nature.

The *Craftsman* ignored Theosophy and occultism as such, but some relevant names stand out. Claude Bragdon wrote two articles in the early years,

ILLUSTRATION 23.2. Gustav Stickley House, Syracuse. Home of the designer, editor, and leader of the Arts and Crafts movement from 1900 to 1905, and from the 1920s until his death in 1942. It is hoped that the house will be restored as a Gustav Stickley museum. *Author's photograph.*

one of them on "A Simple Dwelling" of his design,[22] the other a meditation on the history of art.[23] His theme is the authenticity and beauty of civilizations until the Renaissance, and the subsequent decline of taste and sincerity, until the corner was turned with the Centennial Exhibition (1876). No Theosophist could have missed the unspoken parallel with the founding of their society (1875). Bragdon here makes the sole mention of Hubbard's firm in the entire *Craftsman* (outside the advertising section), which must have brought a smile to Stickley's face. Adapting a line from *HMS Pinafore,* he writes, "Roycroft skim milk often masquerades as Kelmscott cream."[24]

Edward Carpenter found a welcome in the *Craftsman,* as in Hubbard's magazines, for his revolutionary views on art, nature, and the conduct of life,[25] though we hear nothing of his homosexual manifesto, *The Intermediate Sex* (1908). A third character with a well-known presence in the esoteric world was the Jamaican artist Pamela Colman Smith (1878–1951), with a generous article on her fairy painting, her aural-visual synesthesia, and her paintings of the images received from music.[26] Every student of the tarot will recognize the deck of cards she designed in 1909, which remains the most popular of all tarot decks, though unfortunately it does not bear her name.[27]

Craftsman Farms was already draining much of Stickley's considerable income from the firm when he made his fatal move. In 1913 he took on the lease of a newly built skyscraper at 6 East 39th Street, a stone's throw from Bonwit Teller, Tiffany's, and the Century Club,[28] and proceeded to occupy all twelve stories. He filled it with furniture and decorative arts, rooms furnished and painted in suggestive styles, display spaces rented to other manufacturers, a garden center with plants, a floor of building materials, an architectural service, gentlemen's and ladies' clubrooms, and a library where they could relax and meet kindred souls. Those who reached the top floor found a full-service restaurant, supplied from Craftsman Farms. The staff was numerous, the cost enormous (sixty thousand dollars per annum in rent), and the result, after two struggling years, was bankruptcy for the firm called Gustav Stickley The Craftsman Inc.

The *Craftsman* magazine sailed through these end times without any sign of the crisis engulfing Stickley's empire—or Europe. The Arts and Crafts fashion was passing: Colonial- and Federal-period revivals were coming back into favor. Under its editor, Mary Fanton Roberts, the magazine had become less polemical, more open to all periods and styles, and much less moralistic than in the Sargent era. Now Martin Birnbaum could praise the arch-decadent Aubrey Beardsley (1872–1898), even quoting from his erotic novel *Under the Hill*, and saying, "It is not our province to fault his choice of unsavory material"; he was "an artist's artist, and what more could one wish?"[29] D. H. Lawrence's *Sons and Lovers* was reviewed not unkindly, with the caveat that it was "not of particular service to young readers."[30]

For some years before the First World War, the *Craftsman* had been staunchly anti-Kaiser and pacifist. War, when it broke out, was almost welcomed, since it would force Americans into a simpler way of life. After that, very little was said about it. Instead, readers found no fewer than twenty-two articles on wild birds and their legal protection.[31] Another escapist theme was fairies, with articles on how important it was for children to believe in them.[32]

In its last year, 1916, with Stickley desperately trying a new furniture line, all knobbles and colored paint,[33] the magazine secured interviews with the conductors of the Metropolitan Opera, the Boston Symphony, the Philadelphia Orchestra, and the celebrity soprano Yvette Guilbert (1865–1944). At almost its last gasp, it published a poetry issue with poems by Robert Frost, Louis Untermeyer, Carl Sandburg, and Amy Lowell.[34] In short, it was still the place to learn about what was going on in American cultural life, while Europe was otherwise engaged.

Gustav Stickley was not exactly a victim of the war, as the Hubbards were,[35] but rather of the illusion of invulnerability preceding it. He lived on in Syracuse until 1942, lodging with his daughter and son-in-law in the house of his first Arts and Crafts makeover. Today, the firm founded by his brothers Leopold and J. George carries on the family tradition in Manlius and Fayetteville. Craftsman Farms is a Gustav Stickley Museum, and the Roycroft campus again an arts, crafts, and tourist center.

In emphasizing the spiritual side of Hubbard and Stickley, I am aware of two irksome questions. Stickley's few surviving letters show him as an indifferent writer and a bad speller.[36] Scholars agree that his many articles and editorials were mostly ghostwritten by Irene Sargent, Mary Fanton Roberts, and other *Craftsman* staff.[37] Was Stickley in any sense the author behind these mystical effusions? His character is not easy to read, but one of his sub-personalities was certainly the utopian idealist and reformer. There is a Germanic cadence to his attributed writings that a ghostwriter could hardly have faked. Philosophically, I suspect that he was a learner, not a teacher; that he absorbed the aspirations of those educated and articulate women, which then became his faith. This leads to the second question. In the 1890s and 1900s, when "advanced thinkers" of the American middle classes were preoccupied with New Thought, Theosophy, and the wisdom of the East, it made sense to market Arts and Crafts products and style as spiritually superior. Were the Christian Platonism of the *Craftsman* and the mystical pantheism of Hubbard's writings a mere sales ploy? I think not, because the

Arts and Crafts movement, from Ruskin and Morris onwards, *was* ethically superior, and its products aesthetically superior, to the exploitative commercial system. To raise the ethical and aesthetic standards of the public served a cause that many would call spiritual, and only the envious would grudge its rare material rewards.

ILLUSTRATION 24.1. Claude Bragdon, architect, theatrical designer, geometrician, and Theosophist, photographed by Dudley Hoyt, 1897. *Courtesy of Rare Books and Special Collections, Rush Rhees Library, University of Rochester.*

CHAPTER 24

The Rochester Yogi

> The theosophic teaching is that there has never been but one religion in the world, the Ancient Wisdom, and that all differences between faiths are differences of form and not of content, colorations caused by the refracting medium, the mind of man, in receiving and transmitting the white light of a truth received, "in the dark backward and the abysm of time"[1] from spiritual teachers—supermen. Moreover, the same emancipating truth lies dormant in each individual, being slowly stirred into life within the unfolding consciousness through a long succession of correlated lives of ever augmenting intensity. It thus appears that man's spiritual evolution, like all evolutionary processes, is effected both by impulses from without: worldly experience lighted by religious teaching; and from within: the shining of the Inward Light.[2]
>
> *Claude Bragdon,* The Small Old Path, *1911*

When Claude Bragdon (1866–1946) came to write his autobiography, he called it *More Lives Than One* and proceeded to tell in turn "My Personal

Life," "My Architectural Life," "My Theatrical Life," "My Literary Life," and "My Occult Life." If there is a single thread on which all these are strung—and one might add his Geometric, Feminist, and Graphic lives—it is in the dying words of his second wife, Eugenie: "Claude, you must create beauty."

Nowadays anyone who says that beauty is the goal of art (and life) risks a pitying sneer from the sophisticated. But, as we saw in the last chapter, Bragdon's contemporaries in the Arts and Crafts movement still hoped that the dawning century would fulfill this ideal. They looked on America's prospects and destiny with guarded enthusiasm. Would her unprecedented wealth lead to a Periclean age of democracy and public beautification, or would greed and vulgarity make the twentieth century as bad as the nineteenth?

Like Hubbard and Stickley, Bragdon was a self-made man, though from a more intellectual background than they.[3] His mother came from a Congregationalist minister's family with a strong abolitionist history. His father, George Chandler Bragdon, edited local newspapers, moving as opportunity called to Adams, Ithaca, Utica, Watertown, Dansville, Oswego, and finally to Rochester. More an idealist than a businessman, he was an admirer of the transcendentalists, a member of the Theosophical Society, and a poet. Here is a sample of his verse from his collection *Undergrowth*, published privately in Rochester in 1895:

MUSIC OF THE SPHERES.

Could we not hear, had we archangel's ears
  Finely attuned, the vast harmonic flow,
Now all too ravishing for us, of spheres
  Whose cadences, divinely grand and slow,
Are eons long! Do systems not respond,
  Out where immensities are little things
Compared to the immensities beyond,
  To systems chorally, so that there rings
A various symphony from space to space,
  Forever and forever, which shall be
To those exalted by celestial grace,
  In the hereafters of eternity,
Their heaven of sound? and may they not behold
The veil that hides the angelic choirs uprolled?[4]

George Bragdon's muse extended to love poems and nature poems, as well as some folksy ballads and a poem in praise of "Naughty Boys." He indulged Claude as far as the family resources permitted, and the son was soon following in his footsteps. By the age of ten Claude had his own small printing press and was printing magazines and ephemera.[5]

Drawing came naturally to Claude; music not so, though he worked hard at the banjo. Because his father could not afford to send him to college, after high school he found work as a newspaper cartoonist. He then rose, by stages we cannot detail here, to become one of Rochester's premier architects.[6] His greatest, if not his most beautiful work was the New York Central Railroad Station, whose arches were inspired by the driving wheels of a train but whose secret geometry was derived from musical ratios and regulating lines. After an argument with George Eastman, the Kodak king, Claude Bragdon gave up Rochester and his architectural career, moved to New York City, and made a happier if scantier living as a theatrical designer, lecturer, and writer. From 1924 until his death he lived in a studio apartment in the Shelton Hotel.

Although he was a friend of Louis Sullivan and an admirer of Frank Lloyd Wright, Bragdon was no modernist. The houses he designed for the well-to-do citizens of Rochester and Oswego lie between a mild Arts and Crafts and an equally mild neoclassical style. His public buildings are intelligent, even erudite in their geometry and ornament (see illustration at the end of this chapter), but they do not have the flair or memorability of great architecture. His patrons would not have wanted it, so he remained a provincial. His chief surviving monument is the First Universalist Church (1907), now dwarfed by the office blocks of downtown Rochester. Like his Romanesque examplars, Bragdon determined the proportions of the church through harmonic ratios and designed all the details himself, from the ceramic tiles and lighting fixtures to the rivet heads of the exposed steel beams.[7]

Bragdon's originality flowered in the modest fields of posters, tiles, lanterns, textiles, book and magazine covers, and the illustration of his own works. He combined a sense of contrast and mass learnt from Japanese prints (via Toulouse-Lautrec and Aubrey Beardsley) with a vocabulary of geometric patterns that are his trademark. Everything he did shows a flawless facility in drawing. His independent paintings might have won him a place among the geometrical abstractionists, hence as a "fine" rather than "applied" artist (a distinction irrelevant to him), but they are too few and came too late in life to attract notice.[8]

These artistic productions went hand in hand with literary ones. They began as offshoots of his architectural rendering, with studies of local Colonial houses and Italian palaces that he visited on his only foreign tour. He was naturally drawn into the Arts and Crafts crowd: he designed posters and covers for *The Chap-Book*, contributed a poem[9] and a cartoon or two[10] to Hubbard's *Philistine*, and attended Irene Sargent's circle in Syracuse. He was at the head of the table at the famous Philistine Dinner on December 19, 1895, held in honor of Stephen Crane and crashed by "a lot of drunken pseudo-reporters" whom Bragdon claims he "cowed into some semblance of order."[11] The *Buffalo Evening News* reported respectfully that, "The visitors included Mr. Claude Fayette Bragdon, the well-known artist and architect of Rochester, who has become known through his work in the Chap-Book and the Philistine as 'the Beardsley of America,' though a very positive critic of the affectations of the Yellow Book School."[12] This sounds like a coded way of saying that the bachelor Bragdon was not gay, since the recent trials of Oscar Wilde had cast suspicion on the whole aesthetic movement.

Bragdon sensed what a catch he would have been for East Aurora, and how it would have curbed his own ambitions. He did not return Hubbard's friendly overtures because, as he writes, he "could not take him at his own valuation—or perhaps I should say the valuation at which he wanted to be taken: something between Ralph Waldo Emerson and William Morris."[13] Instead, he joined Harvey Ellis in founding the Rochester Arts and Crafts Society, emulating the societies founded the same year (1897) in Boston and Chicago.

While working his way up the professional ladder and keeping company with a lively, bohemian set, Bragdon did not forget his transcendentalist upbringing. Perhaps his father's book of verses was the spur for his one extended poem, "The Golden Person in the Heart," privately published in 1898.[14] This was a recasting of the poetic teachings concerning the higher Self as found in the Upanishads, the Bhagavad Gita, and other books of Eastern wisdom. If we put that together with the doctrine of cosmic harmony expressed in George Bragdon's poem, quoted above, we have the essence of Claude Bragdon's own philosophy.

Bragdon also looked east in a more mundane sense: to Syracuse and Gustav Stickley's factory, where Henry Wilkinson, a young architect, was designing a new line of furniture. One thing led to another, and before long Bragdon was engaged to Henry's sister Charlotte and moving among the wealthy, liberal-minded people to which her family gave him entree. He joined the Genesee Valley Club and built a house on the outskirts of Rochester (called "Cro' Nest" after the local crows and the famous cliff on the Hudson River), at which the new couple entertained in some style. But sadly, their marriage lasted only from 1902 until 1907, when Charlotte died, leaving Claude with a toddler and a newborn baby. He had never changed a diaper or made a pot of coffee but proudly mastered these skills and turned the rest over to a nanny and a cook-housemaid.[15] It was in the wake of this trauma that his "occult life" began in earnest, and I will now concentrate on that.

The catalyst was a series of conversations with a Singhalese Theosophist, Curuppumullage Jinarajadasa (1875–1953; later president of the Adyar Theosophical Society), whom Bragdon heard lecture in Rochester in May 1908. What followed was not so much a conversion as a realization on Bragdon's part that he had always belonged in the theosophical sphere. He set out to read works he had long known of from his father's library, including the *Secret Doctrine* of H. P. Blavatsky and the works of her successor, Annie Besant. Flushed with enthusiasm, he wrote two booklets, one of them an account of Besant's life so far[16] and the other a history of the Theosophical Society.[17] He had them printed at his own expense, and placed copies of the history next to the Gideon Bibles in every hotel room in Rochester.

Bragdon had none of the anguished relation with Christianity that dogged our earlier characters. As a Theosophist, he was unmoved by the sectarian differences and dogmas that were once so important. While never disrespectful of Christianity, he had long sensed that his own path lay in another direction. He confesses in his autobiography:

> Another idea I have about myself is that I am a reincarnated Oriental. Though I have never been to Asia, ever since I read those Theosophical books in my father's library I have felt it to be my spiritual home. Eastern philosophy—Taoistic, Vedantic, Buddhistic—I seem instinctively to understand. Eastern art, even in its humblest manifestations, stirs me emotionally as the greatest masterpieces of Occidental art have never done. . . . I even look like an Oriental.[18]

Jonathan Massey, in the first full-length book on Bragdon, guesses that it was the absence of the churchgoing, Smith College–educated Charlotte that unleashed Claude's new life and mission.[19] In September 1908, Bragdon went to the national convention of the Theosophical Society in Chicago and met Annie Besant and other dignitaries. By November he was attending séances at the Plymouth Spiritualist Church. Spurning Rochester's existing branches of the Theosophical Society (see chapter 18), in 1909 he founded a third, the Genesee Lodge, with himself as its president. With his sister May he started a publishing house, named the Manas Press after the theosophical term for the higher mind.

Their first publication was *My Two Gardens*, a collection of free-verse poems by "A. S." The author was Alice Sprague (1861–1944), the wife of one of Buffalo's captains of industry, Carleton Sprague (1858–1916). The two gardens are of the outer and inner worlds, interpenetrating, and described in the language of nature-mysticism. Here is a sample, for comparison with George Bragdon's *Music of the Spheres*:

> Let me so live that I may hear these great harmonies,
> These fundamental tones;
> Let their rhythm, their sweetness penetrate into my life;
> Let me live in tune with them

> And let their beauty fill my mind and heart;
> Let me hear them above and beyond
> All petty, broken, transient notes.[20]

Bragdon was an attentive reader of Charles Webster Leadbeater, who with Besant headed the movement sometimes called Neo-Theosophy. Leadbeater wrote out of his own clairvoyance about the astral world, reincarnation, life on other planets, the shapes of thoughts and of atoms. Bragdon never swallowed the more extreme claims of this new wave, being more a practitioner than a believer. Through meditation and yoga he had experienced exalted mental states, but mediumship and clairvoyance he regarded as a properly feminine gift. For the women who possessed it he invented the term "Delphic Sisterhood," referring to the ancient Greek oracle of Delphi.

Bragdon's second wife, Eugenie Julier Macaulay (?–1920), whom he married in 1913, had the gift in abundance. She had first tried automatic writing after the death of her first husband, and received the advice to marry again.[21] Claude encouraged her to continue these sessions, though neither was certain whether the source was a distinct entity or Eugenie's own higher self. As usual in such cases, the script and style of the "oracles" were altogether different from the medium's usual ones. "Each message opened with her name, Eugenie; their general tone was kind, even loving, but it was the tone of authority, almost of omniscience, an effect enhanced by the use of the collective 'We' in place of the first person singular."[22] Its basic teaching was of a pantheistic, New Thought variety: "The farthest star is in your heart: the farthest sun shines within you, and to make you understand it is to make the inner the outer."[23] The source was aware of events and trends of the day. It approved Claude's new ventures with sound and light or theater design; it disliked the movies, and was overly optimistic about World War I. "War is not to be," it said on June 23, 1916, "for we are holding the leash and evil shall not pass beyond our control."[24]

Bragdon, understandably, found his wife's oracles far superior to the "appalling invasion from another sphere of a wholly new type of bore"—his words for the recent rash of mediumistic communications.[25] During the same period, communications from a source called "Sano Tarot" were coming to Nancy Fullwood (1870–1939?[26]), an Alabama woman who moved to New York City in 1919. She submitted the scripts to Bragdon, and although he says "the archaic forms of speech employed, the names, the titles, the symbolism, somewhat offended my fastidious taste,"[27] he sponsored their publication. With his foreword to *The Song of Sano Tarot* (1929), he helped to launch Fullwood as a popular author of channeled texts. Another Delphic Sister was Edith Ellis (1876–1960), a "cultivated and charming woman" with a theatrical and literary life behind her.[28] Beginning with *Open the Door!* in 1935, she believed that a Revolutionary War soldier called Wilfred

Brandon was using her to communicate his revelations of the afterlife. Like Fullwood, Ellis went on to become a successful author in this popular genre of the between-wars period.

In Bragdon's later life, Alice Sprague returned to become one of his closest companions and supporters. Although her fortune was much diminished, she helped him financially after his sources of income had virtually dried up.[29] He and Nancy Fullwood would meet in Alice's apartment, where they would sit in a triangle around a rosewood table. Nancy would act as a direct-voice medium, and Claude would write down her words. Whereas Eugenie did not recall what she had written while in trance, Nancy was fully conscious and would sometimes interrupt the "noble and dignified" personality that spoke with a style not her own.[30]

When Alice Sprague's papers came to Bragdon after her death, he found that she too had taken up channeling. The source for which she acted as medium was feminist, theosophical, and practical:

> We are the weavers of destiny. Trust us.[31]
>
> Your religion will be the liberation of woman from ancient traditions that she may become free, even as man has essayed for this.[32]
>
> The permanent atom is the gift of the gods to man. It survives every catastrophe. It never dies. It is that part of the immortal and divine which man has already had. You brought yours over when you came into life, millions of years ago.[33]
>
> Draw in your abdomen and look up. This is an exercise which will develop inner power. Do it often.[34]

His indulgence of mediumship aside, Bragdon's feminism was a natural outgrowth of his esoteric studies, which taught that all things follow the law of polarity. Examples are sun and moon, day and night, fire and water, man and woman. In *The Beautiful Necessity* (1910), he favors the Japanese terms *Yo* and *In*. "Things hard, straight, fixed, vertical are Yo; things soft, curved, horizontal, fluctuating are In, and so on."[35] It is easy to see how this could inform his architectural history, analysis, and creativity. Translated to the personal and social realm, it led to Bragdon's constant effort to redress the imbalances of a male-dominated world. In *The New Image* (1928), one of several collections of essays on the feminine, he opens with a reflection on the momentous changes in women's rights and status that had taken place in his lifetime:

> When the hour struck for woman's emancipation from the thraldom of old folk-ways and outworn conventions, the most sensitive and highly attuned of the sex—those whom I name the Delphic

> Sisterhood—had to revolt, even to the point of destroying their own temple. And this is woman's predicament today, in the countries where the thing has happened: her ancient sanctuary is in ruins, and no new one has arisen. For the moment she is the victim of her own victory: the dark shadow of her new freedom is her new loneliness. Escaped from bondage, questing every sort of knowledge and experience, she has for the moment ethically and culturally outstripped her companion, man, caught in the net of competitive industrialism. She is not understood by him in these new aspects, he resents them, and by him, all unconsciously, she is in her deepest nature tortured and crucified.[36]

Bragdon urged emancipated women not to ape the futile activities of men, but to assert and cultivate their half of the cosmic equilibrium: in a word, love. After World War II he wrote: "It is a mistake to regard love as an emotion, a feeling, a quality; love is an *element*, as air is an element. It is a white fire which burns to destruction, or warms and illumines and promotes growth. It is indeed at the present time the only element of salvation, and the perils of today are as nothing to the perils of tomorrow if we continue to neglect the element of love."[37]

The same equilibrium exists in the individual, for in our essence (Plato's Soul, Carl Jung's Self) we are all androgynes.[38] Yet because we currently inhabit gendered bodies, most of us feel the erotic attraction of our complements. For his time, Bragdon is comparatively frank about sex. In his biography he reveals that he only discovered its real possibilities after his marriage to Eugenie: "She was herself so marvellously beautiful, and had in everything so great a passion for perfection, that she introduced a note of almost supernatural beauty into this most sweetly perilous of all human relations, insisting that all the surroundings and conditions be right for the performance of Love's ritual. . . . It was *Baktai*, Love Yoga, not learned in convents and monasteries, but in the arms of the beloved."[39]

After formally taking up the theosophical path, Bragdon returned to a group of essays published in *House and Garden* in 1902. Titled after Emerson's dictum, "Let us build altars to the Beautiful Necessity," they blended transcendentalist mysticism with practical instruction in design. Bragdon amplified and revised them as "The Theosophy of Architecture" for the *Theosophical Messenger* in 1909, then published them as Manas Press's first full-length book. *The Beautiful Necessity: Seven Essays on Theosophy and Architecture* (1910) explains the metaphysical principles behind architecture, applied geometry, design, and ornament.

Though it cites few contemporary writers, resting its case more on Renaissance theorists like Serlio and Cesarino, Bragdon was drawing on a body of ideas already in the air. Hargrave Jennings's *The Rosicrucians, Their Rites and Mysteries* (1870) had little about the Rosicrucians but much about masculine and feminine symbolism in buildings. James Fergusson's histories of architecture, studies of Indian temples, and his curious books *Tree and Serpent Worship* (1869) and *Rude Stone Monuments in All Countries* (1872) only needed to be read through theosophical spectacles, and all manner of associations would arise. H. P. Blavatsky's own *Secret Doctrine* (1888) used geometrical terms to explain the birth of the cosmos. William Richard Lethaby's *Architecture, Mysticism, and Myth* (1891) interpreted architectural evolution in the light of religious and symbolic values. Louis Sullivan, the modern architect whom Bragdon most admired, was playing with similar ideas in his angry, poetic, stuttering style.[40] It took Bragdon's clarity of thought and genius for didactic illustration to draw these threads together, in what turns out to have been his most lasting contribution to intellectual history.

Although it does not use the term "sacred geometry," *The Beautiful Necessity* was the first textbook on the subject and the impetus for its many developments in the twentieth century. Among these were the geometrical analysis of paintings, whether to confirm the instinctive use of proportions like the Golden Section or to uncover secret messages; the use of geometry as a spiritual discipline, contemplating plane and solid figures as doorways to gnosis; the conspiratorial myth of a secret society that planted its clues in the symbolism and proportions of buildings; the discovery of "ley lines" joining sacred sites, and other geometrical figures detected in the landscape; the search for the ancient units of measure and for the significant numbers that emerged when they were applied to buildings like the Great Pyramid; the science of astro-archaeology, which studies the relation of buildings to the stars and planets; the theories of a geometric "world grid" of energy currents, explaining the placement of sacred sites; and the attempt to restore a cosmic and spiritual dimension to modern architecture, town planning, and landscape design.

Only later in life did Bragdon discover that someone had been there before him: none other than George Felt, who gave a historic lecture on September 7, 1875, at which the founding of the Theosophical Society was first mooted. Felt had written a long manuscript on the geometric canon of the ancients, called *The Kaballah of the Egyptians*. It was announced for publication, but never printed and was presumed to be lost. In 1936 the manuscript resurfaced in the possession of Bragdon's friend Viola de Gruchy. He studied it closely, and the two of them determined to edit and publish it. But it came to nothing. In 1941 the Felt family bought the manuscript back, and now it has vanished again. Marc Demarest calls it "perhaps the most famous lost work of the Victorian occult revival."[41]

Bragdon might not have considered *The Beautiful Necessity* as important as his work on the fourth dimension, which was the subject of the Manas Press books *Man the Square* (1912), *A Primer of Higher Space* (1913), *Projective Ornament* (1915), and *Four-Dimensional Vistas* (1916). Leadbeater and other Theosophists had taught that the etheric and astral worlds exist in dimensions beyond our own, to which clairvoyants have access. This linked up with nineteenth-century speculation about multidimensional geometry and "hyperspace." Linda Dalrymple Henderson's studies show that Bragdon's work was a conduit for fourth-dimensional theory to influence European artists and the early Bauhaus.[42] However, she also explains how the theory collapsed in the face of Albert Einstein's definition of the fourth dimension as time.

ILLUSTRATION 24.2. Bevier Memorial Building of the Mechanics' Institute, Rochester, 1910 (detail). Claude Bragdon, architect. *Author's photograph.*

This did not trouble Bragdon, for he had discovered in the diagrams he drew to explain the fourth dimension a new aesthetic resource. As he writes in *Projective Ornament*, "If after reviewing this literature the reader is disposed to regard the fourth dimension as a mere mathematical convention, it matters not in the least, so long as he is able to make practical use of it. He may likewise, with equal justice, question the existence of minus quantities, for example, but they produce practical results."[43]

While the architect projects three-dimensional objects onto the two-dimensional plane of his diagrams, where they are easily reconstructed by the imagination, Bragdon goes further. He projects fourth-dimensional objects onto the paper and invites one to imagine their reality. Not everyone finds this easy, but anyone can appreciate the practical results of treating them as two-dimensional patterns, yielding a novel vocabulary of ornament. *Projective Ornament*, like all the works Bragdon illustrated himself, is a delightful work of graphic fantasy. He shows how his ornaments could be used to decorate book covers, stained-glass windows, wrought-iron gates, carpets, screens, lanterns, shirts, dresses, floors, balconies, and teacups. In *The Frozen Fountain* (1932) his imagination runs riot in full-page illustrations of a luxurious world, somewhere between theater sets and Art Deco five-star hotels. Ladies with borzoi hounds waft through impossibly high drawing rooms; a bellboy attends an elevator door emblazoned, like the chairs, carpet, and clock, with projective ornament. Even more fantastic are Bragdon's drawings of Sinbad, an allegorical figure named for the hero of the *Arabian Nights*. He wears a black tunic with the sigil that Bragdon had been using since the 1890s: a triple interlace that could also be read as "CB." After being summoned from the ink bottle, Sinbad arrives in "Main Street of an American City of the Dead," lined with historicist buildings and a Louis Sullivan arch. He "Ascends the Isometric Stairs," "Forces the Logarithmic Spiral to Disgorge Its Treasure," "Pushes Asunder the Tesseract Cubes Trying to Find the Fourth Dimension," and so on.

I have not mentioned Bragdon's system of ornament derived from magic squares,[44] nor his theater designs[45] or his experiments in color music.[46] His democratic idealism found expression in festivals of mass singing and light shows that he organized in Rochester and in New York's Central Park.[47] He also wrote on yoga and meditation,[48] on oriental philosophy,[49] and a memoir of the remarkable men he had known.[50] The key to this multifaceted activity is beauty, not just in the arts but in the whole conduct of life. In that sense, Bragdon shared the ideals of the fin-de-siècle aesthetic movement, as well as of the Arts and Crafts community. His uniqueness was in framing them within the esoteric philosophy and global outlook of Theosophy.

ILLUSTRATION 25.1. Archbishop William Henry Francis Brothers ("Father Francis"), restorer of the Church of the Holy Transfiguration of Christ on the Mount, Woodstock. *From the church's website, by permission.*

CHAPTER 25

The Cauldron Refired

Times are different now. We are going through the birth pains of a new era, a better era than the past, and birth pains are always difficult. I have lived long enough to see the handwriting. We are going to disencumber ourselves of Victorian hypocrisy and prudery. I'm not fearful of the young people, if they don't go to church. They come here. You have to be honest with them. You can't throw the book at them, give them a quotation—no matter how beautiful, from the Bible. They are going to ask how do you know it's true? How do you get that way? You have got to exemplify in your life, somehow. I've never had a quarrel with any of them. Some have said, "I don't believe in God."

Four boys from one of the big camps came here, feasted all day, and they said, "Father, we don't believe in God, and neither do our buddies."

"Neither do I," I said, "not any gods your child-minds could conjure up. Let's talk it over."[1]

Father Francis, interviewed in Woodstock, 1966

Innumerable threads stretch forward in time and outward in space, spun by people who were either born in the Upstate region or inspired by the movements that started there.[2] If America had a spiritual center of gravity, it moved west, first to Chicago and then to California, which is another story. As for the region itself, by the time Claude Bragdon left Rochester in 1924 the cauldron had already gone cold. Given over to commerce and concrete, Upstate must have been intolerably dull, and so it remained through the Depression, the Second World War, and the complacent 1950s.

There was Woodstock, though. In 1902 Ralph Radcliffe Whitehead (1854–1929) had started an Arts and Crafts community near the Catskill town, which he called Byrdcliffe. Like Elbert Hubbard's Roycroft, it was inspired by the ideals of John Ruskin and William Morris (whom Whitehead had actually known in his native England), and supported by the private wealth of its founder. Byrdcliffe laid the foundation for Woodstock as the haven for artists and tourists that it still is.

Whitehead's twelve-hundred-acre property included an Episcopalian "chapel of ease" that had been built in 1891 to serve summer visitors to the resort hotels, Mead's Mountain House,[3] and Overlook Mountain House. It looked like a toy version of Upjohn Gothic,[4] picturesquely sited in the woods on Mead's Mountain. After Whitehead's death, his widow, Jane Byrd McCall Whitehead (1861–1955), invited William Henry Francis Brothers (1887–1979) to preside over the chapel. Born in Nottingham, England, and raised in a well-to-do immigrant family in Waukegan, Illinois, Brothers had been the prior of an independent Benedictine order in Fond du Lac, Wisconsin, then in New York City. He was one of the *episcopi vagantes*, "wandering bishops" who claimed apostolic succession but functioned outside the Anglican and Roman Catholic hierarchies. Brothers had been consecrated a bishop in 1916 in the Old Catholic Church, a Dutch sect that had separated from Rome in 1870 over the issue of papal infallibility.[5] Later he was reconsecrated in the Russian Orthodox Church. By the time he died, he was no longer in communion with either of those bodies, but instead with the Ukrainian Autonomous Orthodox Church in Exile.[6] None of this mattered in Woodstock, where Brothers was known as Father Francis or the Archbishop, and many thought him the most exemplary Christian they had ever met.

Brothers called the chapel the Church of the Holy Transfiguration of Christ on the Mount. He restored it with his own hands, installing the Gothic rood-screen from his New York base,[7] hanging up reproductions of Fra Angelico's angels, and living simply in the attached priory. At some point he married; no children are recorded.[8] He was a traditionalist in ritual and a leftist in politics, equally at ease with immigrant workers, down-and-outs, and the celebrities who vacationed in the Catskills, from the Hearsts to

Bob Dylan. When the hippies arrived he became their admirer and defender, and did his utmost to save young men from the draft. Rumor has it that his connections made it possible to hold the 1969 Woodstock music festival on a property outside the town.

In the late 1960s the church would fill on Sundays with a mixture of older Woodstockers, flower people, devotees of Meher Baba,[9] and casual sightseers of all faiths and costumes. While the sanctuary was no bigger than a drawing room, the Mass resembled a high-church Anglican rite, with incense, music from a harmonium, and the noble language of the 1612 prayer book. All were invited to take communion. However, when the Nicene Creed reached its statement about the "Holy Ghost, the Lord and giver of life, who proceedeth from the Father," the Archbishop did not add "and the Son," as the Anglican prayer book does. This had been a point of contention that split the Catholic and Orthodox churches in 1054, and he was now on the latter side. And with the words, "I believe in *one holy Catholic and Apostolic Church*," the usually soft-spoken prelate seemed to be defying the Bishop of Rome himself. Later, he would restore the Western Rite Orthodox Liturgy, after a thousand years of underground use.[10]

Among Father Francis's present-day admirers is Peter Lamborn Wilson (born 1945), who has written on Sufism, Islamic heresies, Irish psychedelics, Hermetic ecology, nonjuring Anglicanism, and much else. In 2010 he commemorated the Woodstock church and its bishop in *7 Churches*, a series of works of "Vanishing Art for the Endarkenment." Wilson describes his own work as "temporary landscape installations—Evanescent Art—an art that in order to exist must disappear, Sacrifices to the spirits of places and epochs (histories) of insurrection and/or surreal grace . . . Neo-pastoral zones. For the re-enchantment of landscapes and the re-paganisation of monotheism . . ."[11] The seven churches chosen for this ritual were St. John in the Wildernesse (Harriman State Park), the Holy Comforter (Poughkeepsie), St. Margaret of Antioch (Staatsburg), Holy Cross Monastery (West Park), the Ascension (West Park), the Stone Church (Cragsmoor), and the Holy Transfiguration (Woodstock).[12] Wilson followed the time-honored principle of sacrificing something of material value (e.g., casting a gold ring into the waters) in order to obtain a spiritual result. The details were governed by the doctrine of correspondences between planets, days of the week, metals, colors, plants, the Seven Churches of Asia, etc., all done in the hermetic spirit of a *lusus serius* (serious play).

Another series of Wilson's poetic actions was linked with his epic poem about the Esopus region, *riverpeople*. The first, at Samhain (October 31) 2009, was near Accord, called Mombaccus by the Dutch settlers and a center of the prehistoric Bear Cult. Another honored Jemima Wilkinson (see chapter 3), and specifically a group of her followers who were left behind when she moved to the Finger Lakes. They settled in the Hudson Valley and communicated with her only in dreams, before and after her (second) death. The other actions took place in the Five Lakes region (honoring the "Jukes," a tri-racial isolated community), Cairo (founding the Fatimid Order of Cairo, New York), Big Indian (refuge and burial place of Winnisook, the seven-and-a-half-foot-tall, eighteenth-century shaman), Phoenicia (in honor of Oscar Wilde's visits to the Catskills in 1882 and 1883), Esopus Island (in honor of Aleister Crowley's residence during the summer of 1918), and a parking lot in Kingston (site of the Esopus Wars of 1659–1664).[13]

Wilson's workings on the Hudson and Esopus rivers might inspire a pilgrimage to the Seven Churches of the Mohawk Valley. Traveling from west to east, they would be Fort Herkimer Church at German Flatts (Dutch Calvinist, built 1753–67); Indian Castle Church at Danube, erected for the Indians by Sir William Johnson (originally Episcopalian, 1769); the Palatine Church near Fort Plain (Lutheran, 1770); the Dutch Reformed Church (1788) and the Lutheran Church (1792) at Stone Arabia, both rebuilt after Johnson's son and his Indian allies had destroyed the earlier churches; the shrine of Saint Kateri Tekakwitha at Fonda, founded by a Franciscan friar in 1938 in anticipation of Kateri's canonization;[14] and the Shrine of Our Lady of Martyrs at Auriesville, founded by the Jesuit Order in 1884 to honor their own martyrs (see chapter 4). Poetic actions aside, they give food for reflection on "non-eccentric" spiritual movements that all claim to be Christian.

In this context, the Rosa Mystica House of Prayer near Edmeston deserves a brief mention. Both inside and out, it looks like a small Catholic parish church, but its origins are bizarre.[15] They go back to an Italian stigmatic, Madre Elena Leonardi of Montechiari (dates unknown; active 1970s–80s), who received apparitions and spoke prophecies from the Virgin Mary. Some of these were apocalyptic warnings; others warned the clergy to mend their ways. Less typically, one prophecy came as an enigmatic sequence of numbers. One of Leonardi's devotees guessed that they were a map reference in longitude and latitude. He consulted an atlas and found that they pinpointed a site in Otsego County. Evidently Mary wished for a chapel to be built there, and dedicated to her as the Mystic Rose. A large tract of field and woodland was bought, and in 1984 some Canadian Franciscans started building a chapel at the specified spot. It has been restored and enlarged more than once since then, and there are reports of healings and other miracles. But since the Vatican has not validated Mother Leonardi's visions and prophecies, Rosa Mystica, like the churchlets of the *episcopi vagantes*, remains outside the Roman fold.

I return now to the late 1960s and to the southern central region of the state. In the hamlet of Valois, on the east shore of Seneca Lake, is a cluster of log buildings, surrounded in late summer by fields of goldenrod and reached through a Japanese *torii* arch. This is Wisdom's Goldenrod Philosophic Center, founded in 1972 by Anthony Damiani (1922–1984). The Dalai Lama, no less, has called him "a truly great man . . . one of my closest spiritual brothers."[16] Damiani grew up in a Sicilian immigrant family in Brooklyn. Among his many jobs he worked at Samuel Weiser's, the best occult bookstore in Manhattan. All the cream (and the sludge) of Eastern and Western wisdom passed through his hands, most of it read by him on the way. After meeting his destined teacher in the English philosopher Paul Brunton (1898–1981), Damiani resolved to make his own philosophical synthesis, as Brunton had done in works such as *The Hidden Teaching Beyond Yoga* and *The Wisdom of the Overself*. To this end, in 1963 Damiani moved his family to an old farmhouse in Valois and took a job with the New York State Thruway Authority. It was the perfect job for a philosopher: by working nights at the lonely exit of Waterloo, at the north end of the lake, he could study undisturbed.

Four years later, Damiani felt the call to share what he had learned. In late 1967 he rented a storefront on the main street of Ithaca. He called it the American Brahman Bookstore, put a Buddha statue in the window, and stocked it from his own library. People wandered in, at first curious, then attracted by his personality and the sense that here was something not taught in universities. One of Damiani's former students takes up the story:

> Soon the number of us eager to discuss spiritual issues or learn the art of meditation with him grew large enough that informal evening classes began in the back room of the store. Anthony often wore his toll-taker's uniform while giving these classes, so that he could rush out at the last minute to drive fifty miles to make his 11:00 night shift on the Thruway. Within two years, his animated classes on Jung's psychology, Hinduism, Buddhism, Christian Scholasticism, Platonism, Paul Brunton's writings, and an exciting new approach to a genuinely spiritual astrology had attracted more people than the store could hold.[17]

Avid for his company and advice, Damiani's students started coming to his house at the weekends, and some of them noticed the pressure this was placing on his wife and family. With his consent, they built a large log cabin on his land, and daily meditations and classes were now held there. Other buildings followed, including a library that came to house Paul Brunton's own legacy of books, manuscripts, and Chinese and Tibetan paintings.

During the 1970s, Tibetan Buddhism was beginning to attract the type of American who had formerly been drawn to Zen Buddhism or to gurus from the Hindu tradition. Ithaca and Woodstock, as it happened, were both central to this development, becoming homes to Tibetan Buddhist monasteries. Some of Damiani's students were active in publishing Tibetan texts and had traveled to Dharamsala in India, where the Fourteenth Dalai Lama (born 1935) lives in exile. The Tibetan leader already knew Brunton, and when he was told of Damiani's work he agreed to visit Wisdom's Goldenrod on his first U.S. tour. In summer 1979 he spent three days there, dedicating the newly built library, a large log building with a distinctly Tibetan look. The Dalai Lama remains the center's patron.

When Damiani died in 1984, there was no possible successor. His students, many of whom had moved to live nearby, continued their meditation and studies on the basis of what he had taught them. They also edited Brunton's unpublished notebooks in sixteen volumes. Wisdom's Goldenrod continues with its publications, classes, study sessions, and retreats, though at a level that is difficult for newcomers to enter. Anthony Damiani's own treatise on philosophical astrology, *Astronoesis*, remains impenetrable to some of his greatest admirers. However, every esoteric teaching seems eventually to filter down to the exoteric level. Brunton once said to the present writer, with a wry smile, "In a hundred years' time there may be a religion around Tony." Stranger things have happened.

Ithaca in the 1970s was a lively center for alternative spiritualities and what was beginning to be called the "New Age." Wouter Hanegraaff defines it as "esotericism in the mirror of secular thought," i.e., the esoteric filtered down into the exoteric. The term is generally credited to the neo-Theosophist Alice A. Bailey, whose "influence on the New Age movement, especially in its early phase, is pervasive."[18] Bailey's stock was high in the 1970s, when her books, channeled from a source calling itself "the Tibetan," were widely studied. Her "Great Invocation" of divine light into the world was practiced in the peace movement and even at the United Nations. One of Bailey's admirers was Mabel Chaffin DeMotte Beggs (1912–2005), who, like Damiani, established a center on her own property outside Ithaca. Bailey had called her foundation the Lucis Trust[19]; Beggs's was the Foundation of Light,[20] and its declared purpose was "meditation, healing, and study." Beggs herself was more a facilitator and educator than a guru, and her center offered a less intellectual, less teacher-centered path than Damiani's. It started in Hubbard's Corner Schoolhouse, then expanded into a newly built lecture hall adjoining the home of Mabel and her second husband, Robert Beggs, a retired Episcopalian priest.[21]Aside from the Foundation of Light's classes, lectures, and regular sessions of yoga and meditation, it houses a unique monument, the Ellis Hollow Stone Circle. This was set out in 1977 by Chuck Pettis, Mike Sweeney, and the Cosmic Monument Study Group. They surely knew the studies of prehistoric stone circles in Britain by John Michell and Alexander Thom, with their talk of earth energies, ley lines, and the complex geometry of megalithic sites. Originally there was a tall central stone and a flat one (for meditating) surrounded by an ellipse of eight boulders aligned to the solstices and equinoxes. In 1997 six new standing stones were inserted, weighing half a ton each, so that the Ellis Hollow circle is now like a miniature Avebury or Callanish. Was Mabel Beggs's property already on a geomantically significant spot, or does such a structure, reinforced by devotion and mental effort, create its own energies? The question could apply to many of the sites in this survey.

The life and career of Jane Roberts (born in Saratoga Springs, lived 1929–1984) are curiously synchronous to those of Anthony Damiani. She lived in Elmira, a short drive from Ithaca or Valois. They both began their public ministry in fall 1967, when Roberts started giving classes in her home and Damiani opened his bookstore, and they both died in fall 1984. Some would say that the resemblance ends there, and admittedly their methods were very different and there was almost no overlap between their groups. Roberts was a trance channeler of an entity called Seth, and although she guarded her privacy, the influence of her books such as *Seth Speaks* (1970) and *The Seth Material* (1972) was worldwide. While the Fourteenth Dalai Lama has vouched for Anthony Damiani, Professor Hanegraaff speaks no less warmly of Roberts/Seth in the standard encyclopedia of Western esotericism:

> The Sethian synthesis is remarkable for its originality and internal consistency. Its optimistic and world-affirming spirituality and its message that all of us have the power to create our own reality by changing our beliefs has strongly appealed to many readers since the 1970s. Detailed analysis of the literature of the New Age movement shows that its basic ideas are modeled after Seth's worldview to such a degree . . . that, without exaggeration, Jane Roberts should be recognized as *one of the major religious innovators in Western society after World War II*. Given her pivotal role in creating the foundations of a comprehensive belief system now widely diffused through Western popular culture, she has been surprisingly neglected by scholars of Western esotericism and of new religious movements.[22]

"You create your own reality," as Seth puts it, means that we are ultimately responsible for what happens to us, because at a higher level of consciousness we have chosen to be what we are. Some take this dictum to mean that if we don't become richer, healthier, more successful in love, etc., we have only ourselves to blame, but they forget that we have first to achieve that higher, causal level of consciousness, which is obstructed by all the lower levels, and from which those goals might not seem so important any more. They are the fool's gold of New Age alchemy, and none knew it better than Roberts herself, who spent her last years physically incapacitated, yet to judge by her own writings a woman of deep wisdom, compassion, and humility.

Another central theme is that "all is mind," meaning that the universe is primarily a mental construct that gives rise to what we perceive as physical reality. This reversal of the scientistic worldview (according to which consciousness is a result of brain chemistry), already a commonplace of Christian Science, was beginning to penetrate the upper reaches of theoretical physics. Some who knew those realms made their way from Cornell University's laboratories to Anthony Damiani's classes, where they listened to his explanations of a "mentalist" as opposed to a materialist philosophy. At the same time, Seth was explaining identical concepts to Jane Roberts's listeners, and soon after to hundreds of thousands of readers.

A third basic idea of this "comprehensive belief system" is the ultimate value and immortality of the individual, not just the human but every conscious being. This defies both scientism, which knows only the ephemeral struggle for physical survival, and the religions that view man as the sinful subject of a god who basks in his own glory. The sources of both Roberts's and Damiani's philosophies speak against this, and even against the Far Eastern concept of the extinction of the individual in the Absolute, as follows:

> You are not fated to dissolve into All That Is. The aspects of your personality as you presently understand them will be retained. All That Is is the creator of individuality, not the means of its destruction.[23]
>
> The self-consciousness thus developed will not be dissolved, extinguished, or re-absorbed into the Whole again, leaving not a trace behind. Rather will it begin a new spiral of evolution towards higher altitudes of consciousness and diviner levels of being, in which it will co-operate as harmoniously with the universal existence as formerly it collided against it.[24]

"Cooperating harmoniously with the universal existence" might serve as motto for almost all the movements surveyed in this book, though they had very different ideas of how to do so. To the Shakers, Mormons, Ebenezers, and other neo-Christians, it was through accepting a new revelation and a distinctive way of life. To the utopians, it was through setting an example of social harmony. To the spiritualists, it was through opening doors into that universal existence, confident that when we die, we will pass through them. To the social reformers, it was through equality and justice. To the occultists, it was through awakening the hidden energies of the human being. To the craftsmen, it was through creating beauty in accord with the natural order. Taken together, these movements helped purge the collective mind of the fear and guilt that the patriarchal religions had exploited, so that even those religions have had to adapt their teachings or risk losing supporters.

The Upstate region, once a creative source, is now more of a receptacle for the spirituality to which it contributed so much. While the expression "New Age" is out of fashion, its activities and attitudes are easily recognizable: holistic healing, yoga, meditation, astrology, tarot, interest in Native American and non-European religions, vegetarianism, deep ecology, self-development, animal communication, Tai Chi, body work, etc. In the Upstate cities they have a subdued presence, being more conspicuous in Rochester and Ithaca. They flourish in the Catskill and lower Hudson counties, where New York City dwellers can spend a weekend or a week recharging their spiritual batteries. In Rhinebeck, the Omega Institute for Holistic Studies offers a gourmet menu of workshops and retreats, from Ayurvedic weight loss to Zen calligraphy. Elsewhere in the state, Lily Dale's summer program adds psychic development and training in mediumship. Pumpkin Hollow Retreat Center in Craryville, like the Foundation of Light, grafts the New Age onto a theosophical heritage. The gazetteer of sites following this chapter also lists some centers of Sufism (esoteric Islam) and Vedanta, the Hindu philosophy brought to America by Swami Vivekananda. But surely the dominant "eccentric" movement, in the sense of being outside the Judeo-Christian mainstream, is Buddhism. There are more than twenty Buddhist monasteries, temples, or centers now operating in the Upstate region.[25] The majority of them belong to the various Tibetan schools; others to the Pure Land school and the Japanese, Chinese, Vietnamese, or Korean Zen traditions. Buddhism suits the current preferences for practice over doctrine, for a philosophy compatible with science, and for self-help rather than obedience to a charismatic leader. All in all, it seems set to become the alternative American religion of the twenty-first century, as spiritualism was for the nineteenth.

Epilogue

This book has followed the convention of historical scholarship in assuming that spirits do not intervene in material reality. I have let the characters speak for themselves about their experiences and beliefs, crediting the former as recognizable psychological states while reporting, and hopefully clarifying, the latter. In this epilogue I will go outside the convention, to satisfy the reader who might be asking, "What do *you* make of all this?"

Although I am at ease with a nonmaterialistic outlook, those who are dead certain that they possess the truth about the unseen world do not convince me. My heart is more with the freethinkers and the Arts and Crafts people. Few of the characters in this book could even agree with one another. Within spiritualism there was heated debate over reincarnation, nonhuman communicators, and the place of Christianity. But every leader offered an investment in a belief system that promised certain rewards. Whether followers bought in because of rapport with him or her, a need for community, or whether they were swept up in mass movements like Millerism and spiritualism, they all belonged to a certain personality type: that which wants to be told what to believe and what not to believe, preferably with salvation on earth or in the afterlife. Without such people, no spiritual leader would stand a chance.

The leaders represent a rarer personality type: one on whose consciousness a metaphysical reality breaks through, whether sought or unsought. We have had examples of waking visions (Joseph Smith, Andrew Jackson Davis, Thomas Lake Harris, Cyrus Teed), near-death experiences (Ann Lee, Jemima Wilkinson, Handsome Lake), and several types of mediumship or possession (the Fox sisters, H. P. Blavatsky, Paschal Beverly Randolph, Amanda Jones, James Peebles, John Murray Spear, Eugenie Bragdon, Jane Roberts). Either they were all pathologically deluded, which is an evasive and degrading judgment, or else there is indeed some other order of reality accessible to select humans. But who is to say what this order is, and who or what is responsible for the contact? For most readers the answer is probably, "None of the above."

To the more open-minded, I suggest two approaches that do not solve these enigmas, but at least allow us to view them dispassionately. The first is the Fortean approach, named for Albany-born Charles Fort (1874–1932). Over years of mining old newspapers and scientific journals for reports of odd occurrences and unexplained phenomena, Fort developed a philosophy of agnostic acceptance of the strangeness of the world. His mission was to resurrect the "damned facts" that do not fit the worldview sanctioned by current science. Like Socrates, Fort held that the beginning of wisdom is to admit one's own ignorance, and he shared the Greek philosopher's scorn for "experts" who claim to know what they do not know.[26] In the philosophical prologue to his *Book of the Damned* (1919) he writes: "We believe no more. We accept."[27] Furthermore, the facts seemed to suggest that humanity is not the only intelligence in the universe, and that others may have interfered in its affairs. "I think we're property" is another of Fort's dicta.[28] We have met a version of this in the "hidden hand" theory of spiritualism's origins, and the self-identified angels and ascended beings who contact humans are perhaps these hidden hands. Jacques Vallee, a post-Fortean thinker who compared Joseph Smith's experiences with those of UFO contactees (see chapter 6), wonders if there is "an alien force that anticipates our own scientific development by decades, mocking our efforts to identify its nature and its long-term intentions."[29] We too might wonder whether some entity with a warped sense of humor set Handsome Lake digging for a great underground beast, Spear building the New Motor, Harris sporting with the Lily Queen, and Teed proving that the earth is a concave sphere.

Fort noted that anomalous phenomena tend to cluster as to time and place. This entire book is evidence of that, but we can sometimes narrow the focus. For example, Hiram Edson's vision of Christ in the cornfield in 1844 (see chapter 8), which became the theological foundation of Adventism, happened between Clifton Springs and Port Gibson. That is about five miles from the Sacred Grove outside Palmyra, where in 1820 Joseph Smith met God the Father and Jesus Christ, and about four miles from Hydesville, where in 1848 the Fox sisters started talking to the dead. So three lasting religious movements—Adventism, Mormonism, and spiritualism—were all sparked off in that little triangle.

Here is another example. Near that triangle, one can draw a straight line south from the thruway junction of Waterloo, where in the 1960s Anthony Damiani spent his nights in deep study of the Neoplatonists, to Elmira, where in the same decade Jane Roberts, speaking as Seth, disseminated an occult philosophy with a distinctly Neoplatonic flavor. Not two miles from either side of this line are the following sites:

- Waterloo itself, where the Congregational Friends believed in an unbroken chain of communication between the Infinite and all beings, and the first women's rights convention was planned at the M'Clintock and Hunt homes;
- The Peter Whitmer Farm, where Joseph Smith finished translating the Book of Mormon, showed the golden plates to the three witnesses, and organized the Church of Jesus Christ of Latter-Day Saints;
- Wisdom's Goldenrod Philosophic Center, founded by Damiani and now under the patronage of the Dalai Lama;
- Watkins Glen, site of the freethought convention at which radicals and spiritualists joined forces against organized religion.

Could this be a ley line, like the ones supposed to link prehistoric monuments and sacred sites in Europe? Is there any significance to it? In

ILLUSTRATION 25.2. Ellis Hollow Stone Circle, at the Foundation of Light, Ithaca. *Author's photograph.*

the Fortean view, everything is significant, since Fort hypothesizes that "all things are of a oneness, which is a state intermediate to unrealness and realness."[30] That is to say, they are neither what he calls the Universal and Seth calls "All That Is," which alone is real, nor are they entirely separate and independent from each other. The Waterloo-Elmira line is something I accept, without having any theory to explain it. Neither real nor unreal, it is an emblem of the interdependence of ancient philosophies, angelic visions, paranormal phenomena, radical social movements, freedom from outmoded dogmas, and possession by spirit entities: in short, the cauldron of our title.

A second approach that I find helpful is the Neoplatonic, which is not agnostic like the Fortean approach but based on mystical experience subjected to philosophical analysis. Rather than taking the physical cosmos as the primary reality, onto which life and consciousness have somehow become grafted, it reverses the relationship. It views humans as primarily souls, undergoing a temporary experience in material bodies. Even more radically, it holds that the material universe depends for its existence and structure on a higher, archetypal order. To this way of thinking, all spiritual movements begin with some sort of contact with a higher reality. Whether the approach comes from above (as in divine revelations) or from activating the higher elements of the human being is for theologians to argue. What is certain is that the interpretation of the experience is colored and limited by circumstances and prior beliefs. For instance, when our nineteenth-century visionaries met a luminous being, they took it to be a dead relative, an angel, or Jesus, and it spoke to them as such. A Neoplatonist of the Greco-Roman era would more likely have called it a daimon: a member of a class of beings intermediate between humans and gods.

Such contact, which happens in all ages and climes, may illuminate, but it may also give the recipient an inflated sense of self-importance. The present book is full of textbook cases in which after the person comes down to earth, or arises reborn, the ego takes over and makes him or her fanatical, domineering, and (however gently) exploitative. This is probably why theurgy, the art of summoning higher beings, was kept so secret in ancient times, and only disclosed to initiates who, presumably, had already proved their psychological fitness. As the excerpts that head many of the preceding chapters have shown, our characters were often plunged into mystical or visionary experiences for which they were philosophically unprepared, and they had to make the best of it.

Neoplatonism assumes that the intentions of the universe are basically benevolent and that all souls aspire to union with the One, which is also the Good. If that is the case, then these experiences should be seen in a more positive light. Daimonic interventions, instead of being a cynical game played by our owners with their "property," may be a periodic infusion of spiritual energies, following a long-term plan for humanity. This was the view of the spiritualists who were sure that in 1848 a "spiritual telegraph" had been opened between heaven and earth, and that the great movement for social justice had been inspired from above. The Theosophists would apply the same interpretation to the great religions themselves, each one having served an evolutionary purpose for its particular time and place. They would be the first to add that once the impulse has been given, the human recipients of these energies, like the discoverers of other, physical energies, may do more harm than good.

How can we judge these movements, without the anachronism of applying current ethical ideals to past eras? Thinking of the two approaches sketched above, I would ask: Did they lead souls closer to the Platonic ideas of the True, the Beautiful, and the Good? A Buddhist might phrase it differently, though in the same spirit: Did they wish for all beings to be happy? Or, taking the darker, Fortean view, did they treat humans in some sense as property?

When I review each eccentric movement and its leader in this light, many of them fall short of the ideal. However, taken as a whole I see them as having contributed to four positive gains on the balance sheet: social, religious, philosophical, and aesthetic. The first and least contestable gain was in social progress in the Western world. During these years, slavery became indefensible and women's rights were on the way to recognition. The second was within American Christendom, where by the dawn of the twentieth century Calvinism was a spent force and God's primary attribute was seen as love, rather than anger. The third was in the philosophical challenge to materialism. Those scientists who study the paranormal, parapsychology, and the higher reaches of physics, with its link to philosophy, continue the challenge. The fourth was in the Arts and Crafts movement, with its dedication to beauty and to the spiritual value of handiwork.

In closing, I would add one more contribution, which has most touched me as an immigrant from history-laden Europe: the rich legacy of these movements to the Upstate region. It is a legacy waiting to be discovered, for most residents and visitors are oblivious to it. The land needs enlivening with these stories, in all their comedy and profundity. A first step is the following gazetteer of about 150 relevant sites in forty-three counties. A few already have the state's blue-and-gold historical markers to explain what happened there. If every site had one, what a difference it would make to public awareness of the past! People would be curious; children would ask questions. There would be tours and pilgrimages, and, who knows, the cauldron might start bubbling again.

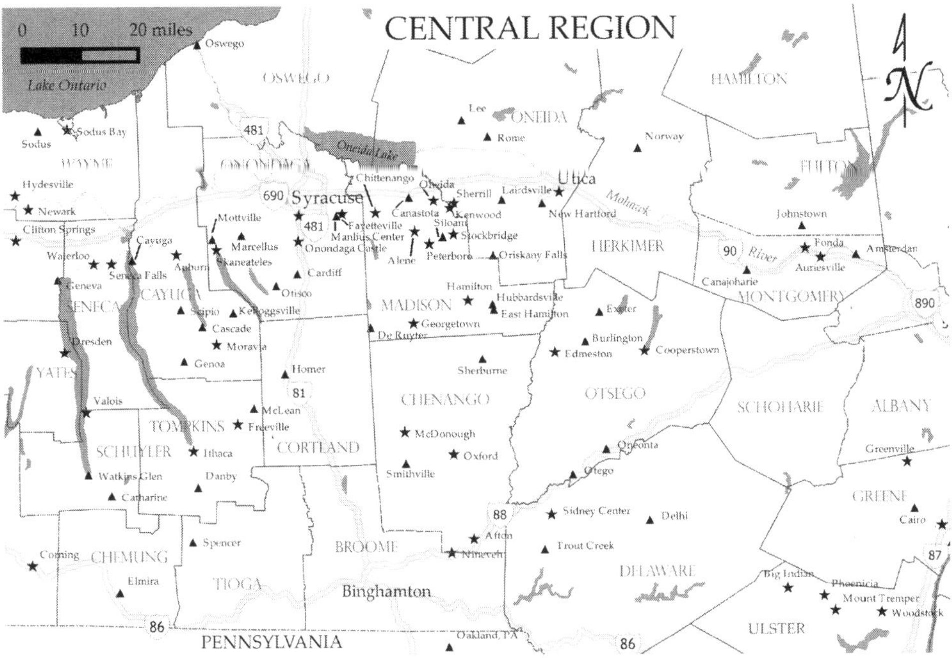

CENTRAL REGION
0 10 20 miles
Lake Ontario
Oswego
OSWEGO
Sodus
Sodus Bay
WAYNE
Hydesville
Newark
Clifton Springs
Waterloo
Seneca Falls
Cayuga
Auburn
Geneva
SENECA
CAYUGA
Dresden
YATES
Valois
SCHUYLER
Watkins Glen
Catharine
TOMPKINS
Ithaca
Danby
Freeville
McLean
Homer
CORTLAND
Scipio
Kelloggsville
Cascade
Moravia
Genoa
Mottville
Marcellus
Skaneateles
Otisco
Cardiff
ONONDAGA
Syracuse
Onondaga Castle
Fayetteville
Manlius Center
Chittenango
Oneida Lake
Oneida
Sherrill
Canastota
Kenwood
Siloam
Stockbridge
Alene
Peterboro
Oriskany Falls
Lee
ONEIDA
Rome
Lairdsville
Utica
New Hartford
Norway
HERKIMER
Mohawk River
HAMILTON
FULTON
Johnstown
Fonda
Auriesville
Amsterdam
Canajoharie
MONTGOMERY
MADISON
Hamilton
Hubbardsville
East Hamilton
Georgetown
De Ruyter
Exeter
Burlington
Edmeston
Cooperstown
OTSEGO
Sherburne
CHENANGO
McDonough
Oxford
Smithville
Oneonta
Otego
SCHOHARIE
ALBANY
Greenville
GREENE
Cairo
Sidney Center
Delhi
Afton
Nineveh
Trout Creek
DELAWARE
Big Indian
Phoenicia
Mount Tremper
Woodstock
ULSTER
BROOME
Binghamton
TIOGA
Spencer
CHEMUNG
Elmira
Corning
PENNSYLVANIA
Oakland, PA

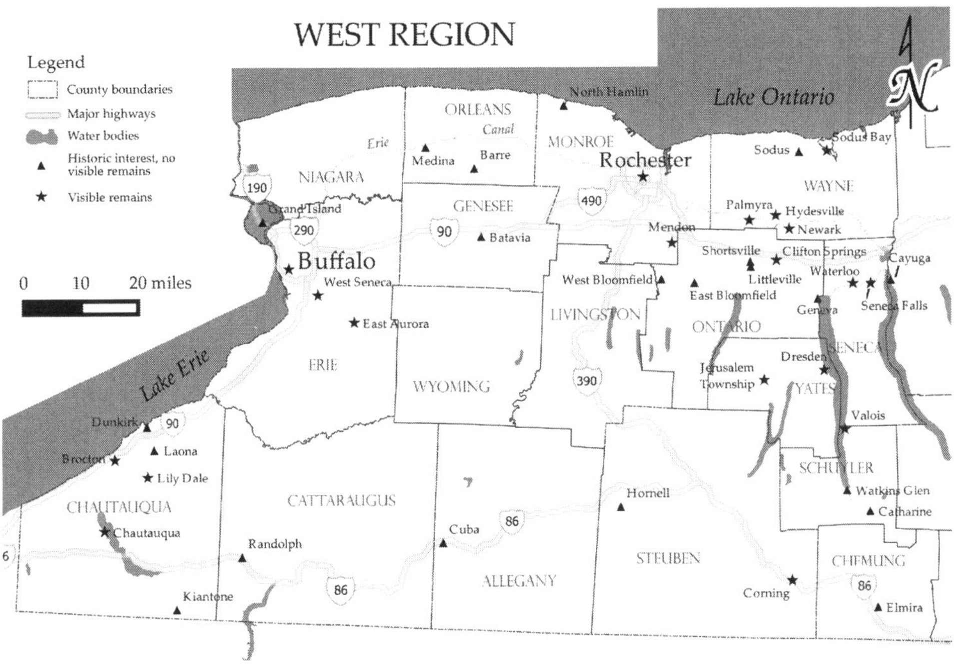

WEST REGION
Legend
County boundaries
Major highways
Water bodies
Historic interest, no visible remains
Visible remains
0 10 20 miles
Lake Ontario
Lake Erie
North Hamlin
ORLEANS
Erie Canal
Medina
Barre
MONROE
Rochester
NIAGARA
Grand Island
Buffalo
West Seneca
East Aurora
ERIE
GENESEE
Batavia
WYOMING
LIVINGSTON
West Bloomfield
Mendon
Sodus
Sodus Bay
WAYNE
Palmyra
Hydesville
Newark
Shortsville
Clifton Springs
Cayuga
Littleville
Waterloo
East Bloomfield
Geneva
Seneca Falls
ONTARIO
SENECA
Dresden
Jerusalem Township
YATES
Valois
SCHUYLER
Watkins Glen
Catharine
Dunkirk
Brocton
Laona
Lily Dale
CHAUTAUQUA
Chautauqua
Kiantone
CATTARAUGUS
Randolph
Cuba
ALLEGANY
Hornell
STEUBEN
Corning
CHEMUNG
Elmira

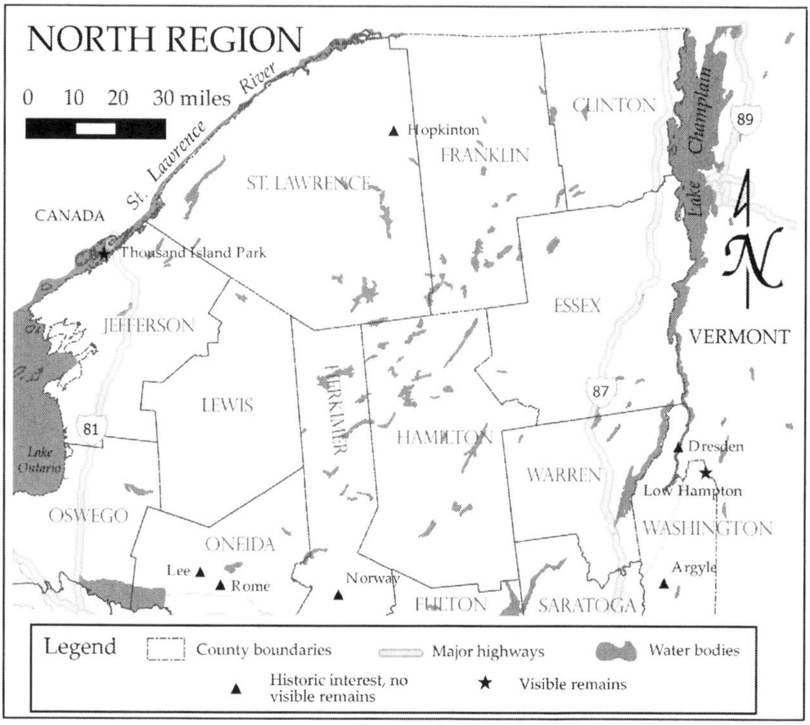
NORTH REGION
0 10 20 30 miles
St. Lawrence River
CANADA
Thousand Island Park
Hopkinton
ST. LAWRENCE
FRANKLIN
CLINTON
Lake Champlain
89
ESSEX
VERMONT
JEFFERSON
LEWIS
HERKIMER
HAMILTON
87
81
Lake Ontario
WARREN
Dresden
Low Hampton
WASHINGTON
OSWEGO
ONEIDA
Lee
Rome
Norway
FULTON
SARATOGA
Argyle
Legend
County boundaries
Major highways
Water bodies
Historic interest, no visible remains
Visible remains

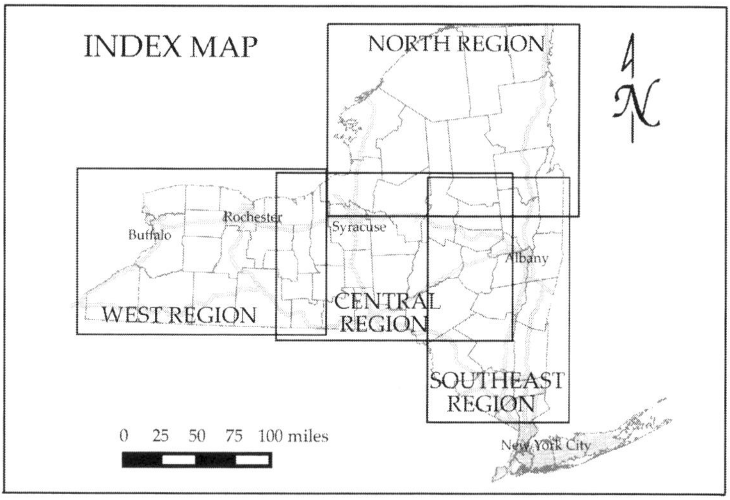
INDEX MAP
NORTH REGION
Rochester
Buffalo
Syracuse
Albany
WEST REGION
CENTRAL REGION
SOUTHEAST REGION
0 25 50 75 100 miles
New York City

SOUTHEAST REGION
N
HAMILTON
WASHINGTON
Norway
Argyle
SARATOGA
HERKIMER
FULTON
Mohawk
River
Saratoga Springs
Cambridge
Johnstown
Ballston Spa
Fonda
Amsterdam
Auriesville
90
Canajoharie
MONTGOMERY
Exeter
SCHENECTADY
Petersburg
Colonie
Albany
Cooperstown
88
RENSSELAER
OTSEGO
ALBANY
SCHOHARIE
Oneonta
New Lebanon
Greenville
Canaan
Cairo
Delhi
Leeds
987G
Catskill
Craryville
GREENE
DELAWARE
Big Indian
River
COLUMBIA
Phoenicia
Woodstock
Mount Tremper
Red Hook
Livingston Manor
Rhinebeck
Shekomeko
ULSTER
Stone Ridge
17
Amenia
Esopus
Mombaccus
Wassaic
SULLIVAN
Hyde Park
Hudson
DUTCHESS
Poughkeepsie
Bethel
Plattekill
Pine Bush
87
Wappingers Falls
Walden
Glen Spey
PUTNAM
ORANGE
Carmel
Blooming Grove
987
84
North Salem
6
WESTCHESTER
0
10
20 miles
684
ROCKLAND
Ossinning

Gazetteer of Sites

* Some visible remains (private house, monument, etc.)
** Public admitted, sometimes with fee, usually seasonal
*** Major site, well worth a visit

Abbreviations of the Counties of New York State

ALB Albany. ALL Alleghany. BRO Broome. CAT Cattaraugus. CAY Cayuga. CHA Chautauqua. CHM Chemung. CHN Chenango. COL Columbia. COR Cortland. DEL Delaware. DUT Dutchess. ERI Erie. GEN Genesee. GRE Greene. HER Herkimer. JEF Jefferson. LIV Livingston. MAD Madison. MNR Monroe. MNT Montgomery. NIA Niagara. ONE Oneida. ONO Onondaga. ONT Ontario. ORL Orleans. OSW Oswego. OTS Otsego. REN Rensselaer. SAR Saratoga. SCE Schenectady. SCY Schuyler. SEN Seneca. STE Steuben. STL Saint Lawrence. TIO Tioga. TOM Tompkins. ULS Ulster. WAR Warren. WAS Washington. WAY Wayne. WES Westchester. YAT Yates.

Afton (CHN)* Site of the house (destroyed) where Joseph Smith the Mormon prophet married Emma Hale in 1827. There is a NYS historical marker beside the Afton Fairgrounds on Route 41. House (private) of Josiah Stowell, patron and friend of Joseph Smith, on Route 7, 4 miles south of Afton. A bronze statue of Joseph Smith stands before the house, which is marked with a plaque (ch. 6).

Albany (ALB) Colony of early perfectionists under John B. Foot and the Annesley sisters, c. 1831 (ch. 10). The Millerites, after their Great Disappointment, hold a conference to determine Adventist doctrine, 1845 (ch. 8). Charles Fort, philosopher of unexplained phenomena, born 1874. Albany Karma Thegsum Chöling (Tibetan Kagyu school). Shambhala Meditation Center. (ch. 25).

Alene (MAD)* Nichols Pond State Park, disputed site of the Champlain Battle, 1615. Explanatory plaque and a NYS marker by a large tribal or sacred stone (ch. 4).

Amenia (DUT)* Thomas Lake Harris's Brotherhood of the New Life, 1863–67. He founds the Bank of Amenia and builds the present M&T Bank building, 1865 (ch. 16).

Amsterdam (MON) In the nearby woods, John Bovee Dods has his first spirit encounters, with his dead father (1809). Home of Benjamin Paul Blood (1832–1919), farmer, mystic, and receiver of the "anesthetic revelation."

Argyle (WAS) Robert Matthews ("Matthias") invades the church and proclaims the "Declaration of Judgment," with himself as its divine agent, 1830 (ch. 8).

Auburn (CAY)** Brigham Young, Mormon leader, works as a carpenter, 1815–17; some of his reputed work is preserved in the Seward House. Kate Fox's visit, invited by Elias Capron, 1849, starts a wave of spirit circles and mediums (ch. 12). The "Apostolic Circle," run by Mrs. Benedict, summons Thomas Lake Harris and James Leander Scott as mediums for St. Paul and others, 1850 (chs. 12, 16). Gustav Stickley, future Arts & Crafts pioneer, directs manufacturing at the state prison, 1890–92 (ch. 23).

Auriesville (MON)** Shrine of Our Lady of Martyrs, 1884, commemorates the Jesuit missionaries martyred in the 1640s (chs. 4, 25).

Ballston Spa (SAR) General Abner Doubleday, later president of the Theosophical Society, born 1819 (ch. 18).

Barre (ORL) Yuh-Heh Magnetic Mineral Springs, a healing center in the 1870s (ch. 17).

Batavia (GEN) Albert Brisbane, American promoter of Charles Fourier's social philosophy and founder of Sodus Bay community, born 1809 (ch. 8). Home of anti-masonic agitator William Morgan until his abduction, 1826 (ch. 7).

Bethel (SUL)* Woodstock Festival, 1969, commemorated by Bethel Woods Center for the Arts, 2006 (ch. 25).

Big Indian (ULS)* Monument to the 18th-century Esopus Indian shaman Winnisook (ch. 25).

Blooming Grove (ULS) Andrew Jackson Davis, the "Poughkeepsie Seer," born 1826 (ch. 11).

Brocton (CHA)* Thomas Lake Harris's Brotherhood of the New Life starts a vineyard, 1867; he lives until 1875 in "Vine Cliff" (private) (ch. 16).

Buffalo (ERI)** St. Paul's Church (replaced by St. Paul's Episcopal Cathedral), where Mordecai Manuel Noah, playwright and politician, dedicates his foundation stone for "Ararat, a Refuge for the Jews," 1826, now in Erie County Historical Society (ch. 7). Revival movements of the Buffalo Creek Prophet and the Tonawanda Prophet, 1830s (ch. 4).

Burlington (OTS) Parley Parker Pratt, Mormon leader, born 1807 (ch. 7).

Cairo (GRE) Fatimid Order of Cairo New York founded, 2010 (ch. 25).

Cambridge (WAS) Robert Matthews ("Matthias"), prophet and accused murderer, born 1788 (ch. 8).

Canaan (COL) Parley Pratt, future Mormon leader, has a vision of a square and compass in the sky, 1830 (ch. 7).

Canajoharie (MON) Susan B. Anthony, woman suffrage leader, teaches at the Academy, 1846–48 (Ch. 13).

Canastota (MAD) General Convention of the New York Perfectionists held, 1835 (ch. 10).

Cardiff (ONO) Site of the burial and exhumation of the "Cardiff Giant," 1868 (ch. 20).

Carmel (PUT)* Chuamg Yen Monastery, home of the Buddhist Association of the United States, 1981 (ch. 25).

Cascade (CAY) The Cascade Hotel (demolished) owned by Mary Andrews, spiritualist medium (ch. 20).

Catherine (SCY) Birthplace of Adeline Eliza Nichols, 1826–1909, later called Lois Waisbrooker, feminist editor, sexologist, protester.

Catskill (GRE) After being transported here, Andrew Jackson Davis meets Galen and Swedenborg in a graveyard on his way back to Poughkeepsie, 1844 (ch. 11).

Cayuga (CAY) J. C. F. Grumbine, founder of the Order of the White Rose, has his first ministry as clerk of the Universalist Society, 1884 (ch. 21).

Chautauqua (CHA)** Chautauqua Institute founded, 1874 (ch. 15).

Chittenango (MAD)* Birthplace (house destroyed) of Lyman Frank Baum, author, 1856 (ch. 21).

Clifton Springs (ONT)** Hiram Edson Farm and Visitor Center, "Theological Birthplace of the Seventh-day Adventist Church" (ch. 8). Clifton Springs Sanitarium Historic District and Foster Cottage Museum, where Amanda Jones communicated with the spirit of Dr. Andrews during her "air cure" (ch. 17).

Colonie (ALB)** First Shaker settlement, 1776. Home of Mother Ann Lee until her death, 1784. The surviving buildings now comprise the Watervliet National Shaker Historic District (ch. 3).

Cooperstown (OTS)** General Abner Doubleday, here known as the inventor of baseball, spends his boyhood, 1830s (ch. 18). Indian grave consecrated 1874, with poem by Rev. W. W. Lord, 1899 (ch. 4). The "Cardiff Giant" rests in the Farmer's Museum (ch. 20).

Corning (STE)* Scottish Rite Cathedral, 1921: the only purpose-built temple of this high-grade Masonic order (ch. 7).

Craryville (COL)* Pumpkin Hollow Retreat Center (Northeast Theosophical Foundation), 1937–present (Ch. 25).

Cuba (ALL) Cora Scott Richmond, much-married spiritualist medium, born 1840.

Danby (TOM) Swedenborgian society or church founded by Dr. Louis Beers, 1816 (ch. 11).

De Ruyter (MAD) Ezra Cornell, founder of Cornell University, born 1807 (ch. 20).

Delhi (DEL) Site of a perfectionist community under Hiram Sheldon, 1830s (ch. 10).

Dresden (WAR) William Miller preaches his first sermon announcing the coming end of the world, 1831 (ch. 8).

Dresden (YAT)** First settlement of the Universal Friend, Jemima Wilkinson, and her followers, 1790–94 (ch. 3). Robert Green Ingersoll, freethinker and humanist, born 1833. His birthplace is now a museum (ch. 20).

Dunkirk (CHA) Anna Cross Kimball, spiritualist medium and sexologist, born 1831. Childhood home from c. 1895 of George Adamski (1891–1965), founder of the Royal Order of Tibet and UFO contactee.

East Aurora (ERI)*** Important site for the history of the Arts & Crafts movement and of utopian thought. Home of Elbert Hubbard and the Roycrofters, 1900. Buildings include the Roycroft Inn, the Roycroft Chapel, the Copper Shop, the Print Shop, and the Elbert Hubbard Roycroft Museum (ch. 22).

East Bloomfield (ONT) Home of Amanda Theodosia Jones, spiritualist and inventor of the vacuum canning process (ch. 17).

East Hamilton (MAD) See Hubbardsville.

Edmeston (CHN)* Rosa Mystica House of Prayer, 1984, located on geodetic instructions from Mother Elena Leonardi (ch. 25).

Elmira (CHM) James Martin Peebles, spiritualist and world traveler, serves as Universalist pastor, 1853–55 (ch. 21). Home of Jane Roberts and Robert F. Butts, medium and scribe for communications from "Seth," from 1963 (ch. 25).

Esopus (ULS)* Burial place of Mary Cragin, beloved of John Humphrey Noyes, drowned 1851 (ch. 10). Summer residence of Aleister Crowley, poet and magus, 1918. Center of Peter Lamborn Wilson's poetic actions, 2009–10 (ch. 25).

Exeter (OTS) Joseph Ball, sleeping preacher, active 1819 (ch. 5).

Fayetteville (ONO)** The Gage House (or Home), residence of Matilda Joslyn Gage, women's rights leader and Theosophist, from 1854. Now seat of the Matilda Joslyn Gage Foundation (ch. 13).

Fonda (MON)** Shrine of Saint Kateri Tekakwitha, the "Lily of the Mohawks" (1656–1680), 1938. (chs. 4, 25).

Freeville (TOM)** Center for New York spiritualist conventions from 1895. Now the Temple of Truth, whose buildings include the Dittman Memorial Chapel, 1952.

Georgetown (MAD)* Spirit House, or Brown's Free Hall (private), built by Timothy Brown on spirit instructions, 1860s; his earlier house (private) 2 miles south, built 1850s (ch. 17).

Geneva (ONT) Perfectionist convention held, 1846.

Genoa (CAY) Important perfectionist convention attended by John Humphrey Noyes, 1847 (ch. 10). James Martin Peebles, spiritualist and world traveler, serves as Universalist pastor, 1846–49 (ch. 21).

Glen Spey (SUL)* Kadampa Meditation Center (New Kadampa tradition), (ch. 25).

Grand Island (ERI) Intended site of Mordecai Manuel Noah's "Ararat," as a refuge for the Jews and all who will accept the Mosaic Law, 1826 (ch. 7).

Greenville (GRE)* Orgyen Cho Dzong Retreat Center (Tibetan Nyingma school) (ch. 25).

Hamilton (MAD)* Mystic Order of Veiled Prophets of the Enchanted Realm (known as MOVPER or the Grotto) founded, 1890. Plaque on the Smith Block, Broad Street (ch. 7).

Homer (COR) Amelia Bloomer, women's rights leader and dress reformer, born 1818. Andrew Dickson White, freethinker and first president of Cornell University, born 1832 (ch. 20).

Hopkinton (STL) "The Little Band," active 1836–1850s, separates from the Congregational church and tries to raise the dead. Rev. Austin Kent, exponent of free love.

Hornell (STE) Birthplace of Alva John Kiehle (1930–2009), investigator and, as John A. Keel, writer on strange phenomena, UFOs, and conspiracy theory.

Hubbardsville (MAD) Includes East Hamilton. George Addison Throop and others attempt to found a Fourierist community at "Hubbard's Corners," 1843 (Throop Papers, Cornell University Library). Perfectionist convention held, 1845. Three families begin semi-communistic living at Beaver Meadow, 1847, before joining the Oneida Community (ch. 10).

Hyde Park (DUT) Boyhood home of Andrew Jackson Davis, the "Poughkeepsie Seer" (ch. 11).

Hydesville (WAY)* Site of the Hydesville rappings, 1848, and the Fox family's rented cottage. In 1916 the cottage is moved to Lily Dale. It burns in 1955 and is commemorated by a stone marker. Around 1980 John Drummond, a Canadian, reconstructs the cottage on the surviving foundations, using material from old barns. This too burns down in 1983. In 1999 the National Association of Spiritualist Churches buys the site, protects the stone foundations with a pavilion, and landscapes the adjacent grove of trees. The bricks around the building record the names of many donors to the project, completed in 2004 with the inauguration of the Hydesville Memorial Park (chs. 12, 15).

Ithaca (TOM)** Dr. Louis Beers founds a Swedenborgian society, 1816 (ch. 11). John Humphrey Noyes, future founder of the Oneida Community, starts his first magazine, the *Witness*, 1837 (ch. 10). Cornell University founded, 1865; the campus includes Andrew Dickson White's house, tomb, and witchcraft collection (ch. 20). Richardson Cottage (destroyed), residence of Hiram Corson, Professor of English, when hosting H. P. Blavatsky, 1875 (ch. 18). Foundation of Light, with Ellis Hollow Stone Circle, 1970s. Namgyal Monastery Institute of Buddhist Studies, North American seat of the 14th Dalai Lama, 1992 (ch. 25).

Jerusalem township (YAT)* Second settlement and house (private) of the Universal Friend, Jemima Wilkinson, and her followers, 1794–1819. (ch. 3).

Johnstown (FUL) Elizabeth Cady Stanton, women's rights leader and freethinker, born 1815 (ch. 13).

Kelloggsville (CAY) James Martin Peebles, spiritualist and world traveler, serves as Universalist pastor, 1846–49 (ch. 21).

Kenwood (MAD)*** Site of primary importance for the history of the communal movement. The Oneida Community Mansion House, begun 1861 and completed in virtually its present form 1878. Home of John Humphrey Noyes from 1848–79 and of the Oneida Community until 1881, when it dissolves and becomes a joint-stock company (ch. 10).

Kiantone (CHA) William Brittingham discovers magnetic healing springs, 1852; John Murray Spear, medium and social reformer, founds Harmonia, or "the Domain," 1853; notorious Free Love Convention held, 1858 (ch. 15).

Lairdsville (ONE) Important perfectionist convention attended by John Humphrey Noyes, 1847 (ch. 10).

Laona (CHA) Home of Jeremiah F. Carter, proto-spiritualist medium, 1845 (ch. 15)

Lee (ONE) Birthplace of Hiram Erastus Butler (1841–1916), author of *Solar Biology* (1887), founder of the Society for Esoteric Culture (Boston, 1887), and leader of the Esoteric Fraternity, a community in Applegate, California (1891–).

Leeds (GRE)* New York Mahayana Temple (Chinese Buddhist), c. 1971 (ch. 25).

Lily Dale (CHA)*** Important spiritualist community with an uninterrupted history as Laona Free Association, c. 1850; Religious Society of Free Thinkers, 1855; Cassadaga Lake Free Association, now called Lily Dale Assembly. Buildings include Marion Skidmore Library, Forest Temple. Extensive summer program of lectures and workshops (ch. 15).

Littleville (ONT) Ontario Union, a Fourierist community, 1843–c. 1844 (ch. 9).

Livingston Manor (SUL)* Dai Bosatsu Zendo Kongo-ji, a Rinzai Zen Buddhist monastery, 1976 (ch. 25).

Low Hampton (WAS)** Home of William Miller, preacher of the end of the world, from 1786. His house, built 1815, is maintained by the Seventh-Day Adventist Church (ch. 8).

Manlius Center (ONO) Perfectionist convention held, 1844 (ch. 10).

Marcellus (ONO) Home of Rachel Baker, most notable of the sleeping preachers, from 1803–57 (ch. 5).

McDonough (CHN)* Palyul Retreat Center (Tibetan Dzogchen school), 1998 (ch. 25).

McLean (TOM) James Martin Peebles, spiritualist and world traveler, serves as Universalist pastor, 1842–46 (ch. 21).

Medina (ORL) First phenomenon of "direct spirit voice." Following noises, a spirit called "Josh" speaks and haunts the family. (Britten 1884, 511–12)

Mendon (MNR)* House built by Brigham Young, Mormon leader, who lived there 1830–32 and was baptized in the adjacent mill pond.

Mombaccus (ULS) Sacred site identified by Peter Lamborn Wilson as derived from "Mask of Bacchus," named by Dutch settlers for an image of Maysingwey, the Algonkan Bear God (ch. 25).

Moravia (CAY)* Houses (private) of the Keelers and their servant and medium, Mary Andrews. Mary Todd Lincoln visits for séances, 1872; Cornell professor Hiram Corson visits, 1874 (ch. 18). The parents of Cyrus Teed (founder of Koreshanity) are settled here and he starts his first community, 1870s (ch. 19).

Mottville (ONO) James Martin Peebles, spiritualist and world traveler, serves as Universalist pastor, 1846–49 (Ch. 21).

Mount Tremper (ULS)* Zen Mountain Monastery, 1980 (Ch. 25).

New Hartford (ONE) Cyrus Teed, founder of the Koreshan Community, spends his youth and works on the Erie Canal, 1850s (ch. 19).

New Lebanon (COL)*** Large collection of Shaker buildings and memorabilia. Joseph Meacham heads the New Light congregation, 1779–80, and joins the Shakers who settle there, 1780. The North Family Village is now the Mount Lebanon Shaker Village, with the Shaker Museum and Library (ch. 3). The South Family Village houses The Abode of the Message (Sufi Order International), 1975 (ch. 25)

Newark (WAY)** Newark-Arcadia Historical Society Museum; material on spiritualism (ch. 12).

Nineveh (BRO)* House (private) of Joseph Knight, friend and disciple of Joseph Smith, on Route 26, south of the Nineveh bridge, marked with a plaque (ch. 6).

North Hamlin (ORL) Clarkson Phalanx, a Fourierist community, 1843–c. 1844 (ch. 9).

North Salem (WES) First pastorship of John Humphrey Noyes, future founder of the Oneida Community, 1833 (ch. 10).

Norway (HER) Home of Dr. Rowland Sears, who cures Rachel Baker of preaching in her sleep, 1816 (ch. 5).

Oakland* (Susquehanna County, Pennsylvania; formerly named Harmony) Site owned by the Church of Jesus Christ of Latter-day Saints, 3 miles west of Oakland on Route 171. The site commemorates the revival of the Aaronic Priesthood (monumental sculpture of John the Baptist with Joseph Smith and Oliver Cowdery), the first baptisms of the Mormon Church, the site of the cottage and acreage owned by Joseph Smith and his wife, Emma Hale, and, on the other side of Route 171, the excavated foundations of the house of Isaac Hale, Emma's father. In the adjacent graveyard are the tombstones of Isaac Hale and his wife, Elizabeth, and of Alvin Smith, the first child of Joseph and Emma, born June 15, 1828 and died the same day (ch. 6).

Oneida (MAD)** Oneida Indian Nation territory. Shako:wi Cultural Center and Sacred Stone of the Oneidas (ch. 4). See also Kenwood, Sherrill.

Oneonta (OTS) James Martin Peebles, spiritualist and world traveler, serves as pastor of the Oneonta Universalist Society, 1889 (ch. 21).

Onondaga Castle (ONO)* Onondaga Indian Reservation. Tomb of Handsome Lake, Seneca chief, visionary, and founder of the Gaiwi'io, reformed Indian religion (ch. 4).

Oriskany Falls (ONE) (formerly called Cassety or Castor Hollow) Union of two local temperance orders to form the Order of Good Templars, open to men and women of all races, 1851.

Ossinning (WES) Heartt Place (destroyed), residence of Benjamin Folger, businessman. As "Mount Zion," it houses the prophet Robert Matthews ("Matthias") and the future abolitionist leader Sojourner Truth, formerly Isabella Van Wagenen, early 1830s (ch. 8).

Oswego (OSW) James Martin Peebles, spiritualist and world traveler, serves as Universalist pastor, 1850s; Amelia Bloomer preaches there in bloomers, (ch. 21).

Otego (OTS) The Three Treasures Zen Center (Korean Kwan Um school) (ch. 25).

Otisco (ONO) Simeon Watson, sleeping preacher, active 1826 (ch. 5).

Oxford (CHN)* James Martin Peebles, future spiritualist and world traveler, educated at Oxford Academy, late 1830s (ch. 21).

Palmyra (WAY)*** Important complex of Mormon sites and monuments. Home of Joseph Smith from 1816. Sacred Grove: site of his first vision, 1820. Hill Cumorah: finding place of the golden tablets, 1823 (retrieved by Smith, 1827). Grandin Press, where the Book of Mormon is printed, 1830. Hill Cumorah Monument by Torleif S. Knaphus, 1935. Latter-Day Saints Temple, 2000. Hill Cumorah Visitors Center, 2002 (ch. 6).

Peterboro (MAD)** House (destroyed), land office, and former free church of Gerrit Smith. National Abolition Hall of Fame (ch. 13).

Petersburg (REN)* Rahob Dharma Center (Tibetan Buddhist), 2002 (ch. 25).

Phoenicia (ULS)* Menla Mountain Retreat (branch of Tibet House, NYC), 2001 (ch. 25).

Pine Bush (ORA)* Site of much UFO activity, 1980s–90s. Dharma Drum Retreat Center, Chan (Chinese) Zen Buddhist (in Ulster County). Blue Cliff Monastery, Vietnamese Zen Buddhist, 2007 (in Sullivan County) (ch. 25).

Plattekill (ULS) Swedenborgian church founded by Dr. Louis Beers, 1817 (ch. 11).

Poughkeepsie (DUT) Home of Andrew Jackson Davis, the "Poughkeepsie Seer," from c. 1840 and site of his first revelations (ch. 10).

Randolph (CAT) John Murray Spear's New Motor, built on spirit instructions, brought from Lynn, Mass., and destroyed by a mob, 1854 (ch. 15).

Red Hook (DUT)* Kunzand Palchen Ling Tibetan Buddhist Center, 2003 (ch. 25).

Rhinebeck (DUT)** Omega Institute for Holistic Studies, 1977; holds an extensive program of lectures, workshops, conferences, and retreats from April to October, (ch. 25).

Rochester (MON)** Sites of Isaac and Amy Post's house, Leah Fox's house, Corinthian Hall, Josephine Cables's house, Plymouth Spiritualist Church, all destroyed by urban renewal (chs. 12, 13, 18). Susan B. Anthony's house, maintained as a museum (ch. 13). American Theosophical Society convention held, 1886, with Josephine Cables as increasingly independent leader (ch. 18). First Universalist Church, Bevier Memorial Building, and other buildings by Claude Bragdon, architect and theosophical writer; other buildings destroyed, including his largest work, the New York Central Railroad Station (ch. 24). Rochester Zen Center founded by Philip Kapleau, 1966 (ch. 25).

Rome (ONE) Charles Grandison Finney, preacher of the Second Great Awakening, invited to lead his first revival, 1826 (ch. 2).

Saratoga Springs (SAR) Jane Roberts, poet, philosopher, and medium for the Seth writings, born 1929; attends Skidmore College, 1947–50 (ch. 25).

Scipio (CAY) Isaac Post, Quaker, abolitionist, and spiritualist medium, born 1798 (ch. 13). Site of Rachel Baker's religious crisis, 1811, and preaching in her sleep, 1813–16 (ch. 5). James Jesse Strang, rival to Brigham Young and founder of a breakaway Mormon sect, born 1813.

Seneca Falls (SEN)** Women's Rights National Historical Park, including the Women's Hall of Fame, the reconstructed Wesleyan Chapel where the first women's rights convention was held, 1848, and the house of Elizabeth Cady Stanton (ch. 13).

Shekomeko (DUT) Site of a chapel built by the Moravians for the first Christian mission to the Mahicans, 1741–44.

Sherburne (CHN) Childhood home of Brigham Young, Mormon leader, 1804–17. NYS marker at intersection of Route 21 and Cole Rd.

Sherrill* (MAD) Principal factory of Oneida Ltd., silverware manufacturer and successor to the Oneida Community on its dissolution in 1880 (ch. 10).

Shortsville (ORL) Amanda Jones, spiritualist medium and inventor, receives the "Crusader Documents" at William Livingston Brown's house, 1872 (ch. 17)

Sidney Center (DEL)* Padmasambhava Buddhist Center (Tibetan Nyingma school). Osmanli Naksh-i'bendi Hakkani Dergahi (Sufi Center), 2002 (ch. 25).

Siloam (MAD) Site of medicinal springs frequented by reformers and spiritualists (ch. 13).

Skaneateles (ONO)* Skaneateles Community, a secular, Fourierist community, 1843–46 (ch. 9). The main house is currently the Frog Pond Bed-and-Breakfast.

Smithville (CHN) Home of James Martin Peebles, Universalist minister, spiritualist, and world traveler, from childhood until c.1842 (ch. 21).

Sodus (WAY) Joseph Howard, sleeping preacher, active 1818 (ch. 5).

Sodus Bay (WAY)* Sodus Bay Phalanx, a Fourierist community, 1844–46. Some buildings survive as part of the Cracker Box Palace Farm Animal Sanctuary (ch. 9).

Spencer (TIO) Swedenborgian society founded by Dr. Louis Beers, 1816 (ch. 11).

Stockbridge (MAD)* House (private) of Paschal Beverly Randolph, author, medium, and Rosicrucian, and Mary Randolph, healer and publisher, 1851–60 (ch. 14).

Stone Ridge (ULS)* Vivekananda Retreat Center (Ramakrishna Order), 1997 (ch. 25).

Syracuse (ONO)* L. Frank Baum's childhood home, Roselawn (destroyed), from 1866. Baum's sister's house on W. Onondaga St. where he met his wife, Maud Gage; to be restored as a museum (ch. 21). J. C. F. Grumbine, pastor of First Universalist Society, 1884–87; runs College of Psychical Sciences & Unfoldment and Order of the White Rose, 1899–1900 (ch. 21). William H. Dower founds Temple of the People, 1898 (ch. 14). Gustav Stickley's factory (Eastwood, 1892), showrooms, and homes. His house on Columbus Avenue (1900) is to be restored as a museum. Irene Sargent holds court at the Yates Hotel (destroyed) to Arts and Crafts pioneers including Claude Bragdon, and edits the *Craftsman*, 1900s (ch. 23).

Thousand Island Park (JEF)* Vivekananda Cottage, where the Hindu spiritual teacher spent the summer of 1895. Acquired by the Ramakrishna-Vivekananda Center of New York, 1946 (ch. 25).

Trout Creek (DEL) Cyrus Teed, founder of Koreshanity and theorist of the concave earth, born 1836 (ch. 19)

Utica (ONE)* Gerrit Smith, landowner, philanthropist, and abolitionist leader, born 1797 (ch. 13). Charles Grandison Finney preaches at First Presbyterian

Church and to mill owners and workers in his first revival campaign, 1826 (ch. 2). Thomas Lake Harris, future founder of the Brotherhood of the New Life, spends his youth, c. 1828–45 (ch. 16). Daniel Cody founds the Knights of Jericho, parent of the Independent Order of Good Templars, 1850. Paschal Beverly Randolph, author and medium, active from about 1852, resident 1862–64; his wife, Mary Jane Randolph, healer, resident through 1872 (ch. 1). Cyrus Teed's first visions and medical practice, 1869–70 (ch. 19). Justus Henry Rathbone, founder of the Knights of Pythias, born 1839; his monument and tomb in New Forest Cemetery, 1899 (ch. 7).

Valois (SEN)* Wisdom's Goldenrod Philosophic Center founded by Anthony Damiani, 1972; Library inaugurated by the Dalai Lama, 1979 (ch. 25).

Walden (ORA)* Tsechen Kunchab Ling Temple of All-Encompassing Great Compassion (Tibetan Sakya school), founded 2001, temple begun 2007 (ch. 25).

Wappingers Falls (DUT)* Kagyu Thubten Chöling Monastery and Retreat Center (Tibetan Kagyu school), 1978 (ch. 25).

Wassaic (DUT) Thomas Lake Harris's Brotherhood of the New Life, 1861–63 (ch. 16).

Waterloo (SEN)** Log house (reconstructed) of Peter Whitmer, where the Book of Mormon was completed, 1829, and Visitor Center. (ch. 6). House of Elizabeth M'Clintock, part of Women's Rights National Historical Park (ch. 13).

Watkins Glen (SCY) Watkins Freethinkers Convention, with maiden speech by women's rights leader Matilda Joslyn Gage, participation of the Theosophist Albert L. Rawson and the Universalist minister James M. Peebles, and arrest of D. M. Bennett, former Shaker and freethinker, for distributing prohibited literature, 1878 (ch. 20).

West Bloomfield (ONT) Bloomfield Association, a Fourierist community, 1843–c. 1844 (ch. 9).

West Seneca (ERI)** Shaker settlement, 1826–c. 1836, then sold to the Community of True Inspiration (Ebenezers), 1843–1860s. Several buildings erected by the community are still in use, including the one housing the West Seneca Historical Society Museum (ch. 9).

Woodstock (ULS)* See also Bethel, Mount Tremper. Church of the Holy Transfiguration of Christ on the Mount, built 1891, presided over by Archbishop William Henry Francis Brothers, c. 1930–84. Byrdcliffe Arts and Crafts community founded by Ralph Whitehead, 1902–29, now under restoration and revival. Karma Triyana Dharmachakra monastery, North American seat of the 17th Karmapa, 1980. Palden Sakya Center for Tibetan Buddhist Studies and Meditation (Tibetan Sakya school). Shadhuliyya Sufi Center Northeast (ch. 25).

Notes

Chapter 1: The Historical Background

1. Information from Pound, xv.

2. Most of this chapter is common knowledge, its facts found in standard encyclopedias and histories and given focus by more specialized reading, e.g., of the works of Barkun, Berleth, Bernstein, Cross, Guarneri, Gutierrez, and Reid (see Bibliography under these names).

3. These sources complement the scholarly literature with rare information, anecdotes, and insights. Examples are the works of Carmer, Klees, Metzger, Winfield, and Zimmer. I have made judicious use of the 1940 WPA guide (see Bibliography under *New York. A Guide*), which, in some respects, is not superseded. DeLorme's topographical atlas (see *New York Atlas*) has also been an indispensable companion.

4. Apollonius of Tyana: first-century Pythagorean philosopher and magician; Marcion of Sinope: second-century Gnostic bishop; Mansur al-Hallaj (c. 858–922): Islamic mystic executed for heresy; Sabbatai Zevi (1626–1676): claimant to being the Jewish Messiah.

5. The Tuscaroras joined the Five Nations in 1722.

6. For the churches, see chapter 25. The Mohawk Valley mansions are Fort Johnson (1749), Johnson Hall (1761–62), the Herkimer Home (1764), and Guy Park (1774).

7. Chaplain to Sullivan's army (Berleth, 275) and founder of Hamilton College (chartered 1812) on land given him by the Oneidas.

8. A commemorative stone in Cooperstown records Clinton's ingenious maneuver.

9. Reid, 132.

10. On the earliest canals, see http://www.nysm.nysed.gov/research_collections/research/history/three/bat4.html

11. Ginseng was grown in New York's forests and exported in great quantities to China. See http://www.dec.ny.gov/animals/7472.html

12. Or so he said; see chapter 11.

13. Bernstein, 350.

14. A trend reversed after the Depression by the state's acquiring derelict farmland for state forests.

Chapter 2: The Religious Background

1. Finney, 20–21.

2. See Reid, 84–97 on the Mohawk chapel at Fort Hunter. The Onondaga chapel was not built.

3. For the history of Queen Anne's gifts of communion plate, see Harris & McKay. For the Mohawk silver, see the website of Christ Church Royal Chapel, http://www.parishoftyendinaga.org/chapelroyal.htm. For the Onondaga silver, see the website of St. Peter's Protestant Episcopal Church, Albany, www.stpeterschurchalbany.org/objects.htm.

4. Lambert, 254.

5. Klein, 166–67.

6. Klein, 169.

7. For distinctions between Calvinists, evangelicals, and revivalists, see Lambert, 27.

8. See especially chapters 9–10 of Lovejoy.

9. Marini, 53.

10. Corliss, 185–86.

11. On Meacham's establishment of Shaker norms, see Marini, 137–35.

12. Paraphrased from the Winchester Profession, adopted at the Universalist Convention in Winchester, NH, 1803. See Robinson, 4, 56.

13. Quoted in Robinson, 29.

14. Ballou, 125.

15. The two sects merged in 1961 into the Unitarian Universalist Association.

16. This summary is based mainly on Dorrien, 1–43, and Robinson, 26–38.

17. Dorrien, 31–33.

18. Dorrien, 38.

19. Hardman, 30.

20. Hambrick-Stowe, 6.

21. Hambrick-Stowe, 9.

22. From "immediately after an early breakfast" until "nearly dinner time." Finney, 16.

23. Hardman, 71.

24. Bratt, 62, citing Ephraim Perkins.

25. Figures in Hardman, 209.

26. Reference is to the Hill Cumorah Pageant, which acts out the history of the Church of Jesus Christ of Latter-Day Saints.

Chapter 3: The Female Face of God

1. *Life, Character, Revelations*, 4–8.
2. French Protestants, persecuted even before Louis XIV revoked the Edict of Nantes in 1685.
3. Whitworth, 13–14.
4. Campion, 49.
5. Campion, 57.
6. Now called Colonie, a suburb adjacent to Albany Airport.
7. White & Taylor, 47–60.
8. Marini, 111–12.
9. Marini, 130.
10. White & Taylor, 101.
11. *Republic* X, 596c.
12. Visitors' reports are collected in Wergland 2007 and Wergland 2010.
13. From a newspaper report, quoted in Wergland 2007, 5.
14. Garrett, 189, 216–17.
15. Garrett, 237–38.
16. Stein, 167.
17. Stein, 167.
18. Stein, 170.
19. Stein, 171.
20. Garrett, 238.
21. Stein, 175.
22. Stein, 177, 180–81.
23. Wisbey 11.
24. Wisbey, 10.
25. Wisbey, 12–13.
26. Marini, 48.
27. Wisbey, 26.
28. Wisbey, 94–96.
29. E.g. Brownell, Hudson.
30. Wisbey, 131, quoting La Rochefoucauld.
31. Wisbey, 168.
32. Wisbey, 144.

Chapter 4: The Indian Tragedy

1. Parker, section 94.
2. Schiavo & Salvucci, I, 13.
3. *New York*, 422, calls it an Oneida fort. According to Schiavo & Salvucci, 405, it was Onondaga.
4. See Giambastini, 49, and Daniel H. Weiskotten's arguments at http://www.rootsweb.ancestry.com/~nyccazen/Shorts/Questions/NicholsPond.html
5. Schiavo & Salvucci, I, 47–48.
6. Schiavo & Salvucci, I, 52.

7. Salvucci & Schiavo, II, 341.
8. Francis Parkman (1823–1893), historian.
9. Salvucci & Schiavo, II, 7.
10. Dennis 1993, 266.
11. Wallace 1972, 73.
12. Wallace 1972, 120.
13. Bellknap, 21, 23–24, quoted in Hauptmann, 48.
14. Hauptmann, 27.
15. *Forest Hill Cemetery*, [11].
16. Hauptmann, 214.
17. Bastine & Winfield, 198–99.
18. See Ezekiel 1:5–10; Revelation 4:6–7.
19. Parker, Introduction, 7.
20. Dennis 2010, 70.
21. Wallace 1972, 89–91.
22. See the transcription made in Cattaraugus, 1906, in Parker, 86–94.
23. Dennis 2010, 96.
24. Dennis 1993, 21.
25. Wallace 1872, 253.
26. Wallace 1972, 261.
27. Wallace 1972, 260.
28. Painting in the Smithsonian American Art Museum. See Dennis 2010, 103.
29. Wallace 1972, 290; Bastine & Winfield, 54–55.
30. Wallace 1972, 292.
31. Dennis 2010, 106, 260 n46.
32. Hauptmann, 176.
33. Wallace 1972, 334.

Chapter 5: Sleeping Preachers

1. Mais, 4–5.
2. See *Devotional Somnium;* Ives.
3. Thanks to Marc Demarest for the genealogical information, and for the idea of Rachel Baker as "proto-spiritualist."
4. *Devotional Somnium*, 17.
5. For examples, see the transcriptions in *Remarkable Sermons*.
6. Mais, 6
7. Mais, 28–29.
8. Mais, 23.
9. *Devotional Somnium*.
10. *Devotional Somnium*, 34. The name is sometimes spelled Mitchell.
11. Mais, 9.
12. Ives, 411.
13. Ives, 407.

14. Obituary in the *Congregational Quarterly* 18 (July 1876), 420, which gives "Sully," presumably a misprint for Tully.

15. *Devotional Somnium*, 34.

16. *Orange County Patriot*, Goshen, NY, Dec. 15, 1818, quoting from *Palmyra Register*, Dec. 2, 1818.

17. *Cooperstown Watch-Tower*, September 16, 1819.

18. *The Album*, Rochester, May 23, 1826. Reprinted in *New York Spectator*, May 26, 1826, and several Upstate newspapers. Some give Watson's name as Simon.

19. See *Devotional Somnium*.

20. Buescher 2004, 90.

21. Ives, 405.

22. Ferdinando Fairfax, letter in *Devotional Somnium*, 295. Italics original.

Chapter 6: Mormon Roots

1. Joseph Smith's address to the Church, September 6, 1842; *Doctrine and Covenants*, sect. 128:20–21.

2. Though seldom mentioned, the existence of God's wives is a logical consequence of LDS doctrine.

3. See Vogel for maps of the regions and the locations of Joseph Smith's early activities.

4. Smith, *History of the Church*, ch. 1:14–19.

5. Smith, *History of the Church*, ch. 1:30–35.

6. Smith, *History of the Church*, ch. 1:51–52.

7. Smith, *History of the Church*, ch. 1:59.

8. Smith, *History of the Church*, ch. 1:56–57; Newell & Avery, 7–8.

9. Roberts 1965, vol. 1, 99, 218; Bushman 2005, 63, 119.

10. Smith, *History of the Church*, ch. 1:67–73.

11. Roberts 1965, vol. 1, 82; Bushman 2005, 48–52.

12. Roberts 1965, vol. 1, 85; Bushman, 59.

13. Roberts 1965, vol. 1, 199–92; Bushman 2005, 109, 115.

14. Smith, *History of the Church*, ch. 1:57–58.

15. Roberts 1965, vol. 1, 157; Bushman 2005, 80.

16. Roberts 1965, vol. 1, 124–25; Bushman 2005, 76–78.

17. *Doctrine and Covenants*, sect. 17:1.

18. Statement printed in the Book of Mormon.

19. Brooke, 138.

20. Brooke, 127–28.

21. Deposition of Peter Ingersoll, Dec. 2, 1833, in Anderson, 134–39; here quoted, 136.

22. Brooke, 31.

23. Deposition of William Stafford, Dec. 8, 1833, in Anderson, 143–46.

24. Deposition of Willard Chase, Dec. 11, 1833, quoting the account of Joseph Smith, Sr., in Anderson, 121.

25. Walters; Bushman 2005, 48–52.

26. Complete court record and associated documents in Morgan, 321–39.
27. See especially Brooke, Quinn, Forsberg.
28. Morgan, 225, citing Lucy Mack's *Narrative*, 18–24.
29. Testimony of Lucy Mack Smith, quoted in Bushman, 2005, 24.
30. Brooke, 162–63; Forsberg, 68–69.
31. Discussion, with a facsimile, in Tanner, 55–57.
32. Tanner, 57, noting that in published editions "of angels" is omitted.
33. Morgan, 247; see explanations in Bushman 2005, 39–41.
34. Morgan, 249. See also Brodie, 21–25.
35. Morgan, 253.
36. Bushman 1984, 58–59; Bushman 2005, 41; Quinn 12–13.
37. Unpublished notes of Evans-Wentz, owned and cited by Vallee 1975, 162, 171; Vallee 2008, 213.
38. Vallee 1975, 167; Vallee 2008, 210–11.
39. Vallee 1975, 170; Vallee 2008, 213.
40. Deposition of Abigail Harris, Nov. 28, 1833, in Anderson, 130.
41. Brodie, 41.
42. Bushman 2005, 58.
43. For varying accounts of the translation, see Givens, 26–37; Morgan 277–88; Bushman 2005, 63–73.
44. Letter VIII of Oliver Cowdery (1834), in Kirkham, 96.
45. Roberts 1965, vol. 1, 110–12.
46. Roberts 1965, vol. 1, 124.
47. Roberts 1965, vol. 1, 147.
48. See I Samuel 28:6, Ezra 2:63, Nehemiah 7:65.
49. Givens, 22, citing Proctor, *History of Joseph Smith*, 139.
50. Morgan, 382 n36, citing *Tiffany's Monthly*, July 1859.
51. Brodie, 40n, citing *Kansas City Journal*, June 5, 1881.
52. Roberts 1965, vol. 1, 92; Brodie, 40.
53. Givens, 22, citing Vogel, *Early Mormon Documents*, 1:508.
54. Roberts 1965, vol. 1, 127–30; Bushman 2005, 69–72.
55. *Doctrine and Covenants*, sect. 17.
56. See later statements by Cowdery, Harris, and Whitmer in Roberts 1965, vol. 1, 142–44.
57. Brodie, 74.
58. Morgan, 393 n36, citing A. Metcalf, *Ten Years Before the Mast* (1888), 7, and John A. Clark, *Gleanings by the Way* (1842), 256–57.
59. Morgan, 394 n39, citing A. Metcalf, *Ten Years Before the Mast* (1888), 73–74.
60. Roberts 1965, vol. 1, 130.
61. See Tanner, 10 on "plural marriage" (with facsimile of 1835 and 1843 editions of *Doctrines and Covenants*), and 39–49 on the exclusion of blacks and the later reversal of the doctrine.
62. Bushman 2005, 291–92.
63. Genesis 5:18–21. The *Joseph Smith Translation of the Bible* adds a long passage on Enoch.

64. See Godwin 1994, 169–86.

65. Letter to Bulwer Lytton, cited in Godwin 1994, 184.

66. First published as *De l'état social de l'homme, ou Vues philosophiques sur l'histoire du genre humain*; later (1824) as *Histoire philosophique du genre humain*. See Bibliography for English translation.

67. Buescher 2008, 21.

68. Buescher 2008, 18–19.

Chapter 7: The Square and Compass

1. Pratt, 45–46.

2. See the verbatim transcriptions of the Endowment rites and the motion picture presentation in Sackett, 22–52.

3. William Morgan's widow, Lucinda, converted along with her second husband, George Washington Harris, and also became one of Joseph Smith's plural wives. See Homer, 24.

4. On these roots, see Quinn, Brooke, and especially Owens.

5. Occasionally known as Mordecai *Manasseh* Noah.

6. On Noah's pretense to Sephardic origin, thought socially superior to Ashkenazic, see Sarna, 2.

7. Broadhurst, pt. 1. Presumably Noah was a Royal Arch Mason, not a Knight Templar since that required one to be Christian.

8. Sarna, ix.

9. Sarna, 3–4.

10. "Essays of Howard, on Domestic Economy," in Noah, 77–104.

11. Noah 1999, 13. On Noah's literary work, see Weingrad, 143–85.

12. On his instruction of a grand jury to indict the antislavery agitators if they caused a breach of the peace, see Karcher, 285.

13. Sarna, 16.

14. The whole story is told in Leiner.

15. Sarna, 25.

16. Allen, 310.

17. Allen, 316. A more elaborate version of the Proclamation in Noah, 111–24.

18. Weingrad, 158.

19. Broadhurst, pt. 4.

20. Allen, 320.

21. Allen, 321.

22. Allen, 324.

23. Noah, 139.

24. Noah, 146.

25. Noah, 154.

26. Noah, 133–34.

27. See Moore for much detail on these movements and illustrations of the lodges, etc.

28. Moore, 86–87.

29. See Pike for one version of the lectures.
30. Moore, 90.
31. Emery & Emery, 3.
32. See McCain, pt. 3.
33. On Dunn, see *Rockford Today*, 122.
34. The M.O.V.P.E.R. ritual is currently accessible at http://www.stichtingargus.nl/vrijmetselarij/grotto_r.html
35. The Grotto's main causes are Children with Cerebral Palsy and Dental Care for Children with Special Needs. See same website.

Chapter 8: Not the End of the World

1. *The Midnight Cry*, Nov. 17, 1842.
2. Biographical information, unless otherwise noted, from Bliss.
3. Bliss, 50.
4. Bliss, 55.
5. Sears, 85.
6. Bliss, 68.
7. Bliss, 85–90.
8. Not to be confused with Dresden, Yates County, where Robert Ingersoll was born (see chapter 13).
9. Illustrations of these and other heavenly phenomena in Sears, 36–57.
10. Bliss, 137.
11. Bliss, 226.
12. Bliss, 136.
13. Possibly designed by the folk portraitist William Matthew Prior. See Oak & Shaw, 20–25, for the connections of Prior and Miller, including two remarkable portraits.
14. Sears, 203, citing verbal sources.
15. Sears, 99–103.
16. Nichol, 204, quoting *The Advent Shield and Review*, May 1844, 90.
17. Bliss, 254.
18. Bliss, 271.
19. Bliss, 293–95.
20. Miller's view. See Bliss, 281.
21. George Storrs's view. See Sears, 242–43.
22. Bliss, 295–97.
23. Nichol 458. This would become the accepted view of the Seventh-Day Adventists.
24. Nichol, 434–35.
25. Bliss, 307–08.
26. Bliss, 267.
27. Revised Standard Version, Introduction to Daniel and note on 8:9–14.
28. See John 1:24–31.
29. At this time the village was called Sing Sing, an Indian name. It adopted the form "Ossining" in 1901 to distinguish itself from the prison on its outskirts.

Chapter 9: Brief Utopias

1. *Jahrbücher*, 18. Sammlung, 16–17. (Author's translation)
2. Shambaugh, 29.
3. Shambaugh, 41.
4. Shambaugh, 299.
5. *Jahrbücher*, 18. Sammlung, 11–12.
6. Scheuner, 191.
7. A "scandalous affair," according to Frank Lankes in *West Seneca*, 9.
8. Scheuner, 195.
9. Shambaugh, 66.
10. Scheuner, 201.
11. Scheuner, 223.
12. Scheuner, 227.
13. Shambaugh, 60.
14. Frank A. Slade, "Home of the Ebenezers," in *West Seneca*, 16–17.
15. Lankes, 44–45.
16. Hoehnle 2003, 22–24.
17. The name occurs in Song of Solomon 4:8. For the Iowa period, see Hoehnle 2003. The "Amana" line of refrigerators and kitchen appliances descends directly from the community's industries.
18. Shambaugh, 76.
19. See Hoehnle 2012, with many illustrations of the site.
20. Fourier, *Oeuvres complètes*, III, 248, from Beecher & Bienvenu, 211–12.
21. For Brisbane's conversion of the Brook Farm community to Fourierism, see Noyes 1870, 200–32.
22. Brisbane 1840, 382n.
23. Bestor 1938, 25.
24. See his autobiography in *Browne's Phonographic Monthly* 2 (1877), 201–05; also Guarneri, 363.
25. Noyes 1870, 267.
26. For a complete list, see Pitzer, 461.
27. Bestor 1938, 263.
28. See Medlicott for evidence.
29. Bestor 1938, 115–18.
30. Bestor 1938, 153.
31. Bestor 1938, 238.
32. Bestor 1938, 249.
33. Bestor 1938, 267.
34. Noyes 1870, 291.
35. Bestor 1938, 280, quoting *Harbinger* 5 (Sep. 18, 1847), 239. See also Noyes 1870, 291–92.
36. Noyes 1870, 167, citing *The Communitist*.
37. Noyes 1870, 162.
38. Douglass 1994, 673.
39. *Social Pioneer*, 5.

40. *Social Pioneer*, 13.
41. *Social Pioneer*, 22.
42. *Social Pioneer*, 63.
43. Wells, 6.
44. Wells, 6. For a longer version, see Noyes 1870, 164–68
45. Wells, 12–13.
46. Wells, 14.
47. Noyes 1870, 173.
48. *Sacramento Daily Union*, August 11, 1851.
49. *Memorial and Biographical History of Northern California*, 214.
50. At Christmas 1870 Collins and his wife hosted the women's rights leader Abigail Scott Duniway. See http://asduniway.org/.

Chapter 10: Perfection in This Life

1. *Annual Report of the Oneida Association*, 1848/1849, 23.
2. Noyes 1923, Noyes 1931, and Noyes 2001. For a more detailed account of the archive, see Lawrence Foster in Noyes 2001, x–xii.
3. See *Utica Post-Standard*, September 10, 2012, on the demise of the Sherrill operation.
4. See photograph in Noyes 1923, opp. 12.
5. Noyes 1923, 60.
6. Carden, 29.
7. Noyes 1923, 68.
8. Noyes 1923, 112, 121, 140.
9. Noyes 2001, 88.
10. Noyes 1847, 276–77, 288–89.
11. Noyes 1847, 337–41.
12. Noyes 1923, 288–90. George Noyes, after reporting all this, adds wryly that 1880 was the year the Oneida Community ended.
13. For the list, see Godwin 2011a, 354–56.
14. Noyes 1923, 411.
15. Noyes 1847, v–viii, 97.
16. Noyes 1847, 104.
17. Noyes 1923, 413.
18. Noyes 1923, 404n.
19. Noyes 1847, 17–19.
20. Noyes 1923, 308.
21. Klaw, 241n.
22. Noyes 1923, 339–40.
23. Noyes 1923, 358. On Ithaca as an early religious center, see Wellman.
24. Noyes 1931, 113.
25. The fable of Onan (Gen. 36:9) had created a taboo against *coitus interruptus* and, by extension, against contraceptive devices even when available.
26. See Wonderley.
27. Matt. 22:30; Mark 12:25; Luke 20:34–36.

28. Examples from Thomas, 33.
29. Thomas, 47.
30. Noyes 1931, 266. The families were those of Joseph C. Ackley, William S. Hatch, and Daniel P. Nash. They do not seem to have been involved in the Hubbardsville-East Hamilton Fourierist plans (see ch. 9).
31. Noyes 1931, 261
32. Noyes 1931, 265.
33. *New York, A Guide*, 488.
34. Pitts & Leonard.
35. Noyes 1831, 393.
36. Pitts & Leonard.
37. Pitts & Leonard.
38. Noyes 2001, 44.
39. Carden, 37.
40. Noyes 2001, 288.
41. Noyes 2001, 285.
42. Klaw, 195.
43. Klaw, 89–90.
44. Noyes 1937, 16.
45. Noyes 2001, 58n.
46. Noyes 2001, 252.
47. Effective against colds and diphtheria, according to *Mutual Criticism*, 71.
48. Noyes 2001, 321.
49. Noyes 2001, 265.
50. Noyes 2001, 208.
51. Fogarty, 60.
52. Noyes 2001, 158.
53. Klaw, 216, 231.
54. Klaw, 233.
55. Klaw, 206.
56. Rainwater, 237. Thanks also to Anthony Wonderley for a talk that explained the return of the stirpicults and their rescue of the company.

Chapter 11: The Poughkeepsie Seer

1. Davis 1885, 30–31.
2. What follows is summarized from Kerner, 1845.
3. Edmonston, 59–60.
4. Darnton, 90n.
5. See for example the study of a somnambulist in Belden.
6. Some influential works are J. C. Colquhoun, *Report of the Experiments on Animal Magnetism Made by a Committee of the Medical Section of the French Royal Academy of Sciences* (Edinburgh: Robert Cadell, 1833) and *Isis Revelata: An Inquiry into the Origins, Progress, and Present State of Animal Magnetism* (Edinburgh: Maclachlan & Stewart, 1836); Baron Dupotet de Sennevoy, *An Introduction to the Study of Animal Magnetism* (London: Saunders & Otley, 1838); and Chauncey Hare Townshend,

Facts in Mesmerism, with Reasons for a Dispassionate Inquiry into it (London: Longmans, 1840).

7. Poyen, 145.
8. Davis 1857, 169.
9. Grimes, 271.
10. Grimes, 271 (my italics).
11. Buescher 2004, 21–23.
12. Buescher 2004, 24.
13. Davis 1857, 215–16.
14. Davis 1857, 227–37.
15. Davis 1857, 240–42.
16. Davis 1857, 243–45.
17. Davis 1857, 250.
18. Davis 1857, 257.
19. Block, 97.
20. Williams-Hogan & Eller, 268.
21. Block, 100.
22. Also spelled Brittain.
23. Review of *The Principles of Nature* in *The Daguerreotype and Foreign Miscellany* 2 (1848), 85–88, citing *The Athenaeum*.
24. See Albanese, 214.
25. C. W. Webber, cited in Noyes 1870, 566–67.
26. Bush 202–03.
27. *The Daguerreotype* 2 (1848), 88.
28. Grimes, 273.
29. Lucas, "Davis, Andrew Jackson," in Hanegraaff 2005, 2:309.
30. The journal was later bought by William Henry Channing (see ch. 13) and renamed *Spirit of the Age*.
31. "Blasphemies of Andrew Jackson Davis," *New Jerusalem Magazine* 21 (1847), 298–304.
32. Davis 1868, 100.
33. "The Emergence of Dr. Davis," *The Psypioneer* 1/5 (2004), 37–38.
34. For two rare examples of a scholarly appreciation of Davis, see Faivre, 137–52, and Gutierrez, *passim*.

Chapter 12: Rapping Spirits

1. Only years later were the memorable words "Mr. Splitfoot" (i.e., the Devil) inserted in retellings of the story.
2. Lewis 1887, 5–7.
3. Capron & Barron, 96.
4. See for example Sawin, 136–39.
5. Testimony of Mrs. Norman Culver, in the *Athenaeum*, April 1851, analyzed at length in Spicer, I, 82–84.
6. Weisberg 244.

7. Weisberg, 256.

8. Lewis 1887, 34–37.

9. (Ann) Leah Fox had been abandoned by her first husband, Bowman Fish (see Stuart, 9), but went by his name. She would subsequently become Mrs. Brown, then Mrs. Underhill.

10. Weisberg, 47–49, summarizing Leah Underhill's account.

11. Spicer, II, 36.

12. Leah mentions him as "Professor E. C. Rogers, a powerful mesmerizer who happened to be lecturing in Rochester at the time, who by his magnetic power and manipulations gave me prompt and complete relief." Underhill, 362.

13. Rogers 1853, 94n.

14. Rogers 1853, 316

15. Rogers 1853, 326.

16. Rogers 1853, 165.

17. Rogers 1853, 184.

18. Rogers 1853, 167–68.

19. What follows is based on Godwin 1990.

20. Olcott 1875, 453–54.

21. *Ghost Land*, 39–40.

22. Harrison, 85.

23. Sinnett 1895, 15–16; revised version published in Sinnett 1896, 437.

24. Leadbeater, 79.

25. Wachtmeister, 9.

26. Lecture to the London Spiritualist Alliance, April 7, 1898, quoted in Guénon, 24–25.

27. Besant, 37–41.

28. Sinnett 1920, 4, 10–11.

29. Guénon, 20. See ch. 14 for more on this Brotherhood.

30. Guénon, 27.

Chapter 13: The Progressives Take Notice

1. Smith 1859, 16.

2. *Rochester City Directory*, 1849, 1851.

3. Photographed in 1936 and pictured at http://www.libraryweb.org/rochimag/roads/underground.htm

4. Isaac was born in Westbury, Amy in Jericho, flanking the hamlet now called Hicksville.

5. Braude, 13.

6. Douglass 1994, 674.

7. Powalski, 6.

8. Isaac Post to Joseph and Mary Robbins Post, November 23 [1848?], quoted in Braude, 10–11.

9. Braude, 11.

10. On what follows, see Powalski, 8–12.

11. Powalski, 18.
12. Letter of April 5, 1850, in *Frederick Douglass Papers*, I, 413.
13. Nell, 533.
14. Garrison calls her "Mrs. Brown, formerly Miss Fish."
15. Garrison, 5.
16. For what follows, see Burdick.
17. Frothingham, 84–85.
18. Smith 1859, 4.
19. Smith 1859, 46.
20. William Henry Channing (1810–1884), eminent Unitarian minister and abolitionist, nephew of William Ellery Channing (see ch. 2), in Rochester from 1852–54.
21. Asa and Huldah Griffin Anthony, distant cousins of Susan B. Anthony. They were in the Rochester circle that met for séances at the Posts'. See Nell, 22.
22. William and Mary Hallowell, also in the Posts' spirit circle. See Nell, 22.
23. Catharine A. Fish married Giles Stebbins while at the Sodus Bay community. They were early activists in Rochester spiritualism and abolitionism.
24. See the M'Clintocks and Hunts, below.
25. Auburn abolitionists active in the Underground Railroad. Mrs. Seward was the wife of William Henry Seward, New York State governor, senator, and secretary of state under Lincoln and Johnson.
26. President of the Oneida Institute in Whitesboro and abolitionist ally of Gerrit Smith.
27. Charles B. Sedgwick, Syracuse lawyer for the abolitionist movement.
28. Samuel Joseph May, Unitarian pastor in Syracuse.
29. Stanton, Anthony & Gage, vol. 1, 465.
30. Goldsmith 48, quoting letter from Willets to Isaac Post, October 23, 1848.
31. As named in Stanton, Anthony & Gage, vol. 1, 67.
32. Both the Hunt House and the M'Clintock House are part of the Women's Rights National Historical Park.
33. Stanton, Anthony & Gage, vol. 1, 68.
34. Goldsmith, 31; Braude, 58.
35. Letter of February 6, 1850, in Mott, 201.
36. Letter of August 30, 1852, Mott, 222.
37. Griffith, 72.
38. University of Rochester Libraries, http://www.lib.rochester.edu/index.cfm?page=4112.
39. Braude, 97.
40. Harper, 918.

Chapter 14: Sex, Drugs, and Mirrors

1. "Passing Glances—No. 2," *The Christian Spiritualist* 1/43 (Mar. 3, 1855), 2.
2. For early biographical facts and surmises, see Deveney 1997b, 1–9, 373–80.
3. An otherwise unrecorded instance. See Randolph 1861–62, 170.
4. Deveney 1997b, 109.

5. Deveney 1997b, 99–101.

6. Four-acre parcel defined in Madison County Deeds, Liber BR, p. 381, as sold on July 5, 1851, for $200. The Madison County Map of 1859, Stockbridge inset, shows the house of "P. B. Randolph."

7. On Randolph's concept of his own race, see Deveney 1997b, 4–8, 378 n. 34.

8. Letter of June 1, 1853, *The Telegraph Papers* 1 (1853), 421–22.

9. Letter of June 24, 1853, *The Telegraph Papers* 1 (1853), 333–35.

10. Letter of July 21, 1853, *The Telegraph Papers* 2 (1853), 20–22.

11. "Harmonial Convention," *The Telegraph Papers* 4 (1854), 49–58.

12. Deveney 1997b, 21.

13. "Clairvoyance and Psychometry," *The Telegraph Papers* 6 (1855), 54.

14. Deveney 1997b, 25.

15. P.B. Randolph, "Jottings by the Wayside. The Earlville Miracles," *The Telegraph Papers* 8 (1856), 266. Dated from Utica, March 22, 1855. This report also reached France, in *Journal du magnétisme* 15 (1856), 43.

16. Often explained away as spider webs, but see the chemical analyses in Boldman.

17. See Deveney 1997b, 143–44.

18. Deveney 1997b, 379–80n., quoting *New York Daily Tribune*, November 25, 1858.

19. Deveney 1997b, 100–01.

20. See Deveney 1997b, 504, n.21.

21. Madison County Deeds, Liber CQ, pp. 47–48.

22. Boston: see Deveney 1997b, 101. Mary Jane Randolph is listed in *Utica City Directory* 1861–62, 1867–68, 1868–69, 1870, 1871, 1872; P. B. Randolph in the volumes for 1862–63, 1863–64,

23. In Randolph 1860, 69, which Mary Jane copyrighted and prefaced, she is called an "Indian Doctress" from a long line of medicine men.

24. Randolph 1861–62, 35–36.

25. Deveney 1997b, 28, 144.

26. Deveney 1997b, 131–32.

27. The house is now demolished, but the adjacent row of houses remains.

28. Randolph 1888, 135.

29. Randolph 1861–62, 115.

30. Randolph 1868, 185.

31. *New York Tribune*, January 26, 1864, 2.

32. Deveney 1997b, 69.

33. See Deveney 1997b, 173, 205.

34. From "The Ansairetic Arcanum," quoted in Godwin, Chanel & Deveney, 241.

35. See Deveney 1997b, 79.

Chapter 15: Chautauqua Follies

1. *New York Tribune*, September 21, 1858.

2. The following information is condensed from the letter by Dr. James P. Greaves (also spelled Greves), written in Milwaukee, January 24, 1853, in *Spiritual Telegraph* 2/1 (May 7, 1853): 1; largely reproduced in Britten, 230–31.

3. Dates from a note by Sherwin Chase, dated 1971, in the Fenton History Center, Jamestown, NY: file "Harmonia—Religious Movement—The Kiantone Movement."

4. Following information from "The Spiritual Spring," *Jamestown Journal*, April 22, 1853.

5. On Sheldon and his later association with John Murray Spear, see Buescher 2006, 194–97.

6. Letter of James F. Greaves, Britten, 231.

7. It is not clear whether this was the same person as the one who discovered the spring on location.

8. "A Spiritualist Convention in Chautauqua," *New York Tribune*, September 21, 1858.

9. On all of these, see Godwin 2011a.

10. On the members both of the spirit association and the twelve mortals chosen as the "General Assembly," see Cronin, 69–81.

11. In Internet sources, a portrait of John Murray is sometimes mistaken for one of Spear, of whom no portrait is known.

12. See Britten 1870, 232; Buescher 2006, 90–91; Cronin 90.

13. Except Constance Noyes Robertson's novel, *Seek no Further*, which blends Spear's and Noyes' communities with Timothy Brown's Spirit House.

14. Buescher 2006, 79.

15. Buescher 2006, 106.

16. Buescher 2006, 132.

17. Buescher 2006, 137.

18. Summarized from Cronin, 101.

19. *New York Daily Times*, May 26, 1857, quoted in Buescher 2006, 167.

20. Chase, 829.

21. Merrill, 143; Duino, 141.

22. P. B. Randolph, writing in the *Christian Spiritualist* in 1855, denied that the New Motor had been destroyed. (Information from J. P. Deveney.)

23. Duino, 150n.

24. See Buescher 2006, 153–54.

25. On these and other details, see Buescher 2006, 177–85

26. Chase, 830.

27. Edson, 947.

28. See Brisset. I thank Antoine Faivre for introducing me to this "*Prince des penseurs*."

29. See Bailey for an account of Staples's excavation.

30. "A Spiritualist Convention in Chautauque [*sic*]," *New York Tribune*, September 21, 1858.

31. See Britten 1870, 233–34.

32. The following is based on McCoy, supplemented by an interview with the 80-year-old Jeremiah Carter and his spirit guide: "Talks with a Spirit. Express

Correspondent has an Interview with Dr. Hedges," *Illustrated Buffalo Express*, June 30, 1895.

33. Watson, 421.

34. Jones, 74.

35. See Watson for many details and names, and for the general history of spiritualist camp meetings, Deveney 2012.

36. Myers, 2.

37. Themes selected from "Legacy of Love," the summer 2012 program of the Lily Dale Assembly. For interviews with present-day residents, see Wicker.

Chapter 16: Open Breathing

1. Respiro, 30, quoting *Herald of Light*, 1853. "Respiro" was Dr. C. M. Berridge, formerly a Church of England minister and a Theosophist, and a prolific interpreter of Harris. Schneider & Lawton, 115n.

2. Cuthbert, 86. "A grocer and auctioneer," according to Trahair, 171.

3. Guerin, 7–8.

4. Trahair, 171. In 1847 the church was sold to a Jesuit congregation, and in 1848 burned to the ground. See *Xavier: Alumnews of Xavier High School*, March 2009, 3.

5. Britten 1870, 215, quoting Charles Partridge in the *Spiritual Telegraph*, Feb. 18, 1860.

6. Buescher 2004, 77.

7. Davis 1868, 95.

8. Cuthbert, 92, 96, 99, 102.

9. Harris 1854, Appendix by S. B. Brittan, 200.

10. Sometimes given as James D. Scott.

11. Britten 1870, 58–59, 208–09.

12. Now in Fayette County, West Virginia.

13. Noyes 1870, 568–69.

14. *The Mountain Cove Journal*, 1/16 (Dec. 30, 1852).

15. For details, see Britten 1870, 210–11.

16. Britten 1870, 212.

17. Britten 1870, 216.

18. Schneider and Lawton, 37, 153.

19. Harris married his second wife, Emily Isabella Waters, in 1855 on his trip to New Orleans. She died in 1885.

20. Harris 1854, x–xi and note.

21. Harris 1854, 15.

22. See Respiro, passim.

23. Guerin, 52–64.

24. Harris 1854, 160–61.

25. Harris 1854, 179. The prophecy referred to is Isaiah 11:6–8.

26. Cuthbert, 132.

27. Author of the epic poem *The Course of Time* (1827).

28. I.e., Alessandro Cagliostro (1743–1795).

29. Harris 1858, iv.
30. Harris 1857, 22–23.
31. Britten 1870, 214–15.
32. Cuthbert, 182; Guerin, 61–62.
33. Schneider and Lawton, 192n.
34. Noyes 1870, 590–91.
35. Wallace 1976, 189.
36. Wallace 1976, 194.
37. See Respiro.
38. Cuthbert, 217–19.
39. Harris 1876, 118–19.
40. Harris 1884, 509.
41. Cuthbert, 9. On the sons, see Schneider & Lawton, 193–94.
42. Schneider & Lawton's fascinating book is an account of their relationship.
43. Respiro, 188.
44. Noyes 1870, 581.
45. Quoted in Schneider & Lawton, 146.
46. Photographs of Vine Cliff in Kurtz, 63–68, McAllister, n.p.
47. LeBaron 1980, 87.
48. LeBaron 1980, 95. It hardly took a seer to discover this, as Emperor Louis-Napoleon had been deposed the previous year, and France had just surrendered to the new German Empire.
49. Emma Tucker, quoted in Schneider & Lawton, 412n.
50. Harris's mansion has been demolished, but the community's round barn in Santa Rosa is still standing.
51. See LeBaron 1976.

Chapter 17: Practical Spirits

1. *The Banner of Light*, January 19, 1897.
2. The following account is abridged from Godwin 2011b, which contains full documentation.
3. They were subsequently painted blue, and are now red.
4. Robertson, 14.
5. Edmonds & Dexter, II, 537.
6. Jones, 266.
7. The following account is largely based on Jones's autobiography. For further details, including Jones's patents, see Pollard.
8. In the 1860s, newspapers in the Buffalo region frequently carried her poems. She also published several books of them.
9. Jones, 53.
10. Jones, 76.
11. Jones, 181.
12. Jones, 217. A fuller description in Oneida County *Gazetteer and Business Directory*, 1868, 50–51.
13. Jones, 193.

14. Jones, 252.

15. Reputed to be the Indian name for life; Jones, 257.

16. "Use the Yuh-Heh Magnetic Mineral Spring Water!" *Syracuse Daily Journal*, September 21, 1872.

17. Jones, 259.

18. Jones, 268.

19. Jones, 262–69, 348.

20. Jones, 342.

21. Jones, 305.

22. Jones, 339.

23. Writer of science textbooks and professor of physics at Vassar College from 1874.

24. Jones, 341.

25. "What Women Are Doing." *New York Press*, October 8, 1892. The news was widely reprinted in Upstate newspapers.

26. Jones, 418.

27. See Pollard for specifics.

28. Jones, 420.

29. Jones, 422.

Chapter 18: Theosophy, from Ithaca to Halcyon

1. Blavatsky Letters, I, 217 (Letter no. 63), translated from the Russian by Boris de Zirkoff.

2. Heustis Street is now called College Avenue. The "Richardson Cottage," where the Corsons hosted Madame Blavatsky, is no longer to be seen.

3. This Mary (Mrs. John) Andrews is not to be confused with Louisa Andrews of Springfield, Mass., with whom both Corson and H.P.B. were corresponding at this time. Mrs. Lincoln's visit to Moravia was reported in *Auburn Daily Bulletin*, February 27, 1872, and recently confirmed by the discovery of her signature in a hotel visitor's book. See Smith 2001, 10.

4. H. Corson, "Modern Spiritualism," *Cornell Review* II/3 (Dec. 1874).

5. For his first letter, January 31, 1875, see Blavatsky Letters, I, 65.

6. Blavatsky Letters, I, 86 (Letter no. 21, February 16, 1875).

7. See Blavatsky Letters, I, 109 (Letter no. 30, March 20, 1875).

8. Corson 1929, 218; Gomes 1987, 112. For the Andrews' activities, see Sheila Tucker, "Who Was the Lady in Black?" *Auburn Sunday Citizen*, December 22, 1974, 37.

9. Olcott 1941, 103.

10. See chronological survey by Boris de Zirkoff in Blavatsky, *Collected Writings*, I, liv–lviii.

11. Letter to her sister Vera, latter half of 1875. Blavatsky Letters, I, 196.

12. Interview with Charles Lazenby in *The Path*, 1910, quoted from Gomes 1987, 112–13.

13. Corson 1929, 26–27.

14. Hiram Corson, quoted in Gomes 1987, 114.

15. For H.P.B.'s aristocratic ancestry, see the genealogical tables in Blavatsky *Collected Writings*, I, lxix–lxxi.

16. On the writing of *Isis Unveiled*, see John Algeo's "Background Essay: The Writing and Publication of *Isis Unveiled*" in Blavatsky Letters I, 330–40; for more detail, Olcott 1941, 202–54.

17. Blavatsky Letters, I, 196–97 (Letter no. 56, latter half of 1875).

18. Letter of November 16, 1875, to Stainton Moses, in Blavatsky Letters, I, 202 (Letter no. 59).

19. Blavatsky Letters, I, 197 (Letter no. 57, October 13–16, 1875).

20. Olcott 1941, 203.

21. Corson 1929, 37.

22. She wrote Corson that she could not control him and had given him up. Blavatsky Letters, I, 233 (Letter no. 64, January 8, 1876).

23. See extract from the address in Blavatsky Letters, I, 221.

24. See Blavatsky Letters, I, 222–29.

25. See Blavatsky Letters, I, no. 67.

26. See Blavatsky Letters, I, no. 126.

27. Author of the epic poem "Hiawatha."

28. Corson 1911, 179.

29. Date from Gomes 1987, 115.

30. Olcott 1941, 208.

31. For an extended treatment of this theme, see Deveney 1997a.

32. We would not grudge Cooperstown the myth that Doubleday also invented baseball.

33. On Doubleday and Theosophy, see Gomes 1991.

34. Later (1889) wife of William Farrington Aldrich (1853–1925), born in Palmyra, N.Y., philanthropist, U.S. representative for Alabama, mine and newspaper owner, for whom Aldrich, Alabama, is named.

35. Eek, 183: Dâmodar K. Mâvalankar to Abner Doubleday, March 24, 1882.

36. As reported in *The Theosophist* IV/2 (1882), Supplement, 2.

37. Gomes 1991.

38. *Theosophical Movement*, 120.

39. List from "Searchers of Mysteries," *Rochester Democrat & Chronicle*, July 1, 1886.

40. "Strange Secret Session," *Rochester Democrat & Chronicle*, July 8, 1886, 6.

41. *The Path* I/5 (August 1886), 159.

42. Thus the report in *Rochester Democrat & Chronicle*, July 23, 1886. The defense of reincarnation, summarized at length in this article, was by Ernest M. Sasvil, M.D. (also known as Sassoville). For his reminiscences of Cables and her group, see "Incidents," *Journal of the American Society for Psychical Research* V (1911), 324–29.

43. Quoted in *Theosophical Movement*, 121.

44. Blavatsky *Collected Writings*, VII, 242.

45. This was the name of the "free gift" of a colored picture offered to newspaper subscribers.

46. Blavatsky *Collected Writings*, VII, 248, 249n.

47. See Godwin, Chanel & Deveney, 7.
48. Godwin, Chanel & Deveney, 87.
49. Godwin, Chanel & Deveney, 196.
50. *Syracuse Daily Journal*, August 31, 1893.
51. See *Theosophical Movement*, 682.
52. See Bibliography, *Theogenesis*
53. [Charles Hillinger], "Hiawatha, Legendary Iroquois Indian Chief, Revered by a Tiny Religious-Philosophical Group in California," *Watertown Daily Times*, August 1, 1974, 4; Gayle Cuddy, "Life of Hiawatha Captured on Canvas," *San Luis Obispo Tribune*, June 2, 2010.

Chapter 19: The Hollow Earth

1. Teed, 15–17.
2. Biographical information compiled from Fine undated, Fine 1975, Hicks, Millner, Ohnemus, Rahn, Sherwood. Accounts of Teed's early life do not always agree.
3. Rahn, 18.
4. [Obituary of Cyrus Teed]. *Auburn Citizen*, December 30, 1908.
5. Smith 1880, I, 237.
6. Testimony of Dr. S. F. Teed, in *Utica Daily Observer*, September 19, 1889.
7. "His portraits of Charles E. Whitman, former Governor of this state and of the late Fra Elbertus Hubbard won him national fame." *The Press*, Binghamton, May 25, 1929, quoted in Fine undated, 8.
8. Their address is given both as 169 and 171 Genesee Street, above Buckingham & Ketchum's Music Store.
9. Teed 1900, 5.
10. Rahn, 21.
11. Places mentioned in Carmer, 269, and by Millner.
12. *Flaming Sword*, 5/7 (Feb. 18, 1893), 98.
13. "Woman's Triumph, or the Great Mystery Revealed," *Flaming Sword*, 5/7 (Feb. 18, 1893): 104.
14. *Flaming Sword*, 5/4 (Jan, 28, 1893): 52.
15. What happened to Jesse's foundry and his water motors? Prominent advertisements in the *Flaming Sword* through 1894 show them still being manufactured in Dayton, Ohio.
16. No. 1, Wolf Building, Onondaga Street. See Hicks, Millner. According to Fine 1975, 215, the Syracuse physicians list does not include him.
17. For details, see Fine 1975, 222–23, 226.
18. Fine 1975, 225.
19. *Flaming Sword*, V/10 (Mar. 1893), 151–52.
20. Koresh, 110.
21. Koresh, 108.
22. Summarized from "Astro-Anthroposophy. Alchemy versus Chemistry." *Flaming Sword* 5/9 (Mar. 4, 1893), 129–36; 5/10 (Mar. 11, 1893), 145–47; 5/11 (Mar. 18, 1893), 161–63.

23. *Flaming Sword* 5/9 (Mar. 4, 1893), 131.

24. "Time Periods." *The Guiding Star* 2/9, 281, reprinted in the *Flaming Sword* 5/15 (Apr. 15, 1893), 225.

25. Goodwillie, 67–68.

26. Goodwillie, 80.

27. Evans, 5.

28. *Flaming Sword*, September 17, 1892; quoted in Goodwillie, 82–83.

29. Goodwillie, 93.

30. Rahn, 54.

31. See Rea, 62–64.

32. See Koresh, 160–65.

33. See Koresh, 179–99.

34. Michell, 45.

Chapter 20: Freethought

1. Ingersoll, 101–02.

2. Information on Bennett is mostly taken from Bradford, supplemented from Boris de Zirkoff's biographical note in Blavatsky, *Collected Writings*, IV, 625–33, and from the website of the Freethought Trail, http://www.freethought-trail.org/.

3. It was really the second such convention. The "Freethinkers' Association of Central and Western New York" had held a convention at Wolcott, Wayne County, on August 17–19, 1877, then changed to the more inclusive name.

4. Amply described in *Proceedings and Addresses*.

5. Laws (1873) against the publication of materials with sexual content, including birth control, fiercely enforced by Anthony Comstock (1844–1915) and not fully repealed today.

6. *Mahatma Letters*, no. 37.

7. Now Hobart and William Smith College.

8. See Rogers 1942, 72–84.

9. Becker, 94, 103.

10. "What does the Lord require of you but to do justice, and to love kindness, and to walk humbly with your God?" (Micah 6:8).

11. "To visit orphans and widows in their affliction, and to keep oneself unstained from the world." (James 1:27).

12. White 1896, I, xii.

13. The following account is based on White 1905, II, 465–85.

14. The carver is identified at http://www.lhup.edu/~dsimanek/carver.htm.

15. Kolmerton, 42.

16. Kolmerton, 47.

17. Kolmerton, 204.

18. The *History of Woman Suffrage* eventually comprised six volumes (1881–1922). The latter three were written by Susan B. Anthony and her disciples.

19. Brammer, 111, on the authority of Anthony and her assistant, Husted Harper.

20. *Proceedings and Addresses*, 213.

21. Stanton, Anthony & Gage, I, 25 (opening page of ch. 1).
22. Kern, 53.
23. Kern 53–54.
24. Blavatsky 1877, II, 586.
25. Kern, 93–94. Massey was too ill to come.
26. Wagner, 61.
27. Wagner, 51.
28. Kern, 132–34
29. See Wagner 64, Kern 170.
30. Stanton 1895/98, I, 12.
31. Stanton 1895/98, I, 133.
32. Stanton 1895/98, II, 72.
33. Stanton 1895/98, II, 106–12. Mathers's work was in turn based on Knorr von Rosenroth's *Kabbala denudata* of 1677/78.
34. Stanton 1895/98, II, 109.
35. Stanton 1895/98, I, 145.
36. Stanton 1895/98, II, 167.
37. Stanton 1895/98, II, 70.
38. Stanton 1895/98, II, 177–78.
39. Stanton 1895/98, II, 67–68.
40. Stanton 1895/98, II, 209.
41. For the responses in detail, see Kern 172–222.
42. Stanton 1895/98, II, 215.

Chapter 21: Oz and Ends

1. The Second National Bank of Syracuse, 1863–73.
2. The location of Roselawn is now a parking lot in the suburb of Mattydale; see http://www.freethought-trail.org/.
3. Rogers 2002, 240.
4. On anti-Oz prejudice even in America, see Hearn, 75–77.
5. Thanks to J. P. Deveney for pointing out the example of General Jinjur.
6. See Rogers 2002, 53.
7. Loncraine, 125.
8. Loncraine, 199.
9. See list in Riley, 266. On Baum's lasting influence on commercial display, see Loncraine 154–57.
10. See Baum's description of Oz, 1910, quoted in Riley, 244.
11. Riley, 147.
12. Loncraine, 93.
13. Hearn, 69–73.
14. See Algeo for details of the Baums' membership and quotations from these editorials.
15. Such Internet sites are so ephemeral that it is pointless to give specific addresses. The interested reader will easily find current examples.
16. Rogers 2002, 51.

17. Loncraine, 250–51. The Baums' house in Chicago, as Matilda confirmed, was haunted. But by what?

18. On Phelon's Atlantis see Godwin 2011a, 223–24.

19. His first foreign trip, in 1868–70, took him to the Near East. He circled the globe westward in 1872–74, 1876 –78, and 1896–97.

20. All accounts of Peebles's early life, including that of Whipple, have had to rely on Barrett, since Peebles did not keep (or had lost) his records from that time.

21. Barrett, 25, 27.

22. *New York*, 644.

23. Speech to Troy Lyceum, reported in *Troy Daily Times*, January 5, 1874.

24. Whipple, 32, 38–39.

25. Whipple, 64–67.

26. Whipple, 542, quoting Dunn's letter of 1897.

27. *Religio-Philosophical Journal* xliii/17 (Dec. 17, 1887). Thanks to J. P. Deveney for this reference.

28. Whipple, 145–46.

29. Whipple, 423.

30. Whipple, 124, 128.

31. Compare Colonel Olcott, who was commissioned after the war to investigate cases of corruption.

32. Whipple, 237.

33. Report of the Universal Peace Society Meeting, *New York Herald*, May 18, 1868.

34. See his comments in Peebles 1898, 359.

35. Peebles 1898, 297.

36. Peebles 1898, 389.

37. On Peebles's curious connections with the Theosophists, see Johnson 1994, 75–79, and an important note by Gomes 1987, 228–29n.

38. See the description of extinct Philadelphia medical schools on the Penn University website: http://www.archives.upenn.edu/histy/features/medical/extinct.html#6.

39. The article cited in note 27 congratulates the spiritualists on losing Peebles to become an "Episcopal bishop," presumably in the Methodist Episcopal Church.

40. See Dunn's official biography and portrait in *Rockford Today*, 121–22, and, less respectfully, Marc Demarest's account at http://ehbritten.blogspot.com/2011_08_01_archive.html.

41. Unpublished research by John Patrick Deveney, to whom many thanks for sharing his findings on Grumbine.

42. *The Universalist Register* 49 (1884), 37.

43. Bruce, II, 516.

44. "As McGlynn a Martyr: Rev. J. C. F. Grumbine to Suffer for His Political Opinions," *Syracuse Daily Standard*, December 10, 1887.

45. *Newtown Register*, December 22, 1887.

46. *Syracuse Standard*, March 31, 1888.

47. *Syracuse Daily Courier*, January 18, 1889.

48. Campbell, 118.

49. *Flaming Sword* 13/33 (July 7, 1899), 14. The advertisement appears regularly for the rest of the year.
50. Grumbine, unpaginated addenda.
51. Peebles 1901, 7.
52. Information from J. P. Deveney's unpublished work.

Chapter 22: The Fra

1. Elbert Hubbard, "Credo," *The Philistine* X/4 (Mar. 1900), i-ii. Often reprinted with *A Message to Garcia*.
2. Dirlam & Simmons, 166, quoting from Hubbard, *White Hyacinths*.
3. Balch, 202–04.
4. See Dirlam & Simmons, 177–78.
5. Quinan, 6–7; Balch, 109–10.
6. Dirlam & Simmons, 54.
7. William McIntosh, lead article in *The Philistine* I/1 (June 1895), 1–2.
8. Unsigned note in *The Philistine* I/1 (June 1895), 20.
9. Dirlam & Simmons, 139.
10. *Song of Songs*, xxvi.
11. See illustrations in Vilain, 25–27, 30.
12. Vilain, 24, 49 n.11.
13. Dirlam & Simmons, 53.
14. Note by "The Pastor," *The Philistine* VIII/2 (Jan. 1899), 33.
15. Claude Bragdon, "A Sonnet of Despair," *The Philistine* I/6 (Nov. 1899), 169.
16. Dirlam & Simmons, 95.
17. See Dirlam & Simmons, 149n; McCarthy, 53.
18. *The Fra* II/3 (Dec. 1908), 37 (summarized).
19. *The Fra* I/2 (May 1908), 19.
20. *The Fra* I/5 (Aug. 1908), 79.
21. "Some Astral Autographs," *The Philistine* VIII/5 (Apr. 1899), 147–50. Here quoted: 149–50.
22. "The Religion of Humanity," *The Fra* I/2 (May 1908), 21–22.
23. "Time and Change," *The Philistine* VI/4 (Mar. 1898), 115–117.
24. "The Brotherhood of Jiners," in Hubbard, *A Message to Garcia*, 67–76.
25. "Consecrated Lives," *The Philistine* XI/4 (Sep. 1900), 104–10. Here quoted: 107–08. Reprinted in Hubbard, *A Message to Garcia*, 89–100.
26. See Stickler, Pollitt.
27. Winfield 1997, 134–55; Winfield 2001, 115–25.
28. Dirlam & Simmons, 141–42. Oxyrhynchus Papyri, 30/77.
29. *The Philistine* X/4 (Mar. 1900), 101.

Chapter 23: The Craftsman

1. Gustav Stickley, "Als Ik Kan," *The Craftsman*, XXI/1 (Oct. 1911), 112–13.
2. Cathers, 224 n.15.

3. Cathers, 23.

4. Cathers, 22–32.

5. Hewitt, 41.

6. *The Craftsman* VII/6 (Mar. 1905), xxvii.

7. "Time's Changes in the Destinies of Art," *The Craftsman* I/2 (Nov. 1901), 33.

8. Cathers, 232 n38.

9. Jessie Kingsley Curtis, "Oriental Rugs: their design and symbolism," *The Craftsman* VI/3 (June 1904), 271–77.

10. Caryl Coleman, "A Mark of Honor," *The Craftsman* V/1 (Oct. 1903), 17–30; "The Sacred Cipher," *The Craftsman* V/3 (Dec. 1903), 207–12.

11. See *The Craftsman* VII/2 (Nov. 1904), passim; photo on 188.

12. Irene Sargent, "The Wavy Line," *The Craftsman* II/3 (June 1902), 131–42. Here quoted: 135.

13. *The Craftsman* III/4 (Jan. 1903), 208.

14. *The Craftsman* III/5 (Feb. 1903), 271.

15. See *The Craftsman* III/5 (Feb. 1903), 265; VII/1 (Oct. 1904), 29, 54.

16. *The Craftsman* XI/1 (Oct. 1906), cover.

17. Gustav Stickley, "Secessionist Art in Europe: Its Growth, Meaning and Failure," *The Craftsman* XIII/1 (Oct. 1907).

18. *The Craftsman* IX/1 (Oct. 1905).

19. *The Craftsman* XIII/1 (Oct. 1907) 114.

20. Hewitt, 7–8.

21. William L. Price, "A Confession of Faith," *The Craftsman* XIX/6 (Mar. 1911), 535–39. Here quoted: 538.

22. Claude Bragdon, "A Simple Dwelling," *The Craftsman* IV/6 (Sep. 1903), 478–85.

23. Claude Bragdon, "The Sleeping Beauty," *The Craftsman* IV/5 (Aug. 1903), 338–47.

24. Bragdon, "The Sleeping Beauty," 343.

25. Bibliography in Hamilton, 71.

26. M. Irwin MacDonald, "The Fairy Faith," *The Craftsman* XXIII/1 (Oct. 1912), 20–34.

27. It is called the "Rider-Waite deck."

28. Smith 1983, 152–53, with illustration.

29. Martin Birnbaum, "Strange Genius of Aubrey Beardsley," *The Craftsman* XXI/3 (Dec. 1911), 245–47.

30. *The Craftsman* XXV/1 (Oct. 1913), 216.

31. By Thomas Gilbert Pearson, future president of the Audubon Society. See Hamilton, 88.

32. See Coningsby Dawson, "The Haunted Wood," *The Craftsman* XXVI/3 (June 1914), 249; Clara T. MacChesney, "The Value of Fairies: what Rackham is doing to save them for the children of the world," *The Craftsman* XXVII/3 (Dec. 1914), 248; [unsigned] "The Sculptor in the Garden: Another chance for the fairies," *The Craftsman* XXX/3 (June 1916), 240.

33. Called "Chromewald."

34. *The Craftsman* XXX/4 (July 1916), passim.

35. Elbert and Alice Hubbard died when the *Lusitania* was sunk by a German torpedo on May 7, 1915.

36. Cathers, 206–07.

37. See Zipf, 143–57.

Chapter 24: The Rochester Yogi

1. Shakespeare, *The Tempest*, act I, scene 2.
2. Bragdon 1911, 10–11.
3. Biographical information compiled from Ellis & Reithmayr; Massey; Bragdon 1938.
4. Bragdon 1895, 52.
5. Illustrations in Ellis & Reithmayr, 94–97.
6. For appraisals of his architecture, see Ellis & Reithmayr, 15–44, and Massey, passim.
7. See Massey, 84.
8. Reproductions in Ellis & Reithmayr, 190–93; Massey, 242, 274, 277.
9. "A Sonnet of Despair," *The Philistine* I/6 (Nov. 1895), 169.
10. Cartoon satirizing *The Lark*, *The Philistine* II/1 (Dec. 1895), 32.
11. Bragdon 1938, 246.
12. Quoted in Dirlam and Simmons, 26.
13. Bragdon 1938, 246.
14. Reprinted in Bragdon 1925, 199–205.
15. Bragdon 1938, 60.
16. Bragdon 1909a.
17. Bragdon 1909b.
18. Bragdon 1938, 135–36.
19. Massey, 124.
20. Sprague 1909, no. XXX.
21. Bragdon 1938, 303.
22. Bragdon 1941, 8.
23. Bragdon 1941, 65.
24. Bragdon 1941, 27.
25. Bragdon 1941, 3.
26. Bragdon, Introduction to Sprague 1946, mentions that Fullwood's last book was published in 1939, "shortly before her death."
27. Bragdon 1938, 309.
28. Bragdon 1938, 312.
29. Massey, 275.
30. Bragdon, Introduction to Sprague 1946, 26.
31. Sprague 1946, 52.
32. Sprague 1946, 63.
33. Sprague 1946, 79.
34. Sprague 1946, 78.
35. Bragdon 1910, 25.

36. Bragdon 1928, 3–4.
37. Bragdon, Introduction to Sprague 1946, 40.
38. See "The Divine Androgyne" in Bragdon 1925, 186–96; reprinted in Bragdon 1936, 114–125.
39. Bragdon 1938, 88.
40. Bragdon arranged for their publication after Sullivan's death as *Kindergarten Chats*.
41. Information from Marc Demarest's paper, "The Fate of the Kaballah of the Egyptians," given at the conference of the Association for the Study of Esotericism, University of California, Davis, July 19–22, 2012.
42. See Henderson.
43. Bragdon 1915, 13.
44. A major topic of Eugenia Victoria Ellis's dissertation. See Ellis.
45. For illustrations, see Ellis & Reithmayr, 171–79; Massey, 251–52, 260–63.
46. For illustrations, see Ellis & Reithmayr, 166–68.
47. See Massey, 178–206; Ellis & Reithmayr, 139–63.
48. See especially Bragdon 1933.
49. See especially Bragdon 1923, 15–56.
50. See Bragdon 1939.

Chapter 25: The Cauldron Refired

1. "Archbishop Francis. Patience and Inspiration," *Woodstock Week*, April 21, 1966. Thanks to Peter Lamborn Wilson for access to this and other clippings from the Alf Evers Archive.
2. The curious may wish to investigate the community on Long Island called Modern Times and the one in Nyack led by "the Omnipotent Oom"; the free-love colony on Lake Ontario; the sexual teachings of Anna Kimball, a "spiritual physician" from Dunkirk, and Lois Waisbrooker, from Catherine; Austin Kent of Hopkinton, early defender of free love; Benjamin Paul Blood of Amsterdam, enlightened through nitrous oxide. Thanks to John Patrick Deveney for generously sharing these subjects of his own research, some of them documented in his *Free Love, Universal Reform and Fraud* (Deveney 2012).
3. Now absorbed into the Karma Triyana Dharmachakra Monastery.
4. The Gothic revival style of Richard Upjohn (1802–1878), much favored for Episcopalian churches.
5. Incidentally, C. W. Leadbeater was consecrated in the same year and the same lineage, stemming from the Old Catholics of Utrecht through Bishop Arnold Harris Mathew. For details, see the list of lineages at http://allengreenfield.wordpress.com/2014/05/24/masonic-dignities-egregoric-successions-updated-april-27-2010/.
6. See http://orthodoxwiki.org/The_Abbey_of_the_Holy_Name_(West_Milford,_New_Jersey).
7. Benedictine community at St. Dunstan's House, 2 Rutherford Place. The rood-screen now in Woodstock is pictured in "Handicraft of Local Monks," *New York Herald-Telegram*, Oct. 23, 1937.
8. Obituary of Mrs. Edna Francis, *Ulster Townsman*, Aug. 12, 1976.

9. Meher Baba (1894–1969) was an Iranian sage who never spoke, but indicated that he was the last avatar and would bring the age to a close.

10. See the church's website, http://wavelinks.net/cottocom.htm. Father Francis's successor, the Venerable John LoBue, follows his work as Metropolitan of North America.

11. *Point d'ironie* 53 (2012), I. My translation from the French. Ellipses in original.

12. Wilson 2010b.

13. See Wilson 2010a. For the Cairo action, *Point d'ironie* 53 (2012), II–III.

14. Kateri was canonized in 2012, as related in ch. 2.

15. For its history, see http://www.rosamysticaofamerica.org/our-story.html.

16. The biographical details that follow are condensed from the introduction to Damiani 1990. The Dalai Lama's quote is on page xv.

17. Editors' introduction to Damiani 1990, xiv.

18. Hanegraaff 1996, 95.

19. *Lucis*: Latin, "of light." It was originally called the "Lucifer Trust," as noted by conspiracy theorists who regard Bailey, and the New Age in general, as agents of the Illuminati.

20. Factual information from www.geo.org/ellis.htm.

21. See the foundation's website, http://www.folithaca.org, for current information.

22. Hanegraaff 2005, 999. Italics mine. The ellipses omit only a reference to another of Hanegraaff's works.

23. Robert F. Butts, introductory notes to Roberts 1977, 13, citing Roberts 1972, 431.

24. Damiani 1993, 261, citing Brunton, 369.

25. The Gazetteer lists only purpose-built centers and established groups. There are many others, and also temples built primarily by and for immigrants.

26. Plato, *Apology of Socrates*, 29b.

27. Fort, 21.

28. Fort, 163.

29. Vallee 2008, 230.

30. Fort, 23.

Bibliography

Albanese, Catherine. *A Republic of Mind and Spirit: A Cultural History of American Metaphysical Religion*. New Haven, Conn.: Yale University Press, 2007.

Algeo, John. "Oz—A Notable Theosophist, L. Frank Baum." *American Theosophist* 74 (1986): 270–73.

Allen, Hon. Lewis F. "Founding of the City of Ararat on Grand Island—by Mordecai M. Noah." *Transactions of the Buffalo Historical Society* 1 (1879): 305–28.

Anderson, Rodger I. *Joseph Smith's New York Reputation Reexamined*. Salt Lake City: Signature Books, 1990.

Bailey, William S. "Kiantone Mystery Solved as Hidden Cave is Unearthed." *Jamestown Journal*, November 18, 1933.

Balch, David Arnold. *Elbert Hubbard, Genius of Roycroft: A Biography*. New York: Frederick A. Stokes Co., 1940.

Ballou, Hosea. *A Treatise on Atonement: in which the Finite Nature of Sin is Argued. . .* 6th ed. Boston: A. Tompkins, 1848.

Barkun, Michael. *Crucible of the Millennium: The Burned-Over District of New York in the 1840s*. Syracuse, N.Y.: Syracuse University Press, 1986.

Barrett, Joseph Osgood. *The Spiritual Pilgrim. A Biography of James M. Peebles*. Boston: Colby & Rich, 1878.

Bastine, Michael, and Mason Winfield. *Iroquois Supernatural. Talking Animals and Medicine People*. Rochester, Vt.: Bear & Co., 2011.

Becker, Carl L. *Cornell University: Founders and the Founding*. Ithaca, N.Y.: Cornell University Press, 1943.

Beecher, Jonathan, and Richard Bienvenu, trans. and ed. *The Utopian Vision of Charles Fourier. Selected Texts on Work, Love and Passionate Attraction*. Boston: Beacon Press, 1971.

Belden, L. W. *Somnambulism. The Extraordinary Case of Jane C. Rider, the Springfield Somnambulist*. London: Simpkin & Marshall, 1834.

Bellknap, Jeremy. *Journal of a Tour from Boston to Oneida, June 1796*. Cambridge, Mass.: John Wilson, 1882.

Berleth, Richard. *Bloody Mohawk. The French and Indian War and American Revolution on New York's Frontier*. Hensonville, N.Y.: Black Dome Press, 2010.

Bernstein, Peter L. *Wedding of the Waters: the Erie Canal and the Making of a Great Nation*. New York: W. W. Norton, 2005.

Besant, Annie. *Talks to a Class*. Madras: Theosophical Publishing House, 1921.

Bestor, Arthur Eugene, Jr. "American Phalanxes. A Study of Fourierist Socialism in the United States (with Special Reference to the Movement in Western New York)." Ph.D. dissertation, Yale University, 1938.

Bestor, Arthur Eugene. *Backwoods Utopias: The Sectarian Origins and the Owenite Phase of Communitarian Socialism in America, 1663–1829*. 2nd enlarged ed. Philadelphia: University of Pennsylvania Press, 1971.

Blavatsky Letters. *The Letters of H. P. Blavatsky, vol. I, 1861–1879*. John Algeo, ed. Wheaton: Theosophical Publishing House, 2003.

Blavatsky, Helena Petrovna. *Collected Writings*. Boris de Zirkoff, ed. 15 vols. Wheaton: Theosophical Publishing House, 1966–91.

Blavatsky, Helena Petrovna. *Isis Unveiled: A Master-Key to the Mysteries of Ancient and Modern Science and Theology*. New York: J. W. Bouton, 1877.

Bliss, Sylvester. *Memoirs of William Miller, Generally Known as a Lecturer on the Prophecies, and the Second Coming of Christ*. Boston: Joshua V. Himes, 1853.

Block, Marguerite Beck. *The New Church in the New World*. New York: Swedenborg Foundation, 1978.

Boldman, Brian. "An Analysis of Angel Hair, 1947–2000." *International UFO Reporter* 26/3 (2001): 10–36.

Bradford, Roderick. *D. M. Bennett: The Truth Seeker*. Buffalo, N.Y.: Prometheus Books, 2006.

Bragdon, Claude and Eugenie. *Oracle*. 2nd ed. New York: Alfred A. Knopf, 1941.

Bragdon, Claude, *An Introduction to Yoga*. New York: Alfred A. Knopf, 1933. (Reissued as *Yoga for You*.)

Bragdon, Claude. *A Brief Life of Annie Besant*. Rochester, N.Y.: Manas Press, 1909. [1909a]

Bragdon, Claude. *Delphic Woman*. New York: Alfred A. Knopf, 1936.

Bragdon, Claude. *Merely Players*. New York: Alfred A. Knopf, 1939.

Bragdon, Claude. *More Lives Than One*. New York: Alfred A. Knopf, 1938. Also published as *The Secret Springs. An Autobiography*. London: Andrew Dakers, 1938.

Bragdon, Claude. *Old Lamps for New. The Ancient Wisdom in the Modern World*. New York: Alfred A. Knopf, 1925.

Bragdon, Claude. *Projective Ornament*. Rochester, N.Y.: Manas Press, 1915.

Bragdon, Claude. *The Beautiful Necessity. Seven Essays on Theosophy and Architecture*. Rochester, N.Y.: Manas Press, 1910.

Bragdon, Claude. *The Frozen Fountain, Being Essays on Architecture and the Art of Design in Space*. New York: Alfred A. Knopf, 1932.

Bragdon, Claude. *The Golden Person in the Heart*. Gouverneur, N.Y.: The Brothers of the Book, 1898.

Bragdon, Claude. *The New Image*. New York: Alfred A. Knopf, 1928.

Bragdon, Claude. *The Small Old Path*. Rochester, N.Y.: Manas Press, 1911.

Bragdon, Claude. *Theosophy and the Theosophical Society*. Rochester, N.Y.: Manas Press, 1909. [1909b] Later, enlarged editions titled *Episodes from an Unwritten History*.

Bragdon, George Chandler. *Undergrowth*. Rochester, N.Y.: Author, 1895.

Brammer, Leila. *Excluded from Suffrage History: Matilda Joslyn Gage, Nineteenth-Century American Feminist*. Westport, Conn.: Greenwood Press, 2000.

Bratt, James D. *Antirevivalism in Antebellum America. A Collection of Religious Voices*. New Brunswick, N.J.: Rutgers University Press, 2006.

Braude, Ann. *Radical Spirits. Spiritualism and Women's Rights in Nineteenth-Century America*. 2nd ed. Bloomington, Ind.: Indiana University Press, 2001.

Bressler, Ann Lee. *The Universalist Movement in America 1770–1880*. New York: Oxford University Press, 2001.

Brisbane, Albert. *Social Destiny of Man: or, Association and Reorganization of Industry*. Philadelphia: C. F. Stollmeyer, 1840.

Brisset, Jean-Pierre. *Œuvres complètes*. Dijon: Les Presses du réel, 2001.

Britten, Emma Hardinge. *Modern American Spiritualism*. New York: Britten, 1870.

Broadhurst, Dale R. "Mordecai M. Noah and the Mormon Zion." http://olivercowdery.com/gathering/ararat2.htm.

Brodie, Fawn M. *No Man Knows My History. The Life of Joseph Smith the Mormon Prophet*. New York: Alfred A. Knopf, 1963.

Brooke, John L. *The Refiner's Fire. The Making of Mormon Cosmology, 1644–1844*. Cambridge: Cambridge University Press, 1994.

Brownell, Abner. *Enthusiastical Errors Transpired and Detected*. N.p.: Author, 1783.

Bruce, Dwight H., ed. *Memorial History of Syracuse, from Its Settlement to the Present Time*. Syracuse, N.Y.: H. P. Smith & Co., 1891.

Brunton, Paul. *The Notebooks of Paul Brunton: Perspectives*. Burdett, N.Y.: Larson Publications, 1984.

Buescher, John Benedict. *Aquarian Evangelist: The Age of Aquarius as It Dawned in the Mind of Levi Dowling*. Fullerton, Calif.: Theosophical History, 2008.

Buescher, John B. *The Other Side of Salvation: Spiritualism and the Nineteenth-Century American Experience*. Boston: Skinner House Books, 2004.

Buescher, John Benedict. *The Remarkable Life of John Murray Spear, Agitator for the Spirit World*. Notre Dame, Ind.: University of Notre Dame Press, 2006.

Burdick, Donna Dorrance. *"Spirited" Women and Men & Their Unpopular Causes*. Peterboro, N.Y.: Peterboro Area Historical Society, 2011.

Bush, George. *Mesmer and Swedenborg; or, The Relation of the Developments of Mesmerism to the Doctrines and Disclosures of Swedenborg*. New York: John Allen, 1847.

Bushman, Richard Lyman, with the assistance of Jed Woodworth. *Joseph Smith: Rough Stone Rolling*. New York: Alfred A. Knopf, 2005.

Campbell, Dudley M. *A History of Oneonta, from Its Earliest Settlement to the Present Time*. Oneonta, N.Y.: G. W. Fairchild & Co., 1906.

Campion, Nardi Reeder. *Mother Ann Lee, Morning Star of the Shakers*. Hanover, N.H.: University Press of New England, 1990.

Capron, Eliab W. and Henry D. Barron. *Singular Revelations. Explanation and History of the Mysterious Communion with Spirits, Comprehending the Rise and Progress of the Mysterious Noises in Western New-York, Generally Received as Spiritual Communications*. 2nd enlarged ed. Auburn, N.Y.: Capron & Barron, 1850.

Carden, Maren Lockwood. *Oneida: Utopian Community to Modern Corporation*. Baltimore: Johns Hopkins University Press, 1969.

Carmer, Carl. *Dark Trees to the Wind. A Cycle of York State Years*. New York: David McKay Co., 1949.

Cathers, David. *Gustav Stickley*. New York: Phaidon, 2003.

Chase, Oliver F. "The Kiantone Movement." In: *Centennial History of Chautauqua County*. Jamestown, N.Y.: Chautauqua History Company, 1904: 826–30.

Corliss, William R. *Handbook of Unusual Phenomena*. New York: Arlington House, 1986.

Corson, Eugene Rollin. *Some Unpublished Letters of Helena Petrovna Blavatsky*. London: Rider & Co., n.d. [1929]

Corson, Hiram. *Spirit Messages. With an Introductory Esay on Spiritual Vitality*. Rochester, N.Y.: Austin Publishing Co., 1911.

Craftsman, The. Eastwood/New York: Gustav Stickley The Craftsman Inc., 1901–1915.

Cronin, Deborah K. *Kiantone: Chautauqua County's Mystical Valley*. Bloomington, Ind.: Author House, 2006.

Cross, Whitney R. *The Burned-Over District: The Social and Intellectual History of Enthusiastic Religion in Western New York, 1800–1830*. Ithaca, N.Y.: Cornell University Press, 1950.

Cuthbert, Arthur A. *The Life and World-Work of Thomas Lake Harris, Written from Direct Personal Knowledge*. Glasgow: C. W. Pearce & Co., 1908.

Damiani, Anthony. *Looking Into Mind. How to Recognize Who You Are and How You Know*. Burdett, N.Y.: Larson Publications, for the Paul Brunton Philosophic Foundation, 1990.

Damiani, Anthony. *Standing in Your Own Way. Talks on the Nature of the Ego*. Burdett, N.Y.: Larson Publications, for the Paul Brunton Philosophic Foundation, 1993.

Dann, Norman K. *Practical Dreamer. Gerrit Smith and the Crusade for Social Reform*. Hamilton, N.Y.: Log Cabin Books, 2009.

Darnton, Robert. *Mesmerism and the End of the Enlightenment in France*. Cambridge, Mass.: Harvard University Press, 1968.

Davis, Andrew Jackson. *Beyond the Valley; A Sequel to "The Magic Staff:" An Autobiography*. Boston: Colby & Rich, 1885.

Davis, Andrew Jackson. *Events in the Life of a Seer; Being Memoranda of Authentic Facts in Magnetism, Clairvoyance, Spiritualism*. 6th ed. Boston: Banner of Light Publishing Co. [1868].

Davis, Andrew Jackson. *The Magic Staff; An Autobiography*. New York: J. S. Brown & Co., 1857.

Dennis, Matthew. *Cultivating a Landscape of Peace. Iroquois-European Encounters in Seventeenth-Century America*. Ithaca, N.Y.: Cornell University Press, 1993.

Dennis, Matthew. *Seneca Possessed. Indians, Witchcraft, and Power in the Early American Republic*. Philadelphia: University of Pennsylvania Press, 2010.

Desjardins, Simon, and Pierre Pharoux. *Castorland Journal: an Account of the Exploration and Settlement of Northern New York State by French Émigrés in the Years 1793 to 1797*. Trans. John A. Gallucci. Ithaca, N.Y.: Cornell University Press, 2010.

Deveney, John Patrick. *Astral Projection or Liberation of the Double and the Work of the Early Theosophical Society*. Fullerton, Calif.: Theosophical History, 1997. [1997a]

Deveney, John Patrick. *Paschal Beverly Randolph: Nineteenth-Century Black Spiritualist, Rosicrucian, and Sex Magician*. Albany, N.Y.: State University of New York Press, 1997. [1997b]

Deveney, John Patrick. *Free Love, Universal Reform and Fraud: The Economics and Transformation of American Spiritualist Camp Meetings in the Nineteenth Century*. Fullerton, Calif.: Theosophical History, 2012.

Devotional Somnium, or, A Collection of Prayers and Exhortations, Uttered by Miss Rachel Baker, In the City of New-York, in the winter of 1815, during her abstracted and unconscious state . . . By Several Medical Gentlemen. New York: S. Marks, 1815.

Dirlam, H. Kenneth, and Ernest E. Simmons. *Sinners, This Is East Aurora. The Story of Elbert Hubbard and The Roycroft Shops*. New York: Vantage Press, 1964.

Doctrine and Covenants of the Church of Jesus Christ of Latter-day Saints. Westport, Conn.: Greenwood Press, 1971 reprint of Salt Lake City: Deseret Books, 1880.

Dorrien, Gary. *The Making of American Liberal Theology. Imagining Progressive Religion 1805–1900*. Louisville, Ky.: Westminster John Knox Press, 2001.

Douglass, Frederick. *Autobiographies*. New York: The Library of America, 1994.

Douglass, Frederick. *The Frederick Douglass Papers, Series Three: Correspondence. Vol. I: 1843–1852*. John R. McKivigan, ed. New Haven, Conn.: Yale University Press, 2009.

Dowling, John. *An Exposition of the Prophecies, Supposed by William Miller to Predict the Second Coming of Christ, in 1843 . . .* Providence: Geo. P. Daniels, 1840.

Duino, Russell. "Utopian Themes and Variations: John Murray Spear and His Kiantone Domain." *Pennsylvania History* 29/2 (1962): 140–50.

Edmonds, John W., and George T. Dexter. *Spiritualism*. 2nd ed. New York: Partridge & Brittan, 1855.

Edmonston, William E., Jr. *The Induction of Hypnosis*. New York: John Wiley & Sons, 1986.

Edson, Hon. Obed. *History of Chautauqua County, New York*. Boston: W. A. Ferguson & Co., 1894.

Edwards, Jonathan, *A Treatise Concerning Religious Affections in Three Parts*. Edinburgh: J. Ogle, 1812. (1st ed. 1746)

Edwards, Jonathan. *The Distinguishing Marks of a Work of the Spirit of God*. Boston: Kneeland & Green, 1741.

Eek, Swen. *Dâmodar and the Pioneers of the Theosophical Movement*. Adyar: Theosophical Publishing House, 1978. (1st ed. 1965)

Ellis, Eugenia Victoria, and Andrea G. Reithmayr, eds. *Claude Bragdon & the Beautiful Necessity*. Rochester, N.Y.: Rochester Institute of Technology/Cary Graphic Arts Press, 2010.

Ellis, Eugenia Victoria. "Squaring the Circle: Regulating Lines of Claude Bragdon's Theosophic Architecture." Ph.D. dissertation, Virginia Polytechnic and State University, 2005.

Emery, George, and J. C. Hermert Emery. *A Young Man's Benefit. The Independent Order of Odd Fellows and Sickness Insurance in the United States and Canada, 1860–1929*. Montreal: McGill-Queen's University Press, 1999.

Evans, F. W. *Shakers and Koreshans Uniting*. Mount Lebanon, N.Y.: Author, 1892. Koreshan Virtual Archives.

Fabre d'Olivet. *Hermeneutic Interpretation of the Origin of the Social State of Man and of the Destiny of the Adamic Race*. Trans. Nayán Louise Redfield. New York: G. P. Putnam's Sons, 1915.

Faivre, Antoine. "Magnétisme et spiritisme dans les États-Unis dans le milieu du XIXe siècle." In Silvia Mancini and Antoine Faivre, eds. *Des Médiums. Techniques du corps et de l'esprit dans les deux Amériques*. Paris: Éditions Imago, 2012 : 135–66.

Fine, Howard D. "The Koreshan Unity. The Chicago Years of a Utopian Community." *Illinois State Historical Society Journal* 48 (June 1975): 213–27.

Fine, Howard David. "The Koreshan Unity; The Early New York Beginnings of a Utopian Community." Undated typescript. Koreshan Virtual Archives.

Finney, Charles Grandison. *Memoirs*. New York: A. S. Barnes & Co., 1876.

Fogarty, Robert S. *Desire and Duty at Oneida. Tirzah Miller's Intimate Memoir*. Bloomington, Ind.: Indiana University Press, 2000.

Forest Hill Cemetery, Utica, New York. Unpaginated booklet, circa 1960.

Forsberg, Clyde R., Jr. *Equal Rites: The Book of Mormon, Masonry, Gender, and American Culture*. New York: Columbia University Press, 2004.

Fort, Charles. *The Books of Charles Fort*. New York: Henry Holt, for the Fortean Society, 1941.

Fra, The. East Aurora, N.Y.: Roycroft Press, 1908–1917.

Freeman, John Crosby. *The Forgotten Rebel: Gustav Stickley and His Craftsman Mission Furniture*. Watkins Glen, N.Y.: Century House, 1966.

Frothingham, Octavius Brooks. *Gerrit Smith: A Biography*. New York: G. P. Putnam's Sons, 1878.

Fullwood, Nancy. *The Song of Sano Tarot*. New York: Macoy Publishing Co., 1929.

Gage, Matilda Joslyn. *Woman, Church, and State. A Historical Account of the Status of Woman through the Christian Ages: with Reminiscences of Matriarchate*. New York: Truth Seeker Co., 1893.

Garrett, Clarke. *Spirit Possession and Popular Religion. From the Camisards to the Shakers*. Baltimore: Johns Hopkins University Press, 1987.

Garrison, William Lloyd. *Modern Phenomena*. Boston: American Liberal Tract Society, 1854.

Ghost Land; or Researches into the Mysteries of Occultism. Trans. and ed. Emma Hardinge Britten. Boston: The Editor, 1876.

Giambastini, Barbara J., ed. *Country Roads Revisited. The Cultural Imprint of Madison County*. Oneida, N.Y.: Madison County Historical Society, 1984.

Givens, Terryl L. *By the Hand of Mormon: The American Scripture that Launched a New World Religion*. New York: Oxford University Press, 2002.

Godwin, Joscelyn, Christian Chanel, John P. Deveney, eds. *The Hermetic Brotherhood of Luxor: Initiatic and Historical Documents of an Order of Practical Occultism.* York Beach, Maine: Weiser, 1995.

Godwin, Joscelyn. "The Hidden Hand, Part I: The Provocation of the Hydesville Phenomena." *Theosophical History* N.S. 3/2 (1990): 34–43.

Godwin, Joscelyn. *Atlantis and the Cycles of Time.* Rochester, Vt.: Inner Traditions, 2011. [2011a]

Godwin, Joscelyn. *The Spirit House, or Brown's Free Hall, in Georgetown, New York: A Short History.* Hamilton, N.Y.: The Upstate Institute at Colgate University, 2011. [2011b]

Godwin, Joscelyn. *The Theosophical Enlightenment.* Albany, N.Y.: State University of New York Press, 1994.

Goldsmith, Barbara. *Other Powers: The Age of Suffrage, Spiritualism, and the Scandalous Victoria Woodhull.* New York: HarperCollins, 1999.

Gomes, Michael. "Abner Doubleday and Theosophy in America: 1879–1884." *Sunrise Magazine,* April–May 1991 (accessed online, unpaginated).

Gomes, Michael. *The Dawning of the Theosophical Movement.* Wheaton, Ill: Theosophical Publishing House, 1987.

Goodwillie, Christian. "Heaven is a Hollow Earth: The Shaker-Koreshan Connection." *American Communal Societies Quarterly* 3/2 (2009): 65–99.

Griffith, Elisabeth. *In Her Own Right. The Life of Elizabeth Cady Stanton.* New York: Oxford University Press, 1984.

Grimes, James Stanley. "Origins of Modern Spiritualism." *Psypioneer* 3/12 (2007): 267–77 (reprinted from J.S. Grimes, *The Mysteries of Human Nature Explained by a New System of Nervous Physiology . . .* Buffalo, N.Y.: R. M. Wanzer, 1857, 346–62).

Grumbine, J. C. F. *Psychometry: Its Science and Law of Unfoldment.* 2nd ed. Syracuse, N.Y.: Order of the White Rose, 1900.

Guarneri, Carl J. *The Utopian Alternative: Fourierism in Nineteenth-Century America.* Ithaca, N.Y.: Cornell University Press, 1991.

Guénon, René. *L'erreur spirite.* 2nd ed. Paris: Éditions Traditionnelles, 1952.

Guerin, Sean P. "The Alternating Utopian Visions of Thomas Lake Harris." B.A. thesis, Hamilton College, 1995.

Gutierrez, Cathy. *Plato's Ghost. Spiritualism in the American Renaissance.* New York: Oxford University Press, 2009.

Hambrick-Stowe, Charles E. *Charles Grandison Finney and the Spirit of American Evangelicalism.* Grand Rapids, Mich.: Eerdman, 1996.

Hamilton, Charles F. *As Bees in Honey Drown. Elbert Hubbard and the Roycrofters.* South Brunswick, N.J.: A. S. Barnes, 1973.

Hanegraaff, Wouter J. *New Age Religion and Western Culture. Esotericism in the Mirror of Secular Thought.* Leiden: E. J. Brill, 1996.

Hanegraaff, Wouter J., Antoine Faivre, Roelof van den Broek, Jean-Pierre Brach, eds. *Dictionary of Gnosis and Western Esotericism.* Leiden: E. J. Brill, 2005.

Hankins, Barry. *The Second Great Awakening and the Transcendentalists.* Westport, Conn.: Greenwood Press, 2004.

Hardman, Keith J. *Charles Grandison Finney 1792–1875. Revivalist and Reformer.* Syracuse, N.Y.: Syracuse University Press, 1987.

Harper, Ida Husted. *The Life and Work of Susan B. Anthony.* Indianapolis: Bowen-Merrill Co., 1899.

Harris, Lauretta, and Tinker McKay. "Chapel Plate for Nova Scotia." *Silver Studies* 28 (2012): 24–33.

Harris, Thomas Lake. *An Epic of the Starry Heaven.* New York: Partridge & Brittan, 1854.

Harris, Thomas Lake. *Arcana of Christianity. An Unfolding of the Celestial Sense of the Divine Word.* New York: New Church Publishing Association, 1858.

Harris, Thomas Lake. *The Lord; The Two-in-One: Declared, Manifested, and Glorified.* Salem-on-Erie: Brotherhood of the New Life, 1876

Harris, Thomas Lake. *The Wisdom of Angels,* Part I. New York: New Church Publishing Association, 1857.

Harris, Thomas Lake. *Wisdom of the Adepts. Esoteric Science in Human History.* Fountaingrove [Santa Rosa: Brotherhood of the New Life],1884.

Harrison, C. G. *The Transcendental Universe: Six Lectures on Occult Science, Theosophy, and the Catholic Faith: delivered before the Berean Society.* Hudson, N.Y.: Lindisfarne Press, 1993. (1st ed. 1894)

Hauptmann, Laurence M. *Conspiracy of Interests. Iroquois Dispossession and the Rise of New York State.* Syracuse, N.Y.: Syracuse University Press, 1999.

Hearn, Michael Patrick, ed. *The Annotated Wizard of Oz.* New York: Clarkson N. Potter, 1973.

Henderson, Linda Dalrymple. "Claude Bragdon, the Fourth Dimension and Modern Art in Cultural Context." In Ellis and Reithmayr, 73–86.

Hewitt, Mark Alan. *Gustav Stickley's Craftsman Farms: The Quest for an Arts and Crafts Utopia.* Syracuse, N.Y.: Syracuse University Press, 2001.

Hicks, Peter. "Cyrus Teed [A Biography]." Koreshan Virtual Archives.

Hoehnle, Peter. "The Amana Church Society: Community, Continuity and Change." *American Communal Societies Quarterly* 6/1 (2012): 22–38.

Hoehnle, Peter. *The Amana People. The History of a Religious Community.* N.p.: Penfield Books, 2003.

Homer, Michael W. "Similarity of Priesthood in Masonry: The Relationship Between Freemasonry and Mormonism." *Dialogue* 27/3 (1994): 1–113.

Hubbard, Elbert. *A Message to Garcia and Thirteen Other Things.* East Aurora, N.Y.: The Roycrofters, 1901.

Hudson, David. *History of Jemima Wilkinson.* Geneva, N.Y., 1821.

Ingersoll, Robert G. *On the Gods and Other Essays.* Buffalo, N.Y.: Prometheus Books, 1990.

Ives, Ansel W., M.D. "A Remarkable Case of Devotional Somnium." *Transactions of the Physio-Medical Society of New York* 1 (1817): 395–412.

Jahrbücher der wahren Inspirations-Gemeinden. Ebenezer bei Buffalo: Community of True Inspiration, 1849-.

Johnson, K. Paul. *The Masters Revealed. Madame Blavatsky and the Myth of the Great White Lodge.* Albany, N.Y.: State University of New York Press, 1994.

Johnson, Paul E., and Sean Wilentz. *The Kingdom of Matthias*. New York: Oxford University Press, 1994.

Jones, Amanda T. *A Psychic Autobiography*. New York: Greaves Publishing Co., 1910.

Karcher, Carolyn. *The First Woman in the Republic: a Cultural Biography of Lydia Maria Child*. Durham, N.C.: Duke University Press, 1994.

Kern, Kathi. *Mrs. Stanton's Bible*. Ithaca, N.Y.: Cornell University Press, 2001.

Kerner, Justinus. *The Seeress of Prevorst*. Trans. Catherine Crowe. New York: Harper & Brothers, 1845.

Kirkham, Francis W. *A New Witness for Christ in America: the Book of Mormon*. 4th ed. Salt Lake City: Brigham Young University, 1967.

Klaw, Spencer. *Without Sin. The Life and Death of the Oneida Community*. New York: Penguin Books USA, 1993.

Klein, Milton M., ed. *The Empire State. A History of New York*. Ithaca, N.Y.: Cornell University Press, 2001.

Klees, Emerson. *The Crucible of Ferment. New York's "Psychic Highway."* Rochester, N.Y.: Cameo Press, 2001.

Kolmerton, Carol A. *The American life of Ernestine L. Rose*. Syracuse, N.Y.: Syracuse University Press, 1999.

Koresh. *The Cellular Cosmogony, or The Earth a Concave Sphere*. Estero: Koreshan Unity, 1983/A.K. 143.

Koreshan Virtual Archives. http://koreshan.mwweb.org/.

Kurtz, Edward T., Sr. *Brocton and Portland*. Charleston, S.C.: Arcadia Publishing, 2007.

La Rochefoucauld-Liancour, François-Alexandre-Frédéric, duc de. *Travels through the United States*. London: R. Phillips, 1799.

Lambert, Frank. *Inventing the "Great Awakening."* Princeton, N.J.: Princeton University Press, 1999.

Lankes, Frank, J. *The Ebenezer Community of True Inspiration*. Gardenville, N.Y.: Author, 1949.

Leadbeater, Charles Webster. *The Astral Plane: Its Scenery, Inhabitants and Phenomena*. London: Theosophical Publishing Society, 1895.

LeBaron, Gaye. *Diaries of Kanaye Nagasawa*. Offprint from a Japanese periodical dated 1980, in Special Collections, SUNY Fredonia.

LeBaron, Gaye. *The Japanese "Baron" of Fountaingrove; A Study of Kanaye Nagasawa and the Japanese Disciples of Thomas Lake Harris*. Santa Rosa, Calif.: Santa Rosa Junior College, 1976.

Leiner, Frederick C. *The End of Barbary Terror: America's 1815 War Against the Pirates of North Africa*. New York: Oxford University Press, 2006.

Lewis, E. E. *A Report on the Mysterious Noises Heard in the House of Mr. John D. Fox, in Hydesville, Arcadia, Wayne County, N.Y. Authenticated by the Certificates, and Confirmed by the Statements of the Citizens of that Place and Vicinity*. Canandaigua, N.Y.: Author, 1848, reprinted Shelburne Falls, Mass.: J. P. Thorndike, 1887.

Lewis, W. Spencer. *Rosicrucian Manual*. 7th ed. San Jose, Calif.: Rosicrucian Press, 1938.

Life, Character, Revelations and Doctrines of the Ever Blessed Mother Ann Lee. Hancock, Mass.: J. Tallcott and J. Deming, 1816.

Loncraine, Rebecca. *The Real Wizard of Oz: The Life and Times of L. Frank Baum*. New York: Gotham Books, 2009.

Lovejoy, David S. *Religious Enthusiasm in the New World. Heresy to Revolution*. Cambridge, Mass.: Harvard University Press, 1985.

Mahatma Letters to A. P. Sinnett from the Mahatmas M. & K. H. 3rd ed. Adyar: Theosophical Publishing House, 1979.

Mais, Charles. *Rachel Baker, Who Prays and Preaches in Her Sleep . . .* New York: Marks, 1814.

Marini, Stephen A. *Radical Sects of Revolutionary New England*. Cambridge, Mass.: Harvard University Press, 1982.

Massey, Jonathan. *Crystal and Arabesque. Claude Bragdon, Ornament, and Modern Architecture*. Pittsburgh: University of Pittsburgh Press, 2009.

Mathers, S. L. McGregor. *The Kabbalah Unveiled*. London: Redway, 1887.

McAllister, Catherine. *The Brotherhood of the New Life. Personal and Public Accounts of Thomas Lake Harris's Communal Vision*. Fredonia, N.Y.: Reed Library, 1995.

McCain, Andrew. "The Incorporation of Fraternalism: American Fraternal Orders at the End of the Victorian Era." http://xroads.virginia.edu/~MA04/mccain/fraternalorders/Homepage.htm.

McCarthy, Fiona. *The Simple Life: C. R. Ashbee in the Cotswolds*. Berkeley, Calif.: University of California Press, 1981.

McCoy, Adrian W. "History of Cassadaga." In H. D. Barrett and A. W. McCoy, eds., *Cassadaga; Its History and Teachings with Histories of Spiritualist Camp Meetings, and Biographies of Cassadaga Prophets and Others*. Meadsville, Pa.: Gazette Printing Co., 1891: 39–61.

McGreevey, Patrick. *Stairway to Empire: Lockport, the Erie Canal, and the Shaping of America*. Albany, N.Y.: SUNY Press, 2009.

Medlicott, Carol. "'We Live at a Great Distance from the Church': Cartographic Strategies of the Shakers, 1805–1835." *American Communal Societies Quarterly* 4/3 (2010): 123–160.

Memorial and Biographical History of Northern California. Chicago: Lewis Publishing Co., 1891.

Merrill, Arch. *Shadows on the Wall: Tales of New York State*. New York: American Book/Stratford Press, n.d.

Metzger, Th. *Selected Strange and Sacred Sites: The Ziggurat Guide to Western New York*. N.p.: Exit 18, 2002.

Michell, John. *Eccentric Lives and Peculiar Notions*. London: Thames & Hudson, 1984.

Millner, Lyn. "Teed's New York Days." Interactive map. http://koreshan.mwweb.org/blog/?p=1135.

Moore, William D. *Masonic Temples. Freemasonry, Ritual Architecture, and Masculine Archetypes*. Knoxville, Tenn.: University of Tennessee Press, 2006.

Morgan, Dale. *Dale Morgan on Early Mormonism. Correspondence and a New History*. John Phillip Walker, ed. Salt Lake City: Signature Books, 1986.

Mott, Lucretia Coffin. *Selected Letters*. Beverly Wilson Palmer, ed. Urbana, Ill.: University of Illinois Press, 2002.

Mutual Criticism. Oneida, N.Y.: Office of the American Socialist, 1876.

Myers, Arthur. "Fox Cottage Burns." Lily Dale Historical Society pamphlet, n.d.

Nell, William Cooper. *William Cooper Nell. Nineteenth-Century African American Abolitionist, Historian, Integrationist. Selected Writings from 1832–1874*. Dorothy Porter Wesley and Constance Porter Uzelac, eds. Baltimore: Black Classics Press, 2002.

New York Atlas & Gazetteer. 6th ed. Yarmouth, Maine.: DeLorme, 2001.

New York. A Guide to the Empire State. Compiled by Workers of the Writer's Program of the Work Projects Administration in the State of New York. New York: Oxford University Press/N.Y. State Historical Association, 1940.

Newell, Linda King, and Valeen Tippetts Avery. *Mormon Enigma: Emma Hale Smith*. Urbana, Ill.: University of Illinois Press, 1994.

Nichol, Francis D. *The Midnight Cry: A Defence of the Character and Conduct of William Miller and the Millerites, who Mistakenly Believed that the Second Coming of Christ Would Take Place in the Year 1844*. Takoma Park, Md.: Review and Herald Publishing Association, 1944.

Noah, Mordecai Manuel. *The Selected Writings of Mordecai Noah*. Michael Schuldiner and Daniel J. Kleinfeld, eds. Westport, Conn.: Greenwood Press, 1999.

Noyes, George Wallingford, compiler and editor. *John Humphrey Noyes: The Putney Community*. Oneida, N.Y.: Author, 1931.

Noyes, George Wallingford, compiler and editor. *Religious Experience of John Humphrey Noyes, Founder of the Oneida Community*. New York: Macmillan Co., 1923.

Noyes, George Wallingford, compiler, Lawrence Foster, ed. *Free Love in Utopia. John Humphrey Noyes and the Origin of the Oneida Community*. Urbana, Ill.: University of Illinois Press, 2001.

Noyes, John Humphrey. *History of American Socialisms*. Philadelphia: J. B. Lippincott, 1870.

Noyes, John Humphrey. *The Berean: A Manual for the Help of Those who Seek the Faith of the Primitive Church*. Putney, Vt.: Spiritual Magazine, 1847.

Oak, Jacquelyn, and Gwendolyn Dubois Shaw. *Artist and Visionary: William Matthew Prior*. Cooperstown, N.Y.: Fenimore Art Museum, 2012.

Ohnemus, Catherine Anthony. "Dr. Cyrus Teed and the Koreshan Unity Movement. *C[ultural] R[esource] M[anagement]* 9 (2001): 10–12.

Olcott, Henry Steel. *Old Diary Leaves, vol. I, America 1874–1878*. Adyar: Theosophical Publishing House, 1941. (1st ed. 1895)

Olcott, Henry. *People of the Other World*. Hartford, Conn.: American Publishing Co., 1875.

Owens, Lance S. "Joseph Smith and Kabbalah: The Occult Connection." *Dialogue* 27/3 (1994): 117–94.

Parker, Arthur C. *The Code of Handsome Lake, the Seneca Prophet* (1913). Internet Sacred Text Archive DVD.

Peebles, James M. "The Pilgrim in War-Paint." *Progressive Thinker* 23/589 (March 9, 1901): 7.

Peebles, James M. *Three Journeys Around the World, or, Travels in the Pacific Islands, New Zealand, Australia, Ceylon, India, Egypt and Other Oriental Countries*. Boston: Banner of Light Publishing Co., 1898.

Philistine, The. East Aurora, N.Y.: Roycroft Press, 1895–1915.

Pike, Albert. *Morals and Dogma of the Ancient and Accepted Scottish Rite of Freemasonry*. Washington: Supreme Council of the Thirty-Third Degree, 1960. (1st ed. 1871)

Pitts, Edward I., and Stephen R. Leonard, Sr. "Oneida Community Chronology." http://oneidacommunity.blogspot.com/.

Pitzer, Donald E., ed. *America's Communal Utopias*. Chapel Hill, N.C.: University of North Carolina Press, 1997.

Pollard, Michelle. "Michelle Pollard's Blog, all about Women and Technology." http://blogs.oregonstate.edu/michellepollard/about/.

Pollitt, Basil H. "My Uncle, Elbert Hubbard." *Rosicrucian Digest* 35 (1957): 425–27.

Pound, Arthur. *Johnson of the Mohawks: a Biography of Sir William Johnson, Irish Immigrant, Mohawk War Chief, American Soldier, Empire Builder*. New York: Macmillan Co., 1930.

Powalski, Caitlin. "Radical Transmissions: Isaac and Amy Post, Spiritualism, and Progressive Reform in Nineteenth-Century Rochester." *Rochester History* 71/2 (2009): 1–25.

Poyen, Charles. *The Progress of Animal Magnetism in New England*. Boston: Weeks, Jordan & Co., 1837.

Pratt, Parley P. *The Autobiography of Parley P. Pratt, One of the Twelve Apostles of the Church of Jesus Christ of Latter-Day Saints*. New York: Parley P. Pratt, Jr., 1874.

Proceedings and Addresses at the Freethought Convention Held at Watkins, N.Y., August 22d, 23d, 24th, and 25th, '78. New York: D. M. Bennett, Liberal Publisher, 1878.

Quinan, Jack. "Elbert Hubbard's Roycroft." In Via & Searl, 1–19.

Quinn, D. Michael. *Early Mormonism and the Magic World View*. Salt Lake City: Signature Books, 1987.

Rahn, Claude J. *A Brief Outline of the Life of Dr. Cyrus R. Teed (Koresh) and of the Koreshan Unity*. Typescript, Estero, 1963. Koreshan Virtual Archives.

Rainwater, Dorothy, and Judy Redfield. *Encyclopedia of American Silver Manufacturers*. 4th ed. Atglen, Pa.: Schiffer Publishing, 1998.

Randolph, Paschal Beverly. *After Death*. 2nd ed. Boston: Author, 1868.

Randolph, Paschal Beverly. *Dealings with the Dead; the Human Soul, Its Migrations and Its Transmigrations*. "Penned by the Rosicrucian." Utica, N.Y.: M. J. Randolph, 1861–'62 [*sic*].

Randolph, Paschal Beverly. *Pre-Adamite Man*. 6th ed. Toledo, Kans.: Randolph Publishing Co., 1888.

Randolph, Paschal Beverly. *The Unveiling: or, What I Think of Spiritualism*. Boston: Mary J. Randolph, 1860.

Rea, Sara Weber. *The Koreshan Story*. Estero, Fla.: Guiding Star Publishing House, 1994.

Reid, W. Max. *The Mohawk Valley. Its Legends and Its History*. New York: G. P. Putnam's Sons, 1901.

Remarkable Sermons and Pious Ejaculations, Delivered During Sleep, Taken in Shorthand. London: E. Cox & Son, 1815.

Respiro [C. M. Berridge]. "Internal Respiration." *The Unknown World* 1/4 (1894): 168–72.

Riley, Michael O. *Oz and Beyond: The Fantasy World of L. Frank Baum*. Lawrence, Kans.: University Press of Kansas, 1997.

Roberts, B. H. *A Comprehensive History of the Church of Jesus Christ of Latter-day Saints*. Provo, Utah: Brigham Young University Press, 1965.

Roberts, Jane. *Seth Speaks. The Eternal Validity of the Soul*. Englewood Cliffs, N.J.: Prentice-Hall, Inc., 1972.

Roberts, Jane. *The "Unknown" Reality: A Seth Book, Vol. 1*. Englewood Cliffs: Prentice-Hall, Inc., 1977.

Robertson, Constance Noyes. *Seek No Further*. New York: Farrar & Rinehart, 1938.

Robinson, David. *The Unitarians and the Universalists*. Westport, Conn.: Greenwood Press, 1985.

Rockford Today, Historical, Descriptive, Biographical. Rockford, Ill.: Rockford Morning Star/Clark Co. Press, 1903.

Rogers, E. C. *Philosophy of Mysterious Agents, Human and Mundane: or The Dynamic Laws and Relations of Man. Embracing the Natural Philosophy of Phenomena Styled "Spiritual Manifestations."* Boston: John. P. Jewitt & Co., 1853.

Rogers, Katharine M. *L. Frank Baum, Creator of Oz*. New York: St. Martin's Press, 2002.

Rogers, Walter P. *Andrew D. White and the Modern University*. Ithaca, N.Y.: Cornell University Press, 1942.

Sackett, Chuck. *What's Going on in There? The Verbatim Text of the Mormon Temple Rituals Annotated and Explained by a Former Temple Worker*. Thousand Oaks, Calif.: Sword of the Shepherd Ministries, 1982.

Salvucci, Claudio P., and Anthony P. Schiavo, eds. *Iroquois Wars II. Extracts from the Jesuit Relations from 1650 to 1675*. Bristol, Pa.: Evolution Publishing, 2003.

Sarna, Jonathan D. *Jacksonian Jew. The Two Worlds of Mordecai Noah*. New York: Holmes & Meier, 1981.

Sawin, Mark Metzler. *Raising Kane. Elisha Kent Kane and the Culture of Fame in Antebellum America*. Philadelphia: American Philosophical Society, 2008.

Scheuner, Gottlieb. *Inspirations-Historie 1817–1850*. Trans. Janet W. Zuber. N.p.: Amana Church Society, 1987.

Schiavo, Anthony P., and Claudio R. Salvucci, eds. *Iroquois Wars I. Extracts from the Jesuit Relations and primary sources from 1535 to 1650*. Bristol, Pa.: Evolution Publishing, 2003.

Schneider, Herbert W., and George Lawton. *A Prophet and a Pilgrim, Being the Incredible History of Thomas Lake Harris and Laurence Oliphant . . .* New York: Columbia University Press, 1942.

Sears, Clara Endicott. *Days of Delusion: A Strange Bit of History*. Boston: Houghton Mifflin, 1924.

Shambaugh, Bertha M.H. *Amana: the Community of True Inspiration*. Iowa City, Iowa: State Historical Society of Iowa, 1908.

Sherwood, Bruce T. Letter to Bruce Pennington, May 4, 1981. Koreshan Virtual Archives.

Simanek, Donald E. "Turning the Universe Inside-Out: Ulysses Grant Morrow's Naples Experiment." http://www.lhup.edu/~dsimanek/hollow/morrow.htm.

Sinnett, A. P. "The Phenomena of Spiritualism Considered in the Light of Theosophical Teachings." *Transactions of the London Lodge of the Theosophical Society* 23 (1895).

Sinnett, A. P. *Some Fruits of Occult Teaching*. London: Theosophical Publishing Society, 1896.

Sinnett, A. P. *Spiritualism as Related to Theosophy*. London: Theosophical Publishing House, 1920.

Smith, Gerrit. *Three Discourses on the Religion of Reason*. New York: Ross & Tousey, 1859.

Smith, Hadden. *History of Chenango and Madison Counties*. Syracuse, N.Y.: D. Mason & Co., 1880.

Smith, J. E. *Legends and Miracles, and Other Curious and Marvellous Stories of Human Nature* . . . London: B. D. Cousins, 1837, 57–62.

Smith, Joseph, Jr. *History of the Church of Jesus Christ of Latter-day Saints*. B. H. Roberts, ed. Salt Lake City: Deseret Books, 1902–1935.

Smith, Joseph, Jr. *Joseph Smith's "New Translation" of the Bible*. Independence, Mo.: Herald Publishing House, 1970.

Smith, Joyce Hackett. *Moravia, New York, "The Mecca of Spiritualism."* Moravia, N.Y.: Cayuga-Owasco Lakes Historical Society, 2001.

Smith, Mary Ann. *Gustav Stickley the Craftsman*. Syracuse, N.Y.: Syracuse University Press, 1983.

Social Pioneer & Herald of Progress, The. Boston: J. P. Mendum, 1844.

Song of Songs, The. East Aurora, N.Y.: Roycroft Printing, 1896.

Spicer, Henry. *Sights and Sounds: The Mystery of the Day: Comprising an Entire History of the American "Spirit" Manifestations*. London: Thomas Bosworth, 1853.

Sprague, Alice. *My Two Gardens*. By A. S. Rochester, N.Y.: Manas Press, 1909.

Sprague, Alice. *Sensitive Horizons*. Rochester, N.Y.: Manas Press, 1946.

Stanton, Elizabeth Cady, Susan B. Anthony and Matilda Joslyn Gage, eds. *History of Woman Suffrage*. 2nd ed. Rochester, N.Y.: Susan B. Anthony, 1889.

Stanton, Elizabeth Cady. *The Woman's Bible*. New York: European Publishing Co., 1895, 1898.

Stein, Stephen J. *The Shaker Experience in America*. New Haven, Conn.: Yale University Press, 1992.

Stickler, Alice. "Elbert Hubbard, the Invincible." *Rosicrucian Digest* 32 (1954): 226–30.

Stuart, Nancy Rubin. *The Reluctant Medium: the Life of Maggie Fox*. Orlando, Fla.: Harcourt Books, 2005.

Tanner, Jerald and Sandra. *Mormonism: Shadow and Reality*. Salt Lake City: ULM, 1987.

Teed, Cyrus R. *Illumination of Koresh. Marvelous Experience of the Great Alchemist Thirty Years Ago, at Utica, N. Y.* Estero, Fla.: Guiding Star Publishing House [1900].

Theogenesis. The Third Section of the Ancient Stanzas of Dzyan, the first two sections having been recorded in the Secret Doctrine by Helena P. Blavatsky under the titles Cosmogenesis and Anthropogenesis. Halcyon, N.Y.: Temple of the People, 1981. (Originally published in parts in *The Temple Artisan*, 1906–18)

The Theosophical Movement 1875–1925: A History and A Survey. New York: E. P. Dutton & Co., 1925.

Thomas, Robert David. *The Man Who Would be Perfect. John Humphrey Noyes and the Utopian Impulse*. [Philadelphia]: University of Pennsylvania Press, 1977.

Trahair, Richard C. S. *Utopias and Utopians: A Historical Dictionary*. Westport, Conn.: Greenwood Press, 1999.

Underhill, A. Leah. *The Missing Link in Modern Spiritualism*. New York: Thomas R. Knox, 1885.

Vallee, Jacques. *Dimensions. A Casebook of Alien Contact*. San Antonio, Tex.: Anomalist Books, 2008.

Vallee, Jacques. *The Invisible College. What a Group of Scientists Has Discovered About UFO Influences on the Human Race*. New York: E. P. Dutton, 1975.

Via, Marie, and Marjorie Searl, eds. *Head, Heart and Hand. Elbert Hubbard and the Roycrofters*. Rochester, N.Y.: University of Rochester Press, 1994.

Vilain, Jean-François. "The Roycroft Printing Shop: Books, Magazines and Ephemera." In Via & Searl, 23–54.

Vogel, Dan. "The Location of Joseph Smith's Early Treasure Quests." *Dialogue* 27/3 (1994): 197–231.

Wachtmeister, Countess Constance. *Spiritualism in the Light of Theosophy*. San Francisco: Mercury Print, 1897.

Wagner, Sally Roesch. *Matilda Joslyn Gage: She Who Holds the Sky*. Aberdeen, S.Dak.: Sky Carrier Press, 2002.

Wallace, Anthony F. C. *The Death and Rebirth of the Seneca*. New York: Vintage Books, 1972.

Wallace, Winchell. "The Mystical Experience of Thomas Lake Harris: the Seer as Creator of His own Visionary World." Ph.D. diss., Hartford Seminary Foundation, Manchester, Conn., 1976.

Walters, Wesley P. "Joseph Smith's Bainbridge, N.Y., Court Trials." *Westminster Theological Journal* 36/2 (1974): 123–55.

Watson, Mrs. Clara. "Lily Dale Spiritualist Assembly." *History of Chautauqua County, New York, and Its People*. Vol. I. Boston: American Historical Society, 1921: 420–25.

Weingrad, Michael. *American Hebrew Literature. Writing Jewish National Identity in the United States*. Syracuse, N.Y.: Syracuse University Press, 2011.

Weisberg, Barbara. *Talking to the Dead. Kate and Maggie Fox and the Rise of Spiritualism*. San Francisco: HarperSanFrancisco, 2004.

Wellman, Judith. *Grass Roots Reform in the Burned-Over District of Upstate New York. Religion, Abolitionism, and Democracy*. New York: Garland Publishing, 2000.

Wells, Lester Grosvenor. "The Skaneateles Communal Experiment 1843–1846." Syracuse: Onondaga Historical Association, 1953.

Wergland, Glendyne R., ed. *Visiting the Shakers, 1778–1849*. Clinton, N.Y.: Richard W. Couper Press, 2007.

Wergland, Glendyne R., ed. *Visiting the Shakers, 1850–1899*. Clinton, N.Y.: Richard W. Couper Press, 2010.

West Seneca Centennial Celebration 1851–1951. West Seneca, N.Y.: West Seneca Centennial Society, 1951.

Whipple, Edward. *A Biography of James M. Peebles, M.D., A. M.* Battle Creek: Author, 1901.

White, Andrew Dickson. *A History of the Warfare of Science with Theology in Christendom*. New York: D. Appleton & Co., 1896.

White, Andrew Dickson. *Autobiography*. New York: Century Co., 1905.

White, Anna, and Leila S. Taylor. *Shakerism: Its Meaning and Message*. Columbus, Ohio: Fred. J. Heer, 1905.

Whitworth, John McKelvie. *God's Blueprints: A Sociological Study of Three Utopian Sects*. London: Routledge & Kegan Paul, 1975.

Wicker, Christine. *Lily Dale. The True Story of the Town that Talks to the Dead*. San Francisco: HarperCollins, 2004.

Williams-Hogan, Jane, and David B. Eller. "Swedenborgian Churches and Related Institutions in Great Britain, the United States, and Canada." In: Robert Larson, ed., *Emanuel Swedenborg. Essays for the New Century Edition of His Life, Work, and Impact*. West Chester, Pa.: Swedenborg Foundation, 2005.

Wilson, Peter Lamborn. *7 Churches Press Release*. N.p., Author, 2010[b].

Wilson, Peter Lamborn. *Vanishing Art Press Releases*. N.p., Author, 2010[a].

Winfield, Mason. *Shadows of the Western Door. Haunted Sites and Ancient Mysteries of Western New York*. Buffalo, N.Y.: Western New York Wares, 1997.

Winfield, Mason. *Spirits of the Great Hill. More Haunted Sites and Ancient Mysteries of Western New York*. Buffalo, N.Y.: Western New York Wares, 2001.

Wisbey, Herbert A., Jr. *Pioneer Prophetess: Jemima Wilkinson, the Publick Universal Friend*. Ithaca, N.Y.: Cornell University Press, 1964.

Wonderley, Anthony. "Making the Bible Argument: John H. Noyes' Mission Statement for the Oneida Community." *American Communal Societies Quarterly* 5/3 (2011): 148–73.

Zimmer, Melanie. *Curiosities of Central New York*. Charleston: History Press, 2012.

Zipf, Catherine W. *Professional Pursuits: Women in the American Arts and Crafts Movement*. Knoxville, Tenn.: University of Tennessee Press, 2007.

Index